The Rough Guide to

The Lake District

written and researched by

Jules Brown

Contents

◀◀ Blencathra on a winter's day ◀ Rowing boats on Derwent Water

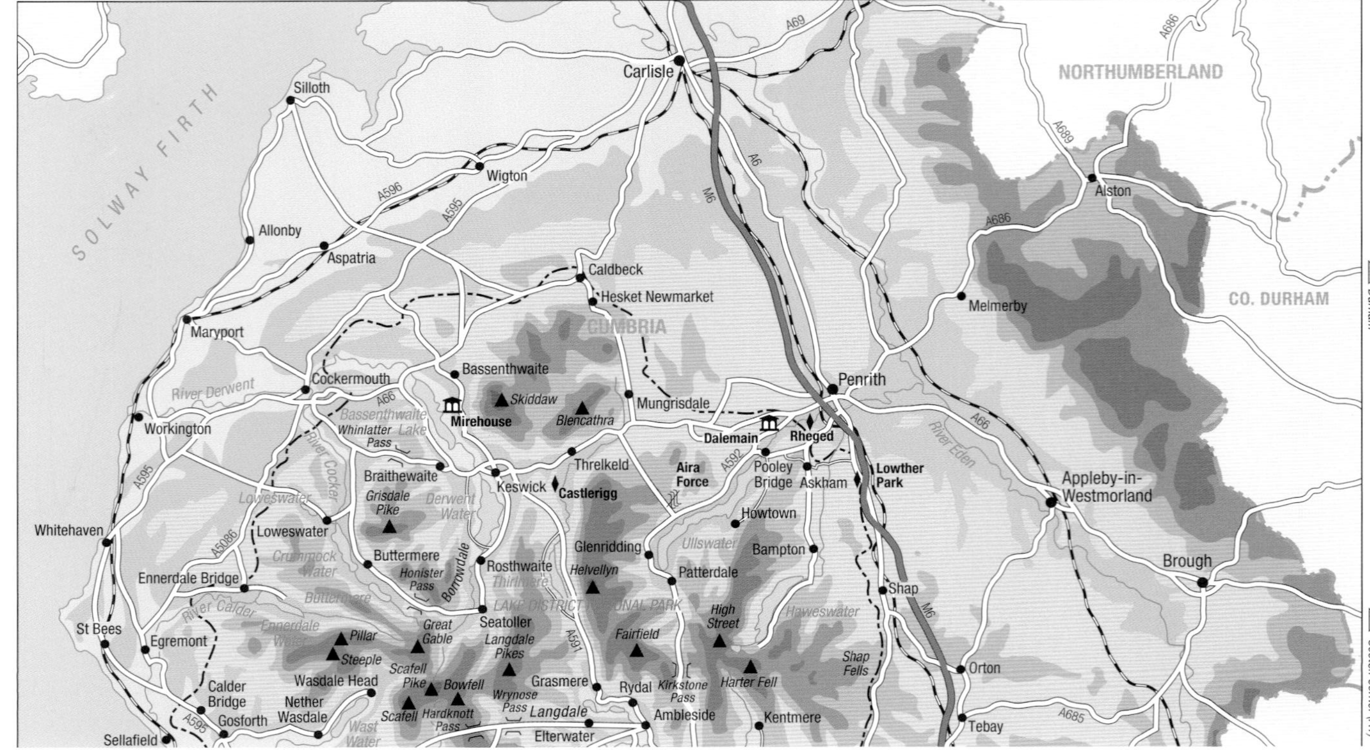
Newcastle
Durham
Scotch Corner (A1)
NORTHUMBERLAND
CO. DURHAM
CUMBRIA
LAKE DISTRICT NATIONAL PARK
SOLWAY FIRTH
Carlisle
Silloth
Wigton
Allonby
Aspatria
Caldbeck
Hesket Newmarket
Maryport
Bassenthwaite
Skiddaw
Blencathra
Mungrisdale
Penrith
Melmerby
Alston
Cockermouth
River Derwent
Mirehouse
Bassenthwaite Lake
Whinlatter Pass
Workington
River Cocker
Dalemain
Rheged
River Eden
Braithewaite
Keswick
Castlerigg
Threlkeld
Aira Force
Pooley Bridge
Askham
Lowther Park
Appleby-in-Westmorland
Grisdale Pike
Derwent Water
Loweswater
Whitehaven
Howtown
Buttermere
Honister Pass
Borrowdale
Rosthwaite
Thirlmere
Glenridding
Helvellyn
Ullswater
Bampton
Patterdale
Brough
Ennerdale Bridge
Crummock Water
Shap
Seatoller
River Calder
Ennerdale Water
High Street
Haweswater
St Bees
Egremont
Pillar
Steeple
Great Gable
Langdale Pikes
Fairfield
Shap Fells
Harter Fell
Wasdale Head
Scafell Pike
Bowfell
Grasmere
Rydal
Kirkstone Pass
Orton
Calder Bridge
Nether Wasdale
Gosforth
Scafell
Hardknott Pass
Wrynose Pass
Langdale
Ambleside
Kentmere
Tebay
Wast Water
Elterwater
Sellafield

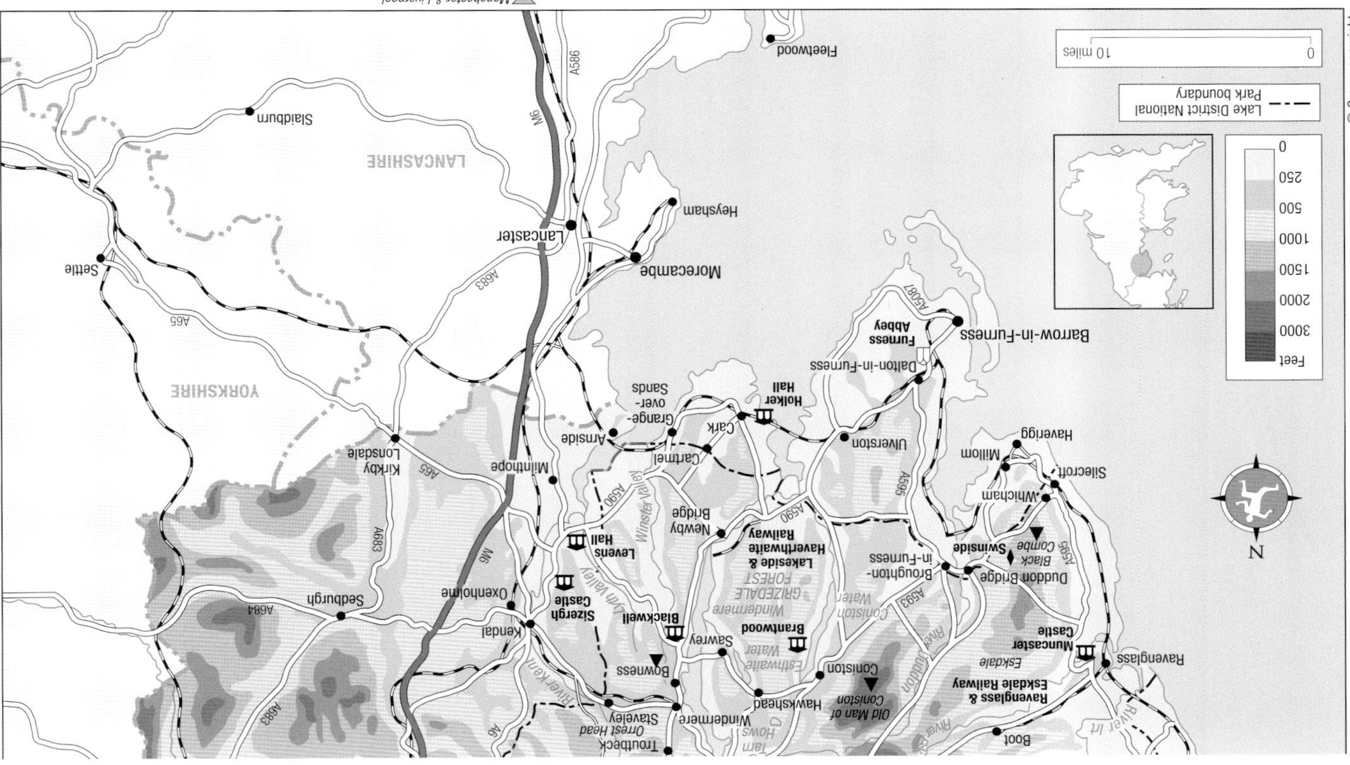
Skipton & Leeds
Manchester & Liverpool
YORKSHIRE
LANCASHIRE
Settle
Slaidburn
Lancaster
Morecambe
Heysham
Fleetwood
Kirkby Lonsdale
Sedburgh
Kendal
Oxenholme
Milnthorpe
Arnside
Grange-over-Sands
Cartmel
Cark
Holker Hall
Levens Hall
Sizergh Castle
Blackwell
Bowness
Staveley
Troutbeck
Orrest Head
Windermere
Hawkshead
Sawrey
Brantwood
Esthwaite Water
Tarn Hows
Newby Bridge
Lakeside & Haverthwaite Railway
GRIZEDALE FOREST
Windermere
Lyth Valley
Winster Valley
River Kent
Coniston
Coniston Water
Old Man of Coniston
Ulverston
Dalton-in-Furness
Furness Abbey
Barrow-in-Furness
Broughton-in-Furness
River Duddon
Duddon Bridge
Swinside
Black Combe
Whicham
Millom
Haverigg
Silecroft
Muncaster Castle
Ravenglass
Ravenglass & Eskdale Railway
Eskdale
Boot
River Esk
River Irt
M6
A6
A65
A683
A684
A586
A590
A593
A595
A5087
Feet
3000
2000
1500
1000
500
250
0
Lake District National Park boundary
0
10 miles
N

Introduction to The

Lake District

The Lake District takes some beating, whether you're looking for a weekend away in the country, a summer "staycation" or an introduction to the best that rural England has to offer. Its famous lakes and mountains, picturesque villages and alpine landscape are celebrated and hyped in equal measure and, to be fair, it's hard to think of a region in Britain with a similar breadth of scenery in such a small area. Popularized by such diverse talents as Wordsworth and the Lake Poets and children's author Beatrix Potter, this little corner of England's northwest presents an instantly familiar face, from quiet country lanes and ivy-clad inns to challenging peaks and tumbling waterfalls. But there's also another side to this typical picture of traditional lakeland life – one of boutique B&Bs, designer hotels, classy gastropubs, high-octane outdoor activities and full-on family fun.

It might only be a small region (just thirty miles across), but tourist numbers are concentrated in fairly specific areas, around the main lakes, famous literary sites and big-ticket family attractions. Even on the busiest of summer days it's relatively quick and easy to escape the crowds by climbing to the higher fells, exploring more remote valleys or visiting one of the Lake District's off-the-beaten-track attractions, from ancient stone circle to Roman fort. The scenery is, of course, the major attraction, and if **hiking and the great outdoors** isn't your bag, it's tempting to say that you're on the wrong holiday. The central lakeland crags – the birthplace of British rock climbing – still lure climbers from far and wide, while the lakes, paths and valleys support an entire industry of adventure activities, from kayaking and windsurfing to pony-trekking and off-road biking.

The region's **literary connections** are justly famous, though you may be surprised to find that it's not all Wordsworth, Coleridge, Southey and De Quincey: writers and poets as diverse as Sir Hugh Walpole, Norman Nicholson and John. Ruskin have left their mark, and their houses, haunts and places of inspiration form the backbone of many a lakeland literary trail. There's a long **industrial history**, too, which manifests itself in scattered mining works, scarred quarry sites, surviving mills (one still working at Stott Park) and a couple of old railway lines – Ravenglass to Eskdale, and Lakeside to Haverthwaite – now converted to tourist use.

The Lake District has one of the country's highest concentrations of classic rural **pubs and inns**, many of them former coaching inns dating back several hundred years. Locally brewed beer is widely available, and a circular walk and a pint in front of a roaring fire at the end of it takes some beating for an afternoon out.

Fact file

- The Lake District National Park was established in 1951 and covers 885 square miles (half a million acres).
- Most of the land within the park (59 percent) is privately owned. The rest is owned by the National Trust (24.8 percent) and water and forestry concerns (12.4 percent), with 3.8 percent under ownership of the National Park Authority itself.
- There are 42,000 people living within the National Park. Up to fifty percent of all jobs are attributable in some way to tourism.
- Farming accounts for just ten percent of the Park's working population – and the National Trust alone owns 91 farms.
- Scafell Pike (3210ft) is England's highest mountain; other major peaks include Scafell (3162ft), Helvellyn (3118ft) and Skiddaw (3053ft). England's deepest lake is Wast Water (243ft), and its largest Windermere (10.5 miles long).

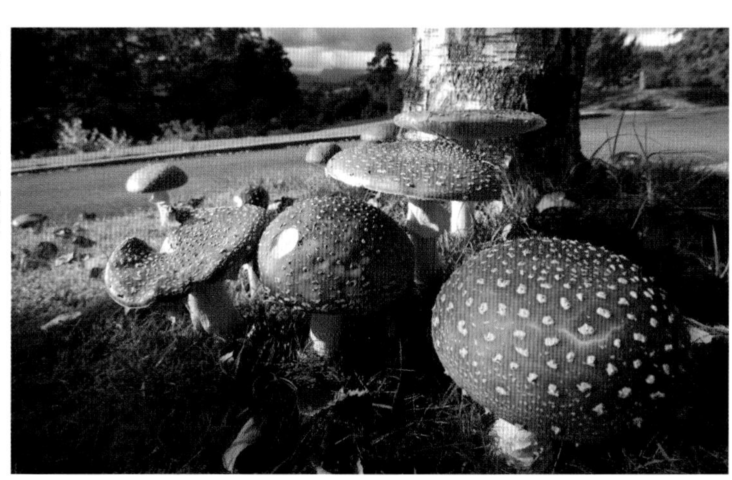

▲ Autumn in the Lake District

Lakeland place names and terms

Many lakeland place names, geographical features and dialect words have origins which go back to Norse, Saxon or even Celtic times. The most common are appended to features you'll see every time you stride out into the countryside – like "fell" (hill, mountain, or high common land), "mere" (lake), "holme" (island), "beck" (stream), "force" (waterfall) and "tarn" (small mountain lake). With other names, it helps to know the derivation in order to figure out exactly what you're looking at, thus place names ending in "-thwaite" (signifying a clearing), or those incorporating the words "ghyll" or "gill" (narrow ravine or mountain stream), "hause" (summit of a pass), "how" or "howe" (rounded hill), "pike" (peak), "raise" (summit of a ridge), "rake" (natural rock passage) or "wyke" (bay). Farming language is deeply rooted in the past – words like "heaf" (grazing area), "garth" (enclosed land or field) or "lath" (barn) have ancient roots – and there was once an entire counting system for keeping tabs on sheep (yan, tyan, tethera, or one, two, three...). That's not to mention scores of dialect words, many still in use, for describing traditional skills and pastimes, from basket-weaving to wrestling.

Stay overnight and you can experience another Lake District speciality, the **country-house hotel**: some of the grandest specimens in England occupy exclusive lake-view positions. Finally, in summer the region hosts many of its annual **sports**, **festivals**, **shows** and **events**, providing a fascinating snapshot of traditional rural life.

Where to go

It's easy to see a great deal of the Lake District in just a few days, even if you are travelling by public transport or getting around on foot. **Windermere** is the longest and largest lake, featuring a cruise service which calls at all points north and south. Two late-Victorian mansions on its shores provide must-see attractions: the National Park's Lake District Visitor

▼ The Wordsworth Hotel, Cockermouth

▲ Tourists browsing in Coniston

Centre at **Brockhole**, and **Blackwell**, whose restored Arts and Crafts interior is one of England's architectural gems. The lake's towns – Windermere, Bowness and, especially, **Ambleside** – have populations of just a few thousand but are among the region's busiest settlements and, given their choice of accommodation, cafés, restaurants and pubs, they make obvious bases. Even if they don't plan to stay there, most people at least pass by Windermere on the way to **Grasmere** and the famous Wordsworth houses of **Rydal Mount** and **Dove Cottage**, or to impossibly pretty Hawkshead and Beatrix Potter's house at nearby **Hill Top**.

Nearby **Coniston** sits at the head of Coniston Water which boasts the **Brantwood** home of art critic and essayist John Ruskin, and cruises on the lake's idiosyncratic wooden launches and steam yacht. Nearby natural attractions include **Grizedale Forest**, where you can cycle or hike the shaded trails, and **Tarn Hows**, many visitors' favourite splash of water in the entire Lakes. Away from the literary trail, there are renowned hikes, peaks and tarns in central **Langdale** – and, arguably, the finest hikers' inn in the region (the *Old Dungeon Ghyll*) from which to explore them. Less dramatic rural pockets in the hills and dales south of Windermere and Coniston offer easy rambles, village visits and pub lunches in the **Duddon**, **Winster** or **Lyth** valleys.

On the whole, the scenery is more dramatic in the north, where four peaks – **Scafell Pike**, **Scafell**, **Helvellyn** and **Skiddaw** – top out at over 3000 feet, and several other equally famous mountains (including **Great Gable** and **Blencathra**) don't lag far behind. The quite different lakes of **Derwent Water** and **Ullswater** provide superb backdrops for a

Kendal Mintcake

You'll see blocks of **Kendal Mintcake** on sale throughout the Lake District, though "cake" is perhaps a misleading term for such a solid confection of molar-shattering properties. It does come from Kendal, though – first produced in the town in 1869 – and it is undeniably minty. As is the way with many great inventions, its initial production came about as a mistake made during the process of combining sugar and peppermint oil for clear mint sweets. It was quickly apparent that the grainy, energy-giving "mintcake" would go far in a region where you often needed a quick boost if you were to scale the local fells and crags. **Romney's of Kendal**, established 1919, is still the biggest producer, famous since Sir Edmund Hillary carried their mintcake up to the top of Everest in 1953. Stick some in your backpack and there's not a Lake District peak you can't knock off before breakfast.

day's cruising and walking. **Keswick**, the main town in the north (with a population of around 5000), is the one major lakeland settlement with real year-round character, and it makes a handy base for exploring: south through delightful **Borrowdale**, a valley for which the word picturesque might have been invented; west over the forested **Whinlatter Pass**; or north to **Bassenthwaite** and its ospreys, nature reserves and animal park.

The summer crowds thin out in the western side of the Park. Although **Buttermere** and **Crummock Water** see a fair amount of traffic, **Wast Water**, **Ennerdale Water** and **Loweswater** lie further off the beaten track. All these lakes provide supreme walking opportunities, from simple lake-circuits to fell-top clambers, and anyone looking for typical rural accommodation – whether a room above a pub, a farmhouse B&B or lakeside hotel – will find the western lakes and fells irresistible. Keep heading west and you find the only part of the Cumbrian **coastline** that lies within the National Park. This stretches twenty miles south from **Ravenglass**, an undistinguished village with a Roman past, but which provides a bucolic route into the heart of dramatic **Eskdale** by either following the snaking road or the **Ravenglass and Eskdale Railway**.

Outside the National Park, most visitors make time for **Kendal** and its excellent museums, the revitalized Georgian port of **Whitehaven**, and the historic market towns of **Ulverston**, **Penrith** and **Cockermouth**, the last also famous as the birthplace of Wordsworth. These are bigger settlements than anywhere in the National Park, so they make useful bases, and they're also rainy-day bolt holes, offering a varied set of attractions from heritage museums to animal parks. On the southern flanks of the National Park **Furness Abbey** and the priory church in the highly attractive village of **Cartmel** provide a glimpse of the erstwhile religious influence on the Lakes, while Cartmel itself is rapidly becoming a boutique getaway.

When to go

▲ Belle Isle, Windermere

High **summer** may be the warmest season – usually – but it isn't the ideal time to visit the Lakes. July and August can see accommodation (and the roads) stretched to capacity as the bulk of the annual visitors descend. If you're thinking of swimming in the lakes, it's worth knowing that late August and September see the waters at their warmest, as they've had time to soak up the summer sun. To be honest, though, you'll barely notice the difference: the inland waters are pretty cold, at best, year-round. Other busy periods include **Easter week**, the few days around **New Year**, and school **half-term holidays** (Feb & Oct). Fewer people visit the Lakes in the **late autumn**, **winter** and **early spring**, so if you're looking for relative peace and quiet, these are the seasons to choose. Many of the indoor sights and attractions remain open year-round, so you shouldn't be unduly inconvenienced, and while some hotels, guesthouses and campsites are closed, those that do stay open tend to offer reduced rates. Spring usually arrives a little later than in the south of England, though in mild seasons you sometimes get the famous **daffodils** flowering as early as February. Mostly, though, before May you might get bright, blue days, but you can also expect chilly mornings, overnight frosts and cold conditions (snow can linger on north-facing slopes as late as June). December has the shortest and rainiest days; November and January aren't much better.

Average daily temperatures in the Lake District

	Jan	Feb	Mar	Apr	May	Jun	Jul	Aug	Sep	Oct	Nov	Dec
Lake District												
°C	4	5	7	10	14	17	19	18	15	11	7	6
°F	38	42	45	50	58	62	65	63	60	52	44	42

15 things not to miss

It's not possible to see everything that the Lake District has to offer in one trip – and we don't suggest you try. What follows, in no particular order, is a selective taste of the highlights of the region. They're arranged in four colour-coded categories, which you can browse through to find the very best things to see and experience. All entries have a page reference to take you straight into the Guide, where you can find out more.

01 **Tarn Hows** Page **136** • The most beautiful spot in the Lake District? Many people think so, but you decide as you stroll the undulating paths around this most serene of tarns.

02 Via Ferrata Honister Page **169** • There's no more thrilling day out than the fixed-rope and zip-wire challenge of England's first "Iron Way".

03 A cruise on Ullswater Page **213** • Steamer trips depart all year round from Glenridding for walks and visits around lovely Ullswater.

04 Blackwell Page **70** • This imposing mansion near Bowness has one of Britain's most glorious Arts and Crafts interiors.

05 Castlerigg Stone Circle Page **152** • The dramatically sited standing stones at Castlerigg, above Keswick, are the most prominent reminder of Lakeland's ancient inhabitants.

06 Great Langdale Page **113** • For the best rugged walking in the central fells, head for the glorious Langdale valley.

07 Grizedale Forest Page **139** • The remarkable sculptures lurking in Grizedale Forest are the backdrop to an adventurous day's walking, cycling or tree-scrambling.

08 Cool camping Page **103** • Glamping - glamorous camping - hits the Lakes, with stylish stays at *Full Circle Yurts* at Rydal Hall, as well as at fab yurts, tipis and bell-tents across the region.

09 The bus ride through Borrowdale Page **164** • The Lakes' most scenic bus route flanks Derwent Water and runs through the stunning valley of Borrowdale.

10 Ravenglass & Eskdale Railway Page **187** • A ride on "La'al Ratty", as the train is known, makes a great family outing, with easy walks possible straight off the platforms of the tiny Eskdale stations.

11 Aira Force Page **215** • The sparkling waterfall with a seventy-foot drop is a cherished location – Wordsworth "wandered lonely as a cloud" among the neighbouring daffodils.

12 Rydal Mount, Grasmere Page **107** • The most famous literary house in the Lake District – the final home of William and Dorothy Wordsworth, containing a wealth of memories.

13 **Wild ospreys, Bassenthwaite Lake** Page **174** • A viewing platform above Bassenthwaite allows you to see these majestic birds at close quarters.

14 **Muncaster Castle** Page **188** • A great family day out, featuring ghosts, gardens and flying owls.

15 **Hardknott Roman Fort** Page **195** • The finest Roman remains in the Lakes stretch across a blustery hillside.

Basics

Basics

Getting there

The Lake District is in the county of Cumbria, in the northwest of England, 80 miles north of Manchester and 270 miles from London. The M6 motorway gets you within a few miles' drive of the eastern side of the region, while public transport links are good, with trains or buses providing reasonably direct access from most major British cities (and from Manchester Airport). The major points of access are Lancaster, Kendal and Windermere to the south, and Penrith and Carlisle to the north.

This section tells you how to reach the Lake District by bus, train or car, and gives all the contact details you'll need for planning routes and booking tickets. The government-sponsored website Ⓦwww.transportdirect.info also has a useful door-to-door **journey planner** for all public and private transport in the country. Touring around the Lakes by either public transport or car is covered in the next section, "Getting around".

Large-scale package-tour operators tend to concentrate on whirlwind trips through the region, bussing passengers in en masse to see the famous lakes and literary sites. Generally speaking, you can do much better than that on your own – either using public transport or booking local tours. But for **outdoor activities or pastime-based holidays** – from cycle-touring to art appreciation – we've picked out some of the more interesting options in the "Walking and climbing" (p.42) and "Organized holidays, courses and outdoor activities" (p.47) sections.

For more guidance on holidaying in the Lake District, contact **Cumbria Tourism**: Ⓣ01539/822222, Ⓦwww.golakes.co.uk. You can also download brochures, useful information and podcasts from the website.

By bus

National Express (Ⓦwww.nationalexpress.com) buses from London's Victoria Coach Station run once daily to Windermere, via Birmingham, Preston and Lancaster, an eight-hour ride (from £35 return). This service continues from Windermere on to Ambleside (15min), Grasmere (30min) and Keswick (45min). There's also a once-daily service to Windermere and the same onward stops **from Manchester**, via Preston (up to 4hr; from £23.50 return), and **from Birmingham** (under 5hr, from £39 return). National Express services from York,

Getting there for overseas visitors

From **Manchester Airport**, northern England's major airport, there are direct train services to Kendal and Windermere. Other services from or via Manchester sometimes require a change of trains either at Lancaster or at Oxenholme, the station for the Lakes on the west-coast main line.

Travelling from Ireland by **ferry**, the most logical port to use is Liverpool (sailings from Belfast and Dublin), from where it's an easy train ride to Manchester and on to the Lakes. Using the Belfast service to Stranraer in Scotland, you'll need to travel first by train to Glasgow then head south from there on the west-coast main line; arriving in Holyhead from Dublin, take the train via Crewe to Oxenholme. From the rest of Europe, using the North Sea crossings makes most sense. Docking at Hull (from Rotterdam and Zeebrugge), take the train to York and Manchester, changing for the onward service to the Lakes; from Newcastle (Hamburg, Amsterdam, Norway and Sweden), take the train to Carlisle, changing for the service south to Penrith and Oxenholme.

Newcastle and Scotland route via Manchester or Carlisle to the Lakes; from the south, east and west you'll have to change in London or Birmingham. The website has all sorts of ticket offers and discounts; it's usually cheapest to book in advance and travel midweek.

Stagecoach (ⓦwww.stagecoachbus.com) has the most useful year-round, direct regional service (#555/556), from Carlisle (three daily) to Keswick and points beyond, or from Lancaster (hourly) to Kendal, Windermere, Ambleside, Grasmere and Keswick.

By train

The main train access is via the **west-coast main-line service** between London and Glasgow. For the Lake District, you change either at Lancaster or **Oxenholme** for the branch-line service to Kendal (3min from Oxenholme) and Windermere (20min). The only other places in the region directly accessible by train are **Penrith** (also on the west-coast main line) and **Carlisle** (west-coast main line, plus connections from Newcastle upon Tyne). There are also direct services from Manchester to Kendal and Windermere; and from Manchester, Preston and Lancaster along the **Cumbrian Coast line** to Ulverston, Barrow-in-Furness, Ravenglass, Whitehaven and Carlisle, providing a leisurely approach to the western Lakes. Various train operators are responsible for the services: **National Rail Enquiries** (ⓣ08457/484950, ⓦwww.nationalrail.co.uk) provides all the timetable, route and service information – the website has a journey planner and links to ticket-sale sites.

From London (Euston Station) there are up to ten departures a day to Windermere, and it's usually around a three hour thirty-minute trip. There are some very good deals if you book in advance (the earlier the better), with one-way fares starting at £11.50. If you buy your ticket on the day, expect to pay more like £85 return, and a lot more if you intend to travel on a Friday or during peak commuter hours. To reach Keswick and the northern Lakes, either take the train from Oxenholme to Windermere and continue from there by bus or stay on the main-line service to Penrith or Carlisle, from where buses also run to Keswick.

From Manchester, the quickest trains to Windermere take one hour forty minutes (advance one-way fares from £4.50, otherwise from £19). Coming from Yorkshire, a longer, more scenic approach is provided by the famous **Settle to Carlisle Railway** (connections from Leeds and Bradford), which runs through stunning Yorkshire Dales countryside. At Carlisle, you'll have to switch to local buses to get you to Keswick, Penrith or Cockermouth.

If you're visiting Cumbria as part of a wider northern England trip, rover tickets offer the best deals on getting to the Lakes: the **North Country Rover** ticket (any 4 days in 8; £72) or the **Freedom of the North West Rover** (any 4 days in 8 £57, or 7 consecutive days £70), are both valid for unlimited travel within Cumbria and the northwest and further afield (as far as Manchester, Newcastle and the Scottish borders) – full details available on the National Rail Enquiries website. Other regional rover tickets are good value for travel between Lancaster, Carlisle, the Cumbrian coast and the Lakes (see Getting Around, next section).

Services **from Glasgow** (2hr 30min–3hr 30min) and **Edinburgh** (3hr–3hr 30min) run to Oxenholme for connections to Windermere, with stops en route at Carlisle and Penrith.

Distances in miles from major cities

	Windermere	Keswick	Penrith
London	270	305	290
Birmingham	150	190	175
Manchester	80	115	100
York	100	115	95
Newcastle upon Tyne	90	80	75
Edinburgh	145	135	115
Glasgow	140	135	115

Six steps to a better kind of travel

At Rough Guides we are passionately committed to travel. We feel strongly that only through travelling do we truly come to understand the world we live in and the people we share it with – plus tourism has brought a great deal of **benefit** to developing economies around the world over the last few decades. But the extraordinary growth in tourism has also damaged some places irreparably, and of course **climate change** is exacerbated by most forms of transport, especially flying. This means that now more than ever it's important to **travel thoughtfully** and **responsibly**, with respect for the cultures you're visiting – not only to derive the most benefit from your trip but also to preserve the best bits of the planet for everyone to enjoy. At Rough Guides we feel there are six main areas in which you can make a difference:

- Consider what you're contributing to the **local economy**, and how much the services you use do the same, whether it's through employing local workers and guides or sourcing locally grown produce and local services.
- Consider the **environment** on holiday as well as at home. Water is scarce in many developing destinations, and the biodiversity of local flora and fauna can be adversely affected by tourism. Try to patronize businesses that take account of this.
- Travel with a purpose, not just to tick off experiences. Consider **spending longer** in a place, and getting to know it and its people.
- Give thought to how often you **fly**. Try to avoid short hops by air and more harmful night flights.
- Consider **alternatives to flying**, travelling instead by bus, train, boat and even by bike or on foot where possible.
- Make your trips "**climate neutral**" via a reputable carbon offset scheme. All Rough Guide flights are offset, and every year we donate money to a variety of charities devoted to combating the effects of climate change.

Advance one-way fares to Windermere from either city start at £7, though considerably more if you buy on the day, or travel on a Friday or at peak times.

By car

The Lake District lies to the west of the M6 motorway, which – as it approaches the hills and troughs of the Lakes and the Eden Valley – displays one of the best feats of road engineering in the country: the section between Kendal and Penrith is as impressive as major highways get in England. Where you come off the motorway depends on your ultimate destination – for Keswick and Penrith, take junction 40; for Kendal and Windermere, take junction 38 (north) or 36 (south); for Cartmel and Ulverston, take junction 36.

Count on a **driving time** of five hours from London and the southeast, an hour and a half from Manchester or Newcastle, two and half hours from York or Birmingham, and three hours from Glasgow or Edinburgh. Once you leave the motorway, the nature of the roads and the summer traffic can slow you right down, so allow plenty of time if you're aiming for the central fells or the western Lakes. Local radio stations carry regular traffic and weather reports. Both the AA (Ⓦwww.theaa.co.uk) and RAC (Ⓦwww.rac.co.uk) have useful route-planning services.

Getting around

Too many people bring cars to the Lake District and, as a consequence, once-quiet valleys and villages can be adversely affected by the amount of traffic. However, over the last few years – recognizing the damage that's being done to the environment – the local authorities have made great improvements to the public transport network within the National Park to encourage people to leave their cars at home. Many of the local bus and lake cruise or ferry services are fully integrated, so you can get around the major destinations easily in a day, and there are lots of very good value "day rider" and other discount tickets available. Bus, boat and train combinations can even get you to the start of most of the best-known hikes and mountain climbs.

The southern, central and northern band – from Windermere and Coniston through Ambleside and Grasmere to Keswick – is the easiest section of the Lakes to tour by public transport. In summer especially, when services are at their peak, there's no longer any real excuse not to use public transport for at least some journeys. In the western Lakes and valleys, and in the far north beyond Keswick, getting around by bus becomes trickier, though nearly everywhere is connected by some sort of service, however limited.

Timetables and information

Major routes and service schedules are listed at the end of each chapter in "Travel details". The best single source of information is the *Cumbria and Lakesrider* **timetable** magazine (available from tourist offices and other outlets), which covers every bus route, ferry service and train line in the Lakes, plus details of all the ticket offers and discounts. You can also pick up individual bus, train and ferry timetables, as well as themed brochures combining bus routes with things like scenic tours, local walks or pub crawls.

For all public transport enquiries in Cumbria – bus, coach, rail and ferry services – call **Traveline** (Ⓣ0871/200 2233, Ⓦwww.traveline.info). Its telephone enquiries service is available daily 7am–8pm, while the website gives access to a searchable database of all public transport services in the area.

By bus

Stagecoach (Ⓣ0871/200 2233, Ⓦwww.stagecoachbus.com/northwest) is the biggest bus operator in the Lakes and Cumbria, though many of its routes are subsidized by Cumbria County Council, the Countryside Agency or the National Parks Authority to ensure services to areas that wouldn't otherwise be economically viable. Routes connect every major town and village, and although travel frequencies vary you can usually count on being able to reach most places at least once a day throughout the year. The most frequent services on all routes are between Easter and the end of the school holidays in August, though some peak-period timetables continue into September and October (often at weekends only). If we say a service is "seasonal" in the Guide, we mean the period from Easter to the end of August.

You can buy tickets on the bus as you go, though the best deal is the **North West Explorer** (one-day £9.75, family £19.50, plus four-day and seven-day options), which is valid on the entire network and available on any bus from the driver. For a week's unlimited travel within Cumbria there's also the **Cumbria Goldrider** card (£23.50, available on the bus), while other special **day-rider tickets** offer really good deals on specific bus routes (like in Borrowdale) or on **bus-and-boat** combinations for Windermere, Coniston and Ullswater – specific details are included in the Guide.

Other services in the Lakes are run by a partnership of agencies and operators, most notably the excellent **Cross-Lakes Experience** (operates Sat & Sun from mid-Feb, then daily Easter–Oct; timetable information from Mountain Goat ⓣ015394/45161 or see ⓦwww.lake-district.gov.uk), which combines boats and minibuses to connect Bowness-on-Windermere with the Beatrix Potter house at Hill Top (£9 return, family £25.80), Hawkshead (£10.20, family £28.65), Grizedale Forest (£13.05, family £36.85) and Coniston Water (£17.55, family £49.50), with connections at Hawkshead and Coniston for Tarn Hows (£3, family £9). The boat-and-minibus service can also carry up to five bikes. The actual timetable changes slightly from year to year, and some years certain route sections may not operate (to Tarn Hows, for example), but the general trend has been to extend the service so that you can explore the central Lakes without the car.

Minibus tours

Lakes Supertours ⓣ015394/42751 or 88133, ⓦwww.lakessupertours.com. All-day 16-seater minibus tours (from £30) – lakes and mountains or literary themes – with some cruises and house entrance fees included.

Mountain Goat ⓣ015394/45161, ⓦwww.mountain-goat.com. Minibus tours (half-day around £25, full-day £35) that get off the beaten track to places such as Duddon Valley and Back o'Skiddaw as well as the usual lakes and passes. Daily departures from Windermere, plus pick-ups in Bowness, Grasmere and Ambleside. Also offers themed four- to seven-night touring holidays (such as the five-night "Spring gardens of the Lake District", £550).

By train

The only place actually in the Lake District National Park you can reach on a regular train service is **Windermere** town, on the branch line from Oxenholme (on the London–Manchester–Glasgow west-coast main-line route) via Kendal and Staveley. Outside the National Park, but still a handy approach to the northern Lakes, **Penrith** is also a stop on the west-coast main-line route, while the Furness and **Cumbrian Coast** branch line from Lancaster runs via Ulverston, Barrow-in-Furness, Millom, Ravenglass and the Cumbrian coastal towns to Carlisle.

Rail passes offer good value for travel within Cumbria, and include the **Cumbria Day Ranger** (£32), the **Cumbria Round Robin** (£25) and the **Cumbria Coast Day Ranger** (£16). There are discounts on all these for children or those with family railcards, and most of the passes are valid after 8.45am Monday to Friday, and all day at weekends and on public holidays – you can buy them at the stations or from conductors on board trains. They all cover slightly different sections of the Cumbrian train network, but you can easily figure out which is most appropriate for your needs by checking with Northern Rail (ⓦwww.northernrail.org) or National Rail Enquiries (ⓦwww.nationalrail.co.uk). Northern Rail also offers "Duo" tickets (basically a second adult return ticket for half-price when two adults travel together), which save you money on the coastal line between Barrow and Carlisle.

There are also two highly scenic steam-train lines in the Lakes. The **Lakeside and Haverthwaite Railway** offers a short jaunt at the southern end of Windermere, while the **Ravenglass and Eskdale Railway** is a fantastic way to explore the more remote western valleys.

By ferry

Windermere, Coniston Water, Derwent Water and Ullswater have **ferry or cruise services**, all of which are covered in detail in the Guide.

Best buy...

...is the Lakes Day Ranger ticket (£17, family £33), valid on all Stagecoach buses in Cumbria and all trains between Lancaster, Penrith, Windermere and Whitehaven. You also get a free Windermere cruise and discounts on Derwent Water, Coniston and Ullswater cruise services and on Lakeside and Haverthwaite and Ravenglass and Eskdale narrow-gauge railways. You can buy it from train station ticket offices or from train conductors: information on ⓦwww.northernrail.org or www.nationalrail.co.uk.

Windermere and Ullswater are the most popular choices for a round-trip cruise; the service on Derwent Water is extremely useful for hopping around the lake and accessing Borrowdale walks; while the Coniston launches and Gondola steam yacht are used mainly as a means of reaching Ruskin's house, Brantwood. The Windermere boats also run from Bowness and Ambleside to the main National Park visitor centre at Brockhole, and down to the bottom of Windermere for the attractions at Lakeside. Combination bus, boat and entry tickets are widely available – basically, if you're planning to take the bus to Windermere or Ullswater, then go on the lake or visit Lakeside's aquarium, Haverthwaite steam train or Brantwood on Coniston, you can save money with an all-in ticket.

By car

While driving around the Lakes might seem convenient, it soon loses its attraction on July and August weekends when the roads are busy, it takes ages to get from village to village and you can't find anywhere to park once you arrive. Leave the car at home, or at your hotel or B&B, whenever you can and you'll get more enjoyment out of the region.

Parking can be difficult throughout the Lakes, especially in the towns and villages. There is free on-street parking in Ambleside, Windermere, Bowness, Coniston, Grasmere and Keswick, but there's not very much of it and it's usually limited to thirty minutes or an hour. Most places have also introduced a **disc parking** scheme, so to park on the street you'll have to nip into a local shop or tourist office and pick up a disc for your dashboard. For longer stays, the best advice, every time, is to follow the signs to the official car parks and pay up. All car parks mentioned in the Guide – and marked on our maps – are **pay-and-display** unless otherwise stated, so a supply of change is a necessity. Expect to pay £1.50–3.50 for up to four hours' parking, and up to £7 or £8 for a full day, even in car parks on National Park Authority and National Trust land in out-of-the-way places. Most town and village hotels and some B&Bs have private parking, mentioned in the reviews where available – if the accommodation is rural, you can take it as read there'll be somewhere free to park.

Most A and B **roads** in the area are in good condition, though single-track driving is common – don't park in passing places. Surfaces on high ground and off the beaten track tend to deteriorate rapidly, being little more than unmetalled tracks in places: many routes can be adventurous at the best of times and downright treacherous in winter or bad weather. The steepest road gradients and most difficult driving are on the following **lakeland passes**: Blea Tarn Road (between Great and Little Langdale), Hardknott Pass (Eskdale and Duddon Valley), Honister Pass (Buttermere and Borrowdale), Kirkstone Pass (Ullswater and Windermere), The Struggle (Ambleside and Kirkstone Pass), Whinlatter Pass (Braithewaite and Lorton Vale) and Wrynose Pass (Duddon Valley and Little Langdale).

Any of the national **car rental** outfits can oblige, but if you'd prefer to rent locally there are rental agencies in the main towns of Kendal, Keswick, Penrith, Ulverston and Windermere, as well as in the county capital of Carlisle. **Taxis** are widely used, as a sort of backup to the public transport network, and there are local taxi firms in the same towns plus Ambleside, Cockermouth, Coniston and Grasmere. All the relevant contact details are given in each town and village's "Listings" section.

By bicycle

Local cycle businesses do much to promote responsible cycling within the National Park, and by following agreed routes, exercising caution and respecting walkers' rights of way you'll help to ensure continued cooperation.

Bike rental outfits are detailed throughout the Guide and can kit you out with all the gear. The going rate is around £20 for a full-day's rental of a mountain bike, with helmets, locks and route maps usually included in the price. Children's bikes, tag-along trailer bikes and tandems are also often available. Good places to go include Whinlatter and Grizedale forest parks, which have dedicated bike rental outlets and special mountain bike trails.

Long-distance tourers have the choice of several routes that cut through Cumbria and the Lake District, including the 72-mile **Cumbria Way Cycle Route** (Ⓦwww.cumbriawaycycleroute.co.uk) from Ulverston to Carlisle and the well-known **Sea-to-Sea (C2C)** cycle route, a 140-mile trip between Whitehaven/Workington and Sunderland/Newcastle (Ⓦwww.c2c-guide.co.uk). Other parts of the National Cycle Network – like the Hadrian's Wall Cycleway or the Reivers Cycle Route – also pass through the region; route details are available from Sustrans (Ⓦwww.sustrans.org.uk).

The best source of **information** for road and family cycling and mountain biking is Ⓦwww.cyclingcumbria.co.uk, which features news, services, events and downloadable routes. There's also cycling information on the Lake District National Park website (Ⓦwww.lake-district.gov.uk), and for more **mountain bike routes** and off-road cycling in the Lakes, check out Ⓦwww.mountain-bike-cumbria.co.uk.

Cycling tour operators

Country Lanes Ⓣ015394/44544, Ⓦwww.countrylaneslakedistrict.co.uk. Bike-touring specialist offering group tours, day-trips and various inclusive multi-day tours, like the 2-night "Taste of the Lakes" self-guided circuit (from £159).

Discovery Travel Ⓣ01904/632226, Ⓦwww.discoverytravel.co.uk. Self-guided cycle tours, including a seven-night Lake District circuit (from £485, B&B basis).

Holiday Lakeland Cycling Ⓣ016973/71871, Ⓦwww.holiday-lakeland.co.uk. Two five-night cycling tours (including hotel accommodation and baggage transfer): "Nine Lakes Tour" (£370) or "Sea to Sea Adventure" (£395), which includes two nights in the Lakes.

Spinnoff Ⓣ015395/67123, Ⓦwww.spinnoff.co.uk. Guided mountain biking for individuals, families and groups, with courses, rides and tours for all abilities. Prices vary, as you can take your own bike or hire one, but skills' days and day rides start at around £50–60, weekends including accommodation from £185.

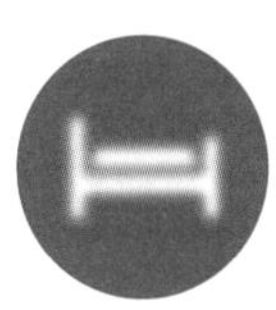

Accommodation

The Lake District has no shortage of accommodation, though it sometimes seems like it at peak periods. At New Year, Easter, public holidays and school holidays (particularly the six-week summer break from late July to the end of August) it's wise to book ahead – though tourist information centres will always be able to find a room for anyone arriving without a reservation. Accommodation listed in the Guide is open year-round unless otherwise stated, though note that, even so, many places close for a few days over Christmas and New Year.

Local information offices all offer a **free room-booking** service where you'll be charged a deposit (usually ten percent) that's then deducted from your accommodation bill. Or you can book accommodation **online** through the Cumbria Tourism website (Ⓦwww.golakes.co.uk), which has a huge database (hotels to campsites) and offers short breaks, special deals and late availability bookings.

Hotels, guesthouses and B&Bs

Bed-and-breakfast (B&B) rates in the Lake District start at around £20–25 per person per night. Even in the most basic of places, you should get a sink, a TV and a kettle in the room. These days, most B&Bs and guesthouses have added en-suite shower and toilet cubicles to their rooms, but you might still have to share or use a bathroom that's down the hall.

Once above these prices – say from £35–40 per person – you can expect a range of services and facilities that you won't get in a standard B&B, from fresh flowers and gourmet breakfasts to king-sized beds and handmade toiletries. Many traditional B&Bs and small guesthouses have revamped their rooms and raised their game in recent years – some are truly excellent and we've highlighted the best choices in every area. Others have retained the cosy familiarity of a B&B but gone down the boutique road, so while you might pay up to £200 a night at places like Ambleside's *Randy Pike*, you're getting a highly individual B&B experience.

Hotels in the Lakes tend to charge what they can get away with, and, as location is everything, lakeside or isolated country retreats can get away with an awful lot – you can easily spend £150–250 for a room in one of the famous country-house hotels, like *Miller Howe*, *Sharrow Bay* or *Gilpin Lodge*. There's a lot of choice in the £80–120 range, though it pays to pick and choose – a classy, personally run B&B often has the edge over a traditional hotel. Again, though, overall standards are improving, as lots of places have had boutique makeovers, adding things like designer fabrics, handmade local furniture, roll-top baths and ipod docks. You no longer have to stay in a flouncy, frilly country-house hotel unless you really want to – more typical of the modern lakeland experience are hotels like Ambleside's town-house-style *Waterhead* or Grasmere's seriously stylish *Moss Grove Organic*.

Rooms are also available in many town-centre and country **pubs and inns**. Often this is traditional B&B in old-fashioned or modernized rooms, starting at around £30 per person, rising to £50 in the best-known traditional hikers' inns (like Langdale's *Britannia Inn* and the *Old Dungeon Ghyll*, and Wasdale's *Wasdale Head Inn*). However, several country inns in particular have gone contemporary, with sharp styling, snappy service and good food now the norm at places like the *Drunken Duck Inn* outside Hawkshead, the *Punch Bowl Inn* at Crosthwaite, Loweswater's *Kirkstile Inn* and Clifton's *George and Dragon*.

Prices in all establishments are often higher at weekends, during summer and over public holidays: conversely, it's always worth asking about off-season **discounts**, which might shave a couple of quid off a B&B room, or up to forty off a hotel.

At weekends, many places insist upon two- or (over public holidays) even three-night **minimum stays**. There again, staying more than a couple of nights in many places brings the standard price down a pound or two a night. There aren't a great many **single rooms** available, and solitary hikers or holiday-makers won't often get much knocked off the price of a double room if that's the only option. Finally, many guesthouses, inns and hotels offer a discounted **dinner, bed and breakfast (D,B&B) rate** which – provided you want to eat there in the first place – is always a better deal than the standard B&B rate: the guide picks out those D,B&B places where the cooking is particularly good. Note, though, that some hotels *only* offer stays on a D,B&B basis, while others are so remote that there's nowhere else to eat anyway.

At all the establishments listed in this book, **payment by credit card** is accepted unless otherwise stated. However, even where credit cards are accepted, American Express cards often aren't – pack another card, just in case.

Accommodation price codes

All **hotel** and **B&B** accommodation in the guide is priced on a scale of ❶ to ❽, indicating the **average price** you could expect to pay per night for a **double/twin room** in high season. **Breakfast** is included, and rooms are **en suite**, unless otherwise stated.

❶ £50 and under
❷ £51–70
❸ £71–90
❹ £91–110
❺ £111–150
❻ £151–200
❼ £201–250
❽ £251 and over

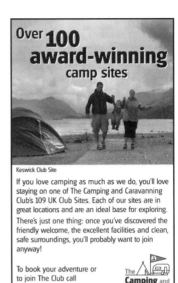

Farm stays

Not surprisingly, one of England's most rural regions offers plenty of opportunity to see country life at close quarters by **staying on a farm**. At its most basic this might be simple farmhouse B&B, offered on many farms as a way of boosting income. Accommodation might be in the farmhouse itself or in cottages on the farm, and you can expect to pay standard bed-and-breakfast rates. Some working farms offer a very special experience – at Coniston's *Yew Tree Farm*, or *Crake Trees Manor* near Penrith, for example, you can expect a glamorous night's stay that's more about chic than sheep. Although there's no obligation, some farms provide a lot more opportunity to muck in, either feeding the animals or finding out more about farming life.

Around twenty farms on **National Trust** land in the Lakes offer B&B. Some of the best are reviewed in the Guide, though the full list and booking details are on the NT website (ⓦwww.nationaltrust.org.uk; click on "Holidays" and then "Bed and breakfast"). Alternatively, check out **Farm Stay UK** (ⓦwww.farmstayuk.co.uk) for more farmhouse options in Cumbria, including a group of superior farm stays marketed as "Luxury in a Farm" (ⓦwww.luxuryinafarm.co.uk).

Hostels, bunkhouses and barns

There are twenty Youth Hostel Association (YHA) **youth hostels** (ⓦwww.yha.org.uk) in the Lake District, three more just outside the park boundaries and a summer-only hostel in the county capital of Carlisle. Several, including those in Ambleside, Keswick and Grasmere, are amongst the most popular in the country, so advance booking is a good idea at any time of the year. Gone are the days of tasks and sackcloth comforts: many hostels have refurbished rooms of two to six beds (linen provided) and nearly all have kitchen, laundry and drying-room facilities, while others have licensed restaurants and wi-fi access. There are still two or three fairly basic hostels based in prime walking country, like *Black Sail* in Ennerdale, but these too have a charm all of their own.

You don't have to be a member to use a YHA hostel, though non-members pay a £3 supplement (under-18s, £1.50) for

the lake district
Cumbria
©Britainonview / Rod Edwards
book your stay in the lakes at golakes.co.uk

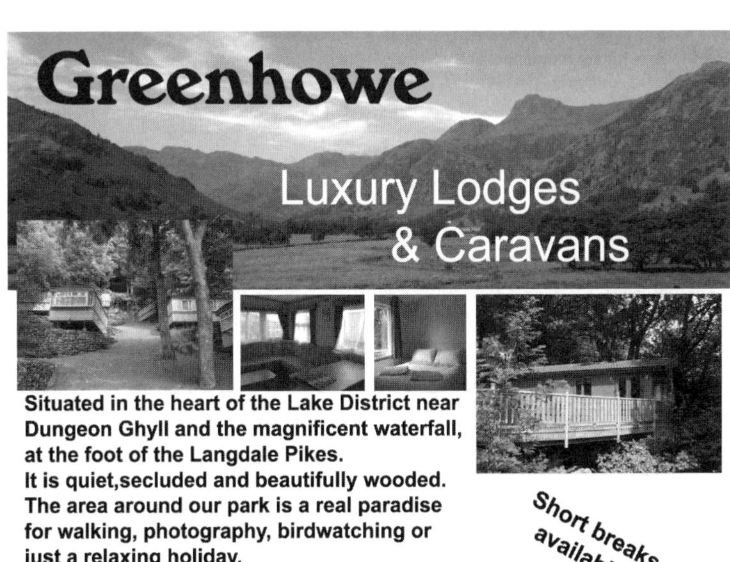
Greenhowe
Luxury Lodges
& Caravans
Situated in the heart of the Lake District near
Dungeon Ghyll and the magnificent waterfall,
at the foot of the Langdale Pikes.
It is quiet,secluded and beautifully wooded.
The area around our park is a real paradise
for walking, photography, birdwatching or
just a relaxing holiday.
Short breaks available
Great Langdale, Ambleside, Cumbria LA22 9JU
Tel: 015394-37231 E-mail: enquiries@greenhowe.com Website: www.greenhowe.com

Best for...

brilliant breakfast – *Howe Keld*, Keswick (p.155).
chic B&B – *Ellergill*, Keswick (p.155).
cool camping – *Full Circle Yurts*, Rydal (p.103).
country elegance – *Armathwaite Hall*, Bassenthwaite (p.176).
designer digs – *Randy Pike*, Ambleside (p.82).
dorm delight – *Grasmere Independent Hostel*, Grasmere (p.103).
family friendly – *Winder Hall*, Lorton (p.203).
farm fancy – *Yew Tree Farm*, Coniston (p.128).
inn style – *Punch Bowl Inn*, Crosthwaite (p.75).
old-school charm – *Old Dungeon Ghyll*, Langdale (p.115).
room with a view – *Miller Howe*, Windermere (p.61).
veggie retreat – *Yewfield*, Hawkshead (p.135).

accommodation and aren't eligible for any other hostel discounts or benefits. If you choose to, you can join the YHA in person at any affiliated hostel on your first night's stay. Overseas visitors who belong to any **International Youth Hostel Federation** (IYHF) association in their own country have automatic membership of the YHA.

YHA **hostel prices** start from £13.95 per night for an adult bed at simple, remote establishments such as those in Ennerdale, rising to over £20 a night at the flagship Keswick and Ambleside hostels in summer. Many hostels have twin or **family rooms** available: couples will pay the current overnight bed price while a typical family room costs between £60 and £80. Breakfast is occasionally included in the price (as at Keswick or Buttermere), but otherwise costs around an extra fiver, as does a packed lunch. Lots of hostels now also offer a three-course dinner (from £11.50), often using locally sourced ingredients and with Cumbrian beers and organic wines available. You can book any YHA hostel online on the website, or call or email the hostels direct. The major YHA hostels are open daily, year-round, though many others have restricted **opening periods** in the winter, which are detailed in the Guide.

The few **independent backpackers' hostels** in the Lakes (in Ambleside, Windermere, Grasmere and Keswick) have similar facilities and are pitched at roughly the same prices as the higher-grade YHA hostels. On the whole, they have a more laid-back feel than the YHA hostels and tend to attract a more international crowd. There are no membership requirements for backpackers' hostels.

Lakeland **bunkhouses** provide simple accommodation for hikers and backpackers. At their most basic, there's a mattress on the floor and a shower room, though others have bunk beds, kitchens, stoves and open fires. You'll have to provide your own sleeping bag and prices run from £6 to £10 per person per night. In a similar vein, there's a series of fifteen **camping barns** in and around the National Park, mostly self-catering converted farm buildings with communal facilities. The cost is £7 per person per night, and although mattresses are provided you'll need your own sleeping bag, foam mat and cooking equipment – some of the farms offer breakfast. For reservations, contact the Lakeland Camping Barn Booking Office (Ⓣ01946/758198, Ⓦwww.lakelandcampingbarns.co.uk).

Holiday property rental

The dream of renting a pretty rural holiday property in the Lakes is easily accomplished. The hardest thing is deciding what you want, with choices ranging from simple stone cottages to large country houses, by way of barn conversions, former mills, town houses and shooting lodges. There are lots of companies out there vying for your custom but all offer the same kind of basic deal. The minimum rental period is usually a week, though outside the summer season and especially in the winter you may be able to negotiate a three-day/long-weekend rate – except, that is, at Christmas, New Year and Easter when prices are at their highest and demand at its most intense. All properties come with a fully equipped kitchen and many (but not all) provide bed linen and towels. Prices vary dramatically – from around £200 a week for the smallest properties to as much as £1000 for a week in a large, luxury property with admission to the local pool and health club thrown in.

Holiday property agencies

Coppermines and Coniston Lakes Cottages ⓣ015394/41765, ⓦwww.coppermines.co.uk. Specialist in the Coniston area, with unique properties in Coppermines Valley as well as around Coniston Water and the Duddon Valley.
Cumbrian Cottages ⓣ01228/599960, ⓦwww.cumbrian-cottages.co.uk. A wide range of over 900 cottages and apartments in the Lake District and Cumbria.
Goosemire Cottages ⓣ01539/731801, ⓦwww.goosemirecottages.co.uk. Forty-five barn conversions or traditional cottages, some with lake views, in the Ullswater, Haweswater, Bassenthwaite, Windermere and Wast Water regions.
Heart of the Lakes ⓣ015394/32321, ⓦwww.heartofthelakes.co.uk. Excellent choice of over 300 quality properties in all corners of the National Park.
Keswick Cottages ⓣ017687/78555, ⓦwww.keswickcottages.co.uk. A good selection of cottages in and around Keswick, Braithewaite and Portinscale in the northern Lakes.
Lakeland Cottages ⓣ017687/76065, ⓦwww.lakelandcottages.co.uk. Period cottages and farmhouses in the northern Lakes, from the Keswick area, through Borrowdale, Lorton Vale, Bassenthwaite and Cockermouth.
Lakeland Hideaways Cottages ⓣ015394/42435, ⓦwww.lakeland-hideaways.co.uk. Cottages, barn and farm conversions in Hawkshead, Sawrey and around Esthwaite Water.
Lakelovers ⓣ015394/88855, ⓦwww.lakelovers.co.uk. A large range of quality properties mainly in the western and southern Lakes, with accommodation generally on the chintz-free side.
National Trust ⓣ0870/458 4422, ⓦwww.nationaltrustcottages.co.uk. Twenty lakeland properties, lakeside cottages to remote farmhouses – mainly around Ambleside, Little Langdale, Eskdale, Loweswater and Penrith.
Wheelwright's ⓣ015394/37635, ⓦwww.wheelwrights.com. Best starting place for cottages in and around Elterwater, Chapel Stile, Langdale, Grasmere and Ambleside.
Windermere Lake Holidays ⓣ015394/43415, ⓦwww.lakewindermere.net. Water-edge apartments and luxury houseboats available on the Windermere shore, sleeping up to six people.

Top 5 YHA hostels

Black Sail (p.201) – hiker's heaven.
Elterwater (p.112) – country calm.
Ennerdale (p.201) – an eco-retreat.
Keswick (p.156) – town -house style.
Wasdale (p.197) – lovely lake views.

Camping and glamping

The Lake District has scores of **campsites**, ranging from back-to-basics hikers' favourites to family-style holiday parks – we've tended to recommend those that favour tents over the large caravan-RV parks. Cumbria Tourism (ⓦwww.golakes.co.uk) has a searchable database of campsites and holiday parks on their website, or consult ⓦwww.lakedistrictcamping.co.uk, a really useful site giving more in-depth details about Lake District campsites. Many sites close between November and March, while in July and August it's always worth booking a pitch in advance if you can (not all accept advance bookings). Prices vary considerably, from a couple of quid for a field site with toilet and cold tap to £10–15 a night for one of the big resort sites, complete with washrooms, leisure facilities, shop and bar.

The **National Trust** (ⓦwww.ntlakescampsites.org.uk) also maintains four campsites – Great Langdale, Low Wray, Wasdale Head and Hoathwaite on Coniston Water (all featured in the Guide) – in fantastic locations. These are incredibly popular and you'll need to book ahead or get there early, especially around summer and bank holiday weekends.

Given the lure of the scenery, it didn't take long for cool camping to make it big in the Lakes, and you can now choose between **yurts**, **tipis** and walk-in **bell-tents** on several campsites, and more will surely follow. Some are stand-alone sites, like the yurts at Rydal Hall, while others put the "glampers" (that's glamorous campers, by the way) in separate areas on established sites, like at the National Trust's Low Wray site. These are upmarket options for camping without a tent, so you can expect futon beds, wood-burning stoves, rugs and hammocks, kitchens and barbecue pits, though you may well have to use the campsite shower-block. They are usually rented in part- or full-week periods, and prices reflect the facilities, from around £250 (part-week) to £450 (week) for something that sleeps 4 or more people. **Camping pods** are also creeping onto many sites, which are eco-friendly, insulated wooden shelters sleeping 2 or 3 people, for around £30–50 a night.

Food and drink

There's been a quiet revolution in Cumbrian food and drink over the last few years, and Michelin-starred restaurants, chilli festivals, artisan bakeries and cookery schools are now just as much part of the scene as the good old cream tea and Cumberland sausage. Pub and café meals in particular have improved immeasurably, while restaurants right across the region pride themselves on using locally sourced ingredients, whether it's farmhouse cheese, organic vegetables or fell-bred lamb. Contemporary tastes are well catered for too – there's a cappuccino machine in even the smallest village – and you're never very far from a café-bar, gastropub or gourmet vegetarian place.

Traditionally, **fine dining** in the Lakes was very much a silver-service roast-and-veg affair, or heavily Anglo-French in character, and this is still the case in some old-fashioned lakeland hotels. But many local chefs have married contemporary tastes and trends with well-sourced local ingredients to produce something slightly different – if not a specific lakeland style of cuisine then at least a welcome change to old-school menus. At the more adventurous places expect to see plenty of pan-searing, chargrilling and slow-roasting, together with ethnic and fusion menu twists, using fresh, local, home-made ingredients. The Lake District currently offers some of the finest **country-house dining**

Best...

café – *Wilf's Café*, Staveley (p.88).
casual dining – *Jumble Room*, Grasmere (p.103).
deli – Lucy's Specialist Grocers, Ambleside (p.84).
dress-up dinner – *Gilpin Lodge*, Bowness-on-Windermere (p.67).
foodie pilgrimage – *L'Enclume*, Cartmel (p.238).
lazy lunch – *Gate Inn*, Yanwath (p.256).
gourmet inn – *Drunken Duck Inn*, Hawkshead (p.135).
organic meal – *George and Dragon*, Clifton (p.220).
restaurant-with-rooms – *Jerichos* at *The Waverley*, Windermere (p.61).
romantic treat – *Lucy's on a Plate*, Ambleside (p.84).
tearooms – *Old Stackyard Tearooms*, Cockermouth (p.252).
veggie dining – *Zeffirelli's*, Ambleside (p.84).

experiences in England, notably the renowned, Michelin-starred foodie locations of *Holbeck Ghyll* and *Sharrow Bay*, though for sheer style, panache and invention nothing beats Simon Rogan's extraordinary restaurant *L'Enclume* in Cartmel, which has few peers in Britain, never mind the Lakes.

Elsewhere, you're as likely to come across good Cumbrian food in a farmhouse **tearoom** or village **café** as in a restaurant, and some of your best memories will be unexpected ones – a scoop of Buttermere ice cream straight from the farm or fresh-baked organic bread in the Mill Yard at Staveley. As a rule, meals in **pubs and inns** are a bit more hit and miss, though many in the Lakes have carved out a good reputation for their food. In the Guide we've picked out our favourite choices for pub meals, whether it's an exceptional sandwich in a town-centre hostelry or gourmet food in a rural **gastropub**, of which there are increasing numbers.

The Cumbria Tourism website (Ⓦwww.golakes.co.uk) is a good place for general **information**, from local food producers to farmers' markets, restaurant news to food festival dates. Otherwise, check out **Ⓦwww.artisan-food.com**, an informative online magazine that throws a highly personal light on Cumbrian food and restaurants. Annual foodie fests include the **Kendal Festival of Food** (October half-term holiday), the celebratory **Damson Day** each spring (Ⓦwww.lythdamsons.org.uk), Dalemain's **Marmalade Festival** (Ⓦwww.marmaladefestival.com) in February – patron, Paddington Bear, obviously – and the **Lakes Chilli Fest** at Levens Hall (Ⓦwww.chillifest.co.uk) in August. For local **markets and farmers' markets**, see the list on p.50.

All cafés, restaurants and pubs listed in the guide serve **lunch and dinner** daily unless otherwise stated. Winter opening hours are notoriously fickle, so a phone call before you set out never does any harm. Listed places all take **credit cards** unless otherwise stated (though this rarely includes American Express).

Local specialities

Beef and pork tends to be overshadowed by the local lamb, particularly by **Herdwick lamb**, the traditional lakeland breed which finds its way onto menus across the county. It also forms the basis of the "tattie pot", a traditional lamb stew topped with potato. The region's biggest **organic meat** producer is the 3000-acre Lowther Park Farm (Ⓦwww.lowtherparkfarms.co.uk), which supplies restaurants and shops across the district, as well as its own *George and Dragon* inn near Penrith. In the south, Holker Hall estate (Ⓦwww.holker.co.uk) specializes in farm-produced cheese, home-reared venison, shorthorn beef and salt-marsh lamb (reared on the salt marshes of Morecambe Bay). For the famous **Cumberland sausage** (see below), the supreme example is that made by Woodall's of Waberthwaite, near Millom (Ⓦwww.richardwoodall.co.uk), suppliers by Royal Warrant to the Queen, and purveyors, too, of fine dry-cured hams and bacon, and a rather special Cumbrian air-dried ham.

For fish, it's usually **local trout** (farmed on Ullswater and elsewhere, as well as found wild) and Morecambe Bay shrimps, though keep an eye out for lake-caught **char**, a trout-like fish peculiar to the Lake District. Landlocked in the Lakes after the last Ice Age, it thrives in the deep, cold waters of Windermere (Daniel Defoe recommended potting this "curious fish" and sending it to your best friend).

Arise, Sir Sausage

The humble breakfast sausage is hardly so humble in the Lake District, where the traditional spiral-shaped **Cumberland sausage** is king. Butchers zealously guard their secret recipes for the perfect blend of pork, herbs and spices, and the matter is taken so seriously that there's a celebratory Sausage Day every July. Meanwhile, on Ⓦwww.traditionalcumberlandsausage.com you can follow the Cumberland Sausage Association on its quest to have the sausage awarded the same protected status as Parma ham and Champagne.

Bread is at its best from the organic, artisan-style Village Bakery, Melmerby, near Penrith (ⓦwww.village-bakery.com), while many outlets also stock **cheese** from the Thornby Moor Dairy, in Thursby (near Carlisle), either made plain (a smooth, creamy variety), smoked, or flavoured with garlic and herbs. The Old Smokehouse at Brougham Hall near Penrith (ⓦwww.the-old-smokehouse.co.uk) **smokes** everything from garlic to goose, and supplies Fortnum & Mason as well as local outlets – try its award-winning smoked Penrith Pepperpot sausage.

Howbarrow Organic Farm (ⓦwww.howbarroworganic.co.uk), near Cartmel, is the region's leading distributor of **organic fruit and vegetables**. You should also keep an eye out at roadside stalls, craft outlets and village shops for locally made honey and preserves – the Lyth Valley's **damson** harvest, for example, ends up in jams, ice cream, chocolate, even beer, gin and vinegar. The Hawkshead Relish Company (ⓦwww.hawksheadrelish.com) and others supply locally made **chutneys and pickles**, often served as part of a ploughman's lunch, and Alston in northern Cumbria provides many outlets with its speciality Cumberland mustards.

The prince of lakeland puddings is Cartmel Village Shop's **sticky toffee pudding** (ⓦwww.stickytoffeepudding.co.uk), though plenty of other places claim the title. People also travel miles for **Grasmere gingerbread** (ⓦwww.grasmeregingerbread.co.uk) and **Penrith fudge and toffee**, (ⓦwww.thetoffeeshop.co.uk) while other old Cumbrian recipes that have been dusted off in shops, cafés and restaurants include things like Borrowdale Teabread (a dried-fruit cake), Cumberland Rum Nicky (a date, ginger and rum pie or tart) and rum butter (with rum, nutmeg, cinnamon and brown sugar). **Windermere Ice Cream** (ⓦwww.windermereicecream.co.uk) is made with organic milk from Low Sizergh Barn (where you can see the cows being milked daily) and comes in over thirty flavours.

No rundown of local treats would be complete without **Kendal Mintcake** (ⓦwww.kendal.mintcake.co.uk), a brutal peppermint confection made by Romney's of Kendal and favoured by strong-toothed hikers and mountaineers – the proud boast is that it was carried to the top of Everest on Hillary's ascent of 1953.

Vegetarians

These days, most B&Bs and hotels at least make a stab at a non-meat breakfast, while several places provide a wholly vegetarian overnight experience, including the *Beech Tree* in Coniston, *How Beck* or *Lancrigg* in Grasmere and *Yewfield* at Hawkshead. There is also a fair number of strictly vegetarian cafés and restaurants in the Lakes, particularly in the main towns – and at places like the gourmet *Quince & Medlar* (Cockermouth), the *Lakeland Pedlar* wholefood café (Keswick) and *Zeffirelli's* pizza and Italian joint (Ambleside) veggies are certainly not getting second best. There are more details about cafés, restaurants, pubs, wholefood shops and accommodation in the useful *Vegetarian Lake District* booklet (ⓦwww.vegetarianguides.co.uk), available in local bookshops or for purchase online.

Cookery courses and foodie activities

Time was, a cookery course in the Lakes might have instructed you in the subtle arts of the microwave, but no more. There's a real interest in broadcasting the best of Cumbrian cuisine to a wider public, starting with **Lucy Cooks** (ⓣ015394/32288, ⓦwww.lucycooks.co.uk), the purpose-built cookery school offshoot of Lucy's of Ambleside, based in the Mill Yard at Staveley (near Kendal). The emphasis is on locally sourced food and ingredients, with subjects taught ranging from bread- and preserve-making to vegetarian or Aga cookery (demos from £30, courses from £110). Another local food champion is Annette Gibbons of **Cumbria on a Plate** (ⓣ01900/881356, ⓦwww.cumbriaonaplate.co.uk), whose one-day "food safaris" (£120) visit local food producers for tastings, topped off by a fancy lunch. Peter Sidwell of Keswick's **Good Taste** café (ⓣ017687/75973, ⓦwww.simplygoodtaste.co.uk) runs a themed cookery day (from £100) once or twice a month, anything from bread-making to Thai cookery, while for something more esoteric Cumbria's food historian Ivan Day (ⓣ01931/716266, ⓦwww.historicfood.com) offers two-day **historic cookery courses**

Here for the beer: Cumbria's 10 best breweries

Barngates Brewery Ⓦwww.barngatesbrewery.co.uk. In-house brewery at the fabulous *Drunken Duck Inn* near Hawkshead, serving beers (Cracker Ale, Tag Lag, Chester's Strong and Ugly) named after dogs that have lived at the inn.

Bitter End Brewery Ⓦwww.bitterend.co.uk. Based at the *Bitter End* pub in Cockermouth, bravely brewing a great range of beers on Jennings' home soil.

Coniston Brewing Company Ⓦwww.conistonbrewery.com. Produces its award-winning Bluebird bitter, Old Man Ale and Bluebird XB pale ale at Coniston's excellent *Black Bull* pub.

Cumbrian Legendary Ales Ⓦwww.cumbrianlegendaryales.com. Beers named after lakeland legends, like the "Buttermere Beauty", as well as great-tasting ales for Loweswater's *Kirkstile Inn*.

Great Gable Brewing Company Ⓦwww.greatgablebrewing.co.uk. The micro-brewery at the wonderful *Wasdale Head Inn* names its refreshing beers after the surrounding mountains.

Hawkshead Brewery Ⓦwww.hawksheadbrewery.co.uk. Founded by former BBC journalist Alex Brodie, now with a brewery (tours available) and great beer-hall in Staveley near Windermere.

Hesket Newmarket Brewery Ⓦwww.hesketbrewery.co.uk. Fully flavoured ales from Britain's first cooperatively owned pub, the *Old Crown*, in Hesket Newmarket.

Keswick Brewing Company Ⓦwww.keswickbrewery.co.uk. There are tours of Keswick's independent brewery, while every pint of Thirst Rescue sold includes a donation to local mountain rescue teams.

Whitehaven Brewing Company Ⓦwww.twbcl.co.uk. Real ale from Ennerdale, made from the brewery's own lakeland spring water.

Yates Brewery Ⓦwww.yatesbrewery.co.uk. One of the longest-standing independent breweries, from Westnewton, Aspatria, a specialist in seasonal beers (Sun Goddess to Winter Fever).

(£280) in his antique farmhouse kitchen at Shap.

Pubs and beer

If you like your pubs with oak beams, slate floors, log fires and country beer gardens, you're in the right part of England. There's a fine selection of old **pubs and inns** throughout the Lakes, many dating back several hundred years. Some have become very well known, either as hikers' bars (like the *Old Dungeon Ghyll* in Langdale or Elterwater's *Britannia Inn*) or for the quality of their food – indeed, some places are more like restaurants-with-rooms these days, such as the classy *Punchbowl Inn* at Crosthwaite or Hawkshead's *Drunken Duck*.

What they all have (or should have) in common is good local **beer**, and these days in the Lakes it's just as likely to have been made on the premises as supplied by a major brewery. There's been a dramatic renaissance in Cumbrian brewing and independent **microbreweries** abound. There are more than twenty in the Lakes now, some little more than single-pub craft brewers (see also feature on p.203), others selling their beers at increasing numbers of pubs across the region.

If you were to visit just one pub in the Lakes for its beer, it should probably be the *Watermill Inn* at Ings (Ⓦwww.watermillinn.co.uk), between Windermere and Staveley, which not only brews its own but has up to sixteen real ales on at any one time. Otherwise, it's **Jennings** (Ⓦwww.jenningsbrewery.co.uk) that has the main lakeland stranglehold. You'll come across its beers everywhere and they also offers brewery tours at their base in Cockermouth. Meanwhile, the local branches of the **Campaign for Real Ale** (links from Ⓦwww.cumbriacamra.org.uk) have useful websites listing real-ale pubs and carrying news about breweries and beer festivals.

Festivals, shows, sports and annual events

There must be more unique festivals, sports and events in the Lake District than in any other region in England. From sheep shows to open-air wrestling, scarecrow festivals to face-pulling competitions, the region shows off its age-old traditions and rugged characteristics in a year-round series of events that often defy description. Most are rooted firmly in the countryside, with the local agricultural show being the annual village highlight in many places, although there's also a thriving arts and culture scene that promotes some internationally recognized festivals.

The month-by-month **festival and events calendar** below picks out the highlights: many traditionally take place on fixed days (often fairly convoluted), so for exact dates either check the websites or contact local information offices or Cumbria Tourism (Ⓣ01539/822222, Ⓦwww.golakes.co.uk). Be aware, too, that the traditional outdoor agricultural shows are particularly susceptible to cancellation due to bad weather or things like foot-and-mouth outbreaks – even some of the most famous shows have been postponed in recent years. There are also hundreds of other events held throughout the year – from guided walks and lectures to craft demonstrations and children's entertainments – many sponsored by the **National Park Authority** (Ⓣ015394/46601, Ⓦwww.lake-district.gov.uk), based at the Lake District Visitor Centre at Brockhole.

Rushbearings and other oddities

The oldest festivals – dating back to medieval times – are the annual **rushbearings**, harking back to the days when church floors were covered in earth rather than stone. The rushes, or reeds, laid on the floors (on which churchgoers knelt or stood) would be renewed once a year. Now the rushes are fashioned into crosses and garlands, decorated with mosses and flowers, and carried in symbolic procession around the village and into the church: the most famous rushbearing festivals (with accompanying bands, hymns, children's sports and races) are held at Ambleside (July) and Grasmere (August).

The **Egremont Crab Fair** (September), held annually since 1267, features such arcane events as greasy-pole-climbing and pipe-smoking competitions and the World Gurning Championship (where contestants stick their head through a horse collar and pull faces). And at a pub in Santon Bridge, Wasdale, the **Biggest Liar in the World Competition** (November) attracts porky-tellers from all over Cumbria (indeed, the world) to a century-old event that celebrates the tallest of tales – see the feature on p.198 for more.

Traditional crafts get an airing at many festivals, but for all things wool and woolly, including the sheep, you need to visit Cockermouth's annual **Woolfest** (June). In Penrith it's pots, or ceramics, celebrated in two extraordinary **Potfests**, the first in the town cattle mart, the second in the grounds of a stately home. Lots of Cumbrian villages also go in for summer **scarecrow festivals**, with the streets of Langwathby (near Penrith) and Millom, among others, filled with Carnival-style scarecrows big and small.

Festivals and events calendar

February

First or second week Word Market Literary Festival, Ulverston Ⓦwww.wordmarket.org.uk.
Third or fourth week Keswick Film Festival Ⓦwww.keswickfilmfestival.org.

March

Second week Words By The Water, Literature Festival, Keswick Ⓦwww.wayswithwords.co.uk.
Third or fourth week (Sat & Sun) Daffodil and Spring Flower Show, Ambleside Ⓦwww.ambleside-show.org.uk.

May

First week Ulverston Walking Festival ⓦ www.ulverstoncouncil.org.uk.
First and second week Ulverston Flag Fortnight ⓦ www.ulverstoncouncil.org.uk.
Second or third week Keswick Jazz Festival ⓦ www.keswickjazzfestival.co.uk.
Third week Keswick Mountain Festival ⓦ www.keswickmountainfestival.co.uk.
Fourth week (bank holiday weekend) Cartmel Races ⓦ www.cartmel-racecourse.co.uk.

June

First week Holker Garden Festival, Holker Hall ⓦ www.holker.co.uk.
First week Ulverston International Music Festival ⓦ www.ulverstonmusicfestival.co.uk.
First week (Sat & Sun) Keswick Beer Festival ⓦ www.keswickbeerfestival.co.uk.
First or second week Boot Beer Festival, Eskdale ⓦ www.bootbeer.co.uk.
Third week Cockermouth Summer Festival and Carnival ⓦ www.cockermouth.org.uk.
Fourth week (last weekend) Woolfest, Cockermouth ⓦ www.woolfest.co.uk.
Fourth week (last Sun) Ullswater Country Fair, Patterdale.

July

First week (Sat) Ambleside Rushbearing Festival.
First week (Sat) Ulverston Carnival ⓦ www.ulverstoncouncil.org.uk.
First week (Sat) Skelton Agricultural Show, Penrith ⓦ www.skeltonshow.com.
First week Coniston Water Festival ⓦ www.conistonwaterfestival.org.uk.
Second week Langwathby Scarecrow Festival ⓦ www.langwathbyscarecrows.co.uk.
Second or third week Furness Tradition Folk Festival, Ulverston ⓦ www.furnesstradition.org.uk.
Third week (Sat) Cumberland County Show, Carlisle ⓦ www.cumberlandshow.co.uk.
Third week Cock Rock, Cockermouth ⓦ www.cockermouthrockfestival.com.
Third or fourth week (Sun) Coniston Country Fair.
Fourth week (last Thurs) Ambleside Sports ⓦ www.amblesidesports.co.uk.
Fourth week (Sat) Cockermouth Agricultural Show ⓦ www.cockermouth.org.uk.
Fourth week Potfest in the Park, Penrith ⓦ www.potfest.co.uk.
Fourth week Maryport Blues Festival ⓦ www.maryportblues.co.uk.

August

First week Potfest in the Pens, Penrith ⓦ www.potfest.co.uk.
First week (Wed) Cartmel Agricultural Show ⓦ www.cartmelagriculturalsociety.org.uk.
First week (Thurs) Lake District Sheepdog Trials, Ings, Staveley.
First week (Fri–Sun) Lowther Horse Trials and Country Fair, Lowther Castle, Askham ⓦ www.lowther.co.uk.
First week (Sat) Grasmere Rushbearing.
First week (Sat) Cockermouth Agricultural Show ⓦ www.cockermouthshow.co.uk.
First weekend Kendal Calling, Lowther Park ⓦ www.kendalcalling.com.
First and second weeks Lake District Summer Music Festival ⓦ www.ldsm.org.uk.
Second week (Thurs) Rydal Sheepdog Trials ⓦ www.rydalshow.co.uk.
Third week (Wed) Threlkeld Sheepdog Trials ⓦ www.threlkeldweb.co.uk.
Third week (Sat) Gosforth Agricultural Show ⓦ www.gosforthweb.co.uk.
Third week (Sun) Langdale Country Fair, Great Langdale.

Woodstock, Glastonbury, Kendal, Silloth...

The Cumbrian summer music scene is now an annual fixture on the festival circuit. The three-day **Kendal Calling** (ⓦ www.kendalcalling.com, August) indie, dance and new music fest gets bigger and better each year, now held in the Lowther Deer Park grounds. **Solfest** (ⓦ www.solwayfestival.co.uk, August) is also a great bash, taking place on a farm close to Silloth on the Cumbrian coast, while big names also drop into nearby Maryport for the **Maryport Blues Festival** (ⓦ www.maryportblues.com, July). Keswick's renowned **Jazz Festival** (May) turns the whole town into a carnival for five days of gigs and street performances, while for home-grown indie-rock and pop there's no better gig than **Cock Rock** (ⓦ www.cockermouthrockfestival.com, July), a three-day farm-field extravaganza in Cockermouth.

Third or fourth week (Sun) Grasmere Sports and Show Ⓦwww.grasmeresportsandshow.co.uk.
Third or fourth week (penultimate Tues) Hawkshead Agricultural Show Ⓦwww.hawksheadshow.co.uk.
Fourth week (last Wed) Ennerdale and Kinniside Show.
Fourth week (Sat before bank holiday Mon) Millom and Broughton Show, Broughton-in-Furness Ⓦwww.millomandbroughtonshow.co.uk.
Fourth week (Sat before bank holiday Mon) Patterdale Dog Day Ⓦwww.patterdaledogday.co.uk.
Fourth week (bank holiday weekend) Cartmel Races Ⓦwww.cartmel-racecourse.co.uk.
Fourth week (bank holiday weekend) Kendal Mintfest Ⓦwww.mintfest.org.
Fourth week (bank holiday weekend) Solfest, Silloth Ⓦwww.solwayfestival.co.uk.
Bank holiday Mon Keswick Agricultural Show Ⓦwww.keswickshow.co.uk.

September

First week Ulverston Beer Festival Ⓦwww.furnesscamra.co.uk.
First week Ambleside Summer Flower Show and Craft Fair Ⓦwww.ambleside-show.org.uk.
First week (Sun) Loweswater Agricultural Show Ⓦwww.loweswatershow.co.uk.
First and second week Ulverston Charter Festival Ⓦwww.ulverstoncouncil.org.uk.
Second week (Thurs) Westmorland County Show, Crooklands, Kendal Ⓦwww.westmorlandshow.co.uk.
Second week (Fri) Kendal Torchlight Carnival Ⓦwww.kendaltorchlightcarnival.co.uk.
Third week (Sat) Egremont Crab Fair and Sports Ⓦwww.egremontcrabfair.org.uk.
Third week (Sun) Borrowdale Shepherds' Meet, Rosthwaite Ⓦwww.borrowdaleshow.org.uk.
Fourth week (last Sat) Eskdale Show, Eskdale Green Ⓦwww.eskdale.info.
Last week Ullswater Outdoor Festival Ⓦwww.ullswater.com.
Last weekend (biennial, odd-numbered years) Lakeland Festival of Storytelling, Staveley Ⓦwww.taffythomas.co.uk.

October

Second week (Sat) Wasdale Head Show and Shepherds' Meet Ⓦwww.wasdaleweb.co.uk.
Third week (Sat) Buttermere Show and Shepherds' Meet.

November

Second week Kendal Mountain Film Festival Ⓦwww.mountainfilm.co.uk.
Third week (Thurs) Biggest Liar in the World Competition, Santon Bridge, Wasdale Ⓦwww.santonbridgeinn.com/liar.
Fourth week (Sat & Sun) Ulverston Dickensian Christmas Festival Ⓦwww.dickensianfestival.co.uk.

December

First week (Sun) Keswick Victorian Fair.

Festivals and events

The main towns host the biggest variety of annual festivals. **Ulverston** in particular – the self-billed "Festival Town" – has something on every month, from flag parade to folk festival, while **Cockermouth** follows its spring Georgian Fair with a long Summer Festival that starts in June and runs right through until the agricultural show at the beginning of August. **Kendal**, too, parties throughout the year, from the street-performance Mintfest extravaganza (June) to the long-established torchlight Carnival parade (September). Winter, meanwhile, sees popular **Christmas and Victorian fairs** in Ulverston and Keswick featuring period costumes, carol-singing, street stalls and strolling Santas.

Lake District literary, film and music festivals are starting to acquire an international reputation, notably Keswick's **Words By The Water** (March), based at the Theatre By The Lake, which offers ten days of writers' and readers' events featuring some high-profile names. There's also the **Keswick Film Festival** (February), showcasing Cumbrian short films, while Kendal's **Mountain Film Festival** (November) is one of the leading festivals of its kind, with screenings, lectures and events all related to films and books about the world's mountains. The **Summer Music Festival** (August) also brings together an international line-up of talent at venues across the region, from early music recitals to big-stage opera.

Naturally, the great outdoors is celebrated too, from the ten-day **Ulverston Walking Festival** (May), or the similar **Ullswater Outdoor Festival** (September), to the bike-, hike- and extreme-sports blowout that is the **Keswick Mountain Festival** (May).

Cumbria's burgeoning independent breweries have promoted a growing attendance at local beer festivals – the longest running is the **Keswick Beer Festival**

(June), but for an example of a smaller event that typifies a real community spirit it's hard to beat Eskdale's **Boot Beer Festival** (June).

Shows, meets and sheepdog trials

Cumbria's most loved annual events take the form of **agricultural shows**, featuring farming equipment, trade and craft displays (including dry-stone walling), food stalls, vegetable-growing and sheepshearing competitions, and prize-winning animals. The separate **Cumberland** (Carlisle, in July) and **Westmorland** (Kendal, September) shows are the largest examples – relics of the days when they were the annual county shows – but the smaller shows (nearly all in July or August) in places such as Gosforth, Coniston, Langdale and Ennerdale are highly enjoyable affairs where it's still very much a case of local communities coming together.

Some very traditional autumn shows (at Buttermere, Borrowdale, Wasdale and Eskdale) are termed **shepherds' meets**, since that's what they once were – opportunities for shepherds to meet once a year, return sheep belonging to their neighbours, catch up on local gossip and engage in competitions, sporting or otherwise. The mainstays of these events are sheep- and dog-judging competitions, bouts of hunting-horn blowing and displays of decorated shepherds' crooks. In addition, there are several annual **sheepdog trials** in August, the main ones at Rydal and Patterdale, where border collies are put through their paces, rounding up sheep into pens at the call and whistle of their owner.

Sports, races and traditional pastimes

Some annual shows specifically announce themselves as **Sports**, such as those at Ambleside (July) and Grasmere (August), the two most important gatherings. At these (but in practice at all of the agricultural shows and meets too) you'll encounter a whole host of special Cumbrian sports and activities, as well as bicycle and track events, carriage-driving, gymkhanas, ferret- or pigeon-racing and tugs-of-war.

Cumberland and Westmorland wrestling is the best known of the local sports, probably dating back to Viking times: two men, dressed in embroidered trunks, white tights and vests, grapple like Sumo wrestlers and attempt to unbalance each other – the first to touch the ground with anything except their feet is the loser, and if both men fall, the winner is the one on top. It's a best-of-three contest that is hugely technical, yet strangely balletic, and has its own vocabulary of holds and grips, like the "hype", the "hank" and the "cross buttock". The winner is declared "World Champion".

Fell-running is basically cross-country running up and down the fells (news and local club links on Ⓦwww.fellrunner.org.uk). It's a notoriously tough business, dominated by local farm workers and shepherds who bound up the fells like gazelles. The famous Joss Naylor of Wasdale is typical of the breed: in 1975 he raced over 72 peaks in under 24 hours; in 1986 he ran the 214 Wainwright fells in a week; and to celebrate his 60th birthday he did the sixty highest lakeland peaks in 36 hours. The sports show races are shorter than these trials, but no less brutal. In a similar masochistic vein is the challenge known as the **Bob Graham Round** (Ⓦwww.bobgrahamclub.co.uk), named after Bob Graham of Keswick who in 1932 completed a traverse of 42 Lake District peaks (and 72 miles) within 24 hours (starting and finishing at Keswick's Moot Hall); around 1400 other people have completed the round since records started being kept in 1960, while the most extreme competitors have extended the round to include as many peaks as possible in 24 hours (the current record is 77).

Hound trailing dates back to the eighteenth century and is derived from the training of foxhounds for hunting. A trail is set across several miles of countryside using a paraffin-and-aniseed-soaked rag and the dogs are then released, with the owners calling them in across a finish line at the show. Trailing (and the heavy betting that accompanies it) occurs most weeks during spring and summer outside the shows – the season runs from April to October, with five main events a year (starting on May Day) and scores of smaller meetings. As in other English rural areas,

fox-hunting proper was long a Cumbrian pastime (on foot in the Lakes, not on horseback), though the controversial 2005 ban on hunting with hounds is supposed to have put paid to the practice. However, the traditional Lake District hunts still meet throughout the autumn and winter, all now claiming to work within the restrictions – ie, the hunts gather for trail-hunting, rather than pursuing foxes.

Children and families

There are few better places in England than the Lakes for children and families. The whole region is something of an outdoor playground, and most of the traditional activities and pursuits – from paddling to rambling – are free. Many festivals and events are timed to coincide with school holidays, and even the capricious weather needn't be a hindrance. Most kids are far less bothered by the rain and mud than their parents, while in any case Cumbria has a terrific selection of wet-weather attractions.

Children pay half-price or go free at most museums, sights and attractions, and there are nearly always discounted **family tickets** available too. The same applies to public transport, boat rides, steam train trips and other activities – it's always worth asking about child/family discounts. Not all **hotels and B&Bs** are so accommodating, and quite a few in the Lakes specifically exclude the under-12s (or children of any age), so you should always check before booking your brood into that dream holiday destination. On the other hand, we've picked out many places in the Guide which are particularly family friendly. Children might also be excluded from some **pubs and restaurants** after a certain time (say 6 or 9pm) – there should always be a sign warning you – and in many country-house hotels you might find that smaller children (again, say the under-12s, however well behaved) are not encouraged to eat dinner with everyone else. If you don't like this attitude, there's no reason to stay at such a place since there are many others where your children will be welcomed.

Outdoor activitites

It's hard to look beyond the **lakes and fells** for keeping active youngsters occupied. The steamers on Ullswater and the solar-powered launches on Coniston Water are particular family favourites, while there are boxed features throughout the Guide on local walks, climbs and rambles, including a list of the dozen best walks in the "Out and About in the Lakes" colour feature (and see the following section on "Walking, climbing and the mountains"). There's always the **beach** as well, never very far away from the hills of the southern and western Lakes, particularly around Millom and Silecroft, or at the sweeping sands of St Bees Head.

The two forest parks at **Whinlatter** and **Grizedale** are excellent stand-alone destinations with their high ropes adventures courses, bike rental and trails, playgrounds and picnic areas. The **Ravenglass and Eskdale Railway** is another great day out, as you can walk and cycle right off the platforms. For wildlife-spotting don't miss **viewing the ospreys** at Bassenthwaite. Local industry is entertainingly covered at places like **Stott Park Bobbin Mill** and **Threlkeld Quarry**, while more hard-core mine tours and daring mountain adventures await at **Honister Slate Mine**.

Whether you visit the famous historic houses and literary sites probably depends on your children's tastes, though **Wordsworth House** in Cockermouth is excellent

Top 6 family excursions

Trotters World of Animals The animal park with a difference. See p.175.

World of Beatrix Potter No real fan – or anyone under 5 – will want to miss this. See p.63.

Lake District Visitor Centre at Brockhole There's something to see and do every day here. See p.70.

Muncaster Castle The most haunted house in England? See p.188.

Lakeside, Windermere Cruise, aquarium, steam train ride and picnic grounds. See p.72.

South Lakes Wild Animal Park Tiger-feeding and kangaroo-spotting in darkest Cumbria. See p.241.

for families, while places like Holker Hall, Dalemain, Muncaster Castle, Hutton-in-the-Forest and Levens Hall also have extensive grounds and plenty of year-round activities on offer. For clambering around old ruins and prehistoric sites, consider **Furness Abbey** (near Ulverston), **Castlerigg Stone Circle** (Keswick) and **Hardknott Roman Fort** (Eskdale).

Outdoor activity operators can take you and your family mountain biking, ghyll-scrambling, kayaking, sailing or horseriding. You'll find all the details and contacts elsewhere in this Basics section. Otherwise, the best single stop is the National Park visitor centre at **Brockhole**, which coordinates hundreds of year-round activities, from guided walks to craft days.

Indoor activities

The skies are dark, the clouds are gathering and it's starting to pelt down – not so good if you're halfway up a mountain, not such a disaster if you head for one of the region's many indoor attractions. At Lakeside's **Lakes Aquarium** you can learn all about lakeland river habitats without setting foot outside – even the otters and ducks are under cover – while Maryport's **Lake District Coast Aquarium** lets kids feed the fish. For fascinating local lore and life there's a range of excellent museums with children's activities, like Coniston's **Ruskin Museum**, Kendal's **Museum of Lakeland Life and Industry**, Keswick's **Cumberland Pencil Museum**, Whitehaven's **The Beacon** and the **Dock Museum** in Barrow-in-Furness. There are shops, crafts and giant-screen 3D movies at **Rheged** visitor centre, just outside Penrith, while in Ambleside you can browse and shop in the region's best selection of **outdoors stores** (not to mention taking the soccer-mad to **The Homes of Football** gallery). Finally, for sheep, ducks and sheepdogs in an entertaining family show, don't miss the **Lakeland Sheep and Wool Centre** in Cockermouth.

Walking, climbing and the mountains

The Lake District was the birthplace of British fell-walking and mountaineering, and hundreds of thousands of people still come to the Lakes every year to get out on the hills. Whatever your level of fitness or expertise, you can find a Lake District walk to suit – from an hour's stroll up to a local waterfall to an all-day circuit, or "horseshoe" route, around various peaks and valleys. If you're not confident about being able to find your own way, or simply want someone else to do the organizing, then it's probably best to join a guided walk or a tour. Various operators run Lake District walking holidays, while local schools and instructors can also introduce you to the arts of rock climbing, mountain navigation and winter hill walking.

Footpaths and walks

Of the long-distance paths, Wainwright's Coast-to-Coast – which starts in St Bees, near Whitehaven – spends its first few sections in the northern Lakes, and the Dales Way finishes in Windermere, but the only true Lake District hike is the seventy-mile **Cumbria Way** (Ⓦwww.thecumbriaway.info) between Ulverston and Carlisle, which cuts through the heart of the region via Coniston and Langdale. The fifty-mile **Allerdale Ramble**, from Seathwaite (Borrowdale) to the Solway Firth, spends around half its time in the National Park area, running up Borrowdale and across Skiddaw, while the 150-mile **Cumbria Coastal Way** runs from Silverdale on Morecambe Bay, all round the Lake District peninsulas and Solway Firth to the Scottish border town of Gretna.

The **walks detailed in this Guide** – often in special feature boxes – aim to provide a cross section of lakeland experiences, from valley bottom to fell top. Some of the most famous mountain ascents are included, as well as gentle round-the-lake strolls. It's vital to note that the brief descriptions in the Guide are not in any sense to be taken as specific route guides, rather as providing start and finish details and other pieces of local information. The colour feature "Out and About in the Lakes" also includes the Rough Guide choice of the ten best all-round walks in the Lake District. For lots of routes specifically designed for those in **wheelchairs or with strollers**, consult the excellent "Miles Without Stiles" section of the National Park Authority (NPA) website (Ⓦwww.lake-district.gov.uk).

There is any number of local **walking guidebooks** and national trail guides on the market: the best are reviewed on p.272.

Useful walkers' websites

Ⓦ**www.bassplace.freeserve.co.uk/wildcamp** Backpacking, camping and walking in Britain, with particular emphasis on the Lake District – click on any of the 214 Wainwright fells for a full description, or check out the pictures, routes, trip reports, camping tips and more.

Ⓦ**www.keswick.u-net.com** Ann Bowker's site claims she's "Mad About Mountains" – and she certainly is. Digital pix, routes and ascents of Skiddaw, her local mountain, plus an incredibly comprehensive photo-gallery of ascents and views of each of the 214 Wainwright peaks.

Ⓦ**www.lakedistrictwalks.com** John Dawson's incredibly detailed Lake District hiking site features over forty classic walks, complete with route descriptions, photos and a distance calculator.

Ⓦ**www.lakelandcam.co.uk** Updated daily, beautiful shots of lakeland scenery and the weather in all seasons and conditions from the roving digital camera of Tony Richards.

Ⓦ**www.stridingedge.net** Sean McMahon's stunning photo diary of fell walks gives a useful first look at the 214 Wainwright and 541 Birkett fells, from route descriptions to summit photos.

Walking equipment, skills and support

Experience isn't always necessary but for any walk you should have the proper **equipment** – Ambleside and Keswick are

Mountain rescue

If you get into trouble on the mountains and someone dials 999, one of twelve Cumbrian **mountain rescue** teams is likely to swing into action. It's an entirely voluntary service, funded by donation – members all live locally, on call 24 hours a day, and each year they save many lives in all weather conditions. Three basic rules, to avoid having to call them: be prepared, check the weather and don't be too ambitious. There's a useful information video and lots more news and advice on the Lake District Search and Mountain Rescue Association website Ⓦwww.ldsamra.org.uk.

the best places in the Lakes to shop for outdoor gear (and some outdoor stores can rent you a pair of boots and a day-pack). Wear strong-soled, supportive walking shoes or boots – you can turn your ankle on even the easiest of strolls. Even in apparently good weather, warm, wind-and-waterproof layered clothing, a watch, water and something to eat are all essential; in winter, make sure you are fully equipped for the conditions.

Bad weather can move in quickly, even in the height of summer, so before starting out on the fells you should check the **weather forecast** – hotels, hostels and most outdoor shops post a daily forecast, or check with one of the forecasting services listed below. Be aware that weather conditions in the valleys are completely different from mountain-top conditions. Above all, take a **map** and, for up on the fells, a **compass** – they're not fashion accessories, so know how to use them. A handheld **GPS** is useful, but can't be relied upon on its own (due to battery failure, loss of satellite signal etc); similarly, carrying a **mobile phone** is no guarantee of safety in the event of trouble as reception in the Lakes is patchy. You might want to join a guided walk or attend a map-and-compass course instead – the NPA runs both in spring and summer, while any of the climbing schools and instructors listed in the next section offer instruction courses on all aspects of mountain skills and safety.

The NPA also does a huge amount of work in the Lakes on **improving access to the countryside**, repairing paths and maintaining rights of way. For the latest news check with the NPA website (Ⓦwww.lake-district-gov.uk) or Fix the Fells (Ⓦwww.fixthefells.co.uk): you can also contact the **Ramblers' Association** (Ⓦwww.ramblers.org.uk), a campaigning organization dedicated to promoting walking in the UK.

Hiking support services

Coast-Coast Packhorse Ⓣ017683/71777, Ⓦwww.cumbria.com/packhorse. Daily, door-to-door baggage and passenger service on the Coast-to-Coast route, plus left-luggage storage for overseas visitors. Service operates Easter until end of Sept.

Sherpa Van Ⓣ0871/520 0124, from abroad Ⓣ00-44-1748/826917, Ⓦwww.sherpavan.com. Daily door-to-door baggage service for walkers and cyclists between overnight stops on the Coast-to-Coast, Sea-to-Sea, Cumbria Way and Dales Way. Service operates Easter until Oct.

Weather forecasting services

Lake District National Park Weatherline Ⓣ0870/055 0575, Ⓦwww.lake-district.gov.uk/weatherline. Five-day advance forecast for fells and valleys, including hiking conditions.

Met Office Ⓦwww.metoffice.gov.uk. Three-day and longer regional forecasts, plus specific Lake District mountain forecasts available.

Walking holidays

Whatever your level of experience, the tour operators listed below are a good place to start looking for an organized walking holiday in the Lakes – all are either locally based or have specialist knowledge of the area. Trips run year-round unless otherwise stated, though there's more choice between Easter and October. Some holidays are self-guided (ie the arrangements are made for you, but you're given a map and walking instructions to follow), while others are fully guided, but there are always baggage transfers and emergency backup services provided where appropriate. The prices below give an idea of

adventurecapital
the lake district
Cumbria
Feeling adventurous?
The breathtaking scenery of the Lake District is a natural adventure playground. Ride the new Altura Trail at Whinlatter forest.
golakes.co.uk/adventure
INVESTING IN
englandsnorthwest
EUROPEAN REGIONAL DEVELOPMENT FUND

Tullie House Museum & Art Gallery
Enjoy a fun-filled day out for all the family!
Something for everyone, from fine art to interactive fun.
We have a variety of exhibitions and events throughout the year.
FREE ADMISSION to ages 18 and under
Tel 01228 618718 or visit
www.tulliehouse.co.uk
TULLIE HOUSE
MUSEUM AND ART GALLERY
CARLISLE
CARLISLE CITY COUNCIL
www.carlisle.gov.uk
Open daily, all year except:
25th/26th December & 1st January
Tullie House, Castle Street, Carlisle CA3 8TP
Tel: 01228 618718 www.tulliehouse.co.uk

what you can expect to pay for certain types of holiday, but note that transport to and from the Lake District is not included (though some operators may be able to arrange it).

Specialist walking-tour operators

Contours Walking Holidays ⓣ017684/80451, ⓦwww.contours.co.uk. Large variety of self-guided walking holidays along the Cumbria Way, Dales Way and Coast-to-Coast, starting at £210 for four nights' B&B, walking from 10–12 miles a day.

Curlew Guided Walking ⓣ01524/35601, ⓦwww.users.globalnet.co.uk/~curlewgw. Small walking groups tackle six- to twelve-mile hikes a day on seven-night tours (five days' walking) in the southern and northern Lakes. Trips cost around £435 B&B, with packed lunch and guide services included. Shorter two- and three-day breaks also available (£160–230).

Discovery Travel ⓣ01904/632226, ⓦwww.discoverytravel.co.uk. Self-guided walking tours, following the Cumbria Way (seven nights, from £445) or a Lakeland Round circuit (eight nights, £525), though Coast-to-Coast (fifteen nights, £845) or a single-centre Keswick or Coniston walking holiday (seven nights, £375) are also available. Prices include B&B accommodation, maps and guides, baggage transfer and emergency support.

Knobbly Stick ⓣ01539/737576, ⓦwww.knobblystick.com. "The easy way to take a walk on the wild side" – basically a range of self-guided walking holidays, say in "undiscovered Cumbria" (8 nights, from £470) or based in comfortable guest-houses, pubs or farms at Ullswater, Keswick and Wasdale (5 nights, from £300). Tailor-made guided walk options too.

Walking Women ⓣ08456/445335, ⓦwww.walkingwomen.com. Women-only guided walking trips to suit all abilities in places like Borrowdale and Grasmere. Two- to four-night tours (£165–325) on a B&B or full-board basis.

Rock climbing and mountain skills

There's probably no better place in England to learn some rock climbing and mountain skills, and certainly no better pool of climbing talent available to teach, at either introductory or advanced level. The **schools and instructors** listed below offer sessions or courses to individuals, families and groups – it's always best to call first to discuss your requirements. Prices vary wildly, depending on the number in the group, the level of training and length of the course, but for a guided walk in the company of someone hugely experienced in the mountains you'll pay from around £120 per day (split between your party). For a day's rock-climbing instruction or abseiling for beginners, you can expect to pay £150, while two-day residential courses start at around £160 per person.

If all you want is a climbing taster, then the indoor **climbing walls** at Kendal (ⓦwww.kendalwall.co.uk) and Keswick (ⓦwww.keswickclimbingwall.co.uk) can offer an hour's unsupervised fun for around £8, or £15 for an introductory training session. There's also a climbing tower (from £3 a session) at the Low Wood watersports centre, near Ambleside.

Climbing schools, walks and instructors

Above the Line *Wasdale Head Inn*, Wasdale ⓣ019467/26229, ⓦwww.wasdale.com. The birthplace of British mountaineering offers a full programme of courses, including hill walking for softies, guided ascents, mountain navigation courses, mountain first aid, and snow and ice techniques. Women's courses (with women instructors) available too, plus accommodation at the inn.

Carolclimb Low Gillerthwaite, Ennerdale ⓣ01946/862342, ⓦwww.carolclimb.co.uk. Carol Emmons and Richard Sagar offer beginners' courses, guided climbs, ghyll scrambles, winter skills training and kayaking. Beginners, children and families welcomed. Accommodation also available.

Glenridding Walking Guides Glenridding, Ullswater ⓣ017684/82957, ⓦwww.glenriddingguides.com. Guide-led walks and climbs for individuals, families and friends, based at the foot of Helvellyn.

Highpoint ⓣ017684/86731, ⓦwww.mountainguides.co.uk. Courses throughout the year concentrating on hill walking, navigational skills and rock climbing – suitable for beginners and improvers as well as more advanced walkers and climbers.

Boating, watersports and swimming

There's plenty of water in the Lake District and plenty of ways to get out onto it. Apart from the ferry and cruise services on Windermere, Derwent Water, Coniston Water and Ullswater, a dozen or so outlets and operators rent out all sorts of craft, from rowboats to sailing boats, kayaks to windsurfers. Most places offer instruction as well as rental.

Rowboat piers are detailed in the Guide and prices start at around £7 per hour; boats usually aren't available in the winter. The main **boating and watersports centres** are listed below. Most offer canoes and kayaks (from around £8 an hour), dinghies and sailing-boats (from £50 half-day, £80 full-day), and small, self-drive motorboats and electric boats (from £50 half-day, £90 full-day). At most places you can expect to pay around £50 for a couple of hours' windsurfing instruction, or £100 a day, and around £80 for an introductory two-hour sailing lesson, or from £180 for a two-day sailing course.

Windermere, Coniston Water, Derwent Water and Ullswater have an overall 10mph **speed limit** (6mph in certain clearly marked zones on Windermere). Powerboats are allowed on the lakes (with the exception of Bassenthwaite), but operators must stick to the speed limits. Any boat with an engine (including an outboard motor) also needs to be registered with the National Park Authority (NPA). For more information about what you can and cannot do on the lakes, call the **Lake Wardens** (ⓣ015394/42753) who enforce the restrictions on Windermere, or the NPA for the other lakes.

The water craft and reservoirs put some areas off-limits for bathers – Loweswater, for example, might seem very tempting but it's classed as a reservoir so there's no swimming allowed. Even where **lake swimming** is permitted, it can be very dangerous, owing to the extremely cold water and steeply shelving sides – people do drown, even on the sunniest, calmest days, most recently on Ullswater in the summer of 2006 when four young men lost their lives in a bathing accident. You might want to stick to local **swimming pools** instead, listed in the town accounts in the Guide (in Windermere, Keswick, Kendal and Ulverston).

Boating and watersports facilities

Coniston Water

Coniston Boating Centre Lake Rd, Coniston ⓣ015394/41366, ⓔconistonbc@lake-district.gov.uk. Rent electric boats, dinghies, rowboats, kayaks and Canadian canoes – there are also sailing lessons and two-day sailing courses available, and a lakeside café. Closed mid-Oct to Feb.

Derwent Water

Derwentwater Marina Portinscale, Keswick ⓣ017687/72912, ⓦwww.derwentwatermarina.co.uk. Sailing, kayaking, canoeing, windsurfing – rental and tuition (and lakeside apartments available too).

Nichol End Marine Portinscale, Keswick ⓣ017687/73082, ⓦwww.nicholendmarine.co.uk. Windsurfing, sailing, canoeing, motorboats and rowboat rental.

Platty Plus Lodore Boat landings, Borrowdale office ⓣ017687/76572, waterfront ⓣ017687/77282, ⓦwww.plattyplus.co.uk. Canoeing, kayaking, sailing and dragon-boating. Closed Nov–Feb.

Ullswater

Glenridding Sailing Centre The Spit, Glenridding ⓣ017684/82541, ⓦwww.lakesail.co.uk. Canoes, kayaks and dinghies; introductory sailing lessons, plus weekend and five-day tuition courses. Closed Nov–March.

St Patrick's Landing Glenridding Pier ⓣ017684/82393, ⓦwww.stpatricksboatlandings.co.uk. Rowboats, motorboats and electric boats. Closed Nov–Feb.

Ullswater Marine Rampsbeck Boatyard, Watermillock ⓣ017684/86415, ⓦwww.ullswatermarine.co.uk. Motorboat rental. Closed Nov–March.

Windermere

Lakes Leisure Rayrigg Rd ⓣ015394/47183, ⓦwww.lakesleisure.org.uk. Canoe, kayak, sailing and windsurfing lessons and courses.
Low Wood A591, Windermere, a mile south of Ambleside ⓣ015394/39441, ⓦwww.elh.co.uk/watersports. Rowboat rental plus sailing, kayaking and motorboat rental or tuition. It's also the only surviving waterski/wakeboard centre on Windermere (within the 10mph limits), suitable for beginners.
Windermere Canoe & Kayak Ferry Nab Rd, Bowness-on-Windermere ⓣ015394/44451, ⓦwww.windermerecanoekayak.co.uk. Canoe and kayak rental; instruction also available.

Organized holidays, courses and outdoor activities

Once you've been out on the fells, climbed the mountains and splashed on the lakes, there's still plenty of scope for an eventful day out. Local tourist offices have details of all sorts of outdoor activities, from horseriding and pony trekking to fishing and go-karting, or check out ideas on the special Cumbria Tourism website ⓦwww.lakedistrictoutdoors.co.uk.

Individuals and small groups are always welcome, though bear in mind that some of the activity days are aimed at the corporate or group market, so you may have to fit in around larger groups. Some operators are particularly good for family days out and can tailor their activities to most ages and levels of experience.

Prices vary wildly, though you can expect to pay from around £25 for an hour's pony trekking, £40 for a half-day's activity session, £50–80 for a full-day's activity, and up to £160 for a day's off-roading or a balloon flight over the Lakes.

Many of the same operators offer residential courses, for those who fancy more than a day's activity, while other businesses offer all-inclusive organized holidays based around various themes, from cycle touring and sketching to cooking and pottery. Note that the prices for organized holidays don't include transport to and from the Lakes, which you'll usually be expected to arrange for yourself.

Arts and crafts

Gosforth Pottery ⓣ019467/25296, ⓦwww.potterycourses.co.uk. Formal instruction in pottery making (wheel-throwing, handwork and decoration), followed by working at your own pace, or opportunities for local rambling and exploring. The pottery – based in Gosforth, in the western Lakes – runs two-night weekend courses (from £235) and one-week courses (from £535) on a full-board basis, tuition and materials included.
Higham Hall ⓣ017687/76276, ⓦwww.highamhall.com. Residential and day-courses at an adult education centre on Bassenthwaite Lake. A huge variety of courses on offer, from local history or art appreciation talks (£12) to two-day wine-tasting seminars (from £180).
Rothay Manor Hotel ⓣ015394/33605, ⓦwww.rothaymanor.co.uk. Two- to five-night themed activity breaks at this agreeable Ambleside hotel include landscape photography, painting (oil and watercolours), music appreciation, gardening and antiques. Available mainly in winter, spring and autumn, from around £275 to £600 per person on a dinner, bed and breakfast basis.

Equestrian centres

Holmescales Riding Centre Holmescales Farm, Old Hutton, near Kendal ⓣ01539/729388, ⓦwww.holmescalesridingcentre.co.uk. Riding instruction, pony trekking and hacking at a 350-acre riding school with indoor and outdoor facilities.
Lakeland Pony Trekking Limefitt Park, Troutbeck Valley ⓣ015394/31999, ⓦwww.lakelandponytrekking.co.uk. Short rides (one- to three-hour) in Troutbeck Valley, near Windermere,

plus a daily pub ride, full-day excursions and two- and three-day trail rides.

Park Foot Trekking Pooley Bridge, Howtown Rd, Ullswater ⓣ017684/86696, ⓦwww.parkfootponytrekking.co.uk. One- or two-hour treks on the northeastern fells, longer trips on request. April–Oct only.

Fishing

Esthwaite Water Trout Fishery ⓣ015394/36541, ⓦwww.hawksheadtrout.com. Boat-fishing on Esthwaite Water, with tuition for beginners (free on certain days), equipment rental/purchase, BBQ and picnic areas (cook your own catch), rowboats, bird-watching, a farm shop and café.

ⓦ**www.lakedistrictfishing.net** A useful resource for all aspects of fishing in the Lakes, with links to courses, clubs and information.

Off-road

Kankku ⓣ015394/47414, ⓦwww.kankku.co.uk. Off-road 4WD expeditions on rough and rocky terrain in Grizedale Forest, Tarn Hows, Langdale and Coniston, with an emphasis on promoting sound driving skills and techniques. Individuals and families welcome – a full day out costs from £150 per vehicle (for up to 4 people), or bring your own 4WD (from £79 a day). Based in Windermere, pick-ups available.

Outdoor activities

Country Adventures ⓣ01254/690691, ⓦwww.country-adventures.co.uk. A varied programme in the Lakes, from a day's scenic walking or cycling to sailing weekends, gorge-scrambling/climbing and multi-activity sessions. Many holidays are youth-hostel-based in places like Ambleside, Elterwater and Borrowdale.

Lake District National Park Authority ⓣ0845/272 0004, ⓔevents@lake-district.gov.uk, ⓦwww.lake-district.gov.uk. Organizes a huge programme of day events throughout the year, mostly free though charges are made for some activities. Highlights include mountain biking with the park rangers, falconry displays, dry-stone-wall building and watersports weekends. Contact the events team or check the events diary on the website.

Outward Bound ⓣ01931/740000, ⓦwww.outwardbound-uk.org. Week-long multi-adventure courses at the Outward Bound Ullswater centre (gorge-walking to kayaking) for 14- to 24-year-olds.

River Deep Mountain High ⓣ015395/28666, ⓦwww.riverdeepmountainhigh.co.uk. Multi-activity holidays (weekend/week-long, self-catering or fully inclusive) incorporating guided walking, canoeing and mountain biking, plus activity days, river trips and instruction.

Rookin House Farm ⓣ017684/83561, ⓦwww.rookinhouse.co.uk. Go-karting, quad-biking, horse-riding, pony trekking, archery and clay-pigeon shooting, not forgetting "human bowling" (one person strapped into a ball, while the others roll it at pins).

Summitreks ⓣ015394/41212, ⓦwww.summitreks.co.uk. Established adventure company offering a year-round programme of activities, from climbing to canoeing, aquasailing (abseiling down waterfalls) to canyoning (descending gorges). Children's multi-adventure days in the school holidays usually incorporate mountain biking, gorge scrambling and canoeing; adults can learn orienteering or join guided walks.

Youth Hostel Association ⓦwww.yha.org.uk. One of the biggest organizers of holidays in the Lakes, the YHA uses its hostels for weekend breaks or longer holidays, with the emphasis on hill walking, rock climbing, kayaking, mountain biking and orienteering – though Coniston's Gourmet Cumbrian food safari is an annual fixture. Accommodation is in bunk rooms (twins and family rooms often available) and most hostels serve budget meals, though self-catering is also available.

Photography

Bill Birkett Photography Courses ⓣ015394/37420, ⓦwww.billbirkett.co.uk. The respected lakeland writer and photographer runs small-group photography courses throughout the year in Langdale and further afield, involving daily walks, mountain photography and technical assistance (bring your own camera and laptop). Either book directly (see website, from £120 per day for up to 3 people) or check the specific day and weekend courses available though Highpoint (ⓦwww.mountainguides.co.uk).

Travel essentials

Costs and discounts

If you're counting the cost, there are plenty of ways to keep to a budget. Nearly all **accommodation** options – from simple B&Bs to luxury hotels – offer special off-season deals or discounts or even free nights for longer stays. It always pays to ask when booking. Youth hostels and self-catering cottages – the Lakes has the most extensive network of either in the country – mean you can save money by cooking for yourself. **Children and senior citizens** get discounts on most forms of transport in the Lakes, and on entrance to the sights, museums and historic houses, and nearly every attraction has a discounted family ticket available. **YHA members** qualify for discounts and special deals on all sorts of activities and at attractions and retail outlets.

As far as **events and activities** go, many of the traditional festivals or local attractions are free, while the National Park Authority organizes free or low-cost activities, courses, walks and events throughout the year. And if you join the **National Trust** (membership Ⓦwww.nationaltrust.org.uk) or **English Heritage** (Ⓦwww.english-heritage.org.uk), you'll get free entry to all relevant sights and attractions.

Hospitals and pharmacies

There are accident, emergency and minor injury services at the hospitals listed below. For minor complaints, you'll find pharmacies in the main towns and villages (all listed in the Guide). These are open standard shop hours, though local newspapers and all pharmacy windows list the pharmacies that stay open an hour or two later on some nights of the week (usually on a rota basis).

Hospitals

Barrow-in-Furness Furness General Hospital, Dalton Lane Ⓣ01229/870870, Ⓦwww.mbht.nhs.uk.
Carlisle Cumberland Infirmary, Newtown Rd Ⓣ01228/523444.
Cockermouth Cockermouth Community Hospital, Isel Rd Ⓣ01900/822226.
Kendal Westmorland General Hospital, Burton Rd Ⓣ01539/732288, Ⓦwww.mbht.nhs.uk.
Keswick Keswick Cottage Hospital, Crosthwaite Rd Ⓣ017687/67000.
Penrith Penrith New Hospital, Bridge Lane Ⓣ01768/245300.

Internet

There's internet provision in all the major towns and villages, though access is rarely cheap (around £2 for 30min is standard). However, local libraries now all have broadband internet, which can be free for short periods or inexpensive. Wireless access is also widespread, even in small B&Bs or hostels – it's often free, though sometimes you have to pay in cafés or larger hotels. If you're taking your own laptop make sure you've got insurance cover for it.

Laundry

Most youth hostels have washing and drying facilities of some sort, and B&B owners can sometimes be persuaded (or offer) to help out. There are self-service laundries in Keswick, Penrith, Windermere and other towns (though none in Grasmere or Coniston), with details included in the relevant listings sections.

Left luggage

Hotels, B&Bs and hostels will all mind guests' luggage for the day (or longer), but there's a distinct shortage of places where you can simply turn up in town and leave your bag or pack for the day. Tourist offices are understandably reluctant to help, given the number of visitors; the only railway stations in the Lakes (at Kendal and Windermere) don't have the facilities; and bus stations are usually little more than roadside stops. Usually, your best bet is to

Rough Guides travel insurance

Rough Guides has teamed up with WorldNomads.com to offer great **travel insurance** deals. Policies are available to residents of over 150 countries, with cover for a wide range of **adventure sports**, 24hr emergency assistance, high levels of medical and evacuation cover and a stream of **travel safety information**. Roughguides.com users can take advantage of their policies online 24/7, from anywhere in the world – even if you're already travelling. And since plans often change when you're on the road, you can extend your policy and even claim online. Roughguides.com users who buy travel insurance with WorldNomads.com can also leave a positive footprint and donate to a community development project. For more information go to Ⓦ**www.roughguides.com/shop**.

ask nicely at local shops, cafés or hotels – buying something first sometimes helps.

Mail

Each town and major village in the Lakes has a single post office where, apart from the usual postal services, you can usually exchange travellers' cheques and foreign currency. Normal opening hours are Monday to Friday from 9am to 5.30pm and Saturday from 9am to 12.30pm, though smaller offices may have restricted hours. It's worth noting that not all post offices are stand-alone businesses – the smaller ones, especially, are often housed in village stores. For information about postal services in Cumbria and the Lakes, or to find a post office address, contact the post office enquiry line on Ⓣ0845/722 3344, Ⓦwww.postoffice.co.uk.

Maps

The best general map of the National Park area is the Ordnance Survey (Ⓦwww.ordnancesurvey.co.uk; OS) Travel Map, Tour no. 3 (1:100,000), with hill shading and principal footpaths illustrated. For more detail of Cumbria as a whole (including Carlisle and the coast), you'll need the (1:50,000) **OS Landranger** series of maps (nos. 85, 89, 90, 96 and 97).

Essential for hikers are the orange (1:25,000) **OS Explorer** series – four maps (nos. 4, 5, 6 and 7) which cover the whole Lake District National Park. There are more rugged, plastic-coated versions of these available too. Some prefer the **Harvey Superwalker** (Ⓦwww.harveymaps.co.uk) series of six waterproof maps (also 1:25,000) covering north, east, west, central, southeast and southwest Lakeland. There's also a good, compact, ring-bound Harvey Lake District **National Park Atlas** (1:40,000), useful for cyclists and general walkers, as well as detailed (1:40,000) fold-out Harvey **route maps** for the Cumbria Way, Dales Way and Coast-to-Coast long-distance paths that all pass through the Lake District.

Most bookshops, outdoors stores and tourist information offices sell the full range of maps, as well as various **local walk map-leaflets**. Recommended series include the packs of *Lakeland Leisure Walks* (five assorted walks in each of the major areas), local fell expert Paul Buttle's various walking booklets, and the National Park Authority's *Walks in the Countryside* leaflets. For **hiking guides** for the Lake District, see p.272.

Markets

Local **markets** are held on: Monday, Cockermouth and Kendal; Tuesday, Broughton-in-Furness and Penrith; Wednesday, Ambleside and Kendal; Thursday, Ulverston; Saturday, Kendal, Keswick, Penrith and Ulverston.

The best regional **farmers' market** is at Orton in the Eden Valley (Ⓦwww.ortonfarmers.co.uk), two miles off the M6 (junction 38; 17 miles north of Kendal), held on the second Saturday of the month. The Orton farmers are also at Pooley Bridge in the summer (April–Sept last Sun) and Rheged visitor centre in the winter (Oct–March last Sun). But it's a growing scene and there are also other farmers' markets at

Carlisle (first Fri of the month), Keswick (second Thurs, plus others), Ulverston (third Sat), Kendal (last Fri, plus others), Whitehaven (second Sat), Cockermouth (first Sat) and Penrith (third Tues).

Media

Local **newspapers** are a good source of information about lakeland events, politics and personalities. Two daily papers carve up the region between them: the *North West Evening Mail* (southern Cumbria, Ⓦwww.nwemail.co.uk) and the *News and Star* (northern Cumbria, Ⓦwww.newsandstar.co.uk). Otherwise, there are weekly papers for each region: the *Westmorland Gazette* (Ⓦwww.thisisthelakedistrict.co.uk), which covers eastern Cumbria and the southern and central Lakes; the *Lake District Herald* (Penrith, Keswick and the northern Lakes); the *Keswick Reminder* (covering just Keswick); and the *Cumberland News* (Carlisle, Keswick and Penrith, Ⓦwww.cumberland-news.co.uk).

Magazines include *Cumbria* (Ⓦwww.cumbriamagazine.co.uk), a small-format monthly magazine, and the bigger, glossier, *Cumbria Life* (Ⓦwww.cumbrialife.co.uk), both of which concentrate on the history, culture and social and natural fabric of the Lakes. The quarterly *Lakeland Walker* is a chatty periodical aimed at hikers and lakeland lovers, featuring walks, news, reviews and equipment-testing.

Local radio stations

BBC Radio Cumbria North Cumbria 95.6 FM/756 AM; West Cumbria 104.1 FM/1458 AM; South Cumbria 96.1 FM/837 AM; Windermere 95.2 FM/104.2 FM.
The Bay North 96.9 FM; Lakes/South 102.3 FM; Cumbria 103.2 FM.
Lakeland Radio South Lakes area 100.1/100.8 FM.

Money

Normal **banking hours** are Monday to Friday from 9.30am to 3.30pm, with some branches in the major towns open on Saturday morning too. Conversely, in smaller lakeland villages, bank branches sometimes only open a couple of days a week. Each of the main settlements in the Lakes has at least one branch of the major banks with an **ATM**, while stand-alone ATMs are increasingly found in village shops and petrol stations, though note that these nearly all charge a fee for withdrawing cash with your card. You can exchange travellers' cheques and foreign currency at major post offices.

Credit cards are widely accepted in shops, hotels, restaurants and service stations, but don't count on being able to use plastic in B&Bs, guesthouses, and some pubs and cafés: we indicate all those that don't accept credit cards in the Guide. Be aware, however – even those that do accept credit cards often don't accept American Express.

Opening hours and public holidays

Full opening hours are given in the Guide for sights, attractions and tourist offices. **Church** opening hours vary considerably, though most of those mentioned open daily between 9 or 10am and 4 or 5pm, but you can't count on it. **Shops and businesses** follow the standard pattern for the UK (Mon to Sat 9am to 5.30pm or 6pm), though you'll find some village stores and local shops open an hour or so earlier or later than these times. **Early closing day** (when the shops shut for the afternoon) is still observed in many towns and villages, usually on Thursday in the Lakes.

Phones

There are public telephone boxes all over the Lake District, even in isolated rural

Public and bank holidays in the UK

January 1
Good Friday (late March or early April)
Easter Monday (as above)
First Monday in May
Last Monday in May
Last Monday in Aug
December 25
December 26

Note that if January 1, or Dec 25 or 26 falls on a Saturday or Sunday, the next weekday becomes a public holiday.

areas, and most take phonecards and credit cards, which is just as well because you'll sometimes find that coverage from your **mobile phone** network is patchy to say the least. The nature of the terrain means you sometimes can't get a signal (though you're usually all right in the main towns and villages), which is one reason why it's not recommended that hikers rely solely on their phones – rather than their navigational skills – to get them out of trouble on the fells. Local telephone codes are included for all numbers listed in the Guide.

Police and emergencies

Dial ⓣ999 for all emergencies: in relevant circumstances ask for Mountain Rescue. If you want to speak to the police but it's not an emergency, call ⓣ0845/330 0247. The addresses of local police stations are given in the relevant town listings and most are only open for limited weekday hours – you'll have to call the non-emergency number above for telephone assistance. There's more information about stations and services at ⓦwww.cumbria.police.uk.

Shopping

There's a fantastic range of local crafts and workshops in Cumbria, from cottage candle-makers to furniture carvers. The website ⓦwww.madeincumbria.co.uk is a good resource, dedicated to Cumbrian crafts, gifts and food, with information and links to craftspeople and local suppliers throughout the region.

Tourist information

For information before you go, contact Cumbria Tourism or the Lake District National Park Authority (NPA), both of which have very useful websites. The Cumbria County Council website is the place to go for local community, transport, leisure and business information, with handy links to other sites.

In the Lake District itself, a series of visitor information offices provides help on the ground – all are listed in the Guide – with the main **National Park Visitor Centre** at Brockhole on Windermere (see below). The other offices are funded and run by the tourist board and the NPA, or by local councils and volunteers: opening hours vary, though in the summer most of the main offices are open daily from 10am to 6pm, sometimes an hour earlier in the morning and an hour later in the evening. Opening hours are reduced in winter and, in some offices, may be restricted to weekends only (usually Fri to Sun) from 10am to 4pm. Local budgetary constraints also sometimes restrict hours and services, but at each office, when it's open, you'll be able to book accommodation, check on local weather conditions, and buy guides and maps.

Visitor information

Cumbria County Council ⓣ01228/606060, ⓦwww.cumbria.gov.uk.
Cumbria Tourism Windermere Rd, Staveley, Kendal, Cumbria LA8 9PL ⓣ01539/822222, ⓦwww.golakesⓦ.co.uk.
Lake District National Park Authority Murley Moss, Oxenholme Rd, Kendal, Cumbria LA9 7RL ⓣ01539/724555; for events and visitor information contact the NPA at Brockhole, Windermere, Cumbria LA23 1LJ ⓣ015394/46601, ⓦwww.lake-district.gov.uk.

Guide

Guide

1

Windermere

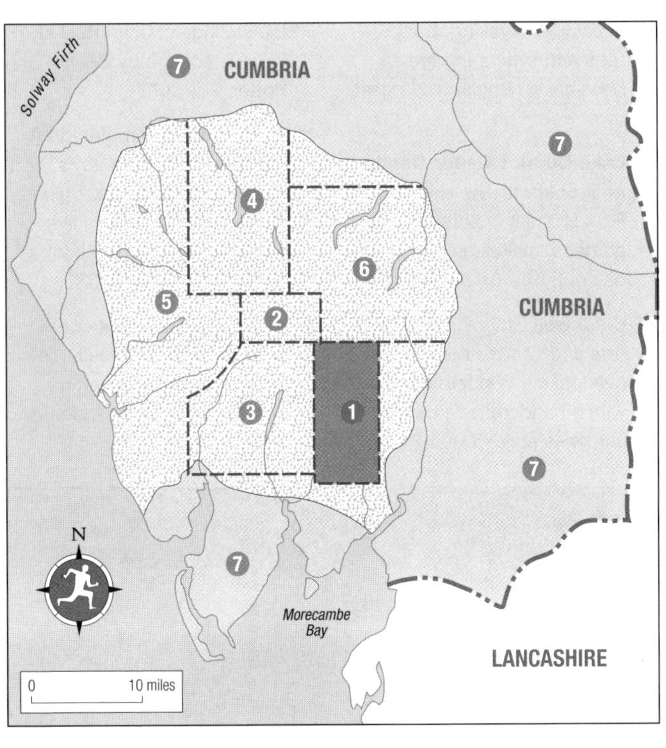

CHAPTER 1

Highlights

* **The view from Orrest Head** The summit of Orrest Head, a short climb from Windermere town, provides stunning views up and down the lake. See p.59
* **Watersports on Windermere** Messing about on the water is easy – kayaking, boat trips and swimming are all possible on England's largest lake. See p.64
* **Lake District Visitor Centre at Brockhole** The National Park HQ, set in acres of gardens, makes a great family day out. See p.70
* **Blackwell** Stunning Arts and Crafts house overlooking Windermere, with a handcrafted interior of immense style. See p.70
* **Lakes Aquarium** Dodge the diving ducks in the underwater tunnel at the entertaining Lakes Aquarium. See p.72
* **Armitt Collection, Ambleside** The lowdown on lakeland literary and artistic life – from the writings of John Ruskin to watercolours by Beatrix Potter. See p.77
* **A night out in Ambleside** A romantic dinner at *Lucy's*, or a meal, a movie or a jazz gig at *Zeffirelli's* – Ambleside is the best place in the Lakes for a big night out. See p.83
* **Kentmere** This quiet corner of the southern Lakes boasts some dramatic walking on the Kentmere Horseshoe trail. See p.89

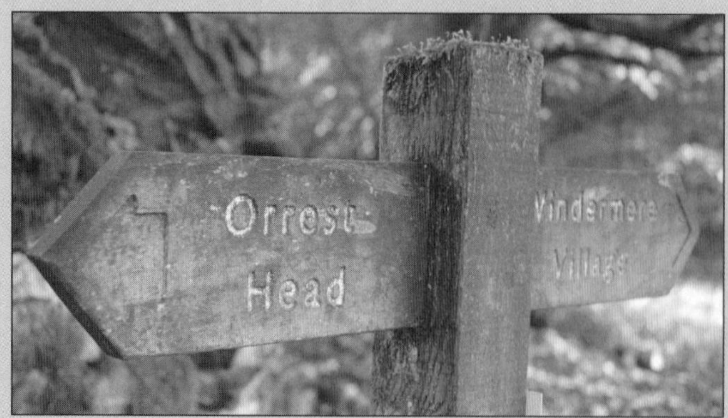

▲ Orrest Head, a short climb from Windermere town

1

Windermere

England's largest and most famous lake rarely fails to impress. The rocky inlets, secluded bays, grassy banks and wooded heights of **Windermere** form the very core of most people's image of the Lake District. And on bitingly cold winter days, or in the dappled spring and autumn sun, there are few finer places in England to soak up the scenery. Hardly surprisingly, it's far too popular for its own good and you're unlikely to find real solitude in any of the three settlements – Windermere, Bowness and Ambleside – which group together on its northeast shore. However, the southern and western reaches of the lake are still remarkably underdeveloped, and their small hamlets, rustic attractions, waterside walks and hilltop scrambles provide some of the most inviting destinations in the southern Lakes.

Most people approaching the central lakes and fells from the south at least funnel through **Windermere town**, getting their first glimpse of the lake at nearby **Bowness** – formerly a medieval lakeside village, though now the National Park's largest resort and boating centre. This also has the pick of the local cultural attractions, most notably the restored Arts and Crafts mansion of **Blackwell** to the south.

William Wordsworth himself thought that "None of the other Lakes unfold so many fresh beauties" and it makes sense to get out on the water as soon as possible. The cruise-boat ride south from Bowness provides access to **Lakeside** and its aquarium, and to the picnic lawns of **Fell Foot Park**, while combined boat-and-train tickets are available for steam trips on the **Lakeside and Haverthwaite Railway**. Heading north from Bowness there are landings at **Brockhole** – whose magnificent gardens form the backdrop for the Lake District Visitor Centre and National Park Headquarters – and at Waterhead for nearby **Ambleside**, a handily sited hiking and touring base that's also the busiest settlement on Windermere.

Away from the lake, the quiet hamlet of **Troutbeck** is strung along a gentle valley that lies between Windermere and Ambleside. There's good walking from here, as there is from the neighbouring **Kentmere** valley, where the River Kent tumbles down through the old mill village of **Staveley**. This is only four miles east of the hubbub at Windermere but it seems like a world apart up on the fell tops or in the even quieter reaches of neighbouring **Longsleddale**.

Windermere town

The completion of the railway from Kendal in 1847 changed the face of Windermere for ever, providing direct access to the lake for Victorian day-trippers and holiday-makers. The hillside hamlet of Birthwaite, lying a good

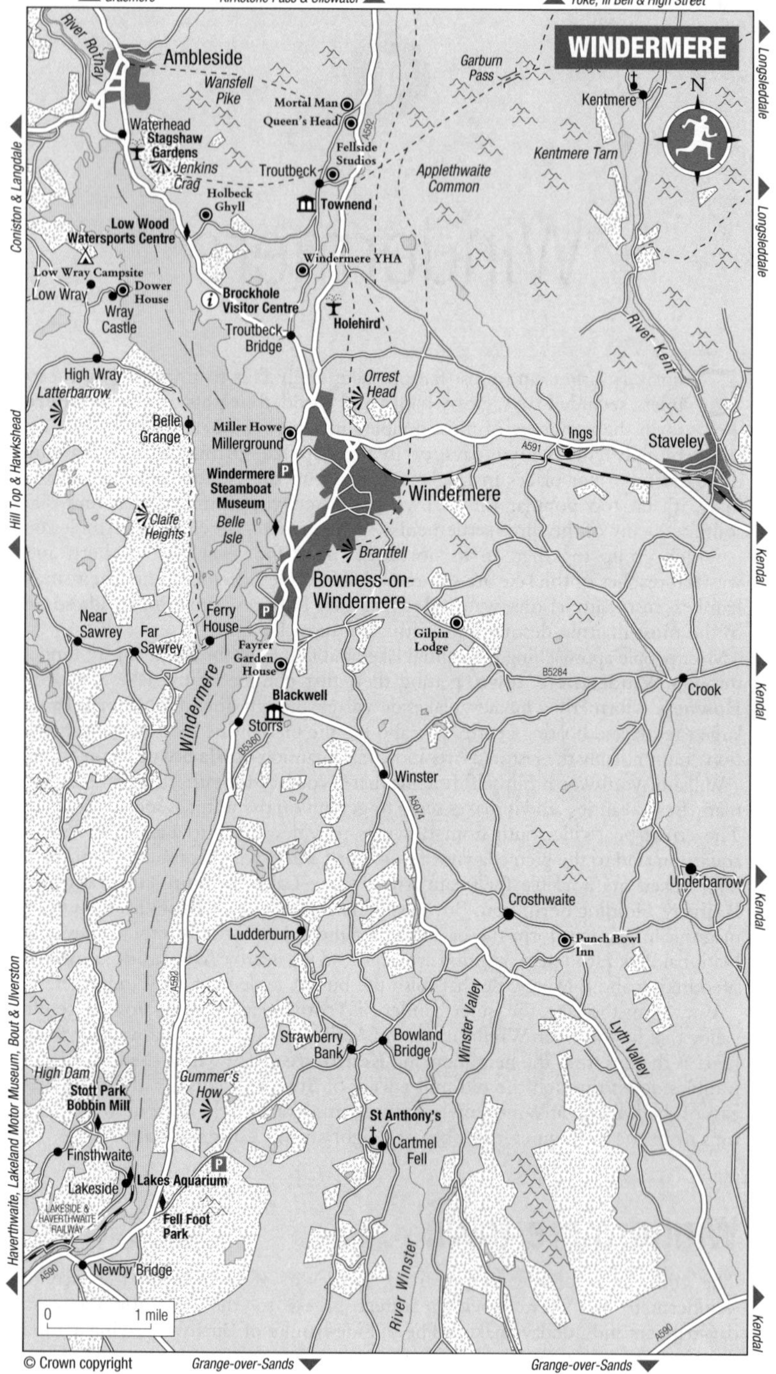
WINDERMERE
Grasmere
Kirkstone Pass & Ullswater
Yoke, Ill Bell & High Street
Longsleddale
Longsleddale
Kendal
Kendal
Kendal
Kendal
Grange-over-Sands
Grange-over-Sands
Coniston & Langdale
Hill Top & Hawkshead
Haverthwaite, Lakeland Motor Museum, Bout & Ulverston
River Rothay
Ambleside
Wansfell Pike
Mortal Man
Queen's Head
Fellside Studios
Garburn Pass
Kentmere
N
Kentmere Tarn
Waterhead
Stagshaw Gardens
Jenkins Crag
Troutbeck
Applethwaite Common
Holbeck Ghyll
Townend
Low Wood Watersports Centre
Windermere YHA
Low Wray Campsite
Low Wray
Dower House
Wray Castle
Brockhole Visitor Centre
Holehird
Troutbeck Bridge
River Kent
High Wray
Latterbarrow
Orrest Head
Belle Grange
Miller Howe
Millerground
Ings
Staveley
A591
Windermere Steamboat Museum
Windermere
Claife Heights
Belle Isle
Brantfell
Bowness-on-Windermere
Near Sawrey
Far Sawrey
Ferry House
Gilpin Lodge
Fayrer Garden House
B5284
Crook
Windermere
Blackwell
Storrs
B5360
Winster
A5074
Underbarrow
Crosthwaite
Ludderburn
Punch Bowl Inn
A592
Winster Valley
Lyth Valley
Strawberry Bank
Bowland Bridge
High Dam
Gummer's How
Stott Park Bobbin Mill
St Anthony's
Cartmel Fell
Finsthwaite
Lakeside
Lakes Aquarium
LAKESIDE & HAVERTHWAITE RAILWAY
Fell Foot Park
A590
Newby Bridge
River Winster
A590
0
1 mile
© Crown copyright

mile from the water, was entirely subsumed within a newly created town, soon named **WINDERMERE** to emphasize the link with the lake itself. Not everyone welcomed the development. William Wordsworth, ever more conservative in his old age, feared the effects of the railway (while conveniently forgetting that his own *Guide to the Lakes* had done much to popularize the district in the first place). The poet attempted to keep out the hordes by means of a sonnet – "Is then no nook of English ground secure from rash assault?" – and by penning rambling broadsides which must have sorely tested the patience of their recipient, the editor of the *Morning Post*. Wordsworth's defence of the "picturesque" had reason behind it, and he can hardly be said to have been wrong in fearing the "railway inundations [of an] Advance of the Ten Thousand". But (like most gentlemen of his day) his real fear was that of the great unwashed, the "imperfectly educated", sullying his back yard with their "wrestling matches, horse and boat races…pot houses and beer shops".

Most of the villas and guesthouses built for the Victorians still stand, and Windermere town remains the transport hub for the southern and central Lakes, but there's precious little else to keep you in the slate-grey streets. Instead, all the traffic pours a mile downhill to its older twin town, lakeside Bowness, and the only reason for not doing the same is to take time to climb the heights of **Orrest Head** (784ft), just to the north of Windermere town. The bare summit gives a famous 360° panorama, sweeping from the Yorkshire fells to Morecambe Bay, the Langdale Pikes to Troutbeck valley. This was the very first lakeland climb made by a young Alfred Wainwright (see p.231), on his earliest visit to the Lake District in 1930 – one that, in his own words, cast a spell that changed his life. It's an easy twenty-minute stroll up through shaded **Elleray Wood**: the signposted path begins just to the left of the large *Windermere Hotel* on the A591, across from the train station. Ten minutes up the path, in Elleray Wood, you'll pass the cottage-studio of **blacksmith** Steve Hicks, where on most days you can grab a cup of tea and browse his creative, handcrafted ironwork.

Practicalities

The A591 between Kendal and Ambleside runs across the northern side of town, past the **train station**. There's a **car park** inside the train station yard and another down in the town on Broad Street by the library; otherwise on-street parking is usually limited to thirty minutes. Windermere is a major **bus terminus**, with all services stopping outside the train station – "Travel details" at the end of the chapter has all the connections, but useful routes include the open-top #599 (to Bowness, Brockhole, Ambleside and Grasmere), the #555 (to Kendal or Keswick), and the #505 (Hawkshead and Coniston). A one-day **Central Lakes Day Rider** ticket (buy from the driver; from £6.50) gives unlimited travel on any service running between Windermere/Bowness and Grasmere/Coniston, while the **Windermere Bus and Boat Rider** (from £9) combines the open-top #599 bus service with a Windermere lake cruise.

A hundred yards away from the station, in the wooden chalet opposite the NatWest bank, stands the **tourist information centre** at the top of Victoria Street (Mon–Sat 9.30am–5pm, Sun 10am–5pm, possibly open later July & Aug; Ⓣ015394/46499, Ⓦwww.lakelandgateway.info).

Accommodation

Good places to look for **B&Bs** are on High Street and neighbouring Victoria Street, with other concentrations on College Road, Oak and Broad streets. At the bottom of town, halfway to Bowness, Lake Road and its offshoots have a line of mid-range **guesthouses** and hotels, but these are a fair walk (or bus ride)

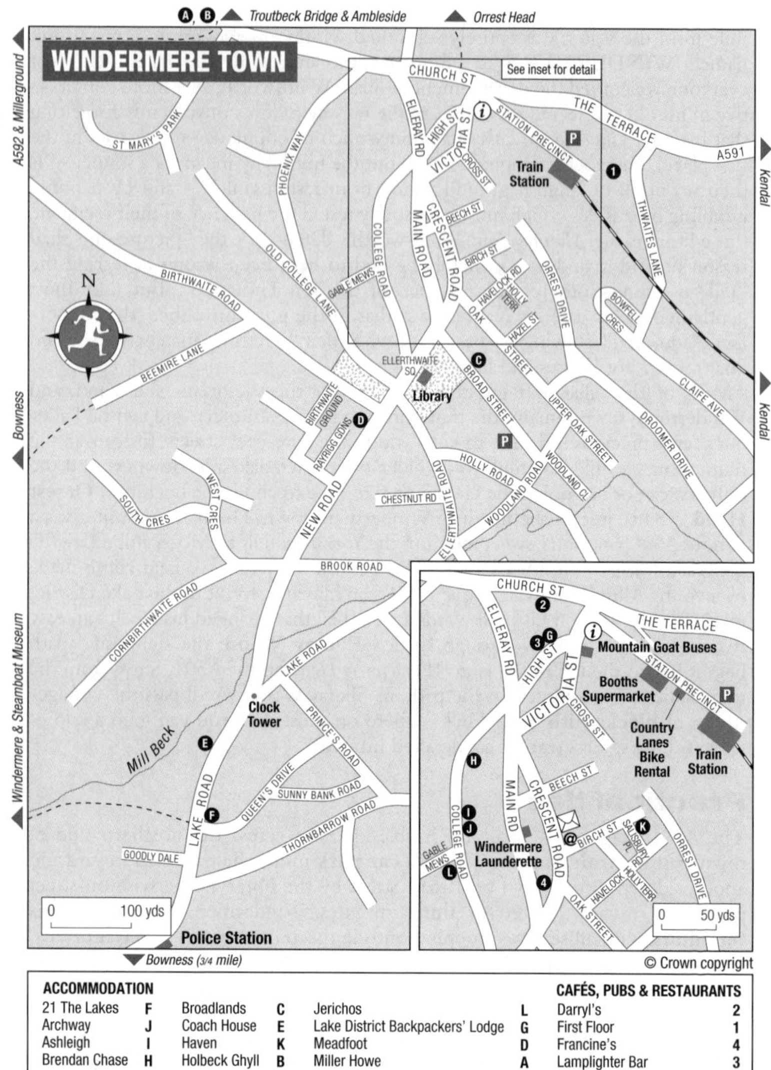

from either Bowness or Windermere. Further out still is a selection of very grand **country-house hotels**, which make the most of their secluded locations, lake views and extensive grounds. Although there's a backpackers' hostel in Windermere itself, the nearest YHA youth hostel is at Troutbeck, while for camping you'll have to head down to Bowness.

In Windermere

Archway 13 College Rd ☎ 015394/45613, Ⓦ www.the-archway.com. Simply a great B&B, with four trim rooms (two doubles, two twin) in a Victorian house, with the best light and views at the front – you know you're in good hands when you get homemade bedside biscuits. It's also known for its breakfasts, serving things like American pancakes, kippers, smoked haddock, omelettes or the traditional full English. Parking. ❷

Ashleigh 11 College Rd ⓣ015394/42292, ⓦwww.ashleighhouse.com. Choose from one of five tasteful rooms, which have been furnished in welcoming country pine. Parking. ❷

Brendan Chase 1 College Rd ⓣ015394/45638, ⓦwww.placetostaywindermere.co.uk. A popular place with backpackers and overseas travellers, who get a warm welcome and a good breakfast. There are eight reasonably priced rooms (some en suite), and if you can fill the spacious family/group rooms, which can sleep up to five, you'll bring the price down to around £20 a night. Also parking and an enclosed yard for cycles. No credit cards. ❷

Broadlands 19 Broad St ⓣ015394/46532, ⓦwww.broadlandsbedandbreakfast.co.uk. For a straightforward night in one of the town's traditional stone-terraced guesthouses, *Broadlands* stands out: a cheerily run family home with five rooms (the top one lovely and light), whose owners can provide local walk leaflets and a car park pass. ❷

Coach House Lake Rd ⓣ015394/44494, ⓦwww.lakedistrictbandb.com. Comfort and contemporary design join hands in this stylish conversion of a Victorian coach house. Five classy rooms with wrought-iron beds, gleaming bathrooms and elegant touches are complemented by a relaxed breakfast with the morning papers, and use of a local leisure club. Parking. ❸

Haven 10 Birch St ⓣ015394/44017, ⓦwww.thehaven.windermere.btinternet.co.uk. Big windows let the light into this handsomely refurbished Victorian house, with the choice of three comfortably appointed rooms (one with a nice antique brass bedstead). Walkers are welcome to use the books, maps and drying facilities. Parking. ❷

Jerichos at the Waverley College Rd ⓣ015394/42522, ⓦwww.jerichos.co.uk. A shift in premises for Chris and Jo Blaydes' acclaimed *Jerichos* restaurant has also added ten good-value rooms in the old *Waverley* temperance hotel. They are modish but unpretentious, restoring the original cornicing and sash windows for example, but adding black leather beds and ipod docks. It's still a food-led operation though, the best in town, offering exciting, seasonally changing Modern British menus (main £16–22), always including a vegetarian option, served in an informal, buzzy, stripped-down restaurant (dinner only, not Thursday; reservations advised). Parking. ❹

Lake District Backpackers' Lodge High St ⓣ015394/46374, ⓦwww.lakedistrictbackpackers.co.uk. Twenty beds in small dorms (available as private rooms on request), a laid-back atmosphere and good facilities, including kitchen with washing machine, internet access, satellite TV, bike storage and lockers. It's a squeeze when full, but the price includes a cereal, tea-and-toast breakfast, and there's information about local tours and work opportunities. No credit cards. Dorm beds from £12.50 (one- or two-night stays £14.50), or £16.50 per person in a private room.

Meadfoot New Rd ⓣ015394/42610, ⓦwww.meadfoot-guesthouse.co.uk. One of the rooms at this friendly family villa opens directly onto the secluded garden, while the others overlook it – as does the dining room and deck where you take breakfast. It makes for a comfortable touring base, with pine-furnished rooms (some with carved four-posters), plus patio and summerhouse. Parking. ❸

21 The Lakes Lake Rd ⓣ015394/44165, ⓦwww.21thelakes.co.uk. The variously themed suites in his boutique hotel aren't everyone's cup of tea, but they certainly make you sit up and take notice. Beds like thrones in some, sunken spa baths and outdoor hot tubs in others, with characters and colours that range from bright-and-white to rich-and-regal. And all behind a most unassuming Victorian frontage (if you ignore the silver globe fountain). If you like this, take a look at the sister hotel in Bowness, *Aphrodite's* (ⓦwww.aphroditeslodge.co.uk), which is, if anything, even more OTT (a fur-clad "Flintstones" cave room anyone?) – guests can use *Aphrodite's* pool in any case. Room rates vary, but start at £70. Parking. ❸–❹, weekends ❺–❻

Around Windermere

Holbeck Ghyll Holbeck Lane (off A591), 3 miles north of town ⓣ015394/32375, ⓦwww.holbeck-ghyll.co.uk. See chapter map for location. One of the stalwarts of the country-house hotel scene in the Lakes, with classically elegant rooms either in the main house (once a hunting lodge for the Earl of Lonsdale) or in detached lodges, suites and houses in the grounds. You get lake views and a sherry decanter in each room, plus seven acres of gardens and woodland with trails, gym and spa, and Michelin-starred food of immense refinement. Room rates start at around £250 (lake view and lodge rooms from £310), but include dinner as well as breakfast. Parking. ❽

Miller Howe Rayrigg Rd (A592), half-mile west of town ⓣ015394/42536, ⓦwww.millerhowe.com. See chapter map for location. The gorgeous Edwardian house, high above Windermere, has long been a byword for lakeland indulgence and new owners have maintained the attraction while sharpening the style. As well as Arts and Crafts furniture and plump armchairs in fire-warmed lounges, there's also an up-to-the-minute sheen throughout and lake views to die for – from classy rooms with their own balconies, or from the bird's-eye terraces and landscaped gardens. Dining is still the highlight, less formal than in the past, with inventive Modern British cooking using locally sourced ingredients; the price includes dinner (otherwise £40 for nonresidents) and a lavish breakfast. Rates start at £210, though superior lake-view rooms (£280) and secluded cottage suites in the grounds (£310) offer an even more memorable experience. Closed 2 weeks in Jan. Parking. 8

Eating and drinking

You don't need to make the trek down to Bowness as there are plenty of **cafés and restaurants** in Windermere. For the finest local dining, consider dinner at *Jerichos at the Waverley*, or lunch or dinner at the more formal country houses of *Holbeck Ghyll* (which has a Michelin star) or *Miller Howe*, all open to nonresidents (see "Accommodation" above, reservations advised for all). *Miller Howe*, particularly, is the pamper-yourself choice for afternoon tea (£14) or Sunday lunch (£25). The main **supermarket** is Booths, by the train station, which also has its own café.

Darryl's 14 Church St (the A591) ⓣ015394/42894. No-frills café for cheap, filling meals – the sort you eat before getting back in your rig and driving across country. Specialities are the all-day breakfast and fish and chips, both under a fiver – served from 8am (the earliest start in town). Daytime only; closed Tues & Wed. No credit cards.

First Floor Lakeland Ltd, behind the train station ⓣ015394/88200. Occupying the first-floor gallery of the kitchen/home-furnishings/design store, this superior café's snacks, lunches and high teas attract peak-period queues. There are always filled baguettes, tortilla wraps, soups, meat and cheese platters, salads, cakes and puddings, while a seasonally changing menu offers dishes such as salmon on a rocket and radicchio salad. Most dishes from £4.50–7.50. Daytime only.

Francine's 27 Main Rd ⓣ015394/44088, ⓦwww.francinesrestaurantwindermere.co.uk. During the day you can drop into this easy-going café-restaurant for anything from a *pain au chocolat* to a big bowl of mussels. Dinner (Wed–Sat only) sees the lights dimmed for a wide-ranging continental menu of pork belly confit to seafood marinara, with an emphasis on fish and seafood, and while most mains run from £9 to £14, a three-course set menu (£17.95) is a steal. Closed Mon.

Lamplighter Bar *Oakthorpe Hotel*, High St ⓣ015394/43547. Very popular local choice for bistro meals, served in the hotel's bar-cum-dining room. English classics (steaks, gammon and egg, rack of lamb and fresh fish) plus a bit of sophistication (crab mornay, oysters or smoked salmon salad), all in big portions at value-for-money prices (most things £10–15); the beer's good too and there's usually live music on Wednesday nights. Closed Sun & Mon lunch.

Listings

Banks NatWest (High St), HSBC and Barclays (all Crescent Rd) have ATMs, and there's an ATM outside Booths supermarket by the station.

Bike rental Country Lanes, The Railway Station (Easter–Oct daily 9am–5pm; Nov–Easter weekends and other times by arrangement; ⓣ015394/44544, ⓦwww.countrylaneslakedistrict.co.uk). Bikes from £19–30 per day, including tandems, tag-alongs and trailers; helmet, maps and routes provided.

Bookshop Fireside Bookshop, 21 Victoria St ⓣ015394/45855, ⓦwww.firesidebookshop.co.uk. Secondhand and antiquarian stockist; good for books on Cumbria and the Lakes.

Car rental Lakes Car Hire, ⓣ015394/44408, ⓦwww.lakeshire.co.uk.

Emergencies The nearest hospital is in Kendal: Westmorland General Hospital, Burton Rd; ⓣ01539/732288.

Internet access Windermere Library, Broad St (Mon, Tues, Thurs & Fri 9.30am–5pm, Sat 10am–1pm, closed Wed & Sun; ⓣ015394/62400). There's also access at the tourist information centre and in Lakeland Ltd by the *First Floor* café.

Laundry Windermere Launderette, 19 Main Rd (Mon–Fri 8.30am–5.30pm, Sat 9am–5pm; ⓣ015394/42326).

Left luggage Available for £1 at *Darryl's* café, 14 Church St (the A591). Thurs–Mon 8am–6pm.
Pharmacy Boots, 10–12 Crescent Rd ☎015394/43093; David Carter, 16 Crescent Rd ☎015394/43417.
Police station Lake Rd, just after the war memorial ☎0845/330 0247, ⓦwww.cumbria.police.uk.
Post office 21 Crescent Rd.
Swimming pool The only public pool actually in the national park is Troutbeck Bridge Swimming Pool, Troutbeck Bridge, 1 mile northwest of Windermere (daily 7.30am–9.30pm, though public admission hours and sessions vary; ☎015394/43243).
Taxis Windermere Taxis ☎015934/42355; plus others in Bowness and Ambleside.

Bowness and the lake

BOWNESS-ON-WINDERMERE – to give it its full title – is undoubtedly the more attractive of the two Windermere settlements, spilling back from its lakeside piers in a series of terraces lined with guesthouses and hotels. Set back from the thumbprint indent of Bowness Bay, a village has existed here since at least the fifteenth century and a ferry service across the lake for almost as long. On a busy summer's day, crowds swirl around the trinket shops, cafés, ice-cream stalls and lakeside seats, but you can easily escape onto the lake or into the hills, and there are several scattered attractions around town to fill a rainy day. Come the evening, when the human tide has subsided and the light fades over the wooden jetties and stone buildings, a promenade around Bowness Bay conjures visions of the Italian lakes.

The Town

What's left of the oldest part of Bowness survives in the few narrow lanes around **St Martin's Church**, consecrated in 1483. The church is notable for its stained glass, particularly that in the east window, now very difficult to make out but sporting the fifteenth-century arms of John Washington, a distant ancestor of first American president George Washington. Outside in the churchyard is the grave of one Rasselas Belfield (d. 1822), "a native of Abyssinia" who was born a slave – and found himself shipped to England – but as a free man became servant to the Windermere gentry.

Most tourists, though, bypass the church and everything else in Bowness bar the lake for the chance to visit **The World of Beatrix Potter**, in the Old Laundry on Crag Brow (daily: Easter–Sept 10am–5.30pm; Oct–Easter 10am–4.30pm; closed 2 weeks Jan; £6.75, all-year family Freedom Pass £27.50; ☎015394/88444, ⓦwww.hop-skip-jump.com). It's unfair to be judgemental – you either like Beatrix Potter or you don't – but it is safe to say that the displays here find more favour with children than the more formal Potter attractions at Hill Top and Hawkshead. Heralded by a fifteen-foot-high bronze outdoor sculpture symbolizing the Potter oeuvre, inside all 23 tales are featured in 3D form (complete with sounds and smells), and there are virtual walks to the places that inspired the author, plus interactive children's attractions, gift shop, garden and themed café.

The other main attraction is the **Windermere Steamboat Museum**, on Rayrigg Road (ⓦwww.steamboat.co.uk), a fifteen-minute walk north of Bowness centre. This is currently undergoing a major restoration which will not only provide new premises for its historic water craft but also include a marine conservation workshop and lake trips on some of the restored steamboats. Museum treasures include the 1850 *Dolly*, claimed to be the world's oldest mechanically driven boat, and exhibits relating to children's author

Arthur Ransome and his *Swallows and Amazons* stories (notably Ransome's own boat, *Coch-y-Bondhu*, which became the boat *Scarab* in *The Picts and the Martyrs*). The new museum isn't expected to open until 2012, but there will be occasional access to parts of the collection during that time – check the website for details.

Out on the lake

All the attractions in Bowness come second-best to a trip on **Windermere** itself – the heavyweight of Lake District lakes, at ten and a half miles long, a mile wide in parts and a shade over two hundred feet deep. As so often in these parts, the name derives from the Norse ("Vinandr's Lake") and since "mere" means lake, references to "Lake Windermere" are tautologous. The views from

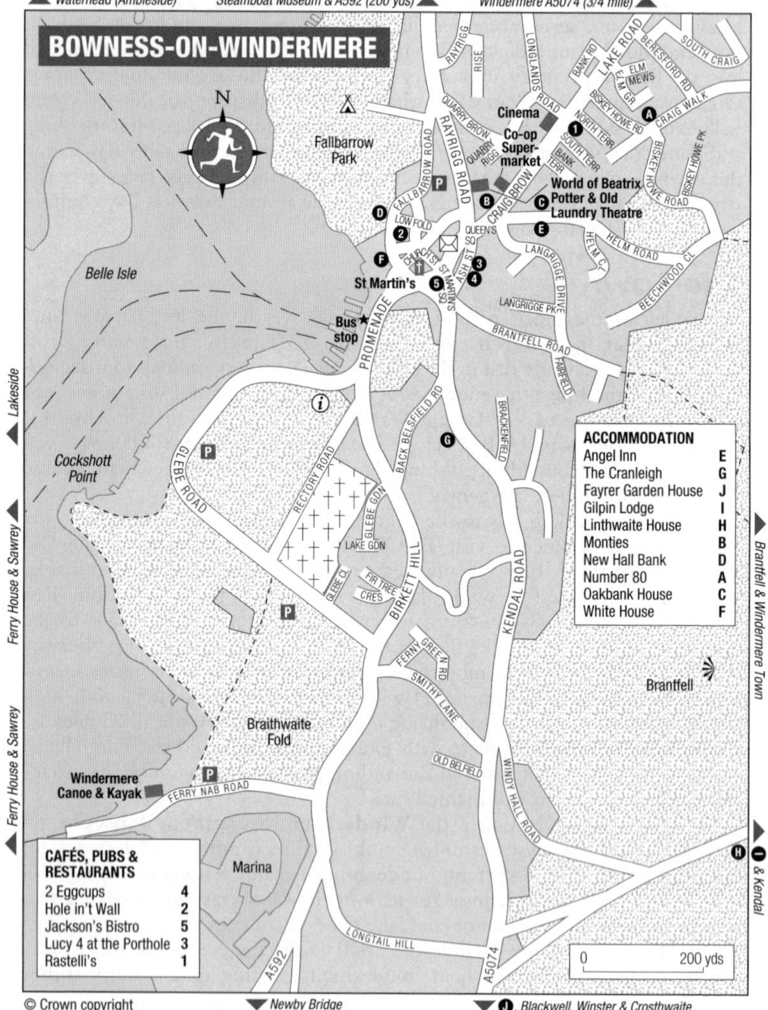

Windermere boat services and cruises

Windermere Lake Cruises (☎015394/43360, ⓦwww.windermere-lakecruises.co.uk) provides a mix of modern cruiser and vintage steamer services around the lake. There are all sorts of options, and you can choose to cruise or to hop-on-hop-off, but basically there are services **from Bowness** run **to Lakeside** at the southern tip (90min "Yellow Cruise", £9.45 return, family £27), **to Ambleside** at the northern end (70min "Red Cruise", £9.15 return, family £26), and on a circular 45-minute **islands cruise** ("Blue Cruise", £6.75, family £18.50). There's also a 45-minute cruise **from Ambleside** which calls at Wray Castle and the Lake District Visitor Centre at Brockhole ("Green Cruise", £6.75 return, family £18.50), and a launch service across the lake **between Bowness pier and Ferry House, Sawrey** (£2.45 one-way, £4.10 return).

If you want to jump off for some walking (Wray Castle to Ferry House, for example, on the shoreline path), you can buy a **Walker's Ticket** (£8.20, family £23.30), which lets you make a circuit from Bowness or Ambleside on the various services. There's also a **Freedom-of-the-Lake ticket** (1-day £16.50, family £45; 3-day £33, family £90) that's valid on all routes. There are also **combination boat tickets** available for the Lakeside and Haverthwaite Railway and the Lakes Aquarium – more information from the pier-side ticket office or respective websites.

Services on all routes are very frequent between Easter and October (every 30min to 1hr at peak times and weekends), and reduced during the winter – but there are sailings every day except Christmas Day. There's discounted **parking** available for customers at Bowness (Braithwaite Fold), Ambleside (Waterhead) and Lakeside.

the water tend towards the magnificent: north to the central fells, or south along a wooded shoreline that is mostly under the protection of the National Trust. The seasons are reflected in the changing colours and tree cover around the lake. Autumn can be a real treat, though global warming has put paid to the spectacular freezing winters of yesteryear – in the 1890s, excursion trains brought astonished sightseers to skate on the lake and marvel at the icicles hanging from the trees.

Many of the private lakeside mansions built for Victorian Lancashire mill owners are now hotels, though **Belle Isle** – the largest of eighteen islets in the lake – is still privately owned. For over two hundred years (until the 1990s), its guardians were various members of the Curwen family who built the island's eye-catching Georgian round house, one of the first of its type in England. The current owners don't allow public access to the island, though the house is visible through the trees if you get close enough on a boat.

The traditional **ferry service** is the chain-guided contraption which chugs across the water from Ferry Nab on the Bowness side to **Ferry House, Sawrey** (departures every 20min; Mon–Sat 7am–10pm, Sun 9am–10pm, final departure in winter 9pm; 50p, bike and cyclist £1, cars £3.50). This provides access to Beatrix Potter's former home at Hill Top and to Hawkshead beyond, but as it can take only eighteen cars at a time queues soon form in summer. The Ferry Nab pier is a ten-minute walk south of the cruise piers, through the parkland of Cockshott Point (or follow the road signs from the promenade). There's also a useful pedestrian **launch service** between Bowness piers and Ferry House, Sawrey (see box above), saving you the walk down to the car ferry.

Rowboats and motorboats are available at **Bowness piers**, with more water-sports outlets further around the bay by the Glebe Road marina, and kayaks available on Ferry Nab Road (see "Listings"). There's a 10mph **speed limit** on the lake (6mph in the more congested areas, where navigation can be hazardous, including Waterhead, and the Bowness Bay and Fell Foot Park areas).

Practicalities

The A592 from the south runs into Bowness along the lake, past the piers, and then continues on, meeting the A591 northwest of Windermere town. There's free two-hour parking on Glebe Road, but otherwise you're going to have to put up with the **car park** charges, either at Glebe Park or Braithwaite Fold (both well signposted). For local information, call in at the National Park's **Bowness Bay Information Centre**, near the piers on Glebe Road (daily: Easter–Oct 9.30am–5.30pm; Nov–Easter 10am–4.30pm; ⓣ015394/42895, ⓦwww.lake-district.gov.uk).

Bus #599 (Easter–Oct daily every 20min; rest of year hourly) leaves Windermere train station for the ten-minute run down Lake Road to Bowness. The bus stops at the piers, which is also the terminus for the #517 (Troutbeck and Ullswater) and the #618 (Newby Bridge, Haverthwaite and Ulverston). For onward routes to Ambleside and Grasmere you have to return first to Windermere station, though the very useful **Cross-Lakes Experience** (Sat & Sun from mid-Feb, then daily Easter–Oct; timetable information from Mountain Goat ⓣ015394/45161 or on ⓦwww.lake-district.gov.uk) provides a direct connecting boat-and-minibus shuttle service from Bowness pier 3 to Hill Top (£9 return/family £25.80), Hawkshead (£10.20/£28.65), Grizedale Forest (£13.05/£36.85) and Coniston Water (£17.55/£49.50).

Accommodation

Be warned that a lake view doesn't come cheap – most places in town with even a glimpse of the water set their prices accordingly, while the local country-house hotels are in uniformly desirable locations. Apart from the places recommended below, Kendal Road has a line of other B&B possibilities. There's no youth hostel in Bowness (your best bet for a lakeside hostel is Ambleside), and neither of the two nearest campsites accept tents.

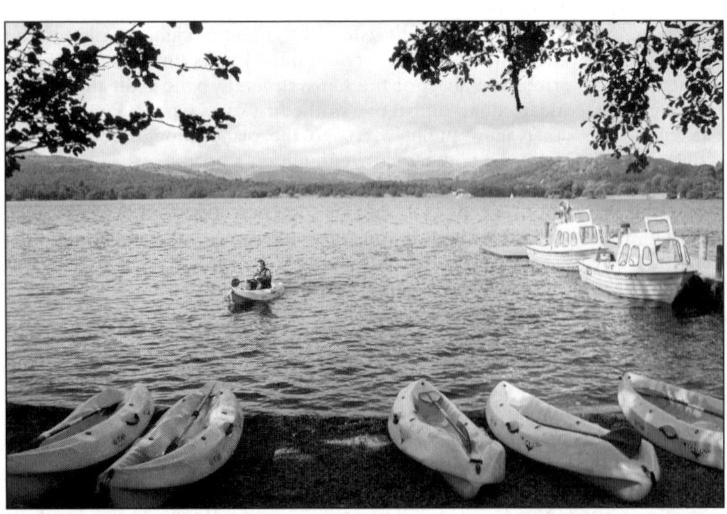

▲ Kayaking on Windermere

Cool swimmings

It might be cold, but it's also cool – swimming in Windermere, that is, now firmly entrenched as part of England's wild swim circuit (see Ⓦwww.outdoorswimmingsociety.com). The British Long-Distance Swimming Association (Ⓦwww.bldsa.org.uk) organizes two official **Windermere swims** every September – a short dash across the lake (first Thursday of the month) and the far more serious ten-mile, length-of-the-lake endurance route (first Saturday), which people use as training for the iconic English cross-Channel swim. There's more of a carnival air to the weekend-long, mass-participation **Great North Swim** (Ⓦwww.greatnorthswim.org), also in September, when thousands plunge in for a one-mile lake swim. Like the equivalent road marathons, it attracts a mix of charity swimmers and medal-winners and you need to register well in advance to take part.

In Bowness

Angel Inn Helm Rd Ⓣ015394/44080, Ⓦwww.the-angelinn.com. A dozen chic rooms – all burnished wood and black leather – above a smooth bar bring a bit of metropolitan style to Bowness. There are also a couple of rooms in the Gatehouse annexe including a huge suite with a help-me-out-of-here sofa, corner bath and a distant lake view. Light bites, wraps and sandwiches and posh pub food (most mains £10–17) are served in the contemporary bar, back restaurant or terraced garden. Parking. ❺

The Cranleigh Kendal Rd Ⓣ015394/43293, Ⓦwww.thecranleigh.com. Indulge yourself in the "guest house with a difference" – the difference being the pampering on offer in super-stylish rooms and suites. They are all different, but share a common core (vibrant fabrics, designer beds, massive flat-screen TVs, ipod docks and space-station-like showers), while larger superior/luxury rooms and suites have private terraces and sitting areas – some, including the eye-popping "Sanctuary", are in adjacent annexe buildings. Parking. ❺, suites ❻

Monties Crag Brow Ⓣ015394/42723, Ⓦwww.montiesbedandbreakfast.com. The standard rooms here are pretty nice as it is, but three others have been given an extra-stylish shot in the arm, with strong colours, good beds and decent bathrooms. All rooms are en suite, save a family room which has a bathroom across the hall. Prices are a bargain and include breakfast in the fab *Monties* café downstairs. ❸

New Hall Bank Fallbarrow Rd Ⓣ015394/43558, Ⓦwww.newhallbank.com. Detached Victorian house with a lake view and a central location (a few yards from the *Hole in't Wall* pub). The en-suite facilities may be tiny, and the dozen rooms themselves not much bigger, but everything is pleasantly decorated, decked out in country pine, with better views the higher you go. Parking. ❸

Number 80 80 Craig Walk Ⓣ015394/43584, Ⓦwww.number80bed.co.uk. Colin and Mandy's quiet town house offers quirky, stylish B&B ("bed then breakfast" they say) in four rather dramatic, earth-toned double rooms. It's a grown-up space for couples (no pets, no children) where you soon feel at ease. Street parking nearby. ❸

Oakbank House Helm Rd Ⓣ015394/43386, Ⓦwww.oakbankhousehotel.co.uk. A cut above your usual traditional B&B – think rugs and flowers, scatter cushions and coordinated furniture, and a welcoming sherry decanter for guests. Some of the rooms have the cherished lake views, and four superior rooms provide a bit more elegance – there's also free use of the pool and facilities at a local country club. Parking. ❹

White House Robinson Place Ⓣ015394/44803, Ⓦwww.whitehouse-lakedistrict.co.uk. A revamped restaurant and bar in the heart of the old village, with half a dozen small but smart en-suite rooms. It's all very modish inside, and there's a slate terrace outside for drinks and meals (most mains £10–17). Parking permit provided. ❸

Around Bowness

Fayrer Garden House Lyth Valley Rd (A5074), 1 mile south of town Ⓣ015394/88195, Ⓦwww.fayrergarden.com. Quiet Victorian country house overlooking the lake, sporting a yesteryear elegance with heavy drapes, fresh flowers and plump cushions in its rooms and lounges. Standard rooms tend to be small and lacking in outlook, so it's best to go for a pricier garden or lake-view room – the latter all with king-sized beds, whirlpool baths and thick robes provided. Rates include dinner. Closed 2 weeks in Jan. Parking. ❻, lake-view ❼

Gilpin Lodge Crook Rd (B5284), 2 miles southeast of town Ⓣ015394/88818, Ⓦwww.gilpin-lodge.co.uk. The relatively small size and long family

Walks from Bowness

While Bowness gets very busy in summer, there are plenty of quieter lakeside spots in the vicinity. Even on the east shore, near the town, you can escape the crowds fairly quickly for an hour or two's stroll, while if you cross to Sawrey using the car-ferry or launch, the whole of the wooded west side as far as Wray Castle (where you can pick up another cross-lake service) makes for an enjoyable circuit.

Rayrigg Meadow and Millerground

A mile north of Bowness (along the A592), past the Steamboat Museum, a path cuts west across **Rayrigg Meadow** to the lakeside and then traces the wooded shore for half a mile to the **Millerground** piers (there's parking here), where you can rejoin the main road. If you're not too muddy, then morning coffee or afternoon tea at nearby *Miller Howe* is a treat. The round-trip from Bowness, including walking along the road, is 2.5 miles, though from Millerground you can walk up through the woods to Windermere town, a mile away, if you want to make a circuit of it.

Brantfell

Best viewpoint is from **Brantfell** (626ft) – "steep hill" – about a mile southeast of Bowness, which takes an hour or so, there and back. Follow Brantfell Road up the hill from St Martin's Square and keep on the path (signposted as the "Dales Way") until you see the diversion up the hillside at Brantfell Farm. The views from the rocks at the top are all-embracing – Belle Isle to Morecambe Bay – and if you rejoin the Dales Way at the farm you could then follow the path east and north all the way into Windermere town (3.5 miles; 2hr, from Bowness) – though it's actually an easier, and nicer, route *from* Windermere to Bowness and the lake, diverting up Brantfell on the way.

Latterbarrow and Claife Heights

The Victorians liked to cross the lake to take tea on the shore below the woods on the west side, and if you're up for an afternoon's walk away from the crowds, this is still the best idea. Cross by car-ferry or launch to Ferry House at Sawrey, from where a gentle path runs two miles north along the shore to Belle Grange. From here you can climb up to **Latterbarrow** (800ft) for lake views before returning along the paths of **Claife Heights** and back to Sawrey. The steep descent through the woods from Far Sawrey to the ferry pier passes the ruins of **The Station**, a castellated viewing platform from which eighteenth-century tourists would view the lake and mountains through a "claude-glass" (named after Romantic landscapist Claude Lorrain), a convex mirror used to "frame" their view. These viewing-stations were very popular until well into the nineteenth century and formed part of any tour of picturesque Lakeland, but the views from this one have been lost to the overarching trees.

See Basics, p.42, for general walking advice in the Lakes; recommended maps are detailed on p.50.

ownership has a lot to do with *Gilpin Lodge*'s success, and warm personal service underpins all that's good here. Elegant rooms in the main house are individually styled, some with four-posters, others with whirlpool baths or private patios – six more contemporary suites have glass-fronted lounges leading to individual gardens with cedarwood hot tubs. It's renowned for its classy, candlelit dining and rates (rooms from £290, garden suites £440) include an extraordinarily lavish breakfast and five-course, seasonally changing dinner (otherwise £55, open to non-guests). Or sample the food, white linen and fine china with a lunchtime bowl of soup, a superior sandwich or a bistro-style dish. Parking. ❽

Linthwaite House Crook Rd (B5284), 1 mile south of town ⓣ015394/88600, ⓦwww.linthwaite.com. An absolute boutique beauty, grafting contemporary style onto an ivy-covered country house set high above Windermere. Rooms are superbly detailed – rich muted fabrics, Shaker-style furniture, king-sized beds with canopies – while in the Loft Suite there's the most beautiful bathroom, a retractable glass roof panel and telescope provided for star-gazing. A conservatory and terrace offer grandstand lake and fell views, and you can work up an appetite for dinner with a walk in the extensive gardens to the hotel's private tarn. Room rates vary according to outlook and size, but run up to £330, suites up to £580, dinner included. Parking. ⑧

Campsite

Fallbarrow Park Rayrigg Rd ⓣ015394/44422. It's caravans and RVs only at this massive lakeside holiday complex, which also has rustic lodge accommodation, plus cottage and van rental. It's a pretty full-on family-oriented affair, with extensive grounds and picnic areas, bar and beer garden, fancy deli and café, wi-fi access throughout, children's play areas, bike rental, you name it. You may never leave, though it's also only a 5min walk from Bowness. Closed mid-Nov to mid-March.

Eating, drinking and entertainment

There are lots of places in Bowness to get a pizza, fish and chips, a Chinese stir-fry or a budget **café** meal – a stroll along pedestrianized Ash Street and up Lake Road shows you most of the possibilities. Finer dining is available at a couple of local **restaurants**, as well as in the dining rooms of the major hotels – *Gilpin Lodge* and *Linthwaite House* (see "Accommodation" above), in particular, get rave reviews (dinner around £55, lunch around half that, reservations advised). The best **pub** by far is the *Hole in't Wall*, while the *Angel Inn* has a great terrace, and for morning coffee or sunset drinks in a more genteel setting you can't beat the lakeside views and cosy lounge of the waterside *Old England* hotel (entrance on Church St).

The Royalty on Lake Road (ⓣ015394/43364, ⓦwww.nm-cinemas.co.uk) boasts the Lake District's biggest **cinema** screen; and the Old Laundry Theatre on Crag Brow (ⓣ015394/88444, ⓦwww.oldlaundrytheatre.co.uk) hosts an annual autumn **Theatre and Film Festival** (from the beginning of September each year) with three months of music, film, comedy and the performing arts.

2 Eggcups 6A Ash St ⓣ015394/45979. Serves the best sandwich in Bowness (including Club, Swiss, Greek or a BLT), plus baked potatoes, omelettes and other daily blackboard specials (£3–6.50). A couple of outdoor tables catch the sun. Daytime only; closed Thurs. No credit cards.

Hole in't Wall Fallbarrow Rd ⓣ015394/43488. How did the town's oldest hostelry get its name (it's officially the New Hall Inn)? Apparently after the hole through which ostlers once had their beer passed to them. Inside are stone-flagged floors, open fires and real ales; outside, a terrace-style beer garden that's a popular spot on summer evenings. The usual bar meals (£9–12) include a daily curry special.

Jackson's Bistro St Martin's Square ⓣ015394/46264. The long-standing local choice for a family dinner or romantic night out, with intimate dining on two floors. Mussels, onion tart, grilled trout and confit of duck provide a classic bistro experience, or choose from the good-value three-course *table d'hôte* menu (£14.95), available all night. Otherwise mains range from £13 to £18. Dinner only.

Lucy 4 at the Porthole 3 Ash St ⓣ015394/42793. Promising the same "devil of a good time" as the original Ambleside establishment, the first *Lucy 4* franchise offers up a winning mix of Mediterranean tapas (£3–7.50) designed for sharing. Longer memories will recall the building as the old Italian *Porthole Eating House*, operatic warbling and all, and the cottage-style nooks and crannies and open fire are still here though there's now a far funkier edge to things. Summer open daily from noon, winter from 5pm (noon at weekends).

Rastelli's Lake Rd ⓣ015394/44227. No surprises, just proper, authentic pizza and pasta (£7–10) in an amiable family-run restaurant – it's good value so you can expect to have to wait for a table in summer. Dinner only. Closed Tues.

Listings

Banks NatWest (Lake Rd) has an ATM and there's a Barclays ATM (though no bank) on Crag Brow, Lake Rd.

Bike and kayak rental There's great off-road biking across the lake around Claife Heights, and all the water you need for a paddle. Windermere Canoe & Kayak, Ferry Nab Rd (daily 9am–5.30pm, ⓣ015394/44451, ⓦwww.windermerecanoekayak.co.uk) have bikes and sit-on kayaks to rent from £20, or choose a combined pedal-and-paddle day from £30.

Emergencies The nearest hospital is in Kendal: Westmorland General Hospital, Burton Rd ⓣ01539/732288.

Pharmacy Lakeland Pharmacy, 5 Grosvenor Terrace, Lake Rd ⓣ015394/43139.

Post office 2 St Martin's Parade.

Taxis Bowness Taxis ⓣ015394/46664; Lakes Village Taxis ⓣ015394/44055.

The Lake District Visitor Centre at Brockhole

The **Lake District National Park Authority** has its main visitor centre at **Brockhole** (Easter–Oct daily 10am–5pm; grounds and gardens open all year; free, though parking-fee charged; ⓣ015394/46601, ⓦwww.lake-district.gov.uk), a late-Victorian mansion set in lush grounds on the shores of Windermere, to the north of Bowness. New developments and attractions are planned for the future, from a watersports centre to interactive cinema, but even now it's the single best place to get to grips with what there is to see and do in the Lakes. Besides the permanent natural-history and geological displays, the centre hosts a full programme of guided walks, children's activities (including a popular adventure playground), garden tours, farmers' markets, special exhibitions, lectures and film shows – the centre, and any local tourist office, can provide a schedule. On a warm day, the **gardens** are a treat, with their little arbours, lakeside paths, grassy lawns, wildflower meadow and picnic areas – the website tells you what's flowering month by month, while woodpeckers, deer, rabbits, foxes and badgers are all regular visitors. The landscaping is among the finest in the Lakes, the work of the celebrated Lancastrian garden architect Thomas Mawson (1861–1933), who also designed the grounds for other Victorian piles at Holehird, Langdale Chase, Holker Hall and Rydal Hall. Inside the former mansion (built originally for a Manchester silk merchant), there's a bookshop – good for local guides and maps – and a café whose outdoor terrace looks down to the lake.

The visitor centre is just off the A591, three miles northwest of Windermere. **Buses** #555 and #599 stop outside, though for a more enjoyable ride come by **Windermere Lake Cruises** launch, which docks at the foot of the gardens. There's a regular service from Waterhead, Ambleside (£6.75 return, family £18.50), which calls at both Brockhole and Wray Castle, on Windermere's opposite shore, and you can usually make a request stop at Brockhole on cruise services from Bowness.

Blackwell

A mile and a half south of Bowness, in an elevated position above the lake, stands the superbly restored mansion of **Blackwell** (daily 10.30am–5pm, Nov–March until 4pm; closed 2 weeks Jan; £6.50, family £17.25; ⓣ015394/46139, ⓦwww.blackwell.org.uk). It's the masterpiece of **Mackay Hugh Baillie Scott** (1865–1945) – less celebrated an architect than his contemporaries, Sir Edwin Lutyens and Charles Voysey, but just as influential in the Arts and Crafts Movement that emerged from the ideas of John Ruskin and William Morris. The house is hugely significant as the only major Arts and Crafts house in such remarkable condition open to the public in Britain. Most are still in private hands, and Blackwell itself has had a variety of owners: from World War II until

You don't always get what you want...

Blackwell's origins – as with so many houses on the shores of Windermere – lie in the nineteenth-century explosion of wealth in the industrial cities. Given free rein by Mancunian brewer and Lord Mayor Sir Edward Holt, who wanted a holiday home in the Lakes, Baillie Scott grasped the opportunity to design an entire house, and Blackwell was completed to his specifications between 1898 and 1900. Taking his cue from Ruskin and Morris, who had championed the importance of traditional handicrafts allied with functionalism, Baillie Scott let Blackwell speak for his ideas and principles – from the almost organic nature of the free-flowing layout to the decorative emphasis on natural motifs and handcrafted designs. The use of natural light, in particular, is revealing, with the family rooms all south-facing, even though this orientates them away from the lake views for which, presumably, Sir Edward had paid a premium. Indeed, there's evidence that the Holts were never entirely comfortable in their designer holiday home. The family (of five children and six servants) soon cluttered Baillie Scott's harmonious interlinked rooms with the paraphernalia of the Victorian gentry – an old photograph shows the main hall encumbered with a heavy chandelier, potted ferns and a stuffed moose's head; and by the end of World War I, as the Arts and Crafts Movement lost its fashionable edge, the Holts visited Blackwell less and less.

the 1970s the house was a girls' school, and was then leased by English Nature until it was bought and restored by the Lakeland Arts Trust.

The house grabs your attention from the very first, as you proceed from the entrance down an oak-panelled corridor, off which is the **main hall**. Baillie Scott's idealized baronial design provides the sort of things you might expect to see in a showpiece country house – vast fireplace, oak panelling, minstrels' gallery and heraldic crests – but lightens the experience with huge dollops of inventive flair. An open-plan room with nooks and corners of varying proportions sports a peacock wallpaper frieze, a bluebell-and-daisy hessian wall-hanging, copper lightshades, Delft tiles and – above all – the recurring carved rowan leaves and berries from the Holt family coat of arms. At the end of the corridor, sun streams into the **white drawing room** and here, and elsewhere in the house, you can sit in the cushioned bay windows and enjoy the garden and lake views. The **bedrooms** upstairs contain changing exhibitions of contemporary and historic applied Arts and Crafts, though the contents of the entire house are display pieces in their own right, from the early twentieth-century carved oak furniture by Simpson's of Kendal to the modern earthenware that is positioned throughout. But it's Baillie Scott's naturalistic touches that perhaps sum up the whole – such as the door handles shaped like leaves or the lakeland birds and flowers that are ever-present in the stained glass and stonework.

The best way to appreciate the overall design is to coincide with the informative introductory talk (usually weekdays at 2.30pm). There's also a pleasant **tearoom**, and a garden terrace where lunches, cream teas and lemonade are served on summer days. A **craft shop** sells works by leading designers, including jewellery, ceramics, scarves and handbags, as well as specialist books on architecture and the Arts and Crafts movement. If you're especially interested, you can head off from Blackwell on an **Arts and Crafts Trail** that links other period houses and sights in the southern Lakes – pick up a leaflet at the house or check the Blackwell website.

Blackwell is on the B5360, just off the A5074, one and a half miles south of Bowness. There's no public transport here, but it's only a 25-minute walk from Bowness; it's along a busy road, though, so take care.

Lakeside and around

From Bowness, cruise boats head five miles down the lake to the piers at **Lakeside**, where gentle wooded hills frame Windermere's serene southern reaches. Combination tickets are available for the boat ride and the two big family attractions on the quayside, namely steam train and aquarium, and the three things together would fill a day. But you can also rent a bike at Lakeside, hike up through the local woods for some views, or catch a launch across the water to Fell Foot Park for a picnic.

Lakeside and Haverthwaite Railway

The quayside is the terminus of the **Lakeside and Haverthwaite Railway** (Easter–Oct 6–7 services daily; £5.90 return, family £16; Ⓣ015395/31594, Ⓦwww.lakesiderailway.co.uk), whose steam-powered engines puff gently along four miles of track along the River Leven and through the woods of Backbarrow Gorge; boat arrivals at Lakeside connect with train departures throughout the day. It's the only surviving remnant of a railway line that once used to stretch all the way to Ulverston and Barrow. There's a billowing rush of smoke in the tunnel – very atmospheric – as you arrive at Haverthwaite, where you'll find parking and a cute station tearoom (closed Jan & Feb). If you get a chance, have a look around the engine shed, where (when it's not out on duty) Britain's oldest working standard-gauge loco, built in Manchester in 1863, is kept. The annual calendar, meanwhile, incorporates steam gala weekends, Victorian evenings, Thomas the Tank Engine days and Santa specials – there's more information on the website. Haverthwaite station itself is on the A590, across the busy main road from the actual village of Haverthwaite – you can reach it on bus #X35 (from Kendal or Ulverston) or #618 (from Ambleside, Windermere, Bowness or Ulverston).

Lakes Aquarium

Also on the quay at Lakeside is the **Lakes Aquarium** (daily: April–Oct 9am–6pm; Nov–March 9am–5pm; last admission 1hr before closing; £8.75, family ticket from £20.20, discounts for online bookings; Ⓣ015395/30153, Ⓦwww.lakesaquarium.co.uk), a very entertaining natural-history attraction centred on the fish and animals found in and along a lakeland river, on the Cumbrian coast, and in other habitats from lake to rainforest. There's a pair of frisky otters (fed every day at 10.30am and 3pm), plus rays from Morecambe Bay and a terrific walk-through tunnel aquarium with huge carp and diving ducks. Educational exhibits, documentaries and daily presentations give the low-down on everything from cockles to pike and leeches

Motoring to a new home

After 30 years located in the old shire horse stables at Holker Hall, the popular **Lakeland Motor Museum** (Ⓣ015395/58509, Ⓦwww.lakelandmotormuseum.co.uk) has a new purpose-built home at Backbarrow, near Newby Bridge, to show off its 30,000-plus motoring history exhibits. It's a dream for petrol-heads and nostalgia buffs alike, who can view the vehicles and memorabilia in rather more fitting surroundings, while a proposed museum halt on the Lakeside and Haverthwaite Railway should open up the collection to a new generation of visitors. Admission details weren't available at the time of writing, but the website has all the latest news.

to lobsters. Enthusiastic staff are on hand to explain what's going on and afterwards you can grab a drink in the lake-view café and enjoy watching the comings and goings of the boats.

Stott Park Bobbin Mill and Finsthwaite

Half a mile up the hill from Lakeside, below Finsthwaite Heights, stands one of England's few working mills, **Stott Park Bobbin Mill** (Easter–Oct Mon–Fri 11am–5pm; last tour 30min before closing; £4.50, family £11.30; Ⓣ015395/31087, Ⓦwww.english-heritage.org.uk). It was founded in 1835 to supply the British textile industry with bobbins – rollers or spools for holding thread – and at one stage employed as many as 250 men and boys. When the cotton industry declined, the mill later diversified, manufacturing pulleys, hammers, mallets, spade handles, yo-yos and even duffel-coat toggles. Commercial production finally ceased in 1971, at a time when plastic had replaced wood for most bobbins. Former workers guide visitors on a 45-minute tour through the processes of cutting, roughing, drying, finishing and polishing on machinery that hasn't changed since it was introduced in the mid-nineteenth century. Note that the steam engine driving the water wheel doesn't operate every day – call for details, if you want to catch it.

From a car park above the mill (follow the road to Finsthwaite) there's a pleasant walk up through the woods to **High Dam**, the reservoir whose water used to drive the mill machinery – allow an hour or so to circle the water and return. Alternatively, if you head for **Finsthwaite** hamlet itself, half a mile above the mill, you can clamber up through the woods of **Finsthwaite Heights** to the naval commemorative tower. The only bus to the bobbin mill or Finsthwaite is a twice-a-week service from Lakeside, Newby Bridge or Ulverston, but the half-a-mile walk up from Lakeside is hardly off-putting.

Fell Foot Park

Across from Lakeside, **Fell Foot Park**, on Windermere's southeastern reach (daily 9am–5pm or dusk; free, though parking-fee charged; Ⓣ015395/31273, Ⓦwww.nationaltrust.org.uk), makes a relaxed picnic spot, where you can lounge on the Victorian landscaped lawns and explore the rhododendron gardens and oak and pine plantations; there's an adventure playground for kids too. There was also once a private mansion here, to go with the grounds, though that's long gone. But the mock-Gothic boathouse still stands and offers rowboat rental, while doubling as a rather superior **tearoom** (opens 11am; closed from Nov until mid-Feb) – from

Bobbins and coppicing

For a time in the nineteenth century the south Lakes' **bobbin mills** formed an important part of the national economy, supplying up to half of all the bobbins required by the booming British textile mills. There were two reasons for the industry's strength in the Lakes: the fast running water from lakeland rivers to drive the mills and the seemingly inexhaustible supply of wood. To make bobbins and other items, **coppiced** wood was required, from trees cut to stumps to encourage the quick growth of long poles, which were then harvested for use. It's a technique that's been used for over five thousand years, and ash, beech, birch, chestnut, hazel and oak were all grown in this way. The bark was peeled off and used in the tanneries, while coppiced wood was also used widely in charcoal-making (another key local industry), thatching and the production of tent pegs, cask bindings, fencing, agricultural implements (such as rakes) and so-called "swill" baskets (cradle-shaped Cumbrian panniers).

the tables outside you can watch the Lakeside and Haverthwaite trains chuff into the station just across the lake. Windermere Lake Cruises run **launches** across to the park from Lakeside (Easter–Oct daily 11am–5pm; £1.50 return), usually every twenty minutes depending on demand and the weather. By car, access is from the A592 (Bowness road), a mile north of Newby Bridge; bus #618, from Ulverston and Newby Bridge to Bowness, passes close by.

An ancient packhorse route from Newby Bridge to Kendal, now a steep and winding minor road, passes to the northeast behind Fell Foot. A mile up, there's free parking by the start of the footpath to **Gummer's How**, the gorse-topped fell which peers over the southern half of Windermere. It's an easy walk up to the little stone trig point on the summit – it'll take an hour there and back, including a rest at the top to gaze down at the Fell Foot marina and the snaking River Leven.

Practicalities

The best way to visit Lakeside is by **boat**, with all the attractions sited just a step or two away from the quayside. Otherwise, the #618 **bus** (from Ambleside, Windermere and Bowness) calls at Newby Bridge and Haverthwaite. Alternatively, contact Country Lanes (daily 9.30am–5.30pm; ⓣ07748/512286, ⓦwww.countrylaneslakedistrict.co.uk) on the quayside, either for full-day **bike rental** (from £19) or a **bike-and-boat** day out (from £15.70) which includes the boat ride from Bowness and a two- or four-hour bike ride (with the latter, you could get as far as Cartmel or Hawkshead and back).

There's limited **accommodation** at Lakeside, though just a mile south of the foot of the lake, down the River Leven, the *Swan Hotel* has a fine riverside location. From here, it's another couple of miles southwest along the A590 to the village of Haverthwaite, which also has a selection of B&Bs.

Accommodation and food

Coach House Hollow Oak, Haverthwaite ⓣ015395/31622, ⓦwww.coachho.com. Friendly B&B in a 200-year-old former coach house and stables, set in appealing gardens. There are only three rooms, two with en-suite facilities, one with its own bathroom down the corridor. The Haverthwaite village pub is just half a mile away and the knowledgeable owners can tell you anything else you need to know about the Lake District. Parking. No credit cards. ❷

Lakeside Hotel Lakeside ⓣ015395/30001, ⓦwww.lakesidehotel.co.uk. A very hospitable four-star hotel with a great location on the lapping shores of Windermere. Some rooms have private gardens or their own terrace, and most overlook the water – they are all country house in feel, with elegant fabrics and marble bathrooms, while nine family rooms (some with separate bunk room for the kids) offer more space. A conservatory runs the length of the hotel, opening onto lakeside lawns and gardens (the ducks are fed daily at 11am!), and there's a large family-friendly indoor pool, as well as hot tub and classy spa facilities. Dining is either in the contemporary *John Ruskin's Brasserie* (*table d'hôte* menu, £33/38) or the elegant but unstuffy fine-dining *Lakeview Restaurant* (£45). Room rates start at £195, while off-season and midweek deals offer good value. Parking. ❼

Swan Hotel Newby Bridge ⓣ015395/31681, ⓦwww.swanhotel.com. This classic old inn, a winding mile or so to the south of Lakeside, has undergone extensive refurbishment to get it up to four-star standard. There's not much left of the traditional inn, which now has classy rooms (including king-sized beds and a sitting room in the executive suites), up-to-date facilities including indoor pool and spa, and a contemporary bar that's more Manchester than muck-and-country. Fusion rules in the River Room restaurant (stone-baked pizzas, rare-breed pork on mixed bean salad, lakeland lamb with tomato salsa, dishes £11–20), or there's a simpler bar menu which you can eat outside at riverside tables by the five-arched bridge. Parking. ❺, weekends ❻

White Hart Bouth, off A590, 1.5 miles northeast of Haverthwaite ⓣ01229/861229, ⓦwww.bed-and-breakfast-cumbria.co.uk. It's a short winding drive off the A590 to this seventeenth-century country inn, with sympathetically upgraded rooms in the eaves that retain their oak beams and idiosyncratic proportions. Locals come here to eat (veggie chilli to fillet steak, £11–18), there's a great choice of real ales, and a kids' playground opposite the pub. Parking. ❸

The Winster and Lyth valleys

From near the foot of Windermere and Fell Foot Park, a minor road runs three miles up to the brow of a hill at **Strawberry Bank**, where the celebrated *Mason's Arms* (see below) is impeccably sited overlooking the low stony outcrops and tidy plantations of the **Winster Valley**. The pub's terrace is a great place for a beer – there are two hundred on offer, from all corners of the globe, including a damson beer made on the premises. Arthur Ransome moved to the Winster Valley in 1925 and it was here that he wrote *Swallows and Amazons*. His house, known as **Low Ludderburn** (not open to the public), can be seen if you take the tortuous bracken- and bramble-lined road north from the pub for a couple of miles. To the south, exactly a mile from the *Mason's Arms* (follow the signposts), **St Anthony's Church** lies tucked into a hollow on the side of Cartmel Fell. The church dates from 1504 – it was built as an isolated, outlying chapel of Cartmel priory – and preserves a characterful seventeenth-century interior: exposed rafters, a triple-decker pulpit and twin "box" pews once reserved for the local gentry.

From Strawberry Bank, the road drops a mile to **Bowland Bridge**, where the *Hare & Hounds* – right by the bridge – is a nice old inn with a sheltered beer garden. Beyond Bowland Bridge, a minor road makes its way north along the upper Winster Valley, before joining the A5074 which runs to Bowness. Where the roads meet there's a sign pointing you northeast towards the tiny village of **Crosthwaite**, whose parish church and adjacent seventeenth-century *Punch Bowl Inn* (see below) nestle in the gentle **Lyth Valley**. Lyth Valley damsons are a staple of the local early summer fruit crop, used in these parts in desserts and preserves (and to flavour beer and gin) – they are a relic of Lakeland's former textile industry, when the fruit was used to make cloth dyes.

Accommodation and food

Brown Horse Inn Winster, A5074 ⓣ015394/43443, ⓦwww.thebrownhorseinn.co.uk. A revamped country inn doing great things with home-produced food from their own Winster valley family farm, just half a mile away from the pub – beat that for food miles. There's a seasonally-changing menu, from beef, lamb and pork to chicken, game and garden veg (mains £10–18). Drink downstairs in the traditional bar, or stay overnight in one of nine handsome rooms, four of which are more contemporary in style. Parking. ❸, weekends ❹

Mason's Arms Strawberry Bank, Cartmel Fell ⓣ015395/68486, ⓦwww.masonsarmsstrawberrybank.co.uk. One of those places you're delighted to have happened upon, especially at lunchtime, when you can look forward to "posh pub" food, from pan-fried pheasant to pork-and-damson sausages (mains £9–15). The cosy, revamped country inn has tables in the stone-flagged bar as well as a contemporary upstairs dining room, and there's also accommodation in two decidedly chic cottages (which sleep 4/6) and five variously priced suites, all available by the night. Parking. Suites ❹–❺, cottages ❻

Punch Bowl Inn Crosthwaite, next to St Mary's Church ⓣ015395/68237, ⓦwww.the-punchbowl.co.uk. Owned by Hawkshead's *Drunken Duck* people, and given a similarly stylish gastro-inn makeover, the *Punch Bowl*'s nine gorgeous earth-toned rooms feature exposed beams, flat-screen TVs, clunky retro bedside radios, and superb bathrooms with clawfoot bathtubs and quite possibly the largest bath towels in Britain. The scrumptious food is modern but unpretentious, locally sourced and seasonal (pot-roast wood-pigeon to local lamb, meals from around £30, plus drinks) and you can eat either in the bar or book for the restaurant (it's the same menu). There's also a salad and sandwich lunch menu served daily, while beer is courtesy of the *Drunken Duck*'s own Barngates Brewery. Room rates vary, but include a superb breakfast and afternoon tea. Parking. ❺–❼, weekends ❻–❽

Ambleside

AMBLESIDE, five miles northwest of Windermere, at the head of the lake, lies at the hub of the central and southern Lakes region. It's a popular, if commercial, base for walkers and tourers, but has lost most of its traditional market-town character over the years. The original market square and associated buildings were swept away in a typically vigorous piece of Victorian redevelopment (though the market cross still stands) and today's thriving centre – more a retail experience than a lakeland town – consists of a cluster of grey-green stone houses either side of the babbling gully of Stock Ghyll, and more outdoors shops, pubs, B&Bs and cafés than you can shake a stick at. Huge car parks soak up the day-trip trade, but actually Ambleside improves with time, boasting some enjoyable local walks and also the best selection of accommodation and restaurants in the area.

The Town

Stock Ghyll once powered Ambleside's fulling and bobbin mills, whose buildings survive intact on either side of Bridge Street, as do a couple of restored water wheels. Straddling Stock Ghyll is the town's favourite building, tiny **Bridge House**, originally built as a covered bridge-cum-summerhouse and used by a local family to access their orchards across the stream. It's had

A most singular woman

Harriet Martineau, a delicate child and hard of hearing, was born into a Nonconformist East Anglian manufacturing family in 1802. Left penniless by the death of her father in 1826, Harriet began to earn a living by writing moral and devotional tales, which she called "**Illustrations**", addressing such weighty matters as slavery, the Poor Laws, taxation, education and emigration. Martineau produced these on a monthly basis between 1832 and 1834 – and, much to the surprise of her publisher, they made her famous overnight. She subsequently travelled widely (with ear trumpet in tow), when it was not easy for a woman of her background to do so, and produced two successful books on America – *Society In America* (1837), lauded by Charles Dickens, and *A Retrospect of Western Travel* (1838). But, never fully well, she collapsed on a visit to Venice in 1839 and remained prone and weak for five years. Often dismissed as an "hysteric", like many Victorian women, Martineau had in fact suffered a prolapse of the uterus, which seriously curtailed her work and travel.

Devoted to the supposed powers of mesmerism, a popular "alternative medicine" of the 1840s, she recovered enough to tour the Middle East and, on her return, visited the Lake District, where she settled, building a house, **The Knoll**, in Ambleside, in which she lived for the rest of her life. Never an orthodox woman, Martineau cut a notable figure in lakeland society. Smoking a pipe or a cigar, she tramped around the fells in men's boots, picking plants for her garden, much to the amusement of the locals. It was said she bathed in the lake by moonlight; certainly she mixed with the lower orders (lecturing in Ambleside to a working-class audience) and harried local officials and churchmen. All this, of course, put her at odds with the conservative Wordsworths – with William, she would argue ferociously, while Mary Wordsworth couldn't stand Martineau and left Rydal Mount every time she came to call.

Martineau continued to write at The Knoll – her *Complete Guide to the English Lakes* (1855) followed the example of Wordsworth – with later works reflecting her loss of faith and turn to humanism. But she continued to suffer from periodic bouts of illness and, after 1855, rarely left her house. By 1866 she was taking opium to relieve the pain of an ovarian cyst and she died at The Knoll in 1876 and was buried in Birmingham with members of her family.

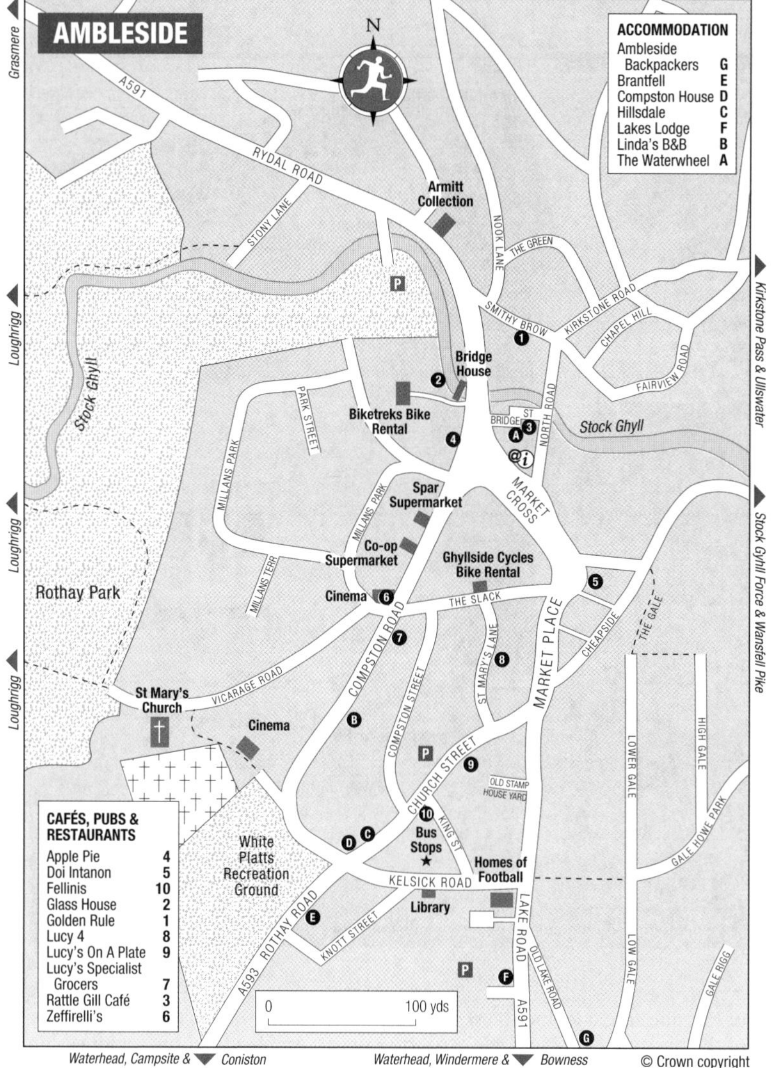

many other uses over the years, mainly for storage, though records show that in the nineteenth century it was briefly home to a family of eight.

For more on Ambleside's history, stroll for a couple of minutes along Rydal Road to the **Armitt Collection** (Mon–Sat 10.30am–4.30pm; £2.50; ⓣ015394/31212, ⓦwww.armitt.com), the town's acclaimed literary museum and historic library. Founded in 1909 (by local society intellectual Mary Louisa Armitt), the collection catalogues the very distinct contribution to lakeland society made by writers and artists from John Ruskin to Beatrix Potter: others, like the redoubtable Harriet Martineau (see box opposite), made their home in the town, and the museum contains cases full of memorabilia – from a life-mask

▲ Bridge House, Ambleside

of Martineau to a lock of Ruskin's hair. There's plenty, too, on the life and work of Herbert Bell (1856–1946), pharmacist of Ambleside turned pioneering lakeland photographer. And anyone driven to distraction by the bunny-and-hedgehog side of Beatrix Potter should be prepared to revise their opinion on viewing the changing selection of her early scientific watercolour studies of fungi and mosses – a beautifully painted sequence donated by Potter herself. At the time of writing, the museum was in talks with the University of Cumbria to take over its management, so displays and admission details may change in future.

The old **market cross** still marks the centre of town, a reminder that – before the coming of the train and the growth of Windermere – Ambleside was the major commercial and business centre in this part of the Lakes. It was to here, for instance, that William Wordsworth had to travel from his house at Rydal Mount when on official duty as the **Distributor of Stamps for Westmorland** (a job he acquired in 1813). A plaque on a building at the top of **Church Street** marks the site of the office he once used.

Further down, at the southern end of town, off Compston Road, you reach **St Mary's Church**, whose rocket-shaped spire is visible from all over town. Completed in 1854, it was designed by George Gilbert Scott – the architect responsible for London's Albert Memorial and St Pancras Station – and contains a mural of the town's annual **rushbearing ceremony**, its figures resplendent in their 1940s finery. The ceremony itself dates from medieval times and derives from the custom of replacing the worn rushes (or reeds) on unflagged church floors. In Ambleside, the event takes places on a Saturday in the first two weeks of July, with a procession through town of decorated rushes and the church congregation singing the specially commissioned Ambleside Rushbearers' Hymn. Behind the church, the green pastures of **Rothay Park** stretch down to the River Rothay, while above loom the heights of **Loughrigg Fell** (1101ft), with the climb to the summit signposted from near the humpbacked bridge at the foot of Rothay Park.

Waterhead

The piers for boats from Bowness lie a mile south of town at **Waterhead**, a harbour on the shores of Windermere that's filled with ducks, swans and rowboats and overlooked by the grass banks and spreading trees of **Borrans Park**. Waterhead was known as Galava to the Romans, who first built a turf-and-timber fort on the lake edge in 90 AD, later superseded by a larger stone structure housing five hundred auxiliary soldiers, which was finally abandoned at the end of the fourth century. The Roman scholar Robin Collingwood excavated the two forts in separate digs between 1913 and 1920 (the Armitt Collection holds many of the objects recovered), though there's little left to see *in situ* as the foundations of various buildings, including a large granary with hypocaust, are now largely grass-covered. But it's an emotive spot, backed by glowering fells and with views across the rippling Windermere waters – the perfect place for sunset-watching or star-gazing. Two or three little cafés by the piers have outdoor seats, while the lawns of the *Wateredge Inn* and *Waterhead* hotel also offer lovely views.

People and places: First loves

The Lake District grabs people in different ways. For photographer Stuart Clarke (born in Hertfordshire, studied in London) it was the wildness and unpredictability of the ancient, golden-brown landscape that dominated his first visit, which he then married to his first true love – football. His terrific cinema-style gallery-cum-shop, The Homes of Football, is now a world-renowned Ambleside fixture with a huge permanent archive, but it started out as a peripatetic exhibition, recording games, grounds, clubs and fans from the Premier League down to the smallest amateur teams. Clarke's view? It's not too grand to say that he sees football as a window on life, but his adopted Lakes keep creeping in and so other photography champions the people and landscapes of this "magic lantern of a place". And this die-hard Watford fan now has other passions. "My heart leaps when I see Cumberland and Westmorland wrestlers so politely going about their craft", admits Clarke, while these days you're as likely to encounter him snapping away at a Cumbrian music festival as the World Cup. The clue is in the title of his book, *Somewhere Across A Promised Land*, which charts the dreams and realities of Clarke's "perfect place", his own backyard of Cumbria.

The Homes of Football, 100 Lake Rd, Ambleside ⓣ015394/34440, ⓦwww.homesoffootball.co.uk. Open daily 10am–5pm; free, though there is occasionally a charge for special exhibitions.

Practicalities

Buses stop on Kelsick Road, opposite the library, with regular local services to and from Windermere, Grasmere and Keswick, plus services to Hawkshead and Coniston (#505), and Elterwater and Langdale (#516). The **Central Lakes Day Rider** ticket (buy on board, from £6.50) covers travel in all the central and southern region. Walking up to town from the **ferry piers** at Waterhead takes about fifteen minutes, though an **electric carriage** shuttle service operates from the piers to the *White Lion* pub in the town centre (weather- and ferry-dependent, but usually daily Easter–Oct, weekends only Nov–Easter, 10.30am–5pm, roughly every 30min; £1.50). The A591 runs right through town and drivers are best advised to make straight for the signposted **car parks**, though be warned that these fill quickly in summer – you may not find a space on your first pass through. The "Hub of Ambleside" **tourist office** is in the Central Buildings on Market Cross (daily 9am–5.30pm; ⓣ015394/32582,

Walks from Ambleside

Ambleside is impressively framed – Loughrigg Fell to the west, the distinctive line of the Fairfield Horseshoe to the north and Wansfell to the east – and even inexperienced walkers have plenty of choice.

Stock Ghyll

The traditional stroll is up Stock Ghyll Lane (which starts behind the *Salutation Hotel*) and through the leafy woods of Stock Ghyll Park (with wonderful daffs in spring) to the tumbling waterfall of **Stock Ghyll Force**, which drops 60ft through a narrow defile. Allow an hour there and back if you linger on the viewing platform and rest on the benches.

Wansfell

Those with loftier ambitions can regain the lane by Stock Ghyll Park and, a little way further up, look for the signposted path (over a wall-ladder) up Wansfell to **Wansfell Pike** (1581ft) – an hour all told to the top, from where there are superb views of Windermere and the surrounding fells. Circular hikers either cut due south from the summit to Skelghyll and return via Jenkins Crag (2hr), or head east across a clearly defined path to Troutbeck and Townend before cutting back (4hr).

Jenkins Crag and Stagshaw Gardens

The viewpoint of **Jenkins Crag**, a mile from Waterhead, gives a glimpse of the lake as well as the central peaks of the Langdales and the Old Man of Coniston – *Country Life* magazine once reckoned this was Britain's most romantic picnic spot. From Ambleside, walk down Lake Road (though there's a handy car park near Hayes Garden World) and follow the signs up Skelghyll Lane, a thirty-minute walk. On the way back you can detour to the National Trust's woodland **Stagshaw Gardens** (Easter–June daily 10am–6.30pm; £2), at its best in spring for the shows of rhododendrons, camellias and azaleas.

Fairfield Horseshoe

The classic hiker's circuit from Ambleside is the **Fairfield Horseshoe** (11 miles; 6hr), which starts just out of town, off Kirkstone Road, and climbs up via High Sweden Bridge and **Dove Crag** (2603ft) to the flat top of **Fairfield** itself (2864ft), before dropping back along the opposing ridge to Nab Scar and Rydal, outside Grasmere. From Rydal, you can avoid most of the road back to Ambleside by following the footpath through the grounds of Rydal Hall. This really is a superb walk on a clear day, not too difficult yet encompassing eight different peaks.

See Basics, p.42, for general walking advice in the Lakes; recommended maps are detailed on p.50.

Out and about in the Lakes

For such a small area, the Lake District packs in a fantastic number of outdoor activities. Not surprisingly, most visitors look to the lakes and mountains for their inspiration, but even if you're not into scenic strolls or hardcore hiking there's plenty on offer throughout the year. The sections in Basics on festivals and events, family excursions, enjoying the mountains, watersports and outdoor activities provide all sorts of contacts and details, but for some general ideas – from great walking routes to lakeland adventures – read on.

Boats at Keswick ▲

Sailing on Windermere ▲

On the water

Almost all the organized cruising and watersports facilities are concentrated on just four lakes – **Windermere** (England's largest lake) and **Coniston Water** in the south and **Derwent Water** and **Ullswater** in the north. Round-the-lake boat services on each offer short cruises, themed tours or ferry drop-offs for hikers and visitors, and the boats run year-round (with local variations) so there's no reason to miss out. If time is short and you have to pick just one lake trip, our vote would be for the **Keswick Launch** (p.161) which provides access to some great walks and dramatic scenery. The same four lakes also have plenty of operators offering dinghy sailing, windsurfing, kayaking or even dragon-boating – the National Park's own **Coniston Boating Centre** (p.125), for example, is a great place to take out a kayak or learn to sail.

Festival time

The region maintains its traditions in unique festivals, agricultural shows and rural events held throughout the old county lands of Cumberland and Westmorland (now Cumbria). Some – like the medieval **rushbearings** in churches at Grasmere and Ambleside – date back centuries, while others show a direct line from the very earliest informal **shepherds' meets**. Put a crowd of lakeland farmers together, plus their dogs and sheep, and it's not long before they're issuing challenges – at all the big summer agricultural "shows" and "sports" you'll see sheepdog trials, hound-trailing, fell running and tugs-of-war, though for sheer spectacle it's hard to beat the hand-to-hand **Cumberland and Westmorland wrestling**. Traditional outdoor events have always been held in

Cumberland and Westmorland wrestling ▼

the summer – particularly August – but there's now a year-round calendar for all interests, from beer and film festivals to spring garden shows and Christmas markets. See p.36 for more on all **annual events**, including a full month-by-month festival calendar.

Outdoor adventures

Given the lure of the ever-present hills and lakes it's hard to come to the Lake District and not have some kind of outdoor adventure. But there are also lots of organized activities on offer – from mountain biking to pony-trekking, fishing to 4WD expeditions – and the only limit is your own stamina. The **Go Ape** high-ropes courses in Grizedale (p.141) and Whinlatter (p.173) forest parks can have the whole family making like a monkey in the trees, and both parks are also great for off-road cycling and hiking. For a thrilling mountain adventure, the sensational **Via Ferrata** at Honister Slate Mine (p.169) lets novices climb the "Iron Way" to the top of Fleetwith Pike. Alternatively, take the narrow-gauge train up Eskdale and then mountain-bike back down the **Eskdale Trail** (p.188) on a great day out on the Ravenglass & Eskdale Railway.

The view from the top

For easy Windermere views, make the short climb up **Orrest Head** (p.59) and soak up the sweeping panorama. In Grasmere, it's **Loughrigg Fell** or **Silver Howe** (see p.100 for both) that offer the best effort-for-view ratio, while from Coniston any decent day demands a dash up **The Old Man** (p.122). Keswick, in the north, is the best base for sampling the serious mountains but even here you can be on the top of **Latrigg** (p.158) within the hour for some wonderful lake vistas.

▲ Walking in the Lakes

▼ Mountain biking

▼ The high-ropes course at Grizedale Forest

The Kirkstile Inn ▲

View from Cat Bells ▲

Distant view of Scafell Pike over Wast Water ▼

Couch potatoes to mountain goats: a dozen walks for all abilities

▶▶ **High-altitude circuit** Keep your head in the clouds on the Coledale Horseshoe. See p.171.

▶▶ **Pub walk** Circle pretty Loweswater and stop off afterwards at the excellent *Kirkstile Inn* for a drink in the beer garden. See p.202.

▶▶ **Mountain peaks** Langdale's most exciting walk is up Crinkle Crags and Bowfell. See p.113.

▶▶ **Round-lake** There are more famous lakes, but the long ramble around Haweswater gets you right off the beaten track. See p.222.

▶▶ **Viewpoint** From Cat Bells – everyone's favourite scramble – you can see for miles. See p.163.

▶▶ **Waterfall hike** Stock Ghyll force is dramatic in spate and an easy walk from Ambleside. See p.80.

▶▶ **Family stroll** There are woodland paths, glistening water and idyllic picnic spots at Tarn Hows. See p.36.

▶▶ **Only for experts** Early start, late finish, guts and stamina required – it's the gruelling Woolpack Walk which covers some of the Lakes' most challenging terrain. See p.192.

▶▶ **Into the valley** Strike off up glorious Grisedale from near Patterdale on Ullswater, with Grisedale Tarn your destination. See p.214.

▶▶ **Wordsworth's footsteps** A tramp in the poet's backyard around Grasmere and Rydal Water. See p.100.

▶▶ **Crowd-free ramble** You'll be on your own in the heart of the Duddon Valley. See p.143.

▶▶ **3000-footer** A must for list-tickers and peak-baggers England's highest mountain, Scafell Pike, tops out at 3210ft. See p.167.

Ⓦwww.lakelandgateway.info), with post office and internet in the same building. For **online information**, consult Ⓦwww.amblesideonline.co.uk, an irreverent but useful community website for the Ambleside area.

Accommodation

Lake Road, running between Waterhead and Ambleside, is lined with **B&Bs**, and there are other concentrations on Church Street and Compston Road, as well as a **backpackers** just on the edge of town – all these are marked on the main Ambleside map. Fancier places tend to lie out of town, or a mile to the south at Waterhead by the lake (see Around Ambleside: Waterhead and Wray map), which is also where you'll find Ambleside's official **youth hostel**. This is one of the most popular in the country and advance reservations are essential during most of the year. The nearest **campsite**, *Low Wray*, is three miles south and also right by the lake – with its pods, bell-tents, yurts and tipis it's fully embracing the cool camping culture.

In Ambleside

Ambleside Backpackers Old Lake Rd Ⓣ015394/32340, Ⓦwww.amblesidebackpackers.com. The independent hostel choice is this extended lakeland cottage, a 5min walk from town, with 66 beds in varying sized dorms. It's a bit frayed at the edges (they cheekily claim "character is built in"), and there's not much space in the dorms, though they do have lockers and washbasins and there's a really well-equipped kitchen, plus dining room and lounge. A cereal, tea and toast breakfast is included in the price, and there's parking outside. Dorm beds from £17, long-stay discounts available.

Brantfell Rothay Rd Ⓣ015394/32239, Ⓦwww.brantfell.co.uk. Soft tones, uncluttered rooms and fell views are the hallmark of this fetching makeover of a Victorian house on the edge of town. Two bigger-than-usual singles, two doubles and two suites with sofas make up the accommodation, all with serious showers. A log fire keeps the guest lounge nice and cosy, and there's free entry to the pool at a local leisure club. Breakfast is a big deal too – choose from traditional, continental or things like smoked salmon, bagels and cream cheese, hash browns, pancakes and kippers. Parking. ❸, suites ❹

Compston House Compston Rd Ⓣ015394/32305, Ⓦwww.compstonhouse.co.uk. Owners Sue and Jerry from New York have cleverly created one of the Lakes' most individual B&Bs inside a traditional lakeland house – hung with iconic American prints, the lovely light rooms are themed after various US states and feature Egyptian cotton bed linen and snazzy small bathrooms. The Stateside feel extends to breakfast, when alongside the traditional fry-up there are also home-made pancakes and maple syrup or fluffy New York-style omelettes. Free parking permit available. ❸, some rooms and weekends ❹

Hillsdale Church St Ⓣ015394/33174, Ⓦwww.hillsdaleambleside.co.uk. Chintz-free B&B, where the refurbished rooms have bold colours, flat-screen TVs and mini-fridges for fresh milk (room 7 has a thoroughly fancy shower-room too). There are also free passes for Low Wood leisure club and private parking. ❷, weekends ❸

Lakes Lodge Lake Rd Ⓣ015394/33240, Ⓦwww.lakeslodge.co.uk. The traditional lakeland slate exterior is no preparation for the lilac/lavender colour scheme inside this fancy urban lodge. A dozen spacious rooms have been given the style treatment, with those at the back sporting views over Loughrigg. A good buffet breakfast (full English, smoked fish, local ham) is served in the informal café-style breakfast room, and you can have dinner or use the pool at Waterhead's *Regent Hotel*. Parking. ❹

Linda's B&B Compston Rd Ⓣ015394/32999. The cheery spirit never flags and the bargain prices – the lowest in Ambleside – go a long way to compensate for the simple facilities. The three rooms (a single, double and a twin) all share a bathroom and a top-floor shower-room, while guests can use the kitchen (a room-only stay brings the price down to as little as £15 a night). There's parking for one car, and a lockable bike shed. No credit cards. ❶

The Waterwheel 3 Bridge St Ⓣ015394/33286, Ⓦwww.waterwheelambleside.co.uk. An ancient, teeny-tiny Ambleside cottage revamped as a romantic bolt hole. There are just three rooms, accessed up a steep staircase, whose signature style is contemporary Victorian – underfloor-heated bathrooms with clawfoot baths, brass bedsteads and flat-screen TVs. Stockgyhll is the priciest and nicest, but from attic-hewn Loughrigg you can see the hills, and in each room is a welcome-back decanter of port and some Kendal mintcake. Last-minute website deals go as low as £60. Parking permit provided. ❹

Around Ambleside

Ambleside YHA Waterhead, A591, 1 mile south of Ambleside ⓣ0845/371 9620, ⓔambleside@yha.org.uk. When does a hostel become a hotel? When it's as good as Ambleside's impressively operated lakeside affair, which boasts over 250 beds divided amongst neatly furnished small dorms, twins, doubles and family rooms. Facilities are first-rate – whether it's swimming off the private jetty, hanging out in the licensed bar and restaurant (drinking local beers and Fair Trade coffee), or grabbing a rental bike – and all the usual hostel stuff is well taken care of too (internet, laundry, drying room etc). There's parking outside. Dorm beds from £15.95, rooms ❷

Dower House Wray Castle, off B5286 (Hawkshead road), 3 miles south ⓣ015394/33211. Sleep the sleep of the just at this very peaceful shoreline house on the Wray Castle estate, and then revel in the view at breakfast – across the lake to the fells. There are four traditionally furnished rooms, including one spacious single – aching hikers should ask for "Fairfield", the only one with a bath (rather than shower). If you got soaked you can get your walking gear dried, and there's also an optional dinner served (BYO wine). Parking. No credit cards. ❸, including dinner ❹

Randy Pike B5286 (Hawkshead road), 3 miles south, just past Low Wray turn-off ⓣ015394/36088, ⓦwww.randypike.co.uk. Andy and Chrissy Hill (of Grasmere's *Jumble Room* restaurant) offer two amazing light-filled B&B suites opening out on to the gardens of what was once a Victorian gentleman's hunting lodge. Seriously, you could live in the stunning designer bathrooms alone, while the hand-crafted beds, pitch-pine floors and quirky, unique furnishings add up to something very special. It's a grown-up, romantic retreat, and you can either stay put with the flat-screen TV, ipod, snack-larder, terrace and gardens, or be whizzed down to the *Jumble Room* for dinner. Parking. ❻

Riverside Under Loughrigg, half-mile west of Ambleside ⓣ015394/32395, ⓦwww.riverside-at-ambleside.co.uk. A charming Victorian house on a quiet lane facing the River Rothay, a 10min walk from town – on foot, take any path across the park, cross the bridge and turn left. Six large, light country-pine-style rooms available (a couple with whirlpool baths), including a river-facing four-poster room and a family room with bunks and a terrific bathroom. Sit outside on the garden deck and plan your day's walking with the library of guides, and then build yourself up with the magnificent breakfast (including home-made preserves, bread, potato cakes and fruit smoothies). Also a tasteful two-bedroom apartment with kitchen-diner at the same address (ⓦwww.gilbertscarfoot.co.uk; sleeps 4). Parking. ❹

Rothay Manor Rothay Bridge, half-mile south of Ambleside ⓣ015394/33605, ⓦwww.rothaymanor.co.uk. Honed to perfection over many years, this impressive Regency-style mansion has been in the hands of the same amiable but unobtrusive family for four decades (and in the *Good Food Guide* for as long). Rooms are larger than average (including decent-sized beds and spacious bathrooms), but the most sought-after "superior" rooms at the front have their own private balcony, while three suites in the grounds provide more space for families. Dinner's a treat, with a contemporary country-house menu (from £34, open to nonresidents) served in the candlelit dining room. Parking. ❻, suites ❼, including dinner ❽

Waterhead Hotel Waterhead, 1 mile south of Ambleside ⓣ015394/32566, ⓦwww.elh.co.uk. Lakeshore city-chic pretty much sums up this designer town-house-style hotel opposite the Waterhead piers. White high-ceilinged rooms feature boutique fabrics and furnishings, with no detail left unattended – from king-sized beds with suede headboards to monogrammed cups for morning tea and a champagne menu in the sparkling slate-and-marble bathrooms. Guests get to use the pool and spa at the nearby Low Wood leisure club, and then it's back for a Pimms in the swanky garden-bar and dinner in the positively metropolitan restaurant (both open to nonresidents, mains £12–20). Parking. ❻–❼

Campsite

Low Wray Campsite Low Wray, off B5286, 3 miles south of Ambleside ⓣ015394/32810, booking enquiries ⓣ015394/63862, ⓦwww.ntlakescampsites.org.uk. The beautiful National Trust site on the western shore of the lake is great for bikers, hikers and kayakers, but it's now also a glam-campers' haven with a choice of wooden camping "pods" for couples and families (£30–45 per night), tipis (part-week rental from £130, weekends £155, contact ⓣ01539/821227 or 07976/ 558602, ⓦwww.4windslakelandtipis.co.uk) and bell-tents (part-week from £225, full week from £345, contact ⓣ07884/315298 or 07813/334865, ⓦwww.long-valley-yurts.co.uk). Tipis and bell-tents are all fully equipped (futons to wood-burners), and you're only 2 miles from a couple of great pubs (including the *Drunken Duck*). Bus #505 (to Coniston) passes within a mile of the site and from the stop it's a nice walk down a country lane. Closed Nov–Easter.

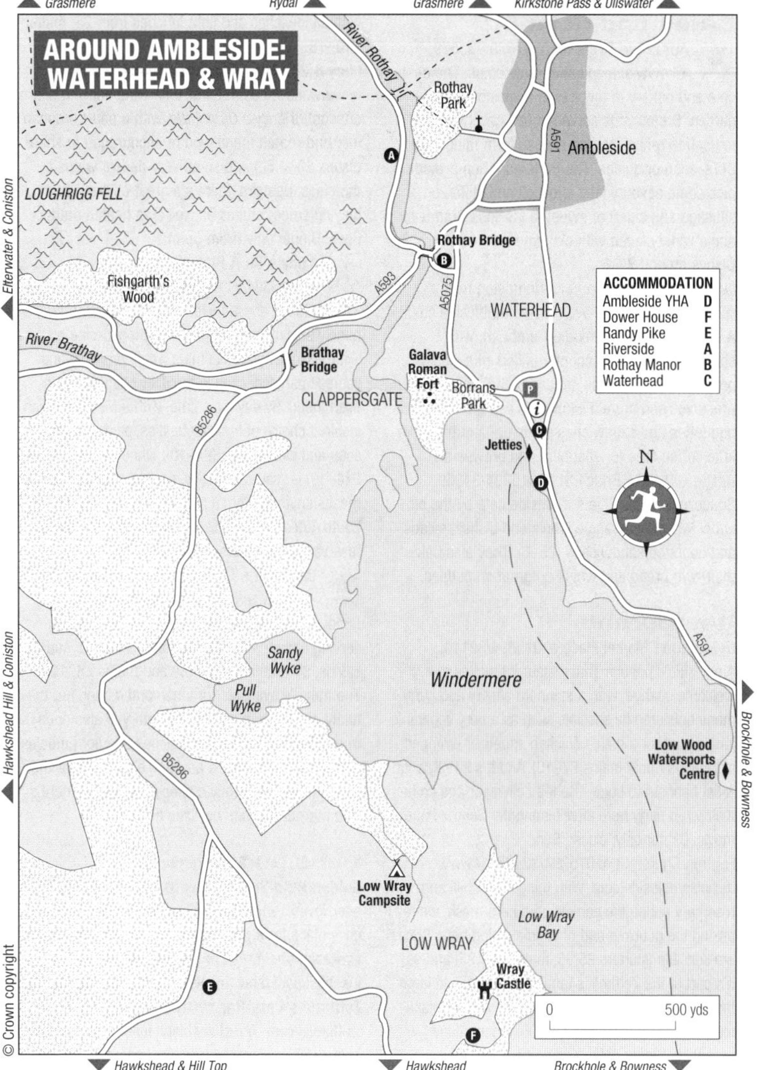

Eating, drinking and entertainment

There's more choice in Ambleside for eating than just about anywhere else in the Lakes, from **cafés** and takeaways to gourmet **restaurants**, which is one of the reasons the town makes such a good base. **Pubs** are plentiful, too, a couple showing real character, though the nicest alfresco drinking is done down at Waterhead. The two small local **supermarkets**, Spar and Co-op, are both on Compston Road, but *Lucy's* deli (see listings) is a far better choice if you're looking to put together a picnic. Zeffirelli's **cinema** (Ⓣ015394/33845, Ⓦwww.zeffirellis.com) has five screens at three locations in town, while for details of Ambleside's annual **festivals** – the Rushbearing (July) and Ambleside Sports (August) – see p.36 and p.39 respectively.

Cafés and delis

Apple Pie Rydal Rd ⓣ015394/33679, ⓦwww.applepieambleside.co.uk. The best café and bakery in town, with a secluded patio-garden. Breakfast is served until 11am (with free tea/coffee refills), or else choose from things like BLTs, soup or quiche. The trademark home-made pies come savoury (say, broccoli and stilton or sausage and cider) or sweet (a luscious Bramley apple variety laced with cinnamon and raisin). Dishes around £5–6.

Lucy's Specialist Grocers Compston Rd ⓣ015394/32223, ⓦwww.lucysofambleside.co.uk. A shrine to all things foodie-Cumbrian, with shelves, baskets and counters filled with classy produce, local cheeses, artisan bread, home-made preserves and more. Picknickers can get fancy baguettes and sandwiches made up, and there's a little coffee area for shoppers and browsers.

Rattle Gill Café Bridge St ⓣ015394/34360. Squeeze into this little streamside café by the old water wheels for veggie wholefood dishes, salads and doorstop sandwiches (£5–6). They also bake their own bread and whisk up great smoothies.

Restaurants

Doi Intanon Market Place ⓣ015394/32119. Ambleside's popular Thai restaurant makes a welcome change, with a standard stir-fry and curry menu bolstered by specials such as a fiery vegetable jungle curry or a grilled chicken appetizer wrapped in papyrus (most mains £7–10). And it's a Hollywood A-list hangout to boot – Renée Zellweger and co had their wrap party here after filming the Beatrix Potter movie. Dinner only; closed Sun.

Fellinis Church St ⓣ015394/32487, ⓦwww.fellinisambleside.com. With things like chilli and rosemary aubergine parcels on a herb mash, we're talking the gourmet end of veggie dining here. Prices are sensible (starters £5.95, mains £10.95) and as it's part of the Zeffirelli's family, no surprise to learn there's a digital art-house cinema on the premises too (meal and movie deal £19.95, reservations essential). Dinner only; restaurant closed Mon.

Glass House Rydal Rd ⓣ015394/32137, ⓦwww.theglasshouserestaurant.co.uk. A very handsome place to eat, with open mezzanine floors chiselled out of a renovated fulling mill complete with water wheel and sunny courtyard. The menu is Modern British (Caesar salad to braised Herdwick lamb), with sandwiches and light lunches from £5, mains £10–18.

Lucy 4 2 St Mary's Lane ⓣ015394/34666, ⓦwww.lucy4.co.uk. Good-time wine bar and bistro offshoot of *Lucy's On A Plate*, with a pan-European mix-and-match menu (you're encouraged to share, dishes £3–7.50) and some very decent wines by the glass. Upstairs, there's a great chill-out bar playing smooth tunes as well as a heated outdoor deck. Dinner only (from 5pm).

Lucy's On A Plate Church St ⓣ015394/31191, ⓦwww.lucysofambleside.co.uk. Quirky doesn't even begin to describe *Lucy's* hugely enjoyable, very informal stripped-pine bistro – if they know you're coming, you'll probably find yourself namechecked in the daily changing, pun-filled menu. By day it's a café, with a Mediterranean-inspired choice of breakfasts, dips, pastas, salads, soup and sandwiches (£4–10); dinner (mains mostly £14–19) is "sourced locally, cooked globally", which means anything from a rack of fell-bred lamb to a South African *bobotie* using Cumbrian beef. Dinner reservations are pretty much essential.

Zeffirelli's Compston Rd ⓣ015394/33845, ⓦwww.zeffirellis.com. *Zeff's* is a star – famous for its wholemeal-base pizzas, but also serving Italian-with-a-twist starters, pastas and salads, all vegetarian (pizzas and mains £8–10). The menu's available for lunch and dinner, but the funky dining room and conservatory is also open from 10am for cakes, sandwiches and light meals; dinner reservations are advised, especially for the popular meal-and-movie special (£17.95). There's also a great upstairs bar (see below).

Pubs and bars

Golden Rule Smithy Brow ⓣ015394/32257. The beer-lovers' and climbers' favourite pub – this is a cosy place for a post-hike pint (six real ales usually available) and a read of the Wainwright, with no jukebox, pool table, meals or other distractions.

Zeffirelli's Café-Bar ⓣ015394/33845, ⓦwww.zeffirellis.com. The shiny black fashionable space above *Zeffirelli's* restaurant is a contemporary jazz and world music bar, with live music most Friday and Saturday nights (often free). You'll catch anything from a local trio to an international act – see the website for advance schedules – and you can eat here too, from a shorter version of the restaurant menu.

Listings

Banks NatWest (Cheapside), Barclays and HSBC (both Market Place) have ATMs.

Bike rental Biketreks, Rydal Rd (daily 9.30am–5pm; ⓣ015394/31245, ⓦwww.biketreks.net);

and Ghyllside Cycles, The Slack (Easter–Oct daily 9.30am–5.30pm; Nov–Easter closed Wed; ⓣ015394/33592, ⓦwww.ghyllside.co.uk). Daily rental from £20, with maps for day rides included in the price.

Emergencies Doctors at Ambleside Group Practice, Rydal Rd ⓣ015394/32693, ⓦwww.amblesidegrouppractice.co.uk. The nearest hospital is in Kendal (Westmorland General Hospital, Burton Rd; ⓣ01539/732288).

Internet access Ambleside Library, Kelsick Rd (Mon, Wed & Fri 10am–5pm, Tues 10am–7pm, Sat 10am–1pm; ⓣ015394/32507), has the most terminals, and there's also access at the tourist office.

Outdoors stores Ambleside is a great place to pick up walking and climbing gear and camping equipment at reasonable prices – there are almost permanent sales on in the outdoors stores. For mountain boots there's F.W. Tyson (Market Place) as well as The Climber's Shop (Compston Corner; walking-boot rental available) and Stewart R. Cunningham (Rydal Rd), while large retailers include Black's (Compston Rd) and Gaynor Sports (Market Cross), the latter the country's biggest outdoors store.

Pharmacy Thomas Bell, Lake Rd ⓣ015394/33345; Boots, 8–9 Market Cross ⓣ015394/33355.

Police station Rydal Rd ⓣ0845/330 0247, ⓦwww.cumbria.police.uk.

Post office Inside the tourist office, Market Cross.

Taxis Abacus ⓣ015394/88285; John's Taxis ⓣ015394/32857; Kevin's Taxis ⓣ015394/32371.

Watersports Low Wood, on the A591, a mile south of Ambleside (ⓣ015394/39441, ⓦwww.elh.co.uk/watersports), is a lakefront watersports centre, for anything from kayaking (from £14 for 2hr) to water-skiing (1hr lesson £65), plus rowboat (from £10 per hr) and motorboat (from £18 per hr) rental.

Troutbeck

Troutbeck Bridge, three miles southeast of Ambleside along the A591 (and just a mile or so from Windermere town), heralds the start of the gentle **Troutbeck valley** below Wansfell, accessed by two roads, one either side of the valley's namesake beck. The main A592 to Patterdale runs north into the valley, passing the Lakeland Horticultural Society's splendid gardens at **Holehird** (daily dawn–dusk; free, though donation requested; ⓣ015394/46008), whose four acres encompass various different habitats, from rock and alpine gardens to rose gardens and shrubberies.

The better route, though, is up a minor road (Bridge Lane) running high above the west side of **Trout Beck** itself. A mile along here is Windermere youth hostel; under a mile beyond is **Townend** (Easter–Oct Wed–Sun plus bank hols, guided tours at 11am & noon, general admission 1–5pm, last admission 4.30pm; £4.20, family £10.50; ⓣ015394/32628, ⓦwww.nationaltrust.org.uk), a seventeenth-century house, built in 1626 for George Browne, a wealthy yeoman farmer, one of that breed of independent farmers known in these parts as "statesmen", after the estates they tended. Remarkably, the house remained in the hands of eleven generations of the Browne family, for more than three hundred years, until 1943 when the National Trust took it over. It's an extraordinary relic of seventeenth-century vernacular architecture, with its round chimneys (of the sort admired by Wordsworth) surmounting a higgledy-piggledy collection of small rooms, some added as late as the nineteenth century. The house is well known for its woodcarvings and panelling, and lavishly embellished beds, fireplaces, chests, chairs and grandfather clocks are scattered around the various rooms. You'll also see the surviving laundry room (complete with ancient mangle), dairy, library and parlour.

Townend is at the southern end of **TROUTBECK** village, really just a straggling hamlet with a post office (which sells cups of tea and ice cream). Several hikes pass through village and valley, with the peaks of Yoke (2309ft), Ill Bell (the highest at 2476ft) and Froswick (2359ft) on the east side forming the

▲ Townend, Troutbeck

barrier between Troutbeck and Kentmere. The most direct route into Kentmere is the easy track over the **Garburn Pass**, while many use Troutbeck as the starting point for the five-hour walk along **High Street**, a nine-mile range running north to Brougham near Penrith. The course of a Roman road follows the ridge, probably once linking the forts at Brougham and Galava in Waterhead.

North of Troutbeck, the A592 makes a gradual ascent to **Kirkstone Pass**, four miles from the village, at the head of which there's a superbly sited pub, the *Kirkstone Pass Inn*, whose picnic tables (across the road) offer terrific views. A minor road from here cuts down directly to Ambleside – so precipitous that it's known as "The Struggle" – while the A592 continues over the pass and down the valley to Ullswater.

Practicalities

Public transport to Troutbeck is limited to bus #517 (Easter–Oct), which runs from Bowness piers and Windermere train station up the A592 and over Kirkstone Pass en route to Ullswater. It makes stops at the *Queen's Head* and the *Kirkstone Pass Inn*.

Traditional **accommodation** in Troutbeck is at one of two famous old inns, the *Mortal Man* or the *Queen's Head,* but there's also superior studio accommodation and some cheaper village B&Bs – local tourist offices should be able to check on space for you. Budget accommodation is at the valley's self-catering **youth hostel**, confusingly known as the *Windermere YHA*, which is a mile up the steep road from the bus stop at Troutbeck Bridge.

Fellside Studios Fellside ⓣ015394/34000, ⓦwww.fellsidestudios.co.uk. A tranquil base for walkers who can set off each day straight from the door of these two excellent self-contained studios (one double, one twin). They're decorated in contemporary style, with oak floors, slate-tiled kitchens and shower-rooms, while attractive living/sleeping areas open directly on to outside terraces. A generous continental breakfast (cold meats, smoked-fish platter, cheese etc) is brought to your door each morning. Parking. ❸

Mortal Man Bridge Lane ⓣ015394/33193, ⓦwww.themortalman.co.uk. Re-opened under new owners, the *Mortal Man* is working hard to restore its reputation. The glorious valley views are still the same, while half of the dozen rooms have been refurbished (with the rest to follow) – wooden four-posters, hung with drapes add a touch of romance to some. The public bar's an age-old beauty, with traditional pub food available here or in the gardens and a more contemporary lakeland dinner in the valley-view restaurant (salmon and tuna fish cakes to duck breast with bubble and squeak, mains £9–18). Parking. ❸, new/4-poster rooms ❹

Queen's Head On the A592 ⓣ015394/32174, ⓦwww.queensheadhotel.com. You're invited to "tuck in and sleep over" at this revamped old coaching inn that simply oozes atmosphere, from the slate floors, oak beams and smoky fires to the carved bar fashioned from a four-poster bed. There are eleven bright-as-a-button rooms in the inn itself (the two largest, with great views, are nos. 10 and 11) and four more, slightly smaller and cheaper, in the converted barn annexe. Dining is a treat, too, with everything from Thai-style mussels to red-onion tarte tatin – most mains cost £11–16 or good-value inclusive D,B&B rates are available. Parking. ❺, including dinner ❻

Windermere YHA High Cross, Bridge Lane ⓣ0845/371 9352, ⓔwindermere@yha.org.uk. Built originally as a private mansion, the house still has magnificent lake views while a major refit has smartened up rooms and facilities. Families like it for its woodland trails, bike rental and outdoor activities, and the food gets good reviews – you can also buy bottled Cumbrian beers and organic wines. Dorm beds from £13.95.

Staveley

Four miles east of Windermere, the little village of **STAVELEY** lies tucked away on the banks of the River Kent. The river has powered mills in Staveley for over seven hundred years, and in the eighteenth and nineteenth centuries there was prosperity of sorts as first cotton was produced and then wooden bobbins were manufactured here in sizeable quantities. These wood-turning skills have survived into modern times, with Staveley woodwork still a thing of beauty. **Peter Hall & Son** (Mon–Fri 9am–5pm, Sat 10am–1pm; ⓣ01539/821633, ⓦwww.peter-hall.co.uk), a mile out on the Windermere road, produces renowned handcrafted furniture and household goods, while many other cottage industries occupy the old mill buildings themselves in **Mill Yard**, off Main Street (see feature). This has become a really popular enclave of craft and food businesses and makes a good stop for a meal or drink.

An easy half-hour stroll around the village starts by the restored tower of **St Margaret's** on Main Street, all that survives of Staveley's original fourteenth-century church. Follow the path at the side of the church tower down to the river, turn left and walk along the riverside path and road to the old bridge, from where you return through the village, passing the replacement nineteenth-century church of **St James** – inside which is a superb Burne-Jones-designed stained-glass window depicting a star-clustered heavenly choir surmounting the crucifixion.

Practicalities

Staveley is bypassed by the A591 – village visitors should follow the signs in to Mill Yard, where there's masses of free **parking**. You can also get here on the train line from Kendal or on the #555 bus, while walkers come past on the Dales Way, which follows the River Kent from Kendal, steers just south of the village and then cuts west across the low fells to Bowness. In fact, Staveley makes a good target for a day on the local fells, either on foot or with a **rental bike** from Wheelbase in Mill Yard (bikes from £16 per day, open Mon–Sat 9am–5.30pm, Sun 10am–4pm; ⓣ01539/821443, ⓦwww.wheelbase.co.uk), the UK's biggest bike store. The bridleways and trails of Kentmere valley (see next section) are easily accessible from here, and the mountain bike centre has showers and changing rooms for cyclists.

Cottage crafts and cups of tea

The ever-expanding collection of businesses at Mill Yard (Ⓦwww.staveleymillyard.com) makes a great target for browsers and buyers, whether you're after a scoop of organic lakeland ice cream courtesy of **Scoop Choc Ice** (Ⓦwww.scoopchocice.co.uk) or a hand-carved dresser from the **Waters and Acland** furniture workshop and gallery (Ⓦwww.watersandacland.co.uk). **Friendly Food and Drink** (Ⓦwww.friendlyfoodanddrink.co.uk) make handmade chutneys, preserves, sauces and mustards, there's yummy artisan-made bread – not to mention decadent choccie "Muddees" – at **More?** (Ⓦwww.morepud.co.uk), while next door at **Organico** (Ⓦwww.organi.co.uk) is the largest organic wine shop in the UK (also with bar and bistro). Come on a Saturday and you can tour **Hawkshead Brewery** (Sat at 1pm, 2pm & 3pm, or by arrangement; Ⓦwww.hawksheadbrewery.co.uk) before getting to grips with brews by the name of "Lakeland Gold" or "Brodie's Prime".

Accommodation

Eagle & Child Kendal Rd Ⓣ01539/821320, Ⓦwww.eaglechildinn.co.uk. The village's nicest inn – right in the centre – has five smallish, but tastefully decorated rooms, some overlooking the River Kent. There's a riverside garden, where you can sip a Cumbrian beer, and good bar meals (using ingredients from village or local suppliers), including home-made soup, well-stuffed baguette and ciabatta sandwiches, Kentmere lamb shanks or the local butcher's bangers with mash (mains around £10). Parking. ❸

Watermill Inn Ings (A591), 1.5 miles west of Staveley Ⓣ01539/821309, Ⓦwww.watermillinn.co.uk. No beer fan should miss the *Watermill*, which has up to sixteen real ales available on tap at any one time, and even more during its various festivals. Add a sun-trap garden and popular bar food and it's no wonder it's won just about every beer award going. The pub was once an old bobbin mill, now imaginatively restored – the bar is fashioned from church pews – and there's a craft brewery on site, as well as eight good-value bedrooms (two with balconies). It's also the venue for regular music nights, plus tall tales once a month (first Tuesday) when the long-standing South Lakeland Storytelling Club meets. Parking. ❸

Eating and drinking

Hawkshead Brewery Beer Hall Mill Yard Ⓣ01539/822644, Ⓦwww.hawksheadbrewery.co.uk. The showcase bar for the excellent beers of the independent Hawkshead Brewery. Peer down into the brew-house and taste before buying, or choose from other guest beers, organic juices, or wines by the glass – and as the bar connects with *Wilf's* you can take your drinks through to the café (or food through to the bar). Live music and other events see occasional evening opening, but otherwise it's open daily noon–5pm (Wed–Sat until 6pm).

Wilf's Café Mill Yard Ⓣ01539/822239, Ⓦwww.wilfs-cafe.co.uk. A classic café for outdoor enthusiasts, cyclists and hikers. It's expanded over the years, but the heart of *Wilf's* was once the bobbin loft of an old wood mill – now there's dining on two floors and terraces out the back overlooking river and weir. The food is good value (most dishes cost £3–6), hearty and mostly veggie – rarebits, chillis, filled baked potatoes, salads and home-made cakes and puddings are mainstays, though there's a blackboard list of daily specials plus themed dinners (£20 a head, BYOB) held once a month. Daytime only.

Kentmere

North of Staveley a narrow road runs its dappled way alongside the River Kent, widening out after three miles into the splendid broad valley of **Kentmere**, with its isolated chapel perched on a bluff in the distance. Houses are few and far between, but the valley has been settled for over a thousand years – remains of a Viking Age farmstead have been identified near the valley head. A later building, Kentmere Hall, a couple of hundred yards up the country lane from the chapel, retains a remarkably well-preserved fourteenth-century turreted pele tower, which you can see from the lane. The heather moorland further up the valley provides a habitat for ground-nesting birds like red grouse, curlew and merlin, while on the high fells, if you're lucky, you'll see wild ponies grazing.

Kentmere is at the junction of several strategic paths and bridleways and is a popular destination for walkers. However, there's only extremely limited parking by the Kentmere Institute hall, behind the chapel, so on good days you'll need to get there early. Easy **hiking routes** head west to Troutbeck (via the relatively gentle Garburn Pass) or east to Sadgill and Longsleddale (see next section) – you can make a six-mile circuit of the latter route by going one way via Green Quarter and Cocklaw Fell. A signposted route also runs up the valley bottom to **Kentmere Reservoir**, a little over two miles from the chapel, which is hemmed in by a ring of dramatic, steep-sided fells. These themselves are all incorporated into the excellent full-day hike known as the **Kentmere Horseshoe** (12 miles; 7hr), a fairly strenuous peak-bagging route along ridges and saddles high above Kentmere Reservoir that takes in Kentmere Pike, Harter Fell, Mardale Ill Bell, Froswick, Ill Bell and Yoke. At one point, crossing Nan Bield Pass, four bodies of water are in view (Haweswater, two tarns and the reservoir), and if you walk the circuit anticlockwise (most people don't) then you'll have magnificent views of Windermere and Morecambe Bay on the home stretch.

Accommodation and food

Maggs Howe Lowfield Lane, Green Quarter, Kentmere ⓣ01539/821689, ⓦwww.maggshowe.co.uk. A half a mile or so east of the chapel (signposted from the bridge) there's either B&B in the house or a mattress on the floor in the bunkhouse next door (£10 per person), which has a couple of showers and a fully equipped kitchen; the bunkhouse is also available for exclusive use by groups (£100 per night, sleeps up to 12). The nearest shop and pub is down in Staveley, but you can arrange to have a big cooked breakfast (£7) or an evening meal (from £15) at the B&B, and walkers can drop in for afternoon tea. Parking. No credit cards. ❷

Longsleddale

If you want to see a really quiet corner of the Lakes, drive or cycle the four miles up the A6 out of Kendal and follow the sign into **Longsleddale** (pronounced "Longsleddle"), next valley to the east after Kentmere. There's only one road, as ridiculously pretty as it is narrow: it peters out after six miles at graceful **Sadgill**

Britain's favourite postie

As millions of British preschoolers know, the postie's job starts "early in the morning, just as day is dawning" – and don't even think of trying to deliver letters without a black-and-white cat in tow. Postman Pat's village of "Greendale" was originally inspired by the rolling countryside and wandering sheep of Longsleddale, which author John Cunliffe got to know well during his time in nearby Kendal. Cunliffe used to live on Greenside in Kendal, just down from which was the Beast Banks post office (next to the *Riflemans' Arms* pub), where he used to chat to the postmaster. It's closed as a post office now (though there's a plaque) but this is where Cunliffe envisaged Pat picking up the mail each morning from Mrs Goggins, in tales that were a big hit on the BBC as soon as they were aired in the early 1980s. Thirty years on, instead of drawing his pension, Pat's been given a new lease of life – the latest programmes have transferred him out of sleepy Greendale to the Special Delivery Service in the busy town of "Pencaster" and given him a helicopter and motorbike (don't worry, Jess the cat gets a sidecar).

Bridge, which is as far as you can go by car. Beyond here rise the encircling fells, where hikers can make their way up to the abandoned Wrengill Quarry and its waterfall and then along the old packhorse trail over Gatesgarth Pass and down to Haweswater. Most of the year you'll not see another soul.

Accommodation and food

Stockdale Cottage Longsleddale ⓣ01539/823716, ⓦwww.stockdalecottage.co.uk. A fantastic retreat for couples and solitude-seekers, with a real sense of arrival after a dramatic drive up a single-track road deep into the heart of the valley. There's only one guest room in Lindy and Harry's country-chic home-from-home and you also get your own lounge and patio, while breakfast can be served on the sunny beck-side terrace. Dinner (2 courses £12, 3 courses £15, BYOB) is available too. The cottage is 10 miles (20min drive) from Kendal but feels like a lot further, with red squirrels and deer on the doorstep and buzzards circling over the looming fells. No credit cards. ❸

Travel details

All timetables can be checked on Traveline ⓣ0871/200 2233, ⓦwww.traveline.info. For Cross-Lakes Experience bus-and-launch information call ⓣ015394/45161, or follow the links to current timetables on ⓦwww.lake-district.gov.uk. Note: see "Windermere" for all stops on the main bus routes #555 and #599.

From Ambleside

Bus #505, "Coniston Rambler" to: Hawkshead (20min), Waterhead Hotel (Coniston Water) for Brantwood boat (30min) and Coniston (35min). Service operates daily: Easter–Oct hourly; Nov–Easter every 1hr 30min–2hr.

Bus #516, "Langdale Rambler" (5–6 daily) to: Skelwith Bridge (10min), Elterwater (17min), Chapel Stile (20min) and Old Dungeon Ghyll (30min).

From Bowness

Bus #517, "Kirkstone Rambler" (3 daily) to: Windermere (8min), Troutbeck Queen's Head (20min), Kirkstone Pass (30min), Brotherswater (45min), Patterdale (50min) and Glenridding (55min). Service operates daily from mid-July to early Sept, otherwise on Sat, Sun & bank hols from Easter to mid-July & Sept–Oct.

Bus #618 (4–6 daily) to: Newby Bridge (15min), Haverthwaite (18min) and Ulverston (30min); or to Windermere (7min), Troutbeck Bridge (11min), Brockhole (14min) and Ambleside (22min).

Cross-Lakes Experience (9 daily): launch from Bowness connects with minibus from Ferry House, Sawrey, to Hill Top (7min) and Hawkshead (15min) – connections at Hawkshead for Grizedale Forest or Tarn Hows, while for Coniston Water change in Hawkshead to the #505 bus, which connects with the Coniston Launch at the *Waterhead Hotel*, Coniston. Service operates weekends from mid-Feb, then daily Easter–Oct.

From Windermere

Bus #555 (hourly) to: Troutbeck Bridge (4min), Brockhole (7min), Waterhead (12min), Ambleside (15min), Rydal (21min), Grasmere (30min) and Keswick (50min); also to Staveley (12min) and Kendal (25min).

Bus #599 to: Bowness (15min); also to Troutbeck Bridge (5min), Brockhole (7min), Waterhead (15min), Ambleside (20min), Rydal (26min), Dove Cottage (38min) and Grasmere (40min). Service operates Easter–Oct every 20–30min, Nov–Easter hourly and only to Bowness or Ambleside.

Bus #618 (4–6 daily) to: Bowness (6min), Newby Bridge (21min), Haverthwaite (25min) and Ulverston (35min); or to Troutbeck Bridge (4min), Brockhole (7min), Waterhead (12min) and Ambleside (15min).

Train (hourly) to: Staveley (6min) and Kendal (14min), and onward services to Oxenholme, Lancaster and Manchester.

2

Grasmere and the central fells

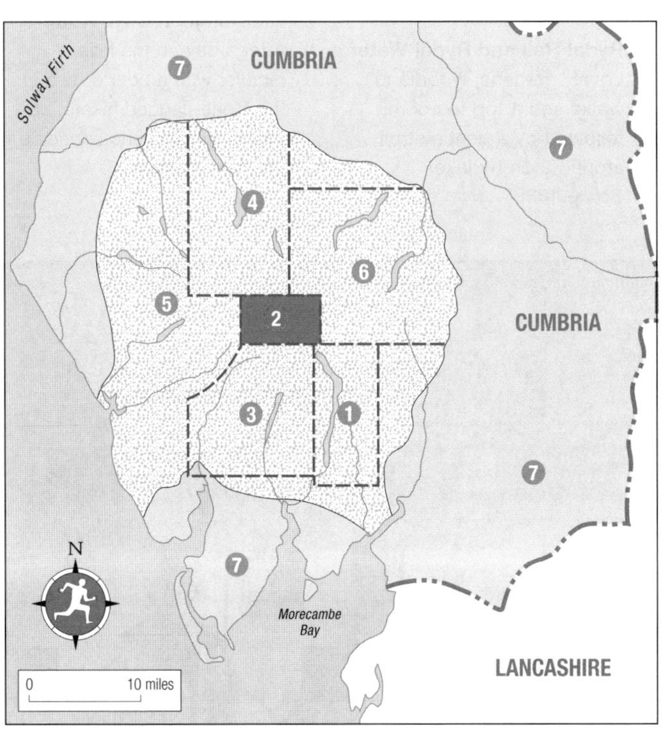

CHAPTER 2

Highlights

* **Visiting Wordsworth's grave, Grasmere** One of England's most famous literary pilgrimages is to the simple grave of the poet Wordsworth. See p.96

* **Dove Cottage, Grasmere** It's an obvious tourist attraction, but you shouldn't miss Wordsworth's first home in the Lake District. See p.104

* **Rydal Hall and Rydal Water** Lovely gardens, woodland walks and a top tearoom, followed by a gentle stroll around a pretty lake. See p.108

* **Elterwater** Stay the night in one of the Lake District's most attractive hamlets. See p.111

* **Walking in Great Langdale** Routes up the famous Langdale Pikes, Crinkle Crags and Bowfell could keep serious hikers occupied for a week. See p.113

* **Old Dungeon Ghyll Hotel** After a day on the fells, recover with a beer or two in the stone-flagged hikers' bar of this atmospheric Langdale inn. See p.115

▲ Pub, Elterwater village

2

Grasmere and the central fells

Grasmere – lake and village – is the traditional dividing line between the north and south Lakes, between the heavily touristed Windermere region and the more rugged fells on either side of Keswick. Rather than for its own charms (which are considerable), **Grasmere** owes its wild popularity to its most famous former resident, William Wordsworth, who first moved here in 1799 and lived in a variety of houses in the vicinity until his death in 1850. Two are open to the public: **Dove Cottage**, where he first set up home in the Lakes with his sister Dorothy; and **Rydal Mount**, on nearby Rydal Water, the comfortable family home to which he moved at the height of his fame. The museum and interpretation centre at Dove Cottage is the Lake District's most important cultural attraction, an essential visit for anyone interested in the English Romantics. It's centred on Wordsworth, of course, but the influence of other famous literary names hangs heavily on Grasmere, too, notably those of Thomas De Quincey, who lived here for more than twenty years and married a local girl; and of the dissolute Coleridges – father Samuel Taylor and son Hartley, whose separate periods of residence often tried the Wordsworths' patience.

Only a few miles west of Grasmere lie the **central fells**, including some of the Lake District's most famous peaks and valleys. Minor roads from Grasmere and Ambleside twist into the superb valleys of Great and Little **Langdale**, overlooked by the prominent rocky summits of hikers' favourites like the **Langdale Pikes**, **Bowfell** and **Crinkle Crags**. It's not all hard going though: there are easier walks to tarns and viewpoints in the bucolic surroundings of **Easedale** and Little Langdale, while hamlets such as **Skelwith Bridge** and **Elterwater** provide classic inns and country B&Bs for an isolated night's stay.

Grasmere

Four miles northwest of Ambleside, the pretty village of **GRASMERE** consists of an intimate cluster of grey-stone houses beside the babbling River Rothay. With a permanent population of under a thousand, and just a handful of roads which meet at a central green, it would be the archetypal, slow-paced,

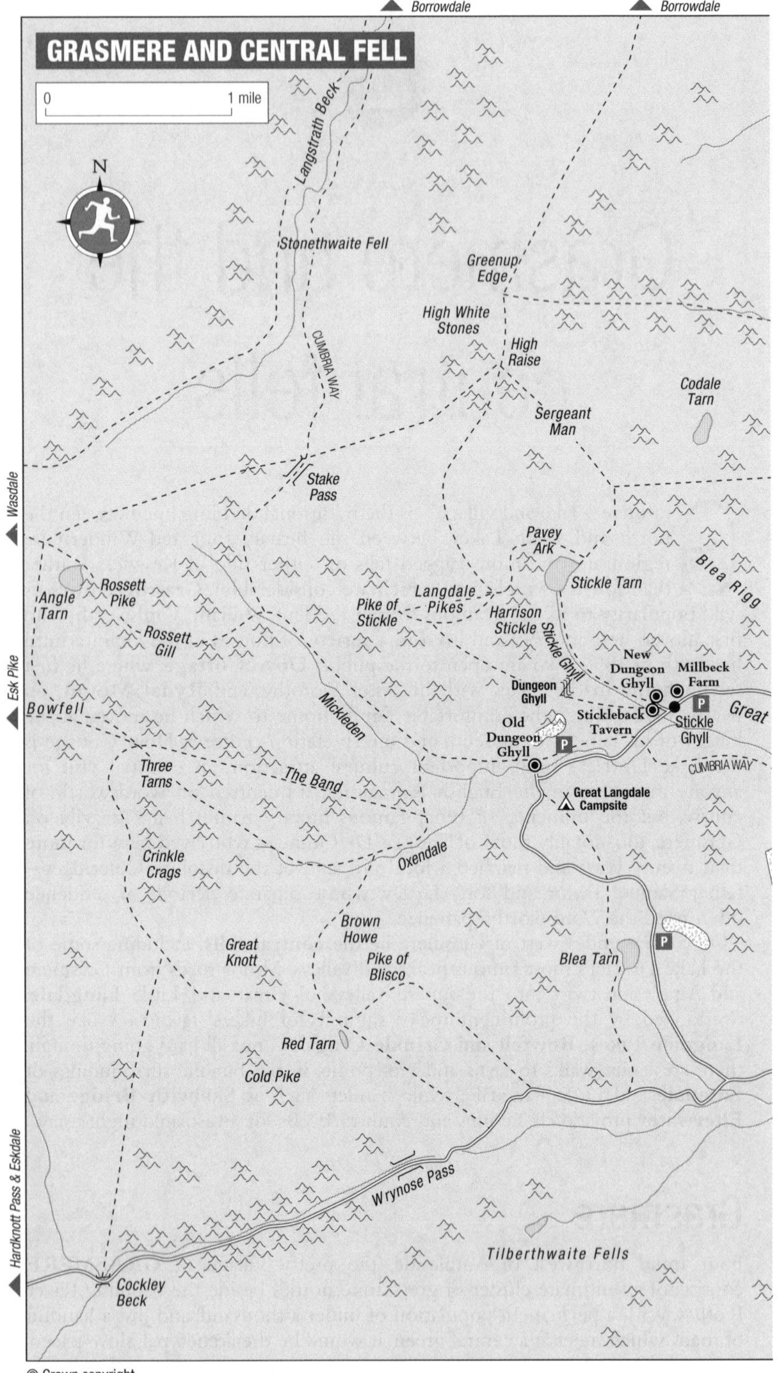
Borrowdale
Borrowdale
GRASMERE AND CENTRAL FELL
0
1 mile
N
Langstrath Beck
Stonethwaite Fell
Greenup Edge
High White Stones
High Raise
CUMBRIA WAY
Codale Tarn
Sergeant Man
Stake Pass
Wasdale
Pavey Ark
Stickle Tarn
Blea Rigg
Angle Tarn
Rossett Pike
Langdale Pikes
Pike of Stickle
Harrison Stickle
Rossett Gill
Stickle Ghyll
New Dungeon Ghyll
Millbeck Farm
Esk Pike
Dungeon Ghyll
Bowfell
Mickleden
Old Dungeon Ghyll
Stickleback Tavern
Stickle Ghyll
Great
Three Tarns
The Band
CUMBRIA WAY
Great Langdale Campsite
Crinkle Crags
Oxendale
Brown Howe
Great Knott
Pike of Blisco
Blea Tarn
Red Tarn
Cold Pike
Wrynose Pass
Hardknott Pass & Eskdale
Tilberthwaite Fells
Cockley Beck

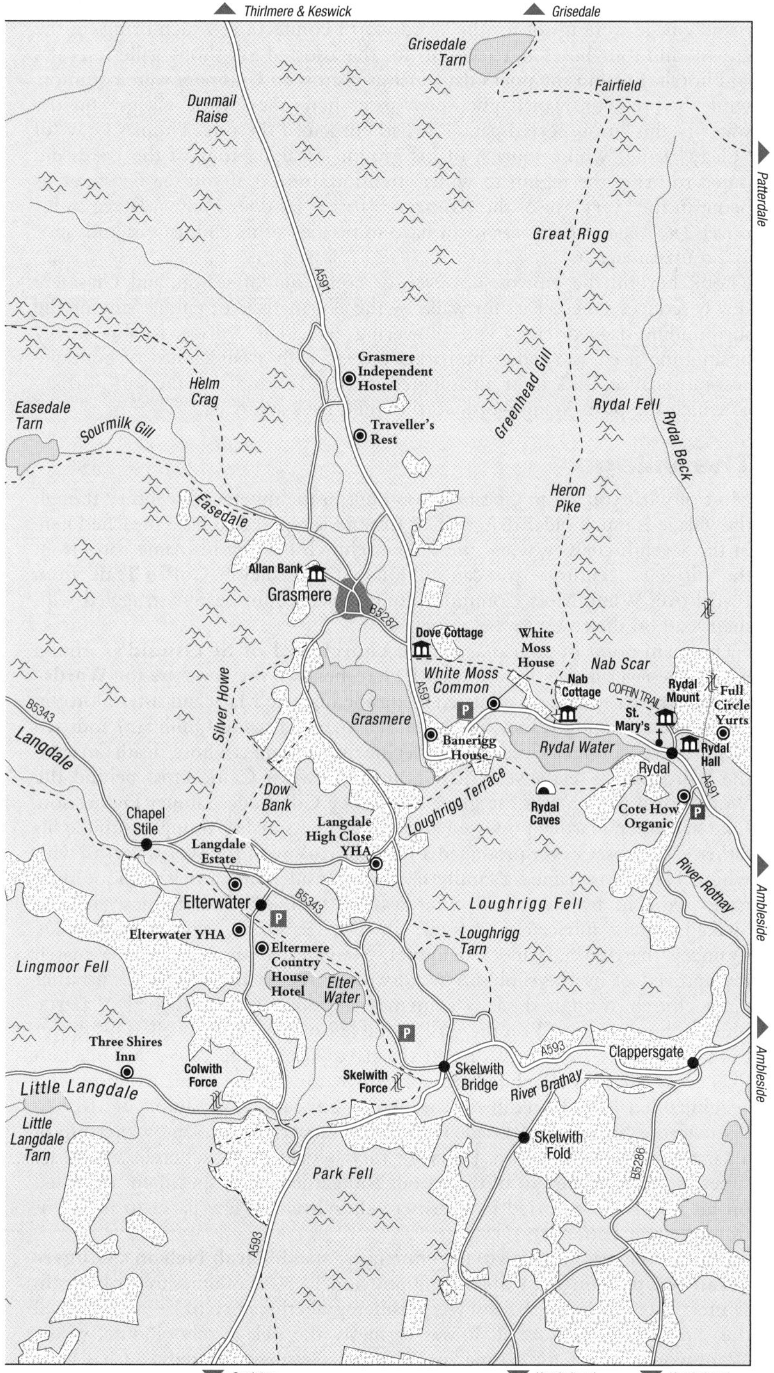
Thirlmere & Keswick
Grisedale
Grisedale Tarn
Fairfield
Dunmail Raise
Patterdale
Great Rigg
A591
Grasmere Independent Hostel
Helm Crag
Greenhead Gill
Rydal Fell
Easedale Tarn
Sourmilk Gill
Traveller's Rest
Rydal Beck
Heron Pike
Easedale
Allan Bank
Grasmere
B5287
Dove Cottage
White Moss House
Nab Scar
Silver Howe
White Moss Common
Nab Cottage
COFFIN TRAIL
Rydal Mount
Full Circle Yurts
B5343
Grasmere
St. Mary's
Langdale
Banerigg House
Rydal Water
Rydal Hall
Rydal
Dow Bank
Loughrigg Terrace
Rydal Caves
Cote How Organic
Chapel Stile
Langdale High Close YHA
Langdale Estate
River Rothay
Ambleside
Elterwater
B5343
Loughrigg Fell
Elterwater YHA
Loughrigg Tarn
Eltermere Country House Hotel
Lingmoor Fell
Elter Water
Ambleside
Three Shires Inn
A593
Clappersgate
Colwith Force
Skelwith Force
Skelwith Bridge
Little Langdale
River Brathay
Little Langdale Tarn
Skelwith Fold
B5286
Park Fell
A593
Coniston
Hawkshead
Hawkshead

rustic village were it not for the Wordsworth connection, which brings in the crowds and tour-buses and accounts for the assorted gift shops, galleries, cafés and hotels. Even in the poet's day curious visitors to Grasmere were common, while before Wordsworth put down roots here, the "white village" on the water in this "unsuspected paradise" had entranced the poet Thomas Gray (of "Elegy" fame) whose journal of his ground-breaking tour of the Lakes did much to bring the region to wider attention. Indeed, if you see Grasmere as being in the "very eye of the Romantic storm" (as does Melvyn Bragg in his novel *The Maid of Buttermere*) you have some idea of its enduring significance as a tourist magnet.

Look beyond the crowds, however, or come out of season, and Grasmere slowly seduces, whether it's for walks by the alluring lake or rambles among the surrounding jagged crags and glowering fells. The village is also slowly positioning itself as a rather upmarket retreat, with a fair choice of boutique accommodation – ideal for a pampered weekend away, if not the sort of thing of which the plain-living Wordsworth would have approved.

The village

Most of what you see in Grasmere was built in the nineteenth century, though the village is much older than that. St Oswald is reputed to have preached here in the seventh century, while the present church bearing his name dates from the thirteenth century – you can still follow the medieval "**Coffin Trail**" from Rydal over White Moss Common, along which coffin bearers struggled with their load on their way to the church.

The main point of pilgrimage is the **churchyard of St Oswald's**, around which the river makes a sinuous curl. Here, beneath the yews, are the **Wordsworth graves** – William is buried alongside his wife Mary and sister Dorothy, his beloved daughter Dora (buried in her married name Quillinan) and two of his much younger children, Catherine and Thomas, whose deaths marred the Wordsworths' early years in Grasmere. A worn Celtic cross behind the Wordsworth plots marks the grave of Hartley Coleridge, Samuel Taylor's son. Like his father, Hartley possessed an addictive personality, though – unlike his father – his lapses never produced a formal break with the Wordsworths, with whom Hartley remained a family favourite. Inside, the church's unique twin naves are split by an arched, whitewashed wall. Wordsworth described its "naked rafters intricately crossed" in *The Excursion*, while Thomas De Quincey married a farmer's daughter, Margaret Simpson, here – a match disapproved of by the snobbish Wordsworths. Associations aside, it's a rather plain church, though there is a memorial plaque to Wordsworth ("a true philosopher and poet") on the wall to the left of the altar, as well as his prayer book on display in a small case in the nave. Also in the case is a medallion likeness of **Sir John Richardson**, surgeon, naturalist and Arctic explorer who accompanied John Franklin on the heroic, but futile, expedition of 1819 to discover the Northwest Passage. Richardson later came into the ownership of a Grasmere country house, Lancrigg in Easedale (now a hotel), where he supervised the laying out of the woods and gardens with specimens collected on his travels. He's buried in Grasmere churchyard (a few paces to the right from the rear entrance).

Right at the rear entrance to the churchyard stands **Sarah Nelson's Gingerbread Shop** (Mon–Sat 9.30am–5.30pm, Sun 12.30–5.30pm, shorter hours in winter; ⓣ015394/35428, ⓦwww.grasmeregingerbread.co.uk) – you'll smell the shop before you see it. It was formerly the village schoolhouse, where Wordsworth taught for a time in 1812, but Grasmere gingerbread has been

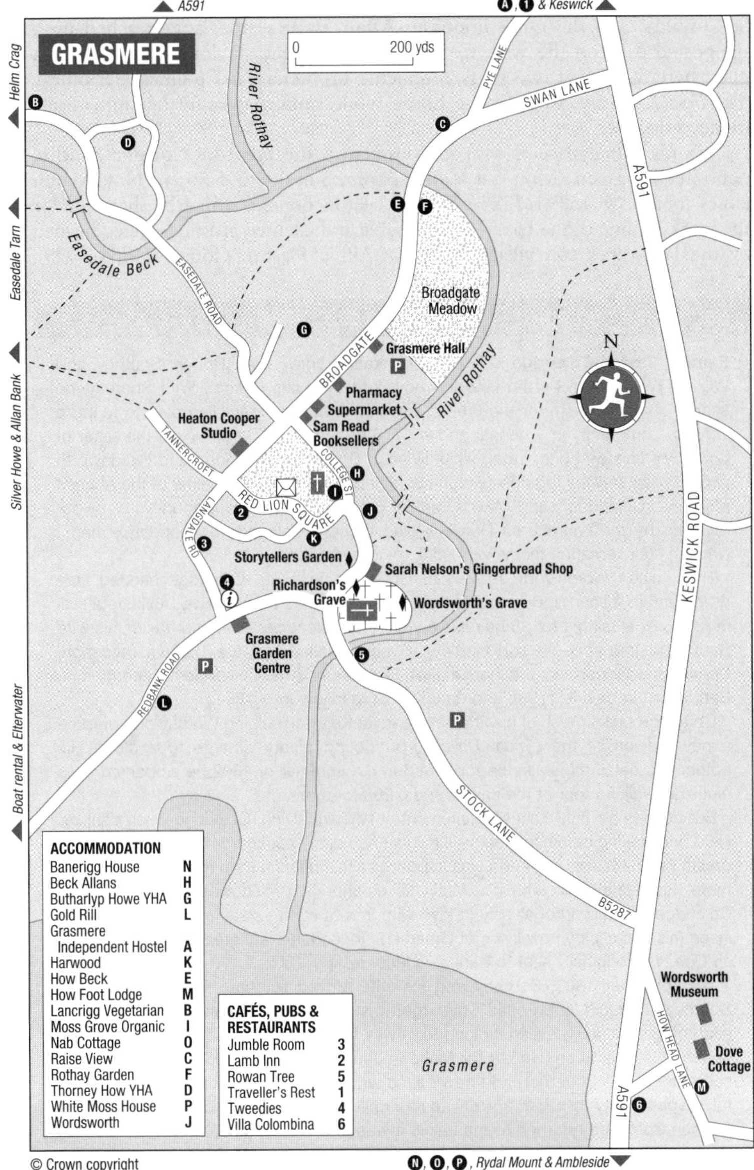

made on the premises since the mid-nineteenth century and the recipe is a closely guarded secret (kept locked in an Ambleside bank vault).

Wordsworth spent most of his Grasmere years living in houses outside the village – Dove Cottage and Rydal Mount – but the five years in between these residences (1808–13) saw the extended Wordsworth family and visiting friends occupying two houses in the village itself. Both are closed to the public, though there's nothing to stop you walking past the **Old Rectory** (opposite

St Oswald's) and the more imposing **Allan Bank** – the latter reached up a signposted path on the walk to Silver Howe. Samuel Taylor Coleridge was a guest here for almost two years, producing his literary and political periodical, *The Friend*, from a room in the house while sinking ever further into drug-induced decline.

The only other place to visit in Grasmere is the **Heaton Cooper Studio**, opposite the green (Mon–Sat 9am–5.30pm, Sun 11am–5.30pm; Nov–March closes at 5pm; ⓣ015394/35280, ⓦwww.heatoncooper.co.uk). It's a showcase for the works of one of the Lakes' most durable and talented artistic families, headed by the landscapes and village scenes of Alfred Heaton Cooper (1864–1929).

Soul, mind and spirit – Coleridge in the Lakes

Samuel Taylor Coleridge (1772–1834) already knew both Robert Southey and William Wordsworth by the time he moved to the Lake District. With Southey, he shared an enthusiasm for the French Revolution and an unfulfilled plan to found a Utopian community in America; and in 1795 he'd married Sara Fricker, the sister of Southey's fiancée Edith. Later, while living in Somerset, Coleridge and Wordsworth wrote *Lyrical Ballads* together, which contained Coleridge's "The Rime of the Ancient Mariner". Coleridge sang Wordsworth's praises at every opportunity; a favour returned by the enamoured Dorothy, who thought Coleridge a "wonderful man... [whose]...conversation teems with soul, mind and spirit".

Thus, when Wordsworth moved to Grasmere in 1799, Coleridge needed little prompting to follow. Having toured the Lakes, he settled on the newly built Greta Hall in Keswick, leasing it for 25 guineas a year. The Coleridges – Samuel Taylor, his wife Sara, and four-year-old son Hartley – were installed by July 1800; a third son, Derwent, was born in the house that September (the Coleridges' second son, Berkeley, had died in 1798); and daughter Sara followed in 1802.

Coleridge spent much of his first two years at Keswick helping Wordsworth prepare a new edition of the *Lyrical Ballads*, but found plenty of time to explore. His notebooks detail the walks he took, and in the summer of 1802 he embarked on a nine-day walking tour of the Lakes; see p.285 for more.

But despite his first flush of excitement at lakeland living, Coleridge wasn't happy. He'd been taking opium for years – if *Kubla Khan* didn't spring from an opium-induced dream no poem ever did – and was in poor health, suffering from rheumatism. What's more, his relationship with his wife was deteriorating – spurred by the fact that Coleridge had fallen hopelessly in love with Wordsworth's sister-in-law, Sara Hutchinson (his "Asra"), by now living at Grasmere. Indeed, his last great poem, *Dejection: an Ode*, was originally sent to Sara as a letter in April 1802.

In September 1803, Southey and his wife arrived to share Greta Hall. As the Southeys had just lost a child Coleridge hoped that the two sisters might comfort each other, but he was also looking for a way to escape so that he might regain his health and inspiration. He left for Malta in June 1804 (where for two years he was secretary to the Governor) and never lived with his family again. Southey assumed full responsibility for Coleridge's wife and children who remained at Greta Hall.

When Coleridge returned to the Lakes it was to live with the Wordsworths at Allan Bank in Grasmere, where he produced a short-lived political and literary periodical, *The Friend*, helped by Sara Hutchinson. When she left, to go and live with her brother in Wales, a depressed Coleridge – once more dependent on drugs – departed for London. Wordsworth, sick of having him moping around the house, had described Coleridge to someone else as an "absolute nuisance", which Coleridge came to hear about: after this breach in 1810, Coleridge only ever made perfunctory visits to the Lakes, avoiding Wordsworth (though the two were later reconciled). He died in London on July 25, 1834, and is buried in Highgate cemetery.

Cooper became a well-known illustrator of guidebooks, especially in the first two decades of the twentieth century, and was succeeded in this by his son, William Heaton Cooper (1903–95), who climbed with the pioneering lakeland mountaineers. William produced paintings and sketches for four topographical Lake District guidebooks and then virtually ensured a dynastic succession by marrying the sculptress Ophelia Gordon Bell. Examples of all their work are on show in the gallery, together with those of current family members – grandson Julian Cooper is the most notable, a climber-artist who produces huge oil paintings of the world's more remote locations.

If you're in the village in summer, you'll be able to see more art at **Grasmere Hall**, up Broadgate from the green, which hosts the annual exhibition of the **Lake Artists Society** (Ⓦwww.lakeartists.org.uk). The society was founded in 1904 by local writer and artist W.G. Collingwood and its summer exhibition – first held in Coniston, subsequently in Grasmere – has been a lakeland fixture every year since. The work displayed is varied, but the society's members are mostly resident in, and take their inspiration from, Cumbria and the Lake District.

The lake and surrounding fells

It's a ten-minute walk from the centre down Redbank Road to the western side of the fell-fringed **lake** itself, also called Grasmere. You can rent a rowboat at the *Faeryland Tea Garden* (March–Oct daily 10am–6pm, Ⓣ015394/35060) by the landing stage – and take a picnic out to the wooded islet in the middle of the lake – or continue walking the mile to the southern reaches where **Loughrigg Terrace** sits under the crags of Loughrigg Fell (look for a track off the road through Redbank Woods, signposted "Loughrigg Terrace and YHA"). From the terrace there are tremendous views back up the lake and across the broad valley, culminating in the pass of Dunmail Raise.

Wordsworth composed most of his poetry during long rambles around the lake and up in the surrounding fells, and – clutching a volume of his collected verse – it's still possible to track down the sources of his inspiration. On the east side of the A591, for example, a path rises to the "tumultuous brook" of **Greenhead Gill**, whose surroundings formed the backdrop to the masterful early lyric poem "Michael" (1800), a moving tale of a shepherd abandoned by his wayward son. However, it's **Easedale** and its tarn (northwest of the village) that conjures the most resonant images. The first version of Wordsworth's autobiographical work, *The Prelude*, was partly composed after long hours tramping up and down the valley, while the tragic deaths of George and Sarah Green of Easedale – who died in a blizzard, leaving behind six children – prompted a memorial poem. ("Who weeps for strangers? / Many wept for George and Sarah Green; / Wept for that pair's unhappy fate, / Whose graves may here be seen.") The Wordsworths even took into care one of the orphans, a story exhaustively chronicled by De Quincey (in *Recollections of the Lakes and the Lake Poets*).

A brisk hike (follow Easedale Rd, past the youth hostel), up the tumbling, fern-clad, Sourmilk Gill to **Easedale Tarn** and back, takes around two hours – from the bridge across Easedale Beck at the start of the path you can also wander up the drive to *Lancrigg Vegetarian Country House Hotel*, which has an organic café and veggie restaurant open to the public (walkers are welcome). You also come this way, up Easedale Road, to climb Grasmere's most celebrated peak, **Helm Crag** (1299ft), which takes about an hour from the village to reach the top.

Walks from Grasmere

Grasmere makes a good base for a wide selection of walks, from lazy round-the-lake rambles to full-on day-hikes requiring a bit of experience. A decent cross section is detailed below, while note that you can also walk the Fairfield Horseshoe circuit clockwise from nearby Rydal.

Around Grasmere and Rydal Water

This is an easy circuit (4 miles; 2hr) that skirts the lake and Loughrigg Fell. From Loughrigg Terrace, the route heads east above **Rydal Water**, passing the dripping maw of Rydal Caves, a disused slate quarry (seen in Ken Russell's *The Lair of the White Worm*), before crossing the A591 to Rydal Mount. Above the house the **"Coffin Trail" bridleway** runs back high above the northern shore of Rydal Water, via **White Moss Tarn** (look out for butterflies), and emerges at Dove Cottage.

Loughrigg Fell

There are all sorts of possible ascents of **Loughrigg Fell** (1101ft) – and it's also easily climbed from Ambleside – but the simplest ascent is straight up the hillside from Loughrigg Terrace: the views are fantastic. A six-mile circuit from the terrace, over the undulating top to Ambleside and then back along the lower slopes via Rydal, takes three to four hours.

Silver Howe

The best direct climb from the village is up to the top of **Silver Howe** (1292ft), above the west side of the lake, from where the views take in the Langdale Pikes, Helvellyn and High Street. The easiest signposted route up from the village passes Allan Bank – it's a two-hour walk, climbing to the summit and then circling round via Dow Bank and down to the lakeside road, emerging just outside the village opposite the *Faeryland* tea garden and boat-rental place.

Helm Crag and High Raise

A reasonably tough high-level circuit to the west of Grasmere (10 miles; 6hr) starts with the stiff climb up to **Helm Crag** (1299ft) – follow the signs from the end of Easedale Road – whose distinctive summit crags are known as **The Lion and The Lamb**, and have thrilled visitors since Wordsworth's day. An undulating ridge walk then runs west to Greenup Edge, and up to **High Raise** (2500ft), popularly regarded as the Lake District's most centrally sited fell. Stay a while for the magnificent views from the summit (marked on maps as High White Stones), before turning back for Grasmere via **Sergeant Man** (2414ft) and then descending past Easedale Tarn and Sourmilk Ghyll.

See Basics, p.42, for general walking advice in the Lakes; recommended maps are detailed on p.50.

Practicalities

Grasmere lies west of the main A591 (Ambleside–Keswick road), with its centre just a few hundred yards down the B5287, which winds through the village. **Bus** #555 (between Kendal and Keswick) and the open-top #599 (from Kendal, Bowness, Windermere and Ambleside) both stop on the village green. A **Central Lakes Day Rider ticket** (from £6.50) allows unlimited stops on the return journey between Bowness and Grasmere, allowing you to visit the Wordsworth houses as a day-trip. The main **car park** is on Redbank Road at the southern end of the village, by the garden centre. There's a second car park on Stock Lane, on the east side as you come in from Dove Cottage. There's no longer an official tourist office in Grasmere, though there is an informal **visitor**

information point in the reception of the *Dale Lodge Hotel* (daily 10am–4pm), up the drive opposite the garden centre.

Accommodation

You should book well in advance for accommodation at any budget, at any time of year, especially the **boutique** places and the popular **youth hostels** and **backpackers' accommodation**. You can walk into Grasmere village and to Wordsworth's Dove Cottage from any of the recommended choices in and around Grasmere. If you stay out at Rydal, you'll be handily placed for the other Wordsworth house, Rydal Mount, though you'll need to drive or catch the bus to the village for food and other services. Grasmere itself has no **campsite**, though the yurts at Rydal Hall are only a couple of miles south or it's seven miles west to the excellent Great Langdale National Trust campsite (see Great Langdale section, following).

In Grasmere

Beck Allans College St ⓣ015394/35563, ⓦwww.beckallans.com. A quality B&B in a modern but traditionally built house in the centre – the more you pay, the larger the room, but all five are smartly furnished, well equipped and boast baths in the en-suite bathrooms. Most have a view over the riverside gardens, while self-catering apartments (including a handsome 1930s caravan) are also available. Parking. ❸

Gold Rill Red Bank Rd ⓣ015394/35486, ⓦwww.gold-rill.com. Lakeside accommodation is at a premium in Grasmere, so the *Gold Rill* is a sought-after spot – soothing rooms have lake or fell views, and there are pretty lakeside gardens with a small heated outdoor pool surrounded by deckchairs. A fire in the lounges keeps it nice and snug in winter. Inclusive dinner rates always offer the best deal. Parking. Closed 2 weeks in Jan. ❻

The Harwood Red Lion Square ⓣ015394/35248, ⓦwww.harwoodhotel.co.uk. Not so much B&B as a boutique "retreat for adults", offering six rustic-chic double rooms with a touch of Swiss-German mountain style. Everything is set up for a cosy getaway, from duck-down duvets and underfloor heating to jacuzzi baths and splash-screen TVs. While all the rooms have a view, a couple also have patios and the duplex suite has a private sun terrace. Breakfast is served in cheery owner Heidi's downstairs namesake deli and coffee house – the boy in the Alpine photo on the back wall is her father. Parking. ❺, suite ❻

How Beck Broadgate ⓣ015394/35553 or 35732, ⓦwww.howbeckgrasmere.com. Two rooms (one double, one twin) are available in this agreeable family house on the outskirts of the village, plus a sun lounge that overlooks the garden and fells. It's a great choice for vegetarians – there's a full veggie breakfast (with home-made bread and preserves) and fruit and flowers in the room, while toiletries are handmade locally from natural and organic ingredients. ❷

How Foot Lodge Town End ⓣ015394/35366, ⓦwww.howfoot.co.uk. The position – a few yards from Dove Cottage – couldn't be better for Wordsworth groupies, and you won't get a better deal on good-quality accommodation in Grasmere than in this light-filled Victorian villa. There's a charming mix of rooms with views over the well-kept gardens, including a spacious suite and (most popular of all, so book in advance) a very appealing room with its own garden-side sun lounge. Thoughtful touches abound (wineglasses and corkscrew provided, fresh milk available for tea and coffee), while guests get a discount on dinner at nearby *Villa Colombina*. Parking. ❸

Moss Grove Organic ⓣ015394/35251, ⓦwww.mossgrove.com. Rarely does a Victorian-era hotel look so stunning, from the luminous lighting that throws a blue glow upon the exterior slate to the luxurious high-concept rooms complete with underfloor heating and Bose sound systems. It's been designed on organic, low-impact lines, so the extraordinary handmade beds are of reclaimed timber, the wallpaper coloured with natural inks, duvets made from duck down and the windows screened by natural wood blinds. The feel is less of hotel and more private house party – there are only eleven rooms and you're encouraged to forage in the kitchen for a buffet-style breakfast (produce largely local, the drinks Fair Trade) and take it back to your room. Parking. ❻

Raise View White Bridge ⓣ015394/35215, ⓦwww.raiseviewhouse.co.uk. There are lovely fell views from every corner of this superior B&B, plus a warm welcome and seven very comfortable rooms (including a cosy single in the eaves). Decor is contemporary country house (think fluffy towels and fetching fabrics), the breakfast's great, and there's dinner by arrangement in spring and autumn. Parking. ❹

Rothay Garden Broadgate ⓣ015394/35334, ⓦwww.rothaygarden.com. The Lake District's newest four-star hotel is a classy mix of town and country, set in quiet grounds by the Rothay River on the edge of the village. Three grades of rooms are in soothing earth tones with dark wood furniture, designer-print wallpaper, thick drapes, and velvet seats and sofas; smart bathrooms have walk-in showers and big, curvy baths. Urban-style attic "loft suites" have the most cachet, though you can't argue with the bright ground-floor "Grasmere" rooms that open out onto a terrace by the babbling river. Service is slick and unobtrusive, while dining is by candlelight in the conservatory restaurant – it's contemporary, using locally sourced cuisine with a four-course dinner included in the room rate. Parking. ❼, suites ❽

Wordsworth College St ⓣ015394/35592, ⓦwww.thewordsworthhotel.co.uk. If you're after a more traditional experience, the four-star "grande-dame" choice in the village presses all the right buttons, from the antique-laden lounge to big, flouncy rooms with a country-house decor and character. It's not a complete time warp though, so you can expect wi-fi access and flat-screen TVs, while the real bonus is the heated indoor pool, jacuzzi, gym and sauna. You can eat in the *Dove & Olive Branch* bistro and bar, or in the more formal *Prelude* restaurant (D,B&B deals are worth considering). Parking. ❻

Around Grasmere

Banerigg House 1 mile south on A591 ⓣ015394/35204, ⓦwww.guesthouse-cumbria.co.uk. See chapter map for location. Grasmere lake views are like hen's teeth so the selling point of this lakeside B&B (a 15min walk from the village, past Dove Cottage) is obvious. There are six rooms (five doubles and a single), most with water views, and even a house canoe that you're welcome to use. Fewer guests take up the option of a morning swim in the lake with your host on his daily plunge. Walkers and cyclists are welcome too (there are drying facilities and a garage for bikes), fuelled by a good breakfast. Parking. No credit cards. ❸

Cote How Organic 3 miles southeast off A591, Rydal ⓣ015394/32765, ⓦwww.cotehow.co.uk. See chapter map for location. A very peaceful retreat, just outside Rydal and set in its own extensive grounds by Rydal Water – turn off the A591 at the "Under Loughrigg" sign and go up past the Pelter Bridge car park. Three characterful rooms retain original fireplaces and antique beds, while in the romantic Rydal Suite (once occupied by American president Woodrow Wilson) you also get original oak beams, a skylight for star-gazing and a vintage roll-top bath with a view. It's a fully certified organic guesthouse, while eco-credentials are unimpeachable, from home-made candles and wind-up torches to discounts to anyone who comes by public transport. The tearooms here are open weekends and bank holidays, usually 11am to 5pm. Parking. ❺

Lancrigg Vegetarian Country House Easedale Rd ⓣ015394/35317, ⓦwww.lancrigg.co.uk. Lancrigg checks all the boxes for a fully organic, vegetarian and vegan-friendly retreat. Half a mile northwest of Grasmere, the isolated country house has trimmed lawns and wildlife-filled woods, while a dozen idiosyncratic rooms have been carved from the well-worn interior, including the former library (now with a lace-draped four-poster and private door into the garden). Veggie breakfast and dinner are included in the price, and dishes tend towards the international, exotic or unusual (like a grilled tofu "TLT" for brekkie) – the *Green Valley* café-restaurant is open all day too for organic drinks, and veggie/vegan snacks and lunches. Parking. ❻

Nab Cottage 2 miles southeast on A591, Rydal ⓣ015394/35311, ⓦwww.rydalwater.com. See chapter map for location. Both Thomas De Quincey and Hartley Coleridge lived in this gorgeous seventeenth-century oak-beamed farmhouse facing Rydal Water. It's now a language school and treatment/workshop venue, but offers B&B in seven rooms (four en suite) when space is available – usually *not* between July and September, but call to check. Light suppers and evening meals available on request (largely organic, and locally sourced or Fair Trade). Parking. ❷

White Moss House Rydal Water ⓣ015394/35295, ⓦwww.whitemoss.com. See chapter map for location. A real slice of old-school hospitality, in a secluded early eighteenth-century, ivy-clad house at the northern end of Rydal Water. Longtime owners, the Dixons, preside over five individually styled, antique-filled rooms (two share a lounge and terrace) that simply beg you to relax in them. It's a glorious spot, to which regulars return year after year, and breakfast is a gourmet treat. Parking. Closed Dec & Jan. ❻

Hostels and yurts

Butharlyp Howe YHA Easedale Rd ⓣ0845/371 9319, ⓔgrasmere@yha.org.uk. Closest of the hostels to the centre, this refurbished Victorian mansion is just 5min north of the green. There are modern bedrooms, plentiful showers and decent facilities throughout, as well as a restaurant (dinner available) overlooking grassy gardens. There's also a children's play area and outdoor games available, and some of the rooms are available for families and couples. Open daily Feb–Nov, weekends only in Dec and Jan. Dorm beds from £17.95.

Full Circle Yurts Rydal Hall, 2 miles southeast, A591 ⓣ07975 671928, ⓦwww.lake-district-yurts.co.uk. See chapter map for location. Tucked into the lovely grounds of Rydal Hall are four authentic Mongolian yurts, sited close to tinkling stream, waterfalls, natural pools and rugged woodland. They sleep up to six, complete with proper beds, rug-strewn wooden floors, wood-burning stove and oven, gas hob and grill, with showers and toilets 100 yards away. Outside each is a raised-deck picnic area, barbecue and brazier, and children's playground nearby, and there's a tearoom at the hall and a decent pub a 5min walk away. The drawback? Only that the yurts are extremely popular, so book well in advance for summer (or consider an autumn/winter break, as the wood-burners keep them really warm). From £265 (Mon–Fri or Fri–Mon rental) or £385 (per week), school and bank hols £285/440.

Grasmere Independent Hostel Broadrayne Farm, A591, half a mile north of the village, past the *Traveller's Rest* pub ⓣ015394/35055, ⓦwww.grasmerehostel.co.uk. See chapter map for location. Boutique in all but name, Grasmere's stylishly presented backpackers' hostel is a real gem. There are 24 beds, all in small, carpeted en-suite rooms – one available as a twin/family room with private bathroom when space allows. Gracious hosts Bev and Jo also provide an impressively equipped kitchen, plus laundry and drying facilities, bike and luggage storage, even a sauna. You can get advice about local walks, or kick back in the comfortable common room, whose large circular window overlooks the valley. Three self-catering cottages also available (by the week) on the farm, each sleeping between two and five people. Dorm beds from £19.50.

Thorney How YHA ⓣ0845/371 9319, ⓔgrasmere@yha.org.uk. Grasmere's smaller, simpler hostel was the first hostel ever bought by the YHA, in 1931. It's still got a bit of old farmhouse character about it, but has been modernized over the years, and is pretty popular with walkers who can set off straight from the front door. It's just under a mile along the road past *Butharlyp Howe*: look for the signposted right turn (and the road's unlit so bring a torch). Evening meal served. Advance bookings required; family groups only Nov–Feb. No credit cards. Dorm beds from £13.95.

Eating, drinking and entertainment

There are plenty of **tearooms and cafés** in Grasmere catering for the mass of tourists that descends every day, and hikers can get sandwiches made up at a couple of places, including *Heidi's*, beneath *The Harwood* on Red Lion Square. Two nearby country tearooms that are worth a special visit are the *Old School Room* at Rydal Hall (see p.109) and *Cote How Organic* (see "Around Grasmere accommodation" opposite). Outside Grasmere's hotels and pubs, good independent **restaurants** are thinner on the ground, though there's enough choice to ring the changes over a few days' stay.

The two big annual summer **events** are the village's rushbearing ceremony and the traditional sports festival, both held in August. Also unique to Grasmere is the **Storytellers' Garden** (ⓦwww.taffythomas.co.uk) at the Northern Centre for Storytelling, which is located in the former National Trust shop opposite the church. Traditional tale-teller and raconteur Taffy Thomas presents open-air events throughout the year (story walks, firelight tales, music and juggling) – call in or check the website for details. Finally, Sunday night is usually **live music** night at *Tweedies* bar, from cover bands to blues guitarists.

Cafés and restaurants

Jumble Room Langdale Rd ⓣ015394/35188, ⓦwww.thejumbleroom.co.uk. Everyone likes this funky, relaxed dining spot, run with a light touch by an amiable Grasmere couple. With tables overlooked by sister-in-law Thuline's dramatic cow and animal oil paintings, the menu ranges the world – say, Tuscan crostini, Thai prawns, local game pie or fish in organic beer batter – and once ensconced, no one's in any hurry to leave. Most mains cost £11–18. Dinner reservations advised. Closed Tues.

Rowan Tree Church Bridge, Stock Lane ⓣ015394/35528. The main draw here is the outdoor terrace in a gorgeous position on a lazy bend in the river, opposite the church. A daytime tearoom menu gives way to Mediterranean-style dining at night, including pizza and pasta choices, plus dishes such as wild mushroom lasagne or sea bass (£8–14). Closed Sun dinner.

Villa Colombina Town End ⓣ015394/35268. The old *Dove Cottage Tearooms* is open during the day for snacks and light meals, and then sports an authentic Italian menu for dinner (mains £10–17) of pizzas, pastas, steak and chicken, as well as mushroom and red pepper risotto and other specials. It's a cheery place to eat at any time, with terracotta-coloured walls under a beamed roof. Closed Jan, and possibly other days in winter; call for details.

Pubs

Lamb Inn Red Lion Square ⓣ015394/35456. The public bar of the *Red Lion* hotel gets packed to the rafters at weekends. There are Theakston's and guest beers on tap, and a queue of local Fast Eddies waiting to drub you at pool.

Traveller's Rest Half a mile north on the A591 ⓣ015394/35604. See chapter map for location. Old roadside inn that's a popular place for Jennings' beers and reasonable bar meals (from Cumberland sausage and mash to Thai curry), and there's a warming log fire in winter.

Tweedies Langdale Rd ⓣ015394/35300, ⓦwww.tweediesbargrasmere.co.uk. Although part of the *Dale Lodge Hotel*, there's more of a country pub feel here than anywhere else in Grasmere, from the stone-flagged floors and wood-burning stove to the big beer garden. It's a CAMRA award-winner for its hand-pumped beers, though if you're after a Pinot Grigio or a Prosecco you'll be fine. The locally sourced menu is also definitely on the gastropub side of things, from black pudding salad to slow-cooked pork belly, potted shrimps to sea bass (mains £12–20). The same menu is also served in the hotel's *Lodge* restaurant, if you want a bit more formality.

Listings

Banks There's no bank in Grasmere, though there is an ATM inside the post office.

Bike rental The nearest bike-rental outlets are in Ambleside.

Bookshop Sam Read Booksellers (junction of College St and Broadgate, ⓣ015394/35374, ⓦwww.samread.co.uk) is a fine independent bookshop, especially good for local interest books, guides and maps, and the works of the Lake Poets.

Emergencies The nearest doctors' surgery is at Ambleside Group Practice (Rydal Rd ⓣ015394/32693, ⓦwww.amblesidegrouppractice.co.uk), the nearest hospital is in Keswick (Keswick Cottage Hospital, Crosthwaite Rd ⓣ017687/67000).

Outdoors stores Outdoor equipment and walking gear from Edge of the World (Red Lion Square), Stewart R Cunningham (Broadgate) and Summitreks (College St).

Pharmacy Grasmere Pharmacy, 1 Oak Bank, Broadgate ⓣ015394/35553.

Post office Red Lion Square

Taxis Grasmere Taxis ⓣ015394/35506.

Dove Cottage

On the southeastern outskirts of Grasmere village, in the former hamlet of Town End, stands **Dove Cottage** (daily 9.30am–5.30pm; closed early Jan to early Feb; £7.50, family ticket £17.20; ⓣ015394/35544, ⓦwww.wordsworth.org.uk), home to William and Dorothy Wordsworth from 1799 to 1808 and where Wordsworth wrote some of his best poetry. The house stands just off the A591 – there's limited parking, though it's an easy walk from the village while buses #555 and #599 stop close by on the main road.

Wordsworth first saw the house in November 1799 while on a walking tour with his friend Samuel Taylor Coleridge, with whom he had published *Lyrical Ballads* the previous year. Keen for a base in the Lakes, Wordsworth negotiated a rent of £8 a year for what had originally been an inn called the *Dove & Olive-Bough*; he and his sister moved in just before Christmas of that year. It was a simple stone house with a slate roof – Wordsworth at this time was far from financially secure – where the poet could live by his guiding principle of "plain living but high thinking". But its main recommendation as far as Wordsworth was concerned was one that is no longer obvious: the views he had enjoyed to the lake and fells were lost when new housing was erected in front of Dove Cottage in the 1860s. When the Wordsworths left in 1808, their friend Thomas De Quincey took over the lease and Dove Cottage is as much a monument to his happiest days in Grasmere (he married from here) as it is to Wordsworth's plain living; the house has been open to the public since 1917.

The **cottage** forms part of a complex administered by the Wordsworth Trust, whose guides, bursting with anecdotes, lead you around the rooms, little changed now but for the addition of electricity and internal plumbing. There's precious little space and – downstairs, at least – hardly any natural light: belching tallow candles would have provided the only illumination. William, not wanting to be bothered by questions of a domestic nature, kept to the lighter, upper rooms or disappeared off on long walks to compose his poetry. De Quincey later reckoned that Wordsworth had walked 175,000 to 180,000 miles in the course of his poetry writing – "a mode of exertion which, to him, stood in the stead of wine, spirits, and all other stimulants whatsoever to the animal spirits". Wordsworth married in 1802 and his new wife, Mary Hutchinson, came to live here, necessitating a change of bedrooms for everyone; three of their five children were later born in the cottage (John in 1803, Dora in 1804 and Thomas in 1806). Sister Dorothy kept a detailed journal of daily life and the endless comings and goings of visitors, notably Coleridge and his brother-in-law Southey, but also Walter Scott, William Hazlitt and, once he'd plucked up the nerve to introduce himself, Thomas De Quincey (see box, p.106). The garden behind the cottage was tamed, while William chopped wood for the fire, planted runner beans, built a summerhouse and hid the disliked cottage whitewash behind a train of roses and honeysuckle. And with all this going on, Wordsworth produced a series of odes, lyric poems and sonnets that he would never better, relying on Dorothy and Mary to make copies in their painstaking handwriting. After eight years at Dove Cottage it became clear that the Wordsworths had outgrown their home and, reluctantly, the family moved to a larger, new house in Grasmere called Allan Bank – Wordsworth had watched it being built and referred to it as a "temple of abomination". They were never as happy there, or in the Old Rectory to which they later relocated, and it wasn't until 1813 and the move to Rydal Mount that the Wordsworths regained the sense of peace they had felt at Dove Cottage.

Most of the furniture in the cottage belonged to the Wordsworths, while in the **upper rooms** are displayed a battered suitcase, a pair of William's ice skates and Dorothy's sewing box, among other possessions. There are surprisingly few reminders of De Quincey's long tenancy, save a pair of opium scales, yet he lived here far longer than did the Wordsworths. In the nearby **museum and art gallery** there's much to be learned about Wordsworth's life and times. It's full of paintings, portraits, original manuscripts (including that of "Daffodils"), pages from Dorothy's journals and more memorabilia, most poignantly Mary's wedding ring. The museum ticket allows entry to any special **exhibitions** currently running, while in good weather the Wordsworth's much-loved **garden** is open for visits as well.

Wide-ranging as the museum is, it can only present a fraction of the complete collection held by the Wordsworth Trust, which amounts to some 70,000 manuscripts, first editions, books, letters, portraits and other items.

Sex, drugs and confessions —Thomas De Quincey in the Lakes

The direct object of my own residence at the lakes was the society of Mr Wordsworth.

Thomas De Quincey, *Recollections of the Lakes and the Lake Poets*.

The young **Thomas De Quincey** (1785–1859) was one of the first to fully appreciate the revolutionary nature of Wordsworth's and Coleridge's collaborative *Lyrical Ballads*, and as a student at Oxford in 1803 he had already written to Wordsworth praising his "genius" and hoping for his friendship. In reply, Wordsworth politely invited him to visit if he was ever in the area. It took De Quincey four years (and two abortive visits, abandoned out of shyness) to contrive a meeting, eventually through the auspices of Coleridge, a mutual friend.

De Quincey first came to Dove Cottage in November 1807 to meet his hero, trembling at the thought: the meeting is recorded in one of the more self-effacing chapters of his *Recollections*. When the Wordsworths moved to Allan Bank the following year, De Quincey – by now a favourite with the Wordsworth children – went too, staying several months. His small private income enabled him to take over Dove Cottage in February 1809, which he filled with books (in contrast to Wordsworth, who had very few). He also demolished the summerhouse and made other changes in the garden which annoyed the Wordsworths, while the relationship further cooled after 1812 following the deaths of young Catherine and Thomas Wordsworth. De Quincey was particularly badly affected by the loss of Catherine, his "sole companion", and for two months after her death passed each night stretched out on her grave in Grasmere churchyard.

The truth is, De Quincey wasn't a well man. Since his university days, he had been in the habit of taking opium in the form of laudanum (ie dissolved in alcohol), and at Dove Cottage he was taking huge, addictive doses – the amount of alcohol alone would have been debilitating enough. He closeted himself away in the cottage for days at a time, complaining that Wordsworth was spoiling the books he borrowed from him, and began an affair with Margaret (Peggy) Simpson of nearby Nab Cottage, a local farmer's daughter who bore him an illegitimate child. The drug-taking was bad enough for the upright, snobbish Wordsworths, but when De Quincey married Peggy in 1817 (at St Oswald's Church, Grasmere) any intimate relationship was at an end.

De Quincey was never suited to regular employment, and following a disastrous stint as editor of the *Westmorland Gazette* he became a freelance critic and essayist for various literary periodicals. His *Confessions of an English Opium-Eater* (1821) first appeared in the *London Magazine* and made his name, and he had sufficient resources to take on another house (Fox Ghyll, south of Rydal) for his growing family (he eventually had eight children), retaining Dove Cottage as a library. Growing success meant De Quincey spent less and less time in the Lakes, giving up Fox Ghyll in 1825 and finally abandoning Dove Cottage in 1830 to move to Edinburgh, where he lived for the rest of his life. It was only between 1834 and 1839 – long after he'd left the area – that De Quincey started writing his Lake "recollections", offending Wordsworth all over again.

These are stored in the adjacent **Jerwood Centre**, a £3-million facility opened in 2005 by Seamus Heaney, which is accessible to scholars and researchers. The centre hosts various related displays and events, while Dove Cottage is the headquarters of the **Centre for British Romanticism**, which together with the Wordsworth Trust sponsors major exhibitions on cultural themes, as well as a respected poetry programme, family activities, residential conferences, talks and workshops attracting some top names – call for details or check the website.

Rydal Mount

Following the deaths of their young children Catherine and Thomas in 1812, the Wordsworths couldn't bear to continue living in Grasmere's Old Rectory. In May 1813 they moved a couple of miles southeast of the village to the hamlet of Rydal, little more than a couple of isolated cottages and farms set back from the eastern end of Rydal Water. Here William rented Rydal Mount from the Flemings of nearby Rydal Hall, where he remained until his death in 1850. Buses #555 and #599 stop on the A591 at Rydal Church, 200 yards from the house. Parking (on the road alongside Rydal Hall) is minimal.

Rydal Mount (March–Oct daily 9.30am–5pm; Nov–Feb Wed–Sun 11am–4pm; closed Jan; £6, garden only £4, family ticket £15; Ⓣ015394/33002, Ⓦwww.rydalmount.co.uk) is a fair-sized family home, a much-improved-upon Tudor cottage set in its own grounds, and reflects Wordsworth's change in circumstances. At Dove Cottage he'd been a largely unknown poet of straitened means, but by 1813 he'd written several of his greatest works (though not all had yet been published) and was already being visited by literary acolytes. More importantly, he'd been appointed Westmorland's Distributor of Stamps, a salaried position which allowed him to take up the rent of a comfortable family house. Wordsworth, Mary, the three surviving children (John, aged 10; Dora, 9; and William, 3) and Dorothy arrived, plus his wife's sister Sara Hutchinson, by now living with the family. Later the household also contained a clerk, a couple of maids and a gardener. Dances and dinners were held, the widowed Queen Adelaide visited, and carriage-loads of friends and sightseers came to call – a far cry from the "plain living" back at Dove Cottage.

Wordsworth only ever rented the property, but the house is now owned by descendants of the poet, who have opened it to visitors since 1970. It's a much

▲ Wordsworth's sofa, Rydal Mount

less claustrophobic experience than visiting Dove Cottage and you're free to wander around what is still essentially a family home – summer concerts feature poetry readings by Wordsworth family members, and there are recent family pictures on the sideboard alongside more familiar portraits of the poet and his circle. In the light-filled **drawing room** and **library** (two rooms in Wordsworth's day) you'll find the only known portrait of Dorothy, as an old lady of 62, and also Mary's favourite portrait of Wordsworth, completed in 1844 by the American portraitist Henry Inman. Memorabilia abounds: Wordsworth's black-leather sofa, his inkstand and despatch box, a brooch of Dorothy's and, upstairs in the attic, their beloved brother John's sword (recovered from the shipwreck in which he drowned) and the poet's own encyclopedia and prayer book. **William and Mary's bedroom** has a lovely view, with Windermere a splash in the distance; in daughter **Dora's room** hangs a portrait of Edward Quillinan, her Irish dragoon, whom she married in 1841, much against Wordsworth's will. The couple spent their honeymoon at Rydal Mount, while the delicate Dora – often ill and eventually a victim of tuberculosis – later came home to die in the house in 1847. The other bedroom was Dorothy's, to which she was virtually confined for the last two decades of her life, suffering greatly from what was thought to be a debilitating mental illness – an underactive thyroid is the current opinion. She died at Rydal Mount in 1855; Mary died there in 1859.

Many people's favourite part of Rydal Mount is the four-and-a-half-acre **garden**, largely shaped by Wordsworth who fancied himself a gardener. He planted the flowering shrubs, put in the terraces (where he used to declaim his poetry) and erected a little rustic summerhouse (for jotting down lyrics), from which there are fine views of Rydal Water. Lining the lawns and surrounding the rock pools are rhododendrons and azaleas, maples, beeches and pines. If you're looking for an unusual souvenir, head for the Rydal Mount **shop**, which sells fell-walking sticks fashioned from the wood found in the garden. There's a tearoom over the road, in the grounds of Rydal Hall (see opposite).

Rydal and Rydal Water

Rydal sits at the foot of its own valley, whose beck empties into the River Rothay. As a hamlet, it's hardly any bigger than it was in Wordsworth's day; though, having seen the poet's house of Rydal Mount, you may as well wander back down the road for the other local sights – namely Rydal's lake, church and hall and, under a mile west, Nab Cottage, the former home of Hartley Coleridge.

There was no local church in Rydal until **St Mary's** (at the foot of Rydal Mount on the main A591) was built in 1824 – Wordsworth was churchwarden here for a year in the 1830s. A swing gate by the church entrance leads into **Dora's Field** (always open; free), a plot of land bought by Wordsworth when he thought he might have to leave Rydal Mount because the owners, the Flemings, wanted it back. Wordsworth planned to build a house here instead, but when the Flemings changed their minds, he gave the land to his daughter. On Dora's death in 1847, the heartbroken Wordsworths planted the hillsides with daffodils.

Across from the church, a driveway leads to **Rydal Hall** (Ⓦwww.rydalhall.org), erstwhile home of the Flemings. The hall has a sixteenth-century kernel but was considerably renovated during Victorian times; it's now a residential conference centre owned by the Diocese of Carlisle. You're welcome to walk in to visit the wonderfully restored **gardens** (open dawn to dusk; donation requested; parking available), originally laid out on classical lines by celebrated landscape gardener and architect Thomas Mawson in 1911. There are captivating views of Rydal Water from the terrace, while the more informal woodland gardens include a restored walled kitchen garden and orchard as well as summerhouse, ice house and game-larder. You could easily spend much of the day in the grounds, which also feature waterfalls, ponds, woodland walks and an adventure playground, not to mention the *Full Circle Yurts* (see Grasmere accommodation), while around the back of the hall, the *Old School Room* **teashop** (daily 10am–5pm, closes earlier in winter) has picnic tables from where you can watch Rydal Beck tumble under a moss-covered packhorse bridge. They make soup, scones and sandwiches here every day, and if you come in winter you can warm up by the wood-burning stove.

Few people bother much with **Rydal Water**, one of the region's smallest lakes at under three-quarters of a mile long and only fifty feet deep in parts. It's handsome enough – though it was considerably quieter before the A591 traced its northern shore – and there's a nice easy walk along the southern shore, back to Grasmere past Rydal Caves. For the best views of the water itself, follow the original route to Grasmere, along the "**Coffin Trail**", which starts directly behind Rydal Mount and runs west under the craggy heights of Nab Scar (1450ft). Medieval coffin bearers en route to St Oswald's would haul their melancholy load along this trail, stopping to rest at intervals on the convenient flat stones.

Nab Cottage, less than a mile west of Rydal on the A591, overlooks Rydal Water. This was the family home of Margaret Simpson before she married Thomas De Quincey; and it was rented much later by the sometime journalist and poet Hartley Coleridge, a Wordsworth family favourite ("O blessed vision! happy child!") despite his trying ways. Abandoned by his father and effectively brought up in Robert Southey's Keswick household, Hartley was a frail, precocious child who took to the demon drink and failed to live up to his early promise. But Wordsworth always retained a soft spot for him, and when Hartley died in Nab Cottage in 1849 Wordsworth picked out a plot for him in Grasmere churchyard. The cottage is now a language school, with B&B usually available outside the summer months (see Grasmere accommodation).

Skelwith Bridge and Little Langdale

Langdale ("long valley") is a byword for some of the region's most stunning peaks, views and hikes, and the route there starts at **SKELWITH BRIDGE**, a cluster of buildings huddled by the bridge over the River Brathay, around three miles south of Grasmere and the same distance west of Ambleside. Slate has been quarried in the area since the nineteenth century and is still used for everything from kitchen work surfaces to tombstones. The main reasons to stop here are for the local waterfall walks and lunch at *Chesters Café By The River* (local daily 10am–5.30pm, lunch served noon–4pm; ⓣ015394/32553, ⓦwww.chesters-cafebytheriver.co.uk), which serves up excellent cakes and very superior café meals (crispy squid, mushroom and

People and places: Mountain man

If anyone knows Langdale it's Bill Birkett who conducts what he calls "a life-long love affair with the hills" through his climbing, walking, writing and photography. It's pretty much in his blood – born and bred in the valley, son of climbing legend Jim Birkett – but Bill also has developed a strong bond with both place and people, which pours from every page of his photographic essay, *A Year in the Life of the Langdale Valleys*. He's out in the mountains in any weather, with camera in hand, and has covered every Lake District hill and mountain more than 1000ft high in his encyclopedic *Complete Lakeland Fells*. This started out as a personal challenge, so it came as a bit of a surprise to find that people were buying the book and knocking off the 541 "Birketts", like they do with the more famous 214 Wainwrights. "I'm really pleased a lot of people are finding it inspiring and useful", says the man whose main motivation is communicating his passion for the hills to others. To this end, he'll take you with him on his walking-and-photography courses and show you what it is about the mountains that captivates him – from the wind on his face and the sun on his back to the pure buzz of the physical landscape.

For more about Bill Birkett, his photography, books and courses, go to Ⓦwww.billbirket.co.uk.

leek risotto, wild boar bangers and mash and so on for £8–12.50): it's a real treat to sit outside on the sunny riverside terrace with a glass of crisp white wine. **Bus** #505 from Ambleside or Coniston stops at Skelwith Bridge, as does the #516 "Langdale Rambler" between Ambleside and the *Old Dungeon Ghyll* in Great Langdale.

From the bridge, there's a riverside stroll along a signposted footpath to Elterwater, a mile away, passing the fairly unimpressive gush that is **Skelwith Force**. For a finer waterfall altogether follow the hilly footpath west of Skelwith Bridge (it starts on the south side of the river) the mile or so to **Colwith Force**, hidden in the woods off the minor road to Elterwater. A circuit taking in both falls and Elterwater won't take more than a couple of hours. There's also another local walk from Skelwith, north through Neaum Woods to pretty **Loughrigg Tarn**, which sits under the crags of Loughrigg Fell.

Heading west, a very narrow minor road off the A593 twists into **Little Langdale**, a bucolic counterweight to the dramatics of Great Langdale to the north. The bedrooms at the *Three Shires Inn* (Ⓣ015394/37215, Ⓦwww.threeshiresinn.co.uk; ❹), about a mile west of Colwith Force, make the most of the valley views, and the inn is the traditional starting point for local rambles, notably the stroll down to the old packhorse crossing of Slater Bridge and to **Little Langdale Tarn**. A longer route – shadowed by a very minor road – runs north over **Lingmoor Fell** (1530ft) via **Blea Tarn** (where there's parking) into Great Langdale – the eight-mile circuit, returning to the *Three Shires Inn* via Elterwater, takes around four hours. The name of the inn, incidentally, is a reference to the fact that it stands near the meeting point of the old counties of Cumberland, Westmorland and Lancashire.

West from Little Langdale, the ever-narrower, ever-hairier road climbs to the dramatic **Wrynose Pass** (1270ft), before dropping down to Cockley Beck for the Duddon Valley or on to the Hardknott Pass.

Elterwater and Chapel Stile

ELTERWATER village lies half a mile northwest of its water, named by the Norse for the swans that still glide upon its surface. It's one of the more idyllic lakeland beauty spots, with its riverside setting, aged inn, spreading maple tree and aimless sheep getting among the sunbathers on the pocket-sized green. Historically, the village made its living from farming, quarrying and lace-making, though these days it's almost entirely devoted to the passing tourist trade: only around a quarter of the houses here are lived in, the rest are used as holiday cottages. There are no sights here, as such, just the quiet comings and goings of a country hamlet, albeit one inundated on fine summer days and bank holidays with vehicles disgorging hikers. Before you head off, you might spare some time first for **Judy Boyes' Studio** (Easter–Oct Wed–Sat 10am–5pm; Nov & Dec Thurs–Sat 10am–4pm; free; Ⓦwww.judyboyes.co.uk), near the inn, which displays a changing exhibition of the artist's locally inspired watercolours.

Elterwater sees its fair share of Langdale-bound hikers – not least because of the two local youth hostels – and numerous fell or riverside walks start straight from the village. Everyone should make the easy half-mile stroll northwest up the river – through the slate-quarry workings, still in use after over 150 years – to **CHAPEL STILE**, where a simple quarrymen's chapel sits beneath the crags. There's a pub and café for those that need a target and, suitably refreshed, you can push on from Chapel Stile, either on the level walk alongside the beck into the lower reaches of Langdale or up through the crags to the north and across Silver Howe to Grasmere.

Practicalities

The #516 "Langdale Rambler" **bus** stops by Elterwater village green. There's **parking** on the common outside the village and more limited space close to the bridge in the centre. Overnight **accommodation** is relatively thin on the

An exile in Langdale

German abstract and performance artist **Kurt Schwitters** (1877–1948) was forced to flee Hitler's Germany in 1937 as his challenging, subversive collages were considered "degenerate" by the Nazis. He moved first to Norway and then to Britain in 1940 where, initially, he was interned as an enemy alien. He spent the later war years scratching a living in London before arriving in the Lake District in 1945 – impoverished, ill and largely unknown. Schwitters became a familiar figure in Ambleside, painting local portraits and landscapes, though it is his **Merzbauten** (Merz buildings) for which he's remembered. Schwitters had already produced three earlier versions of this pioneering form of installation art, in Germany and Norway, and the fourth was begun in 1947 in an old stone barn just outside Elterwater. Constructed from discarded, salvaged and organic materials, the Lake District "Merzbarn" was an embodiment of Schwitters' long-standing "Merz" concept that art could spring from cast-off, found or otherwise useless objects. Schwitters died of pneumonia in 1948 – there's a memorial stone in Ambleside churchyard – and the unfinished Merzbarn was left abandoned, though the artwork on the end wall was removed to the Hatton Gallery at Newcastle University in the 1960s. Plans are in place to restore the Merzbarn itself, install a replica of the missing artwork and eventually open a study-centre and Schwitters museum. You can follow progress on Ⓦwww.merzbarn.net, which also has details of occasional opening times for public visits while the work continues.

ground, though there are plenty of **self-catering cottages** available by the week (sometimes less during winter); contact the Langdale Estate (see below) or Wheelwright's (Ⓣ015394/37635, Ⓦwww.wheelwrights.com), who should be able to fix you up with something in the vicinity. The **village shop** and **post office**, Maple Tree Corner (open daily), opposite the inn, has basic grocery supplies and can sell you a newspaper or a map. In nearby Chapel Stile, the **Langdale Co-operative** (open daily), in business since 1884, has everything else – from cornflakes to hiking boots. If boutique pampering is more in mind, you can get day membership (from £9.50) to use the pool and **spa facilities** at the Langdale Estate, and **rent bikes** from here too.

Accommodation

Britannia Inn Elterwater Ⓣ015394/37210, Ⓦwww.britinn.co.uk. The hugely popular pub on Elterwater's green has nine cosy rooms available – cosy being the operative word, since there's not a lot of space in a 500-year-old inn. But they are charming and quirky, fitted into every available nook, while half have been newly refurbished and offer a bit more than basic comfort. The stone-flagged back-room bar is where the hikers congregate, while the merest hint of good weather fills the outdoor tables on the slate-covered terrace. There's a wide range of beers and good-value food – from home-made pies and Cumberland sausage to seared scallops and Hawkshead trout (mains £10–14) served either in the dining room (booking advised) or cosy front bar. Limited parking available outside the inn. ❹, weekends ❺

Eltermere Country House Elterwater Ⓣ015394/37207, Ⓦwww.eltermere.co.uk. An imposing country house (just a little way past *Elterwater YHA*) with grounds stretching down to the lake. Its seventeenth-century origins are well hidden, though some of the fifteen rooms still sport exposed oak beams, while others have been given a more contemporary look. Many also have uninterrupted lake views, and if you fancy a splash on the water you can borrow the hotel boat. There's a bar and terrace for afternoon teas and bistro meals, while dinner (£25) is served in the lake-view restaurant. Parking. ❹, superior rooms ❺

Elterwater YHA Ⓣ0845/371 9017, Ⓔelterwater@yha.org.uk. A converted farmhouse and barn, just across the bridge from the *Britannia*, provides simple hostel facilities in two- to six-bedded rooms. It's not at all fancy, but it's beautifully sited in great hiking country – walking and activity weekends are held here year-round. While you can unload here, you'll have to park overnight in the village car park. There's a basic self-catering kitchen, and evening meals are served, or the pub's just down the road. Open daily March–Oct, and most weekends in winter – call to check availability. Dorm beds from £13.95.

Langdale Estate Elterwater Ⓣ015394/37302, Ⓦwww.langdale.co.uk. Spreading up the valley, north of the village, this fancy hotel and spa resort blends in well with its surroundings. Set in the grounds of a former woollen mill and gunpowder works, it contains a variety of quality B&B rooms in converted estate cottages, barns and buildings, plus self-catering Scandinavian-style lodges, a glam indoor pool and spa, gym, games room, squash court, two restaurants and a café-bar – plus an estate pub (*Wainwrights Inn*) within walking distance. It's never anything less than pricey, though there are good last-minute website rates (down to £90 B&B). Parking. ❹, weekends ❻

Langdale YHA High Close, Loughrigg, 1 mile northeast of Elterwater Ⓣ0845/371 9748, Ⓔlangdale@yha.org.uk. This rather grand Victorian mansion set in its own grounds sits high on the winding road over Red Bank to Grasmere. It's popular with schools, groups and families, though individuals are welcome (but should book in advance to be sure of a bed). Open fires are lit in winter and there's an evening meal available. Closed Nov–Feb. Dorm beds from £11.95.

Eating and drinking

Brambles Langdale Co-operative, Chapel Stile Ⓣ015394/37500. The store's upstairs café serves large breakfasts as well as sandwiches and lunches (£3.50–6.50), while hikers can buy a picnic pack and get their flasks filled with tea or coffee. Daytime only; closed 1 week in Jan.

Wainwrights Inn Chapel Stile Ⓣ015394/38088. Welcoming slate-floored pub with local beers on tap and popular bar meals of the lamb shoulder and Cumberland sausage variety (mains around £10–12) – the terrace outside is a good spot to rest weary feet.

Great Langdale

Beyond Chapel Stile you emerge into the wide curve of **Great Langdale**, flanked by some of the Lake District's most famous peaks – Crinkle Crags, Bowfell and the Langdale Pikes. It's a dramatic, yet sobering, valley, one of the few in the Lakes where you get a real sense of scale from the lie of the land. It's

Walks in Great Langdale

Walking in Great Langdale isn't necessarily an expeditionary undertaking, but you do need to be more aware than usual of time, weather conditions and your own ability before setting off on a hike. Once you leave the valley bottom there's nothing much that's simply a stroll – then again, of the classic routes picked out below, all save Jack's Rake are within the average walker's ability.

Pavey Ark

Behind Stickle Tarn stands the fearsome cliff face of **Pavey Ark** (2297ft), which can actually be climbed relatively easily if you approach it up the grassy path to its rear (north). Gung-ho walkers make the more dramatic climb up the cleft that is **Jack's Rake**, which ascends the face right to left and is the hardest commonly used route in the Lake District – in parts it's effectively rock climbing and requires a head for heights and steady nerves. An alternative climb, up Easy Gully (it isn't), starts from near the base. However you get up, count on it taking an hour from Stickle Tarn.

The Langdale Pikes

From the top of Pavey Ark it's a straightforward walk on to the renowned "pikes" (from the Viking word for a summit): first, **Harrison Stickle** (2414ft), then down to the stream forming the headwaters of Dungeon Ghyll and then slowly up to **Pike of Stickle** (2326ft). To make a long walk of it, aim then for **Stake Pass** to the northwest and return down the old Langdale packhorse route. Or you could walk the Pikes the other way round, starting with the approach up Dungeon Ghyll and finishing with a descent from Stickle Tarn. Either way, the walking is around seven miles and takes about five hours.

Pike o'Blisco

For a short(ish), sharp climb out of Langdale, **Pike o'Blisco** (2304ft) is a tempting target – you can see its summit cairn from the valley floor, and you'll be on the top in ninety minutes glorying in the views. The easiest route follows the path from the *Old Dungeon Ghyll* road-end, through Stool End farm, and then crosses Oxendale Beck to climb up via Brown Howe to Red Tarn (1hr) for the final push to the pike. Total walk is five miles, a three-hour round trip, but experienced hikers won't find it any problem to incorporate Pike o'Blisco in a full-day Crinkle Crags and Bowfell circuit (see below).

Crinkle Crags, Bowfell and Esk Pike

The orthodox route up to the distinctive **Crinkle Crags** (2816ft) – the name, as you'll see, is deserved – is via Oxendale and Red Tarn. From the summit, an exciting ridge walk north along the "crinkles" drops down to Three Tarns (from where there's a possible descent down The Band to Langdale) or you continue north instead up to the rocky, conical summit of **Bowfell** (2960ft) – one of Wainwright's half-dozen favourite fells. From Bowfell, descend via Ore Gap to **Angle Tarn**, and then back to the *Old Dungeon Ghyll* down Rossett Gill and Mickleden Beck. This is a nine-mile (6hr) circuit, though determined peak-baggers will also want to add **Esk Pike** (2903ft) to the route, after Bowfell (total 11–12 miles, 7–8hr), before swinging back round and down to Angle Tarn.

See Basics, p.42, for general walking advice in the Lakes; recommended maps are detailed on p.50.

▲ Crinkle Crags, Great Langdale

also one of the oldest occupied parts of the region, the evidence in the shape of Stone Age axes found in "factory" sites in the upper valley. A footpath from Elterwater (signposted as the Cumbria Way) runs up the valley to its head – eight miles from Ambleside – from where there are popular onward hiking routes over the passes to Wasdale and Borrowdale. Parking by the side of the B5343 road is discouraged, and drivers should make for either of the valley's main (signposted) car parks, depending on their target for the day.

From the car park at **Stickle Ghyll**, where the Langdale Pikes and Pavey Ark form a dramatic backdrop, Stickle Ghyll itself provides a stiff hour's climb up to **Stickle Tarn**, following a wide stone-stepped path that's been put in place to prevent further erosion of the hillside. Another obvious target is the dramatic sixty-foot waterfall of **Dungeon Ghyll**, around half an hour's climb from the car park – the "dungeon" in question is a natural cave, and after rain the thundering fall itself is an impressive sight. The other car park, a mile further west up the road by the **Old Dungeon Ghyll Hotel**, is the starting point for a series of more hardcore hikes (see box, p.113) that are among the best in the Lakes.

Practicalities

The #516 "Langdale Rambler" **bus** from Ambleside runs via Skelwith Bridge, Elterwater and Chapel Stile to the road end at the head of the valley: the Central Lakes Day Rider ticket (from £6.50) is valid, using any service from Bowness/Windermere. The bus passes all the **accommodation** reviewed below en route and turns around by the *Old Dungeon Ghyll*. The local **campsite** is immensely popular with climbers, hikers and cool campers, so you'll need to book in advance whether you want to pitch a tent, hole up in a pod or lounge in a yurt. **Eating and drinking** in Langdale isn't a problem – all the hotels and pubs serve food – though for groceries and supplies of any kind you'll have to head back down to Elterwater or Ambleside. For local **information** consult Ⓦwww.langdaleweb.co.uk.

Hotels and B&B

Millbeck Farm ⓣ015394/37364, Ⓦwww.millbeckfarm.co.uk. "What you see is what you get", says the owner – basically, three small, country-style rooms in the farmhouse (all sharing a bathroom and toilet), a big breakfast and glorious valley views. You can also buy the farm's own Herdwick lamb and Angus beef. The farm is up the narrow lane by the bridge, just before the *New Dungeon Ghyll*. Parking. No credit cards. ❷

New Dungeon Ghyll ⓣ015394/37213, Ⓦwww.dungeon-ghyll.com. Victorian-era hotel near Stickle Ghyll, beneath the Langdale Pikes. It's a more modern experience than the "Old DG", a mile up the road, and though rooms are a few pounds pricier they've all got nice bathrooms and expansive views. There's a restaurant (dinner £27.50) that's open to non-guests, and good bar meals available in the *Walker's Bar* or on the outdoor terrace (most mains £9–11). Parking. ❺

Old Dungeon Ghyll ⓣ015394/37272, Ⓦwww.odg.co.uk. Langdale's most famous inn is decidedly old-school in character and appearance – well-worn oak, floral decor, vintage furniture and assorted dubious watercolours – but walkers have long appreciated its unrivalled location, while plump armchairs and an open fire in the lounge do much to soothe the day's aches and strains. The en-suite rooms (not all are) offer the best value. Everyone is welcome for snacks and meals: coffee and flapjack served from 9am and dinner (£25, reservations essential) in the dining room at 7.30pm, though all the action is outside on the terrace or in the barebones, stone-flagged *Hikers' Bar*, which has a range of real ales and hearty casseroles and chips-with-everything meals (from £8.50). Parking. ❹

Campsite

Great Langdale ⓣ015394/37668, booking line ⓣ015394/63862, Ⓦwww.ntlakescampsites.org.uk. The National Trust's stupendously sited Langdale campsite has always been popular, but it's gone stellar since fancy camping pods (£30–45 per night, sleeps 2 adults and 1 child, contact the campsite) and luxury yurts (part-week from £285/full week £385, school and bank hols £325/460, contact Long Valley Yurts ⓣ07884/315298 or 07813/334865, ⓦwww.long-valley-yurts.co.uk) were added into the mix. The site's also got a separate family camping field, as well as laundry, drying room, well-stocked shop and kids' playground, while at night boozers decamp to the nearby *Old Dungeon Ghyll*, a 5min walk away.

Bunkhouse and pub

Sticklebarn Tavern ⓣ015394/37356. Langdale's backpacker choice is next to the *New Dungeon Ghyll*, with a sunny slate terrace outside the bar for drinks with grand views. There are sixteen beds available in the bunkhouse, which is centrally heated and carpeted, big breakfasts are served every day (from 9am) and bar meals (from £8.50) available all year round, plus *glühwein* and hot chocolate for those chilly days. Parking. Dorm beds from £12.

Travel details

All timetables can be checked on Traveline ⓣ0871/200 2233, ⓦwww.traveline.info.

From Grasmere

Bus #555 to: Dove Cottage (2min), Rydal (5min), Ambleside (20min), Brockhole (30min), Windermere train station (35min), Kendal (1hr); or to Keswick (20min). Service operates every 30min–1hr.
Bus #599 (open-top service) to: Dove Cottage (2min), Rydal (5min), Ambleside (20min), Brockhole (30min), Windermere train station (35min), Bowness piers (45min). Service operates Easter–Oct every 20–30min.

To Langdale

Bus #516, "Langdale Rambler" from Ambleside (5–6 daily) to: Skelwith Bridge (10min), Elterwater (17min), Chapel Stile (20min), Old Dungeon Ghyll (30min).

3

Coniston Water, Hawkshead and the south

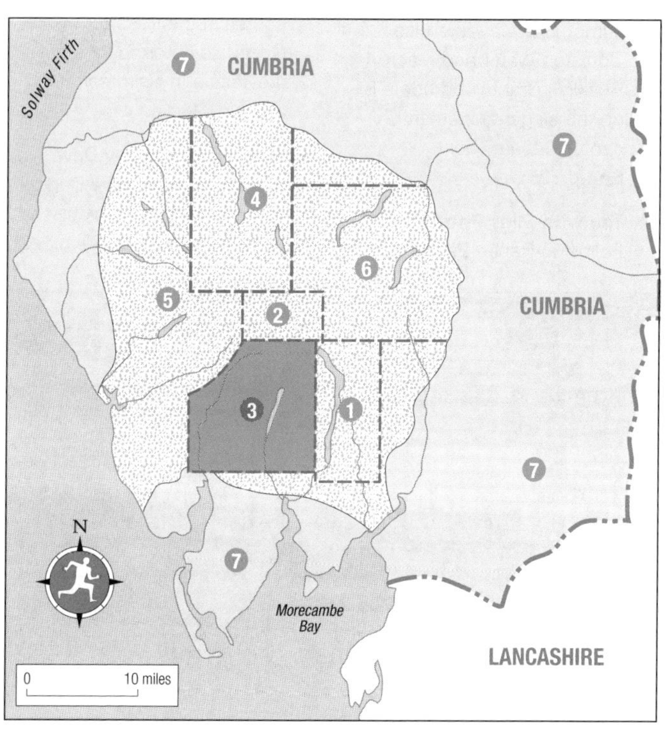

CHAPTER 3

Highlights

* **Climbing the Old Man of Coniston** The finest single climb in the area for anyone who wants to say they've been up a classic Lake District mountain. See p.122

* **Ruskin Museum, Coniston** The best of Coniston – its history, trades, pastimes and personalities – all under one roof. See p.124

* **Steam Yacht Gondola** The sumptuous way to cruise Coniston Water and reach Ruskin's Brantwood home is on the elegant nineteenth-century steam yacht. See p.125

* **Tea with Miss Potter** Follow in Renée Zellweger's footsteps at Coniston's gorgeous *Yew Tree Farm*. See p.128

* **Hill Top, Near Sawrey** No serious Beatrix Potter fan should miss touring the house she bought with the proceeds of her first book, *The Tale of Peter Rabbit*. See p.137

* **Go Ape in Grizedale Forest** The high-wire adventure course in the trees of Grizedale Forest brings out the Tarzan in visitors young and old. See p.141

* **The Duddon Valley** Drive – or better still, walk – the Duddon Valley, one of the region's best-kept secrets. See p.142

▲ Ruskin Museum, Coniston

3

Coniston Water, Hawkshead and the south

Coniston Water – five miles west of Windermere as the crow flies – is not one of the most immediately imposing of the lakes, yet it's one of the oldest settled parts of the Lake District. For as long as there has been human habitation, there has been industry of sorts around Coniston, whether fishing in the lake by the monks of Furness Abbey, copper-mining and slate-quarrying in the northwestern valleys and fells, or coppicing and charcoal-making in the forests to the south and east. The lake's understated beauty – and very possibly its association with these traditional lakeland trades – attracted the Victorian art critic, essayist and moralist John Ruskin, who moved here in 1872. **Brantwood**, his isolated house on the lake's northeastern shore, provides the most obvious target for a trip, and no one should miss a boat ride on the National Trust's elegant steam yacht, *Gondola*, or on the lake's wooden motor-launches.

Those wanting to stay in the area usually look no further than the cute cottages and cobbled streets of **Hawkshead**, three miles east of Coniston Water, with its connections to the big two literary lakeland names of William Wordsworth (who went to school here) and Beatrix Potter (whose husband's former office has been turned into an art gallery). Certainly, the former mining village of **Coniston** itself has to work hard to keep visitors in the face of such stiff competition, but it grows on some after a while and is the usual base for an ascent of the **Old Man of Coniston**, the distinctive peak that backs the village. Wherever you stay, there are easy side trips: to the renowned local beauty spot of **Tarn Hows**, the woodland paths, bike trails and sculptures of **Grizedale Forest**, or Beatrix Potter's former house of **Hill Top** – the latter one of the most visited attractions in the Lake District. Routes south towards the Furness peninsula take you through the pretty **Duddon Valley** – immortalized by Wordsworth in a series of sonnets – and to the quiet market town of **Broughton-in-Furness**, on the southern edge of the National Park.

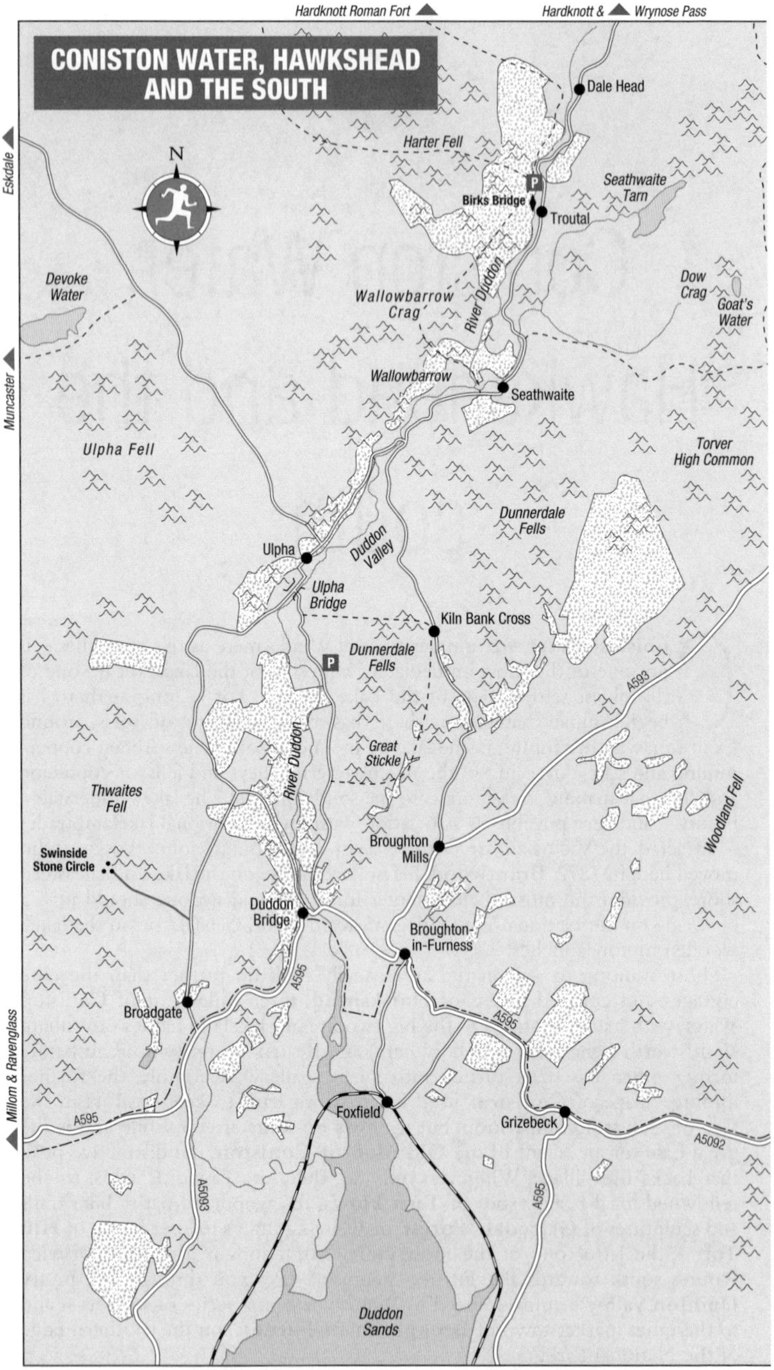

CONISTON WATER, HAWKSHEAD AND THE SOUTH

Hardknott Roman Fort
Hardknott & Wrynose Pass
Eskdale
Muncaster
Millom & Ravenglass
Dale Head
Harter Fell
Seathwaite Tarn
Birks Bridge
Troutal
Devoke Water
Dow Crag
Goat's Water
Wallowbarrow Crag
River Duddon
Wallowbarrow
Seathwaite
Ulpha Fell
Torver High Common
Dunnerdale Fells
Ulpha
Duddon Valley
Ulpha Bridge
Kiln Bank Cross
Dunnerdale Fells
A593
Great Stickle
River Duddon
Thwaites Fell
Woodland Fell
Broughton Mills
Swinside Stone Circle
Duddon Bridge
Broughton-in-Furness
A595
Broadgate
A595
A595
Foxfield
Grizebeck
A5092
A5093
A595
Duddon Sands
Millom & Ravenglass
Barrow-in-Furness

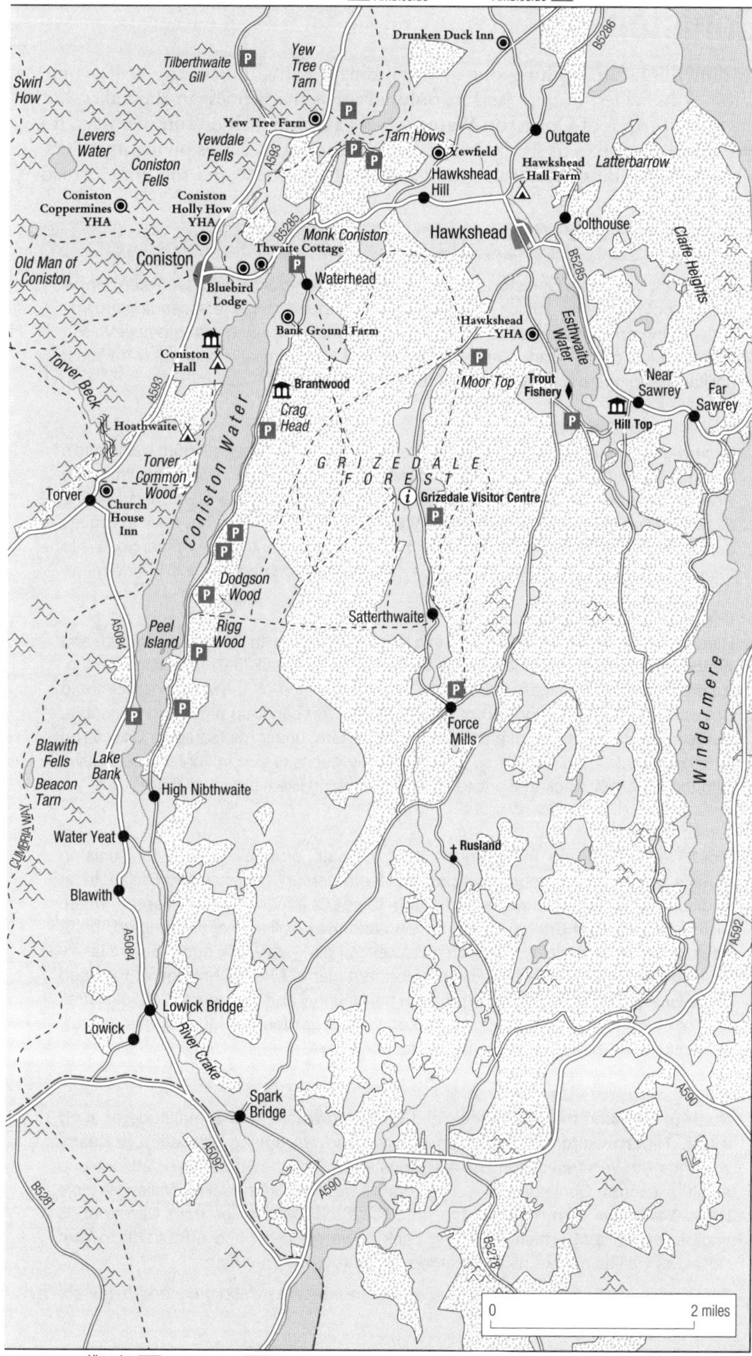
Ambleside
Ambleside
Drunken Duck Inn
Tilberthwaite Gill
Yew Tree Tarn
Swirl How
Yew Tree Farm
Levers Water
Yewdale Fells
Tarn Hows
Yewfield
Outgate
Coniston Fells
Hawkshead Hill
Hawkshead Hall Farm
Latterbarrow
Coniston Coppermines YHA
Coniston Holly How YHA
Colthouse
Hawkshead
Claife Heights
Monk Coniston
Thwaite Cottage
Old Man of Coniston
Coniston
Waterhead
Bluebird Lodge
Bank Ground Farm
Hawkshead YHA
Esthwaite Water
Coniston Hall
Torver Beck
Brantwood
Moor Top
Trout Fishery
Near Sawrey
Far Sawrey
Crag Head
Hill Top
Hoathwaite
Coniston Water
Torver Common Wood
GRIZEDALE FOREST
Torver
Church House Inn
Grizedale Visitor Centre
Dodgson Wood
Satterthwaite
Peel Island
Rigg Wood
Windermere
Force Mills
Blawith Fells
Lake Bank
Beacon Tarn
High Nibthwaite
CUMBRIA WAY
Water Yeat
Rusland
Blawith
Lowick Bridge
Lowick
River Crake
Spark Bridge
0
2 miles
Ulverston
Ulverston
A593
B5285
B5286
A5084
A5092
A590
A592
B5281
B5278
© Crown copyright

Coniston

Its dimensions are nothing out of the ordinary – five miles long, half a mile across at its widest point – and its only village is the plainest in the Lakes, but the glassy surface of **Coniston Water** weaves a gentle spell on summer days. It's one of the best lakes to see by boat, with two separate services plying its waters, while the spreading Grizedale woodland on the east side and the limited road

Walks from Coniston

The classic walk from Coniston village is to the top of the Old Man of Coniston, which is tiring but not overly difficult – Wainwright's flippant reference to ascending crowds of "courting couples, troops of earnest Boy Scouts, babies and grandmothers" isn't that far wide of the mark. Other Coniston walks are similarly accessible to most abilities, ranging from lakeside strolls to ghyll scrambles.

Old Man of Coniston

Most walkers can reach the summit of the **Old Man of Coniston** (2635ft) – England's seventh-highest mountain, if you need an excuse – in under two hours from the village, following the signposted path from Church Beck. It's a steep and twisting route, passing though abandoned quarry works and their detritus, but there's a pause on the way up at Low Water tarn while the views from the top are tremendous – to the Cumbrian coast and Morecambe Bay, and across to Langdale and Windermere.

Old Man circular routes

Hardier hikers combine the Old Man in a ridge-walk loop with **Swirl How** (2630ft) and **Wetherlam** (2502ft) to the north – a seven- or eight-mile walk (5–7hr). Wetherlam, too, is pitted with caves, mines and tunnels, requiring caution on the various descents to Coppermines Valley. Or instead of heading north you can loop around to the south, descending via **Goat's Hause** and Goat's Water tarn, under the fearsome **Dow Crag** (a famed lure for rock climbers). This eventually deposits you in Torver (see below), with the full circuit back to Coniston being something like eight miles (5hr).

Lakeside walks

From Coniston village the Cumbria Way footpath provides access to Coniston Water's west side. The route runs past sixteenth-century Coniston Old Hall (note its traditional circular chimneys) and through Torver Common Wood to **Torver**, where there's the excellent *Church House Inn* pub and the possibility of climbing up Torver Beck to see its waterfalls. There are also several park-and-walk spots on the lake's east side – nearest to the village is the northern pier of **Monk Coniston** at the head of the lake – with trails and picnic tables in the National Trust woodland. You can stroll up from here to the newly restored National Trust **gardens** of Monk Coniston Hall, known for their exotic conifers, and on to Tarn Hows.

Tilberthwaite Gill and Yewdale

North of Coniston the crags, beck and tarn of **Yewdale** offer a multitude of short walks. **Tilberthwaite Gill** is a quiet, narrow glen set among dramatic old quarry workings – there's free parking up a signposted lane off the Ambleside road (one and a half miles from Coniston), or you can walk here from Coppermines Valley via Hole Rake. **Yew Tree Tarn**, right on the Ambleside road (two miles from Coniston), is another pretty spot – there's parking back down the road, and a footpath to Tarn Hows, as well as a great hikers' tearoom at nearby *Yew Tree Farm*.

See Basics, p.42, for general walking advice in the Lakes; recommended maps are detailed on p.50.

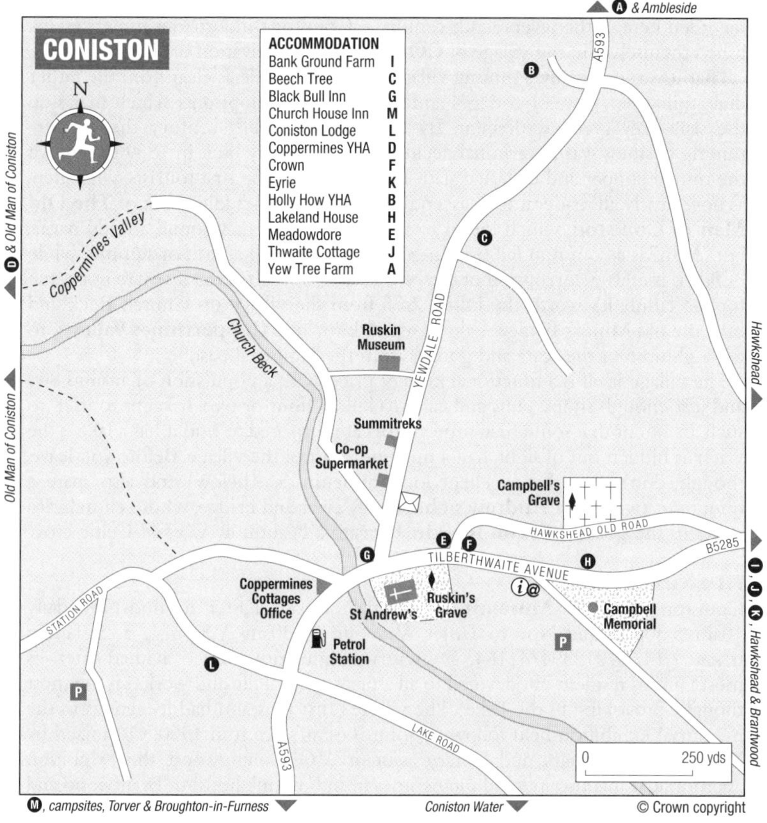

access mean it's easy to lose the worst of the crowds. The lake is also indelibly associated with two famous names. At the end of the nineteenth century, **Arthur Ransome** spent his childhood summer holidays near Nibthwaite at the southern end, and was always "half-drowned in tears" when it was time to leave. His vivid memories of messing about on the water, camping on the islets, befriending the local charcoal-burners and playing make-believe in the hills surfaced later in his children's classic, *Swallows and Amazons*, when Peel Island became the "Wild Cat Island" of the book. The sheltered Coniston waters also attracted speed-adventurer Sir Malcolm Campbell, who set the world water-speed record here (of 141mph) in 1939; his record-holding son, **Donald Campbell**, was to perish on the lake in 1967 in pursuit of an ever faster time, and the story rumbles on today with the ongoing restoration of his crashed powerboat *Bluebird*.

Coniston village

Copper has been taken from the Coniston fells since the Bronze Age, though the Romans were the first to mine it systematically. The industry again flourished in the seventeenth century, and by the nineteenth century hundreds of workers were employed in the local copper mines – producing ore used for the "copper-bottoming" of the wooden hulls of ships. Together with slate-quarriers – first recorded here in the seventeenth century – Coniston's industrious miners established themselves in the village of **CONISTON** (a derivation of "King's Town").

That it was originally a mining village, pure and simple, is clear from the rather drab, utilitarian, rows of cottages and later Victorian shopfronts which make up the slate-grey-green settlement. By the late nineteenth century the copper-mining business was in terminal decline and the railway, built in 1859 to remove the mined copper and quarried slate, began to bring the first tourists, who then, as now, nearly all made time to ascend the craggy, mine-riddled bulk of **The Old Man of Coniston**, which looms to the northwest. It may sound an odd name, but "Man" is a common fell term hereabouts, signifying a peak or summit, while "Old" is merely a corruption of the Norse "alt", or high. Even if you're not game for the climb, it's worth the initial stroll from the village up Church Beck and over the old Miner's Bridge – along what's known as **Coppermines Valley** – to get a glimpse of the scars and gouges from the industrial past.

The village itself is a functional kind of place, with a population of around 800 and just enough shops, pubs and cafés to kill an hour or two. It keeps to itself to such an extent that some first-time visitors are surprised to find it has a lake – the water is hidden out of sight, half a mile southeast of the village. Before you leave, though, don't miss the excellent local museum (see below) and also spare a minute or two for **St Andrew's church**, by river and bridge, whose churchyard contains the **grave of John Ruskin**, beneath a beautifully worked Celtic cross.

Ruskin Museum

Coniston's **Ruskin Museum**, on Yewdale Road (Easter to mid-Nov daily 10am–5.30pm; mid-Nov to Easter Wed–Sun 10.30am–3.30pm; £5.25, family ticket £14; ⓣ015394/41164, ⓦwww.ruskinmuseum.com) – named after its most famous resident but devoted to all aspects of local life and work – is the most thought-provoking in the Lakes. The village's first museum had its genesis in the memorial exhibition held following John Ruskin's death in 1900. Organized by his longtime secretary and literary assistant W.G. Collingwood, the exhibition appropriated manuscripts and mementoes from Ruskin's house at Brantwood and raised sufficient funds for a permanent museum, largely devoted to Ruskin himself. This was housed in Coniston's Mechanics Institute, a local cultural society supported by Ruskin during his life. The latest building stands at the back of this, and is still first port of call for anyone interested in tracing Ruskin's life and work. In relating his ideas and theories to local trades and pastimes the museum also doubles as a highly effective record of Coniston's history through the ages.

The museum begins with a walk-through timeline, placing the village and Ruskin within the wider historical context. Stone and Bronze Age artefacts give way to an exposition of the local geology, essential for an understanding of why Coniston became an important mining and quarrying district. The slate quarried locally has been used for centuries to roof buildings and build bridges and walls – here in the museum, it flags the floors. You'll learn about dry-stone walling (there's a fine example outside the museum) and sheep farming, as well as about the traditional trades that Ruskin himself promoted as a means of sustaining local employment, notably woodcarving and the making of **Langdale linen** and the famous **Ruskin lace** – examples of these are contained in slide-out panels and drawers. In the museum's separate **Ruskin Gallery** are found artefacts from the original memorial exhibition (including a pair of his socks and his matriculation certificate from Oxford), alongside a mixed bag of letters, manuscripts, sketchbooks and a series of Ruskin's own watercolours. Most enterprisingly of all, an interactive side-gallery lets you view pages of Ruskin's sketchbooks at the click of a mouse.

Ruskin linen and lace

Encouraged by John Ruskin, who had his own theories about the sanctity of traditional labour, a local woman, Marion Twelves, revived the trade of flax hand-spinning in Elterwater in 1884. It had almost died out in the Lake District, and the flax itself had to be imported from Ireland. The **linen trade** flourished, assisted financially by Ruskin's own Guild of St George, though contemporary tastes dictated that the finished article would be more attractive to purchasers if it was embroidered. Ruskin provided a series of designs inspired by those of Renaissance ruffs, and hand-cut **lace** was attached to the plain linen to make cushion and sideboard covers and bedspreads. Ruskin's own name was used to promote the work after 1894; his funeral pall (displayed in the museum) was a particularly fine example. The industry continued until the 1930s, though by then few were relying upon it as a principal means of income.

The museum is also the place to track the latest developments in the reconstruction of Donald Campbell's powerboat **Bluebird**, whose wreckage was lifted from the bottom of Coniston Water in 2001. The boat will eventually be displayed here in a purpose-built gallery, though for now the original *Bluebird* engine, plus photographs of Campbell, his funeral and the recovery of the craft are on display, along with related mementoes, like Campbell's crash helmet and overalls.

Coniston Water

It's a ten-minute walk down Lake Road from the village to **Coniston Water** and its piers. The pebble shoreline and grassy verges are very popular on sunny summer days, while the National Park's **Coniston Boating Centre** (Ⓣ015394/41366; free parking available) can provide the wherewithal for fooling around on the water, either in rowboats (from £9 per hr), electric motorboats (£18 per hr), sit-on kayaks (£10 for 2hr) or Canadian canoes (£18 for 2hr). Coniston's sheltered waters also lend themselves to learning to sail, and the centre hires out dinghies or offers lessons and weekend courses. Also right by the lake here is the *Bluebird Café* (Ⓣ015394/41649, Ⓦwww.thebluebirdcafe.co.uk), a nice place with outdoor tables, serving meals, snacks, ices and drinks.

Boat speeds are limited to 10mph, a graceful pace for the sumptuously upholstered and quilted **Steam Yacht Gondola** (Easter–Oct roughly hourly departures 10.30am–4.15pm, weather permitting; £8 round trip, family ticket £20; Ⓣ015394/41288, Ⓦwww.nationaltrust.org.uk/gondola). This was first launched in 1859 but has been fully restored by the National Trust, and now even claims to be "green steam" as the boiler burns sustainable wood-waste logs. The boat leaves Coniston Pier for 45-minute circuits of the northern half of the lake, with stop-offs at Ruskin's Brantwood and Monk Coniston. There are also longer 90-minute lunchtime cruises around the whole lake a couple of times a week (£15, family ticket £39), on which you're invited to bring a picnic – call or check the website for current details.

The other lake service is the similarly eco-friendly **Coniston Launch** (Easter–Oct hourly departures 10.15am–5pm; Nov–Easter up to 5 daily depending on demand and weather; Ⓣ017687/75753, Ⓦwww.conistonlaunch.co.uk), whose solar-powered wooden vessels "Ruskin" and "Ransome" operate on two routes around the lake. The most regular service is north to the *Waterhead Hotel* pier, Torver and Brantwood (50min; £8.50 return, family ticket £22), and there are two daily services south on the longer route to Torver, Lake Bank, Sunny Bank

Speed king

It was an attempt too far for speed king **Donald Campbell** (1921–67) when he returned to Coniston Water at the beginning of 1967. Three years earlier, he'd set both land- (403mph) and water-speed (276mph) world records in Australia, and on January 4, 1967, his latest water-speed attempt on Coniston was looking promising. A first run had touched almost 300mph, but on the return his jet-powered *Bluebird K7* hit a patch of turbulence at an estimated 320mph. The craft went into a somersault and sank, and Campbell was killed immediately. His body and boat lay undisturbed on the lake bed until both were retrieved in 2001 by a team led by diver Bill Smith. Campbell's belated funeral was held at St Andrew's church, before the blue coffin (the colour of his boat) was carried by horse and carriage to the small church cemetery behind the *Crown Hotel*, where his **grave** lies today. There's also a **memorial plaque** dedicated to Campbell (and his chief mechanic, Leo Villa), which dominates the small green in the village centre, and a second plaque down near the piers by the lake.

The retrieval of *Bluebird*, and the ongoing restoration of the craft, have been controversial to say the least; the full story and the arguments are rehashed on the **Bluebird Project** website Ⓦwww.bluebirdproject.com. The restoration team plans to restore *Bluebird* to its pre-crash condition, using as much of the original material as possible. It will be a fully working boat and special dispensation has already been received to run trials on Coniston Water (which otherwise has a 10mph speed limit), probably in 2011.

and Brantwood (1hr 45min; £11.90 return, family ticket £27.50). You can stop off at any pier on either route (there are walk leaflets available onboard), while special **cruises** twice a week (Easter–Oct; £11.50; see website for details) concentrate on the various sites associated with *Swallows and Amazons* and the speed-racing Campbells.

Practicalities

Most **buses** – principally the #505 "Coniston Rambler" (from Kendal, Windermere, Ambleside or Hawkshead), the #X12 (Ulverston) and the #X31 (Hawkshead and Tarn Hows) – stop by the *Crown Hotel*, on the main road (B5285) through the village. A **Ruskin Explorer ticket** (from £14.50, buy on the bus) gets you return bus travel on the #505, plus use of the Coniston Launch and free entrance to Brantwood. The seasonal **Cross-Lakes Experience** minibus shuttle (daily Easter–Oct) runs as far as the *Waterhead Hotel* pier (for Brantwood and lake services), at the head of Coniston Water, half a mile out of the village; you can also connect with the #X31 here, which shuttles into Coniston and on to Hawkshead and Tarn Hows.

Drivers will come in on either the A593 (Ambleside road) or the B5285 (from Hawkshead) – the latter runs through the village as Tilberthwaite Avenue. The main **car park** is signposted; it's right in the centre (off Tilberthwaite Avenue), next to the excellent community-run **Coniston Information Centre** on Ruskin Avenue (daily: Easter–Oct 9.30am–5pm; Nov–March 9.30am–4pm, though hours may vary; Ⓣ015394/41533, Ⓦwww.conistontic.org). There's also useful online information on Ⓦwww.coniston-net.com.

Accommodation

Accommodation is plentiful and, for the most part, reasonably priced, while just outside Coniston are some fantastically appealing places, from farmhouse B&B to gourmet inn. There's one unique self-catering option – an apartment with a view in Ruskin's house, Brantwood (see review below) – while other holiday **cottages** also linked with the area's heritage are available through *The Coppermines* (Ⓣ015394/41765, Ⓦwww.coppermines.co.uk), namely a series of converted dwellings in the old sawmill in Coppermines Valley. Note that access to these, and to the Coppermines **youth hostel**, is up a steep and largely unsurfaced road. The nearest **campsite** to the village is busy *Coniston Hall*, a mile south by the lake, but for a smaller, quieter, family experience the National Trust has just established a fourth Lake District campsite at shoreside *Hoathwaite* (Ⓦwww.ntlakescampsites.org.uk), 2 miles south near Torver.

In Coniston

Beech Tree Guesthouse Yewdale Rd Ⓣ015394/41717. Coniston's former vicarage, 150 yards north of the village, makes a charming vegetarian base. Decorated with zest, half of the eight rooms have their own showers, the others (priced a pound or two less) share a bright bathroom; and there's a garden, with fell views, where you can have tea. Parking. No credit cards. ❷

Black Bull Inn Coppermines Rd, by the bridge Ⓣ015394/41335, Ⓦwww.conistonbrewery.com/black-bull-coniston.htm. The village's best pub has a variety of reasonably spacious B&B rooms, either in the main building or in the renovated Old Man and Bluebird cottages. Those two names are a familiar sight in the pub itself (they're two of the beers brewed on the premises), while the hearty bar meals are very popular – there's always home-made soup and a veggie dish, with local lamb, sausage and trout the menu mainstays (dishes £8.50–15). Parking. ❸, weekends ❹

Coniston Holly How YHA Far End, A593 Ⓣ0845/371 9511, Ⓔconistonhh@yha.org.uk. The closest youth hostel to the village is in a big old slate house (with some four-bedded family rooms) set in its own gardens just a few minutes' walk north of the centre on the Ambleside road. It's popular with schools and families, and is accordingly well equipped (laundry, café, bar service, outdoor activities), and it gets good reviews for its food and eager-to-please staff. Dorm beds from £15.

Coniston Lodge Sunny Brow, Station Rd Ⓣ015394/41201, Ⓦwww.coniston-lodge.com. Six immaculate cottage-style rooms (with bath as well as shower) occupy the extension of the Robinsons' comfortable family home, just 1–2min from the village centre. There's a very cosy, genteel feel inside – the lounge is stuffed full of antiques and mementoes – while a veranda overlooks the garden. Parking. ❹

Crown Inn Tilberthwaite Ave Ⓣ015394/41243, Ⓦwww.crowninnconiston.com. It's nothing fancy but the refurbished rooms at the *Crown* offer a fair amount of space for your money, and many have both baths and showers, a boon for aching walkers. There's a traditional bar downstairs (with meals) and an outdoor terrace looking across the churchyard. Two- and five-night breaks (including dinner) are a bit of a bargain. Parking. ❹

Lakeland House Tilberthwaite Ave Ⓣ015394/41303, Ⓦwww.lakelandhouse.com. A good, centrally located budget option accustomed to walkers and cyclists – bike storage, drying facilities and packed lunches are all available. The ten rooms have all been upgraded and many have decent views, while downstairs there's an internet café serving up big breakfasts, burgers, soup and sarnies (£3–7). ❷

Meadowdore Café Hawkshead Old Rd Ⓣ015394/41638, Ⓦwww.meadowdore-cafe.co.uk. The B&B available at the café is of a high quality and excellent value – there are two en-suite rooms and one with a lovely private bathroom, all three are tastefully furnished, and two have great views. Breakfast is in the café, which has a conservatory extension and slate patio – walkers can have sandwiches made up to take away, and the café's open until late in summer. Parking. ❷

Around Coniston

Bank Ground Farm Coniston Water, east side, north of Brantwood Ⓣ015394/41264, Ⓦwww.bankground.com. See chapter map for location. *Bank Ground Farm* is beautifully set on its own part of the shoreline, 2 miles by road from Coniston. There's atmosphere in abundance (low ceilings, exposed wood and open fires), and it was the original model for Holly Howe Farm in *Swallows and Amazons* and later used in the 1970s film. Seven traditionally furnished rooms in the main house, five of them en suite, have oak beams, carved beds and heavy furniture, and many have sweeping views, especially room 8 which has three windows overlooking lake and fells. Also several self-catering holiday cottages and converted barn, plus a farmhouse tearoom (this open daily in school summer holidays, otherwise weekends only from Easter until Oct). ❸

Church House Inn Torver, 2 miles south of Coniston ⓣ015394/41282, ⓦwww.churchhouseinntorver.com. See chapter map for location. Ziggy Stardust's loss is Coniston's gain – Mike Beaty, once personal chef to David Bowie, has returned to his Cumbrian roots with this fine gastropub, just minutes from the lake. The five B&B rooms are small but charming, and very good value (and there are hook-ups for a few motorhomes out the back), while excellent food is served in the snug real-ale bar or dining room (reservations advised for both). At lunch, it's seasonal soups and superior sandwiches (£4–8); dinner is also locally sourced and strong on the classics (mussels, potted shrimps, local "tattie" hot pot, steak and ale pudding, fish pie, mains £12–18), while service and presentation are spot on. Parking. ❸

Coniston Coppermines YHA Coppermines Valley ⓣ0845/371 9630, ⓔcoppermines@yha.org.uk. See chapter map for location. The hikers' favourite is perfectly placed for ascents of the Old Man and Wetherlam – you're basically halfway up a mountain already by the time you get here. It's fairly basic, with 26 bunks in four-, six-and eight-bedded rooms and few frills, but the dramatic setting can't be beaten, meals are served and you can buy a local beer or organic wine. It's a steep mile and a quarter from the village – follow the "Old Man" signs past the *Sun Hotel* or take the small road between the *Black Bull* and the Co-op; both routes lead to the hostel. Easter–Oct, may be closed some nights; also closed all Nov–March. Dorm beds from £17.95.

The Eyrie Brantwood, Coniston Water, 2.5 miles from Coniston ⓣ015394/41396, ⓦwww.brantwood.org. See chapter map for location. What a find for art-lovers and Ruskin enthusiasts – a very handsomely restored self-catering flat on the upper floor of beautiful Brantwood, available for overnight stays or longer. There's a double bedroom, kitchen-diner and a drawing room with the same lake views that used to inspire Ruskin himself; the gardens outside, and the Brantwood collections when open, are yours to explore. Parking. ❺

Thwaite Cottage Waterhead, B5285, half a mile east of Coniston ⓣ015394/41367, ⓦwww.thwaitcot.freeserve.co.uk. See chapter map for location. The very picture of a pretty English cottage, set back from the Hawkshead road up a little lane (10min walk from the village). Three cosy rustic rooms, slate flags, oak beams and panelled walls, plus a log fire in the guests' lounge and a couple of acres of peaceful gardens. Parking. No credit cards. ❷

Yew Tree Farm A593, 2 miles north of Coniston ⓣ015394/41433, ⓦwww.yewtree-farm.com. See chapter map for location. The best and classiest farmhouse B&B in the Lakes

People and places: Tea with Miss Potter

You know how it is – working farm to run, B&B guests to look after, breakfasts to cook – so what's your reaction when you walk into your messy kitchen to discover Renée Zellweger? "I was horrified!" laughs Caroline Watson, who with husband Jon farms belted Galloway cattle and Herdwick sheep at Yew Tree Farm, just outside Coniston. The Watsons have been at the farm since 2002 and are the current guardians of a most singular property, since Beatrix Potter herself owned and furnished the farm in the 1930s (it subsequently passed to the National Trust). This at least explains finding Bridget Jones in your kitchen – Yew Tree Farm doubled as Potter's house Hill Top in the lavish *Miss Potter* biopic, yet the Watsons managed to live and work through the several weeks of pre-production and two days of filming. Renée may be gone, but Beatrix still makes her presence felt daily in the farm's parlour tearoom, which she established for the original tenants. Everything is still home-made on the farm, from cheese scones to Herdwick lamb moussaka, and business is brisk in summer as walkers and curious film fans follow the Potter trail. Inside the parlour (now the breakfast room for B&B guests), the furniture, paintings and ornaments are all Potter's, along with the Bible box and grandfather clock in the hall. But Caroline's favourite is the Cumberland dresser with the white plates with the motto "Persevere" – appropriate for a farm business she thinks, even one with the spirit of Miss Potter flitting through the kitchen.

Yew Tree Farm tearoom (ⓦwww.yewtree-farm.com) is open Easter–Oct plus school hols daily, otherwise weekends only, 11am–4pm. It's a working farm with very limited parking, and tearoom visitors are advised to come on foot or by bike.

– we're not just talking munching sheep in the garden but also a private outdoor hot tub for guests. Three hugely atmospheric rooms are tucked away amid the creaking floors and mind-your-head oak beams: it's period (1690) in feel – the solid doors have clunky wooden latches and there are hand-crafted beds – but with a contemporary touch, including some bold paintwork and stylish green-slate-floor bathrooms. There's an excellent breakfast sourced from the farm (which sells its own-produced meats), walks straight from the gates (Tarn Hows is only half a mile away), and a decanter of port waiting for you in front of the fire. For the tearoom, see feature opposite. Parking. ❺

Eating, drinking and entertainment

All-day **breakfasts** are served at the *Meadowdore* and *Lakeland House* cafés, while a couple of other **cafés** and bakeries take care of lunch and snacks. For a drive, cycle or walk with a café at the end of it, the *Jumping Jenny* at Brantwood, and the tearooms at *Bank Ground Farm* or *Yew Tree Farm* are all worth a special trip. The outdoor tables at the *Black Bull* are perfect for a pint after a day on the fells, while the single best local dining destination is Torver's *Church House Inn*. The Co-op **supermarket** on Yewdale Road has basic supplies, but for anything more exotic you'll have to go to Ambleside.

Annual festivals include the week-long **Coniston Water Festival** (beginning of July), a celebration of arts, sports, leisure, food and drink, and the **Coniston Country Fair** (end of July), when all manner of traditional country trades, crafts, contests and entertainment take place in the grounds of Coniston Hall. The **Coniston Walking Festival** (September) is also going from strength to strength, with walks for all abilities, events and outdoor activities spread across a long weekend.

Listings

Banks There are ATMs in the petrol station and post office (fee charged at both), but not one at the bank (Barclays, Bridge End; open Mon, Wed & Fri only). Otherwise, the nearest facilities are in Ambleside.
Bike rental The closest places to rent bikes are Hawkshead and Grizedale Forest.
Emergencies The nearest hospital is in Kendal (Westmorland General Hospital, Burton Rd; ⓣ01539/732288, ⓦwww.mbht.nhs.uk).
Internet access There's wi-fi access at the information centre (donation required) and terminals and wi-fi access at the café at *Lakeland House* (see "Accommodation").
Outdoor stores Two or three places in the village sell all the walking gear you might need; Summitreks on Yewdale Rd also rents out boots, rucksacks and waterproofs.
Pharmacy The nearest pharmacy is in Hawkshead (Collins & Butterworth, Main St ⓣ015394/36201).
Post office Yewdale Rd.

Brantwood

If you come to Coniston, you shouldn't miss **Brantwood** (mid-March to mid-Nov daily 11am–5.30pm; mid-Nov to mid-March Wed–Sun 11am–4.30pm; £6.95, family ticket £14.50; garden only £4.95, family £9.50; ⓣ015394/41396, ⓦwww.brantwood.org.uk), the magnificently sited home of **John Ruskin** (1819–1900), which nestles among trees on a hillside above the eastern shore of the lake. It's only two and a half miles by road from Coniston, off the B5285, though the approach is greatly enhanced if you arrive by either the Steam Yacht Gondola or Coniston Launch. Ask for a voucher on the Gondola and you'll get 50p off the Brantwood entry; meanwhile, the Ruskin Explorer ticket (see Coniston's "Practicalities") combines bus and launch travel and Brantwood entry, and there's also a combination Coniston Launch and Brantwood ticket available which you can buy on board the boat.

Family business – the Collingwoods

Few families have had as sure a feel for the Lake District as the **Collingwoods**, whose home was at Lanehead at the northern end of Coniston Water. Local scholar, historian and artist William Gershorn **(W.G.) Collingwood** (1854–1932) was born in Liverpool, but visited the Lake District on holiday as a child and moved here as soon as was practicable. He became an expert on lakeland archeology, the Vikings and early Northumbrian crosses (his *Northumbrian Crosses of the Pre-Norman Age*, published in 1927, is a classic), writing his own guide to *The Lake Counties* (1902) and even a lakeland saga, *Thorstein of the Mere*, largely set around Coniston. While at Oxford University, Collingwood had studied under John Ruskin (who was Professor of Fine Art) and was immediately impressed by his mind and ideas; later, Collingwood became Ruskin's trusted secretary and literary assistant. It was W.G. who designed Ruskin's memorial cross and established the first Ruskin Museum in Coniston. The family befriended the young Arthur Ransome, who was of a similar age to W.G.'s son **Robin Collingwood** (1889–1943). Robin was later to become an Oxford professor of philosophy, influential historiographer and an authority on Roman Britain – he excavated the Galava site and fortifications at Waterhead near Ambleside. W.G.'s wife **Edith** and two daughters, **Barbara** and **Dora**, were also highly talented: Edith and Dora as painters, Barbara as a sculptor. Barbara's bust of the elderly Ruskin is on display in the Ambleside Museum. The family graves all lie, with Ruskin's, in Coniston's churchyard.

Ruskin lived here from 1872 until his death: at first sight he was captivated though by the stunning mountain and lake views and not by the house itself which he complained was "a mere shed". Indeed, the house today bears little resemblance to the eighteenth-century cottage bought for £1500 in 1871 from Radical engraver William James Linton. Ruskin spent the next twenty years expanding it, adding another twelve rooms and laying out its gardens. Thus adapted, Brantwood – "brant" is a Cumbrian dialect word meaning steep – became Ruskin's lair, where the grand old *éminence grise* of Victorian art and letters gardened, wrote, painted and pontificated.

The precocious only child of a wine merchant, Ruskin was from a wealthy background and could afford to indulge his passion for art from an early age, travelling in Europe with his parents and maintaining diaries and sketchbooks. He went up to Oxford in 1836, publishing his first book, *The Poetry of Architecture*, a year later when he was just 18. He made his name as an art critic with the publication of the first part of his celebrated *Modern Painters* (1843), conceived as a defence of J.M.W. Turner, whose work he had admired (and collected) since his student days. Later a champion of the Pre-Raphaelites and, after his wide European travels, a proponent of the supremacy of Gothic architecture, Ruskin came to insist upon the indivisibility of ethics and aesthetics. He was appalled by the conditions in which the captains of industry made their labourers work and live, while expecting him to applaud their patronage of the arts. "There is no wealth but life," he wrote in his study of capitalist economics, *Unto the Last* (1862), elaborating with the observation: "That country is richest which nourishes the greatest number of noble and happy human beings."

Drawing a distinction between mere labour and craftsmanship, he intervened in the lakeland economy by promoting a revival of woodcarving, linen and lace-making, and ventures like this as well as his architectural theories did much to influence such disparate figures as Proust, Tolstoy, Frank Lloyd Wright and Gandhi. Nonetheless, not all Ruskin's projects were a success, partly because of his refusal to compromise his principles. A London teashop, established to provide employment for a former servant, failed since Ruskin refused to advertise; meanwhile, his street-cleaning and road-building schemes, designed to instil into his students (including Arnold Toynbee and Oscar Wilde) a respect for the dignity of manual labour, simply accrued ridicule. Perhaps more relevant today is the very Ruskinian notion of ecological conservation – some see him as the first "Green" – espoused in his opposition to the expansion of the railways and the creation of Thirlmere reservoir.

House and gardens

Once you've paid to go in the **house**, you're free to wander around the various rooms. Ruskin's study (hung with handmade paper to his own design) and dining room boast superlative lake views; they are bettered only by those from the Turret Room where Ruskin used to sit in later life in his bathchair – itself on display downstairs, along with a mahogany desk and Blue John wine goblet, amongst other memorabilia. A twenty-minute video expands on the man's philosophy and whets the appetite for rooms full of his watercolours, as well as for the surviving Turners from Ruskin's collection that weren't sold off after his death. Other exhibition rooms and the Coach House Gallery display Ruskin-related arts and crafts, while there's also a well-stocked **bookshop** for those

Ruskin's life and death at Brantwood

John Ruskin was certainly looking for something other than mere bricks and mortar when he acquired **Brantwood** in 1871. Following his father's death in 1864 he was independently wealthy, lauded for his works, and regarded as the country's foremost authority on art and architecture – indeed, he had just been appointed Slade Professor of Fine Art at Oxford University. But Ruskin's personal life was complicated by two singular relationships, which perhaps led him to seek simplicity and harmony in the lakeland fells.

His **marriage** to Euphemia (Effie) Gray in 1848 – they honeymooned in the Lakes – had been annulled in 1854, with the divorce a cause célèbre of the day, sensationally alleging Ruskin's impotence. Euphemia eventually married the artist John Everett Millais, which – given Ruskin's unflinching support of the Pre-Raphaelites – was a hard blow. Ruskin later formed a long attachment with the young **Rose La Touche**, who was almost thirty years his junior. Her parents disapproved (a proposal in 1866 came to nothing) and when Rose died in 1875, Ruskin was affected badly. Retreating to his lakeland house, he suffered the first of a series of mental breakdowns in 1878.

At Brantwood he was looked after by his married cousin Joan Severn and her husband Arthur, whose family moved into the house in the early 1880s, supervising Ruskin's visits from the Victorian great and good. **W.G. Collingwood**, for one, was always suspicious of the Severns' influence and it's clear that they eventually restricted the number of Ruskin's visitors. The Severns would argue it was to protect Ruskin's health and they had a point, since the last years of his life were punctuated by bouts of depressive illness and mental breakdown. From 1885, he began to produce sections of his **autobiography**, *Praeterita*, and, eventually, it was the only thing Ruskin would work on. Tellingly selective in content, there was no mention of his former wife, Effie. Ruskin broke down again in 1889 and fell into silence, writing nothing after this time, rarely receiving visitors or even speaking. He caught influenza and died at Brantwood on January 20, 1900. **The Severns** inherited Brantwood, ignored Ruskin's wishes that the house be open to the public for a set number of days each year and sold off many of his paintings. Joan died in 1924, Arthur in 1931, following which the house and its remaining contents were sold to **J.H. Whitehouse**, founder of the Birmingham Ruskin Society, who began the task of restoration.

who want to bone up on the Pre-Raphaelites or the Arts and Crafts Movement. There's a summer **theatre** season here, held in the grounds, and various other lectures, recitals and **events** scheduled throughout the year – Thursday is usually "activity day", always a good time to visit, when there might be children's craft sessions or lace-making demonstrations (the website has all the details).

The 250-acre estate surrounding the house boasts a nature trail, while paths wind through the lakeside meadows and into eight distinct **gardens**, some based on Ruskin's own plans. You can potter about, as did Ruskin, among the native flowers, fruit, herbs, moorland shrubs and ferns – his slate seat is sited in the Professor's Garden – or climb the heights behind the house to Crag Head for some splendid views. Free guided garden walks take place several times a week (Easter–Oct, no reservations required).

The *Jumping Jenny* **tearoom** (Ⓣ015394/41715; open same days as the house) – named after Ruskin's boat – serves very nice (mostly veggie) food, especially its soups, cakes and flans, and there are more fine views from the outdoor terrace. You can eat here without paying to go inside either house or gardens.

Hawkshead

HAWKSHEAD, midway between Coniston and Ambleside, wears its beauty well, its patchwork of whitewashed cottages, cobbles, alleys and archways backed by woods and fells and barely affected by modern intrusions. This is partly due to the enlightened policy of banning traffic in the centre. Large car parks at the village edge take the strain, and when the crowds of day-trippers leave, Hawkshead regains its natural tranquillity. It's a handy base in any case for the big local draws of Tarn Hows and Beatrix Potter's Hill Top, while in the quiet country lanes just to the north are some of the finest boutique dining and lodging experiences in the whole region.

The Village

The Vikings were the first to settle the land here, Hawkshead probably founded by and named after one Haukr, a Norse warrior. In medieval times it became an important wool market, the trade controlled by the monks of Furness Abbey, and this early wealth explains the otherwise puzzling presence in such a small community of **Hawkshead Grammar School** (Easter–Sept Mon–Sat 10am–12.30pm & 1.30–5pm, Sun 1–5pm; Oct same days, but closes 4.30pm; £2; Ⓣ015394/36735). This was founded in 1585 and – even by Wordsworth's day, when the wool trade had much declined – was considered to be among the

Fishing on Esthwaite Water

Hawkshead's quiet lake, **Esthwaite Water**, isn't troubled by too many visitors, though Wordsworth, who rambled and splashed here as a boy, always remembered it fondly. Best view of the water is from the car-park access point on the far south-western shore, two miles from Hawkshead, near which budding anglers can find **Esthwaite Water Trout Fishery** (Ⓦwww.hawksheadtrout.com). You don't need any experience as there's tuition and tackle available, and a children's catch-your-own pond, as well as barbecue and picnic facilities. There's also loch-style day-fishing from boats (various permits and packages available), catching trout all year and pike in the winter.

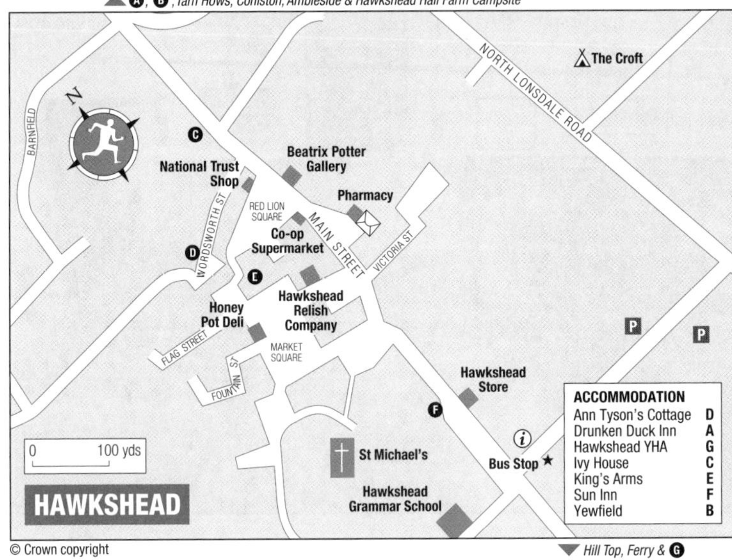

finest schools in the country. Wordsworth and his brother Richard were sent here following the death of their mother in 1778 to acquire an expensively bought education; "grammar" of course being Latin grammar, knowledge of which was the mark of every gentleman. In the simple schoolroom the Wordsworth boys were taught geometry, algebra and the classics at timeworn wooden benches and desks (some date back to the school's foundation); you'll be shown the desk on which the rapscallion William carved his signature – a foolhardy stunt given the anecdote that miscreants were suspended from a pulley in the centre of the room to be birched. He also wrote his first surviving piece of poetry, a paean to the bicentenary of the school's foundation, before leaving in 1787 to go up to Cambridge. The only other things to see are the headmaster's study upstairs, a small exhibition on the history of English grammar schools and a few quills and nibs. The school closed in 1909.

During his schooldays Wordsworth attended the fifteenth-century church of **St Michael's** sited above the school, which harks back to Norman and Romanesque designs in its rounded pillars and patterned arches. It's chiefly of interest for the 26 pithy psalms and biblical extracts illuminated with cherubs and flowers, painted on the walls during the seventeenth and eighteenth centuries. Wordsworth's other connection with the village is that during term-times he lodged with a local woman, **Ann Tyson** – someone he remembered kindly as "my old Dame" in *The Prelude*. Her Hawkshead cottage is now a guesthouse, though the Tyson family, and Wordsworth, actually lived for longer in another (unknown) house after 1783 when they moved half a mile east to Colthouse.

From its knoll the churchyard gives a good view over the village's twin central squares, anchored by a couple of pubs and several cafés. Past the *Queen's Head* on Main Street, the **Beatrix Potter Gallery** (Feb half-term to Easter daily except Fri 11am–3.30pm, Easter–Oct daily except Fri 10.30 or 11am–5pm; £4.40, family ticket £10.50, discount available for Hill Top visitors; ⓣ015394/36355, ⓦwww.nationaltrust.org.uk) hoovers up all

▲ Hawkshead Grammar School

Hawkshead's remaining visitors; admission is by timed-entry ticket. The gallery occupies rooms once used by Potter's solicitor husband, William Heelis, whom she met while purchasing land in the Hawkshead area. There had been a Heelis law firm in the village since 1861 and William was a partner in the family firm from 1900 until he died in 1945, when the building passed to the National Trust (Heelis's prewar office is maintained downstairs). If you were ever going to crack the enduring mystery of his wife's popularity you'd think this would be the place, since the upstairs rooms contain an annually changing selection of Potter's original sketchbooks, drawings, watercolours, letters and manuscripts. Although never formally schooled, she had drawn fossils, fungi and pet animals since childhood and her work is certainly closely observed. Her animals aren't caricatures, but neither are they "art" in any meaningful sense (Potter herself thought it "bosh" to think so), and to a non-Potterphile the paintings and drawings are pleasant without ever being more than mere fluff: the less devoted will find displays on her life as a keen naturalist, conservationist and early supporter of the National Trust more diverting. Potter bought eighteen fell farms and large parcels of Lake District land, which she bequeathed to the Trust on her death.

Practicalities

The main **bus service** to Hawkshead is the #505 "Coniston Rambler" between Windermere, Ambleside and Coniston, while the seasonal #X31 shuttles up to Tarn Hows and on to Coniston. These are complemented by the seasonal **Cross-Lakes Experience** (daily Easter–Oct), whose minibuses run from Hawkshead down to the Beatrix Potter house at Hill Top and on to Ferry House, Sawrey, for boat connections back to Bowness. The B5285 between Coniston and Sawrey skirts the eastern side of Hawkshead; no traffic is allowed in the village itself, but everything lies within five minutes' walk of the **car parks**. The locally run **tourist information centre** (daily 9am–5pm; Ⓣ015394/36946, Ⓦwww.hawksheadtouristinfo.org.uk) is by the main car park.

Accommodation

Reserve a long way ahead if you want to stay in and around Hawkshead during the peak summer season. For **cottages**, barn and farm conversions in Hawkshead and the surrounding area, contact Lakeland Hideaways Cottages near the National Trust office on The Square (ⓣ015394/42435, ⓦwww.lakeland-hideaways.co.uk).

In Hawkshead

Ann Tyson's Cottage Wordsworth St ⓣ015394/36405, ⓦwww.anntysons.co.uk. Wordsworth briefly boarded here and the old street has changed little since, though the house has been upgraded over the years. There are now three rooms in the main house, plus a ground-floor single, and one superior room in what was formerly an adjoining chapel – this has slate floors, underfloor heating, sleigh bed and smart bathroom. Also one self-catering cottage available at the same address. Parking permit available. ❷, superior room ❸

Ivy House Main St ⓣ015394/36204, ⓦwww.ivyhousehotel.com. Elegant Georgian house whose rotunda lights up the country-house-style interior. There are six rooms, some with four-poster beds and two that can be used as family rooms, while the restaurant is open for lunches, Cumbrian cream teas and dinner (mains £10–20). Parking. ❹

King's Arms Market Square ⓣ015394/36372, ⓦwww.kingsarmshawkshead.co.uk. Bags of character here, with the nine rooms retaining their oak beams and idiosyncratic proportions; bathrooms and furnishings, though, are reassuringly up to date. There's a snug little bar with a fire and a fine beer selection, while good-value meals include sarnies, salads and hot lunches (£5–10) as well as a wider-ranging dinner menu (£9–15) featuring the likes of fell-bred lamb, hot smoked salmon and venison steak. Free parking provided in the village. ❹

Sun Inn Main St ⓣ015394/36236 or 0845/643 5674, ⓦwww.suninn.co.uk. Eight revamped rooms in a family-run seventeenth-century inn – think exposed stone and original panelling combined with designer fabrics and locally crafted furniture. Their eco-hearts are in the right place too, with a carbon-offset policy, and food and other products sourced locally where possible, including meat traditionally reared on Cumbrian farms – so, no qualms tucking into a tasty steak, rack of lamb or Cumberland sausage (most mains £9–13), sitting outside on a sunny day on the little front terrace. ❹

Around Hawkshead

Drunken Duck Inn Barngates crossroad, 2 miles north of Hawkshead off B5285 ⓣ015394/36347, ⓦwww.drunkenduckinn.co.uk. See chapter map for location. This 400-year-old inn – more a restaurant-with-rooms these days – is many people's favourite in the Lakes, and it's easy to see why. The sixteen bedrooms mix antiques and cool colours with bold contemporary design; standard rooms in the inn itself are on the small side (midweek rates here are the cheapest on offer), but there's more spacious superior and deluxe accommodation across the courtyard, including an open-beamed Garden Room with sensational views and a balcony. Food shifts from classic sandwiches and bistro meals at lunch to a modish, fab and fresh seasonal dinner menu – starters around £8, mains £14–25. To the whole experience you can add sharp but unstuffy service, award-winning beers from their own Barngates Brewery, a sun-trap garden with private tarn and glorious valley views. What's not to like? Parking. ❺, superior/deluxe rooms ❻–❼

Hawkshead YHA Newby Bridge Rd, 1 mile south of Hawkshead ⓣ0845/371 9321, ⓔhawkshead@yha.org.uk. See chapter map for location. The local hostel is sited on Esthwaite Water's west side, housed in a Regency mansion which retains many of its original architectural features. There are over 100 beds and, with 14 three- or four-bedded rooms, and a separate family annexe, it's very popular with families and small groups. Evening meals and bike rental available. The Cross-Lakes Experience bus passes by. Dorm beds from £13.95.

Yewfield Hawkshead Hill, 2 miles northwest of Hawkshead off B5285 ⓣ015394/36765, ⓦwww.yewfield.co.uk. See chapter map for location. Splendid vegetarian guesthouse set amongst organic vegetable gardens, orchards and wildflower meadows. The house is a Victorian Gothic beauty, whose owners have filled it with Eastern artefacts, contemporary art and photography from their travels, and many of the rooms have been delightfully refurbished with Herdwick wool carpets and some lovely oak panelling and headboards from sustainable sources. There are ten rooms in total (including a tower suite), and two self-catering apartments, split between the main house and the old coach house and stables. Breakfast is either a full cooked veggie blowout or wholefood continental buffet. Parking. Closed Dec & Jan. ❸, superior rooms ❹, suite ❺

Campsites

The Croft North Lonsdale Rd, beyond the car parks on the edge of the village ⓣ015394/36374, ⓦwww.hawkshead-croft.com. The closest site to the centre is a caravan and camper van place – billed as family- and couple-friendly – though there are tent pitches too, and static caravans to rent. It's pricey but you get a lot of facilities, including a big shower block, coin-op laundry and games/TV room. Closed Nov to mid-March.

Hawkshead Hall Farm half a mile north of Hawkshead on the Ambleside road ⓣ015394/36221. See chapter map for location. Escape the crowds and noise at this basic, tap-and-toilet farm-field campsite, which is strictly families only; bus #505 passes the farm on the way into Hawkshead. Closed Dec–Feb.

Eating, drinking and entertainment

Outside the gourmet destination that is the *Drunken Duck Inn*, Hawkshead's **pubs** provide the main eating options, the top choices being the *King's Arms* or *Sun Inn*. There are also a couple of **cafés** in and around the village square and a small **supermarket**, while a couple of places offer picnic supplies and **local produce**, namely the Honey Pot deli (for bread, sandwiches, preserves, biscuits, smoked meats and cheese, ⓦwww.honeypotfoods.co.uk) and the Hawkshead Relish Company (ⓦwww.hawksheadrelish.com), where there are free tastings of their chutneys, relishes, mustards, pickles, preserves and dressings.

Rural activities and entertainment are offered each August during the **Hawkshead Agricultural Show**, while up at *Yewfield* guesthouse at Hawkshead Hill there are free monthly classical **concerts** and recitals (see website for details).

Listings

Banks There's no bank in Hawkshead, though there are ATMs inside the Co-op and the tourist information centre. Otherwise, the nearest banking facilities are in Ambleside.
Bike rental Bikes are available at nearby Grizedale Forest.
Emergencies The nearest hospital is in Kendal (Westmorland General Hospital, Burton Rd; ⓣ01539/732288, ⓦwww.mbht.nhs.uk).
Outdoor stores The village is the home of the country-and-outdoor-wear store Hawkshead (ⓦwww.hawkshead.com), which now has branches nationwide, but the first, flagship store is still trading here on Main Street – considerably extended over the years, and now with a café too.
Pharmacy Collins & Butterworth, Main St ⓣ015394/36201.
Post office Main St (Easter–Oct Mon–Sat 9am–5.30pm, Sun 10am–3pm; Nov–Easter Mon–Fri 9am–5.30pm, Sat 9am–12.30pm).

Tarn Hows

A minor road off the Hawkshead–Coniston road (B5285) winds the couple of miles northwest to **Tarn Hows**, a beautiful body of water surrounded by spruce and pine, circled by paths and studded with grassy picnic spots. The land was donated to the National Trust by Beatrix Potter in 1930 – one of several such grants – since when the Trust has carefully maintained it. It takes an hour to walk around the tarn on its well-kept paths, during which you can ponder on the fact that this miniature idyll is in fact almost entirely artificial – the original owners enlarged two small tarns to make the one you see today, planted and landscaped the surroundings and dug the footpaths. It's now a Site of Special Scientific Interest – keep an eye out for some of the Lakes' (and England's) few surviving native **red squirrels**.

Tarn Hows is one of the Lake District's most popular beauty spots, and the best way to appreciate it is to walk there, so that its charms are gently unveiled as you approach. It's about two miles on paths and country lanes from either Hawkshead or Coniston, and there's a new route to the tarn through the Monk Coniston gardens and grounds (north end of Coniston Water). There's usually an ice-cream van at the tarn car park (April–Oct) or it's just a half-mile or so walk from the tarn to the tearoom at *Yew Tree Farm* (see p.128).

Bus services come and go, though at the time of writing the seasonal #X31 **Tarn Hows Tourer** (daily Easter–Oct; £3 return) was running here up to half a dozen times a day from Hawkshead (also connections from Coniston and the Coniston Launch Pier at the head of Coniston Water). Or you can ask to get off the Cross-Lakes Experience bus at High Cross (at the top of Grizedale Forest) and follow the three-quarter-mile footpath north past Wharton Tarn. Drivers will have to pay to use the designated National Trust car park.

Hill Top

It's two miles down the eastern side of Esthwaite Water from Hawkshead to the twin hamlets of Near and Far Sawrey, overlooked by the woods and tarns of Claife Heights. Near Sawrey in particular – a cluster of flower-draped white-washed cottages in a shallow vale – receives an inordinate number of visitors since it's the site of Beatrix Potter's beloved house, **Hill Top** (daily except Fri: Feb half-term to Easter 11am–3.30pm; Easter–Oct 10.30am–4.30pm; £6.50,

The Tale of Beatrix Potter

A Londoner by birth, **Beatrix Potter** (1866–1943) spent childhood holidays in the Lakes, first at Wray Castle on Windermere and later in houses with grand gardens, at Holehird (Troutbeck) and Lingholm (Derwent Water). Her landscape and animal sketching was encouraged by Canon Rawnsley, a family friend (and founder member of the National Trust), who inspired her to produce her first book, *The Tale of Peter Rabbit*. Potter had this privately printed in 1901 before it was taken up by Frederick Warne publishers. It was an instant success, and with the proceeds, Potter – remembering her happy holidays – bought the lakeland farmhouse at Hill Top in 1905. There were to be 23 tales in all, with half a dozen of the later books set in and around Hill Top, though Potter still lived for much of the year in London. Following her marriage to a local solicitor in 1913, when she was 47, Potter retained the house as her study but installed a manager at Hill Top to oversee the farm. Only known locally as Mrs Heelis the farmer (rather than Beatrix Potter the author), she lived down the road in another house, Castle Cottage (not open to the public), but visited Hill Top most days, usually to work on business associated with her increasing portfolio of farms, which took up more and more of her time. She actually wrote very few books after her marriage, preferring to develop her interest in breeding the local Herdwick sheep, for which she won many prizes at local shows. When she died, her ashes were scattered locally by the Hill Top farm manager: the place has never been identified and there's no other memorial to her, save the house and, now of course, the movie. The **Miss Potter** biopic was largely filmed in Cumbria, presenting Renée Zellwegger as Beatrix in "the most enchanting tale of all", namely her early love affair with her publisher Norman Warne (Ewan McGregor), which ended with his untimely death, after which Potter moved to Hill Top and married in later life. Fans can check out all the film location sites on the website ⓦwww.visitmisspotter.com.

family ticket £16; shop and garden, entry free on Fri when house is closed, and also open Nov & Dec; ⓣ015394/36269, ⓦwww.nationaltrust.org.uk). This has always been a popular attraction, to say the least, but since the 2007 film *Miss Potter* the crowds and queues have grown even more. Entry is by timed ticket, you'll probably have to wait in line to enter the small house, and sellouts are possible, especially in school holidays (and you can't book in advance). There's also limited free parking, and you're encouraged to use the seasonal Cross-Lakes Experience bus-and-launch service, which runs directly here from Bowness or, on its way back, from Hawkshead. One final word for anyone who's seen *Miss Potter* – this house is not the one in the film; Yew Tree Farm near Coniston was used instead.

When you do get in to Hill Top, you'll discover a modest house whose furnishings and contents have been kept as they were during Potter's occupancy – a condition of her will. The carved oak bedstead and sideboards, the small library of bound sets of Gibbons and Shakespeare, and the cottage garden are all typical of well-to-do, if unexceptional, Edwardian taste – though the few mementoes and curios do nothing to throw light on Potter's character. But if you love the books then Hill Top and the Sawrey neighbourhood will be familiar (many of the house fixtures and fittings, for instance, appear in scenes in the books, while the *Tower Bank Arms* next door is the inn in *The Tale of Jemima Puddle-Duck*). And where better to buy a Mrs Tiggy-Winkle salt-and-pepper shaker or a Peter Rabbit calendar than Hill Top's own souvenir-stuffed gift shop?

Near and Far Sawrey

The little hamlet of **NEAR SAWREY** regains its equilibrium once the Beatrix Potter house of Hill Top has closed for the day. It makes a lovely overnight stop if you can find a room (many places have Beatrix Potter connections), and if you can't, you can console yourself with a drink in the pub, the *Tower Bank Arms*, the very model of an English country inn. A mile or so away, across the hay fields, lies **FAR SAWREY**, an equally miniature hamlet, though this time with a church, shop and post office, and also with a pub, the *Sawrey Hotel*, which has a beer garden. From here, tracks fan out across **Claife Heights**, past its little tarns and down through the woods to the western shore of Windermere – the most direct route runs steeply downhill to Sawrey ferry pier, where you can catch the car-ferry or passenger launch across to Bowness. It must be the only route in England signposted in Japanese (the Japanese have a special fondness for Beatrix Potter). Coming from the lake, it takes about an hour to walk from the ferry pier to Near Sawrey and Hill Top; going back downhill, slightly less.

Accommodation and food

Buckle Yeat Near Sawrey ⓣ015394/36446, ⓦwww.buckle-yeat.co.uk. Gorgeous seventeenth-century cottage close to the Potter house (and illustrated in Potter's *The Tale of Tom Kitten*), offering six cosy, country-style double/twin rooms. There's always a colourful display of flowers and baskets outside the cottage; inside, the guest lounge has a slate-flagged floor, big armchairs and a log fire. Parking. ❸

Ees Wyke Near Sawrey ⓣ015394/36393, ⓦwww.eeswyke.co.uk. Georgian country house – Beatrix Potter stayed here on childhood holidays – most of whose eight elegant rooms have matchless views across the fields to Esthwaite Water. Dinner (included in the price) is the high point, with more lovely views accompanied by five courses served from a refined daily-changing menu. Parking. ❻

Tower Bank Arms Near Sawrey, next to Hill Top ⓣ015394/36334, ⓦwww.towerbankarms.co.uk. Hill Top's local pub, owned by the National Trust, looks the very part, with its oak beams, slate floors and cast-iron range. Upstairs are three simple but smart rooms, named Yan, Tan and Tethera (Cumbrian dialect for one, two, three); totter downstairs for an acclaimed array of beers and good food, from local lamb to Esthwaite trout (mains £9–14). And if you can't tell the Beatrix Potter joke in this pub (what do you call a lager-juggling female ceramicist…?), where on earth can you? Parking. ❸

Grizedale Forest

Grizedale Forest extends over the fells separating Coniston Water from Windermere, and the picnic spots, open-air sculptures, children's activities, cycle trails and high-wire adventure course make for a great day out away from the main lakes. There's always been thick forest here, though by the

▲ Sculpture, Grizedale Forest

eighteenth century successive generations of charcoal-making, coppicing and iron-smelting had stripped the fells and dales virtually bare. Regeneration by the Forestry Commission has restored dense oak, spruce, larch and pine woodland to Grizedale and now red deer are seen occasionally, while the forest also provides a habitat for badgers and squirrels, grouse, woodcock and woodpeckers.

Arthur Ransome

Arthur Ransome (1884–1967) was born in Leeds and spent early childhood holidays with his brother and sisters at Nibthwaite by Coniston Water. His boyhood holiday pursuits were all put to use in his books, though it was the friendship he made with the outgoing Collingwood family as a young man of 20 which cemented his love affair with the Lakes – sailing with them on Coniston Water, picnicking on Peel Island, and visiting the local copper mines.

Ransome's first job was with a London publisher, though he was soon published in his own right, producing critical literary studies of Edgar Allan Poe and Oscar Wilde, and an account of London's bohemia. He met and **married** Ivy Constance Walker and they had one daughter, Tabitha, in 1910, but the marriage was never happy. In part this prompted a bold solo move to Russia in 1913, after which his marriage was effectively at an end. Ransome was keen to learn the language and had a special interest in Russian folklore – a well-received translation and adaptation of various fairy tales (*Old Peter's Russian Tales*) appeared in 1916.

During World War I, ill health prevented him joining up and he was hired as a **war correspondent** by the *Daily News*. Consequently, when the Russian Revolution broke out, he was well placed to report on events. Ransome clearly knew his Russian politics and was a sympathetic but critical observer of the Bolshevik Revolution, producing two books of on-the-spot reportage. He interviewed Lenin and other leading figures, and was introduced to Trotsky's secretary, Eugenia, who – on the final break-up of his first marriage – became his second wife.

Ransome spent much of the following ten years in Russia and the Baltic States, latterly as special correspondent for the *Manchester Guardian*, for whom he travelled widely. In 1925 he bought his first lakeland house at **Low Ludderburn**, in the Winster Valley, and, having eventually abandoned journalism, it was here he wrote **Swallows and Amazons** (published in 1930). This was the first of twelve books he produced in the series (the last in 1947), most, but not all, set in the Lake District – spells in Norfolk and Suffolk provided the background for *We Didn't Mean To Go To Sea* and *Coot Club*.

Ransome was inspired to write for and about the five children of the **Altounyan family**, whose father, Ernest, brought them to the Lake District on holiday in 1928. Ernest Altounyan, married to Dora Collingwood, a longtime Ransome family friend, bought two boats (one called *Swallow*) and he and Ransome first taught the children to sail. That the Altounyan children were models for the "Swallows" is now accepted – the first edition of the book was dedicated to them – though when the relationship cooled in later years, Ransome denied this and withdrew the dedication. Other friends and local characters appeared in the books, while Coniston locations figured heavily – Peel Island as "Wild Cat Island", the Coniston fells and mines in *Pigeon Post* and the Old Man of Coniston as "Kanchenjunga". Ransome and Eugenia lived in Coniston itself between 1940 and 1945, but settled in retirement at a house called Hill Top in Haverthwaite. He died on June 3, 1967.

Eugenia donated various effects and mementoes of her husband's to Abbot Hall in Kendal, which maintains an Arthur Ransome exhibition and doubles as the HQ of The Arthur Ransome Society (TARS), whose zealous members keep his flame alive by means of literary events, publications and activities. For more information, contact the museum or visit the expansive Arthur Ransome website: ⓦwww.arthur-ransome.org.

The best starting point is the visitor centre (see "Practicalities"), which is the hub of the waymarked **hiking trails** that spread across both sides of the Grizedale Valley. These extend for between two and fourteen miles on undulating tracks, with the longest, the **Silurian Way**, linking the majority of the ninety-odd remarkable stone and wood **sculptures** scattered amongst the trees. Since 1977 artists have been invited to create a sculptural response to their surroundings using natural materials. Some of the resulting works are startling, as you round a bend to find pinnacles rising from a tarn, sculpted wooden ferns, a hundred-foot-long wave of bent logs or a dry-stone wall slaloming through the conifers.

On a bike (available for rent at the forest centre), you can see much of Grizedale in a day, and while there are climbs involved on every route you'll be rewarded by some excellent views. There are five general waymarked cycle routes and the rather more challenging ten-mile **North Face Trail** on the west side of the forest, which gets rave reviews from serious mountain-bikers.

If there's shrieking from the skies above, that's the daredevils on the zip-wires of **Go Ape** (daily Easter–Oct, Nov weekends only, closed Tues in term-time & closed Dec & Jan; from £25; advance booking essential, online or by phone ⓣ0845/643 9215, ⓦwww.goape.co.uk), an aerial adventure course through the tree canopy, starting near the visitor centre. After a safety briefing you're let loose to negotiate the inter-linked rope bridges, Tarzan swings and scramble nets – fantastic fun at an adrenaline-inducing 59ft above floor level. It takes a good two hours to get around – there's a minimum age of 10 and a minimum height of 4ft 7in, but apart from that anyone can do it.

Two miles south down the road from the visitor centre, the forestry hamlet of **Satterthwaite** has a pub, the *Eagle's Head* while, hidden away in the narrow lanes a further two miles beyond, is the rustic **Rusland church**. Surrounded by undulating grazing land, it's a serene setting for the simple graves of children's writer **Arthur Ransome** and his wife Eugenia.

Practicalities

Access to the forest is easiest from Hawkshead, which is just two and a half miles northeast of the visitor centre, or you can walk through the forest from the east side of Coniston Water, from Monk Coniston and from Brantwood. There's a bus, the seasonal #X30 **Grizedale Wanderer** (4 daily, Easter–Oct), which runs from Hawkshead via Moor Top, and connects with the Cross-Lake Experience service (so you can come direct from Bowness-on-Windermere and still have time for a decent day out).

The bus stops by the impressive **Grizedale Visitor Centre** (daily: Easter–Oct 10am–5pm; Nov–Easter 10am–4pm; free; ⓣ01229/860010, ⓦwww.forestry.gov.uk/grizedaleforestpark), and there's also a big car park nearby (fee charged). The centre is the forest's information and activity hub, where you can find out about anything from hiking conditions to entertainment programmes, including summer outdoor theatre. Across the courtyard is the **Café in the Forest** (open from 9.30am, meals £4–7.50), which is both restaurant and coffee shop, with a big outdoor terrace overlooking an excellent children's playground. There's a takeaway and ice-cream counter too.

For bike rental, follow the signs to **Grizedale Mountain Bikes** (daily from 9.30am, last rental at 3pm, though hours/days may vary; ⓣ01229/860369, ⓦwww.grizedalemountainbikes.co.uk), which has a wide variety of models available (from £15 for 4hr, full-day rental from £22), including "tag-alongs" and trailers for kids, as well as route maps and cycling gear.

Broughton-in-Furness

Southwest of Coniston Water, a quiet triangle at the southern edge of the National Park is anchored by the small market town of **BROUGHTON-IN-FURNESS**. It dates back to medieval times, though its aspect is pure Georgian. Tall houses surround an attractive square, complete with spreading chestnut tree, commemorative obelisk, stone fish slabs and stocks. In the eighteenth century the market was a staging post for wool, wood and cattle, shipped out of the area from the nearby Duddon estuary. Follow Church Street to the edge of town and you'll reach the **church of St Mary Magdalene**, originally twelfth century though now much restored. The town's only literary connection is a slight one: the scapegrace Brontë brother, Branwell, taught here briefly before terminally pickling himself in Haworth.

Just west of the village at **Duddon Bridge** is the turning off the A595 for Ulpha and the Duddon Valley (see next section), and it's only another mile or so beyond to the minor Broadgate turn-off (keep an eye out, it's on the right) for access to the wonderful **Swinside Stone Circle** (always open; free). A mile up the narrow road you can park by the verge at Cragg Hall and then follow the rough Swinside Farm track another mile on foot (there's a bridleway sign, 20min walk) to the fifty-odd ancient stones, which stand in a natural amphitheatre surrounded by undulating fells. It's a magical spot, with the local name for the stones, Sunkenkirk, reflecting an old belief that the devil sunk the stones of an ancient church (kirk) into the ground. Hardy pagan souls troop up here for a winter solstice ceremony each year.

Practicalities

Broughton is only ten miles from Coniston (along the A593, via Torver) and it's a handy stop en route to Ulverston or up the west coast towards Ravenglass. The most frequent **bus services** to Broughton are from the south on the #511 (not Sun), from Ulverston, every hour and a half, or twice a day from Millom.

The community-run **Broughton Information Centre** is in the old town hall on The Square (daily 10am–12.30pm & 1.30–4pm; ⓣ01229/716115, ⓦwww.broughton-in-furness.co.uk), while down Princes Street is a range of proper local shops, including butcher, greengrocer and fantastic **bakery-café**, the *Broughton Village Bakery* (closed Mon; ⓣ01229/716284, ⓦwww.broughtonvillagebakery.co.uk), which uses organic flour and Fair Trade ingredients in a terrific range of breads, cakes, quiches, soups and sandwiches. There are a couple of pleasant old **pubs**, like the *Manor Arms* on The Square, and **B&B** across from here at the *Square Café*, at Annan House (ⓣ01229/716388, ⓦwww.thesquarecafe.biz; ❷). You'll find more rooms at the *Black Cock Inn* on Princes Street (ⓣ01229/716529, ⓦwww.blackcockinncumbria.com; ❸) – this is the local favourite for bar meals (mains £8–15), while the best country-pub choice is the venerable *Blacksmiths' Arms* (ⓣ01229/716824, ⓦwww.theblacksmithsarms.com) at **Broughton Mills**, just over two miles to the north off the A593.

The Duddon Valley

A mile west of Broughton, a minor road leads from Duddon Bridge up the stunning **Duddon Valley**, twisting and turning its increasingly dramatic way northeast to the foot of the Wrynose and Hardknott passes. Wordsworth wrote a sequence of 34 sonnets about the valley (published as *The River Duddon* in

Walks in the Duddon Valley

Duddon Valley seems like a million miles from the main lakeland tourist spots, even though Coniston Water is within tramping distance away to the east. Consequently, local walks are likely to be enjoyed alone and the two classics below show you very different terrains and views.

Harter Fell and Hardknott

If you just want to knock off a peak, you can climb from the car park at Birks Bridge through the forestry land to the west to ascend **Harter Fell** (2140ft), whose summit is a jumble of rocky outcrops with excellent views. It'll take a couple of hours, up and down. But a good, rugged circular walk (7 miles; 4hr) from Birks Bridge climbs first north to **Hardknott Pass** and then down to the Roman fort there, which is a good place for a picnic. Then you climb again to reach Harter Fell from around the back, followed by a final descent through the plantation land to the bridge and the river.

A Dunnerdale Round

The rolling, rounded **Dunnerdale Fells**, east of Ulpha, have some fantastic views up into the central Lakes and south to the Duddon estuary and the glinting sea. An easy **Dunnerdale Round** (5 miles; 2hr 30min) starts from just south of Ulpha Bridge, up the signposted bridleway to Kiln Bank Cross. You walk east over towards the minor Kiln Bank Cross road and then climb up to **Stickle Pike** and across to **Great Stickle** for some wonderful views, before returning to the Ulpha Bridge road via Black Stones.

See Basics, p.42, for general walking advice in the Lakes; recommended maps are detailed on p.50.

1820), his conclusion – "Still glides the Stream, and shall for ever glide" – a comment on the ephemeral nature of man. Lofty thoughts indeed as you navigate around the rocky outcrops and through the wandering sheep crowding the road.

On warm days cars line the verges at **Ulpha Bridge**, five miles north of Broughton, as picnics are spread on the riverbanks and kids plummet from the bridge into the water. A small post office/shop a little way up from the bridge (near the Eskdale road junction) sells ice cream. At **Seathwaite**, another three winding miles along the road, there's the excellent *Newfield Inn* (see p.144), and a popular short walk to **Wallowbarrow Crag**, below which the river tumbles through a gorge. Beyond Seathwaite the road is ever more tortuous, though there's parking and picnic space a couple of miles further north close to **Birks Bridge**, an ancient crossing which spans a twenty-foot-deep chasm teeming with brown trout. Shortly after Birks Bridge the head of the valley widens dramatically at Dale Head, whose "Big Sky" perspective is quite out of keeping with the confined Lakes – more New Zealand than Cumbria. The river is at its widest here, and at the bridge and junction of **Cockley Beck** you can debate the dubious pleasures of attempting your onward route: west over Hardknott Pass into Eskdale or east over Wrynose Pass to Little Langdale; both passes require careful driving or, in the case of out-of-condition cyclists, an oxygen tent. *Cockley Beck Farm* (Ⓣ01229/716480) by the bridge has a farmhouse tearoom. Writer John Pepper spent several winters in a simple farm cottage here, recounted in his classic "back to nature" book, *Cockley Beck*, marvelling at a place where "peaks rose into the stars like psalms" but enduring temperatures that "plummeted so dramatically, even dreams froze".

Practicalities

There's a very slow early-morning **postbus** once a day (not Sun) from Broughton-in-Furness to Cockley Beck, via Ulpha and Seathwaite; a quicker afternoon service (Mon–Fri) only goes as far as Seathwaite. Realistically, though, you need your own transport to see much of the Duddon Valley – or be prepared to walk or cycle. There's plenty of **information** on ⓦwww.duddonvalley.co.uk, including links to lots of local B&Bs and holiday cottages.

Accommodation and food

Newfield Inn Seathwaite ⓣ01229/716208, ⓦwww.seathwaite.freeserve.co.uk. One of those classic lakeland country inns, with a dark, rustic interior, slate floors, local beers on tap and a garden which looks up onto the fells. Food is a hearty mix of things like steak pie, farmhouse ham-and-eggs and blackboard specials (served daily between noon and 9pm, dishes £5–10). Two inexpensive self-catering flats are also available by the night. Parking.

Troutal Farm Seathwaite ⓣ01229/716235, ⓦwww.troutalfarm.co.uk. Up the road towards Birks Bridge is this working Herdwick sheep farm, where a couple of pretty B&B rooms are available in the Victorian farmhouse. Feel like mucking in? The owners offer sheepdog handling courses (from £40, see ⓦwww.lakedistrictsheepdogexperience.co.uk) with the farm collies. Parking. No credit cards. ③

Travel details

All timetables can be checked on Traveline ⓣ0871/200 2233, ⓦwww.traveline.info.
For Cross-Lakes Experience bus-and-launch information call ⓣ015394/45161, or follow the links to current timetables on ⓦwww.lake-district.gov.uk.

From Coniston

Bus #505 "Coniston Rambler" to: Hawkshead (16min), Ambleside (35min), Brockhole (41min), Windermere (47min). Service operates Easter–Oct roughly hourly; Nov–Easter frequency is much reduced.
Bus #X12 (Mon–Sat 7 daily) to: Torver (7min), Ulverston (40min).
Cross-Lakes Experience (up to 10 daily): services from Coniston *Waterhead Hotel* to Hawkshead (14min), with connections on to Hill Top and Ferry House, Sawrey (for launch to Bowness). Service operates Sat & Sun from mid-Feb, then daily Easter–Oct.

From Hawkshead

Cross-Lakes Experience (up to 9 daily): minibus to Hill Top (7min) and Ferry House, Sawrey (15min, for launch connection to Bowness); also to Coniston *Waterhead Hotel* (14min, to connect with the Coniston Launch service to Brantwood and Coniston). Service operates daily Easter–Oct.
Bus #X30, "Grizedale Wanderer" (4 daily): to Moor Top (5min) and Grizedale Visitor Centre (10min). Service operates daily Easter–Oct.
Bus #X31, "Tarn Hows Tourer" (Mon–Fri 8 daily, Sat & Sun 3 daily): to Tarn Hows (10min). Service operates daily Easter–Oct.

Writers and artists

The Lake District stands out on the literary and artistic map of England, as prominent as Shakespeare's Stratford-upon-Avon, the Brontë's Haworth and Constable's Stour Valley. But it's not just "Wordsworth's Grasmere" that's the draw, though the poet, his homes and his extended circle form the undoubted focus of most visits. Since the eighteenth century, a wide variety of artists and writers have been drawn to every corner of the region, all looking for inspiration in its unrivalled combination of light, lakes and mountains.

Samuel Taylor Coleridge ▲

Wordsworth's final home, Rydal Mount ▼

The Lake Poets

Wordsworth, Coleridge and Southey are the "Lake Poets" of popular description, a clique of fluctuating friendships with a shared passion for the Lake District at its core. Only **William Wordsworth** (1770–1850) – born in Cockermouth, schooled in Hawkshead, longtime resident of Grasmere – could be considered a true local, but it was actually as a young man in England's west country that he first forged his relationship with **Samuel Taylor Coleridge** (1772–1834), with whom he published the landmark *Lyrical Ballads* in 1798. When Wordsworth moved to Grasmere the following year, Coleridge soon followed as, later, did Coleridge's brother-in-law **Robert Southey** (1774–1843), who settled in nearby Keswick, and the interconnections between the three played out across the years. There's an argument, too, for extending the bounds of the renowned triumvirate to include **Dorothy Wordsworth** (1771–1855), the poet's sister. She devoted her life to her brother and his work, and William placed great reliance on the observations recorded in her journal.

Not just Wordsworth…

Grasmere's towering presence isn't the only literary name in the Lakes. Journalist, critic, essayist and "opium-eater" **Thomas De Quincey** moved to the Lakes specifically to meet the famous poet and even lived in the Wordsworths' former home, Dove Cottage (see p.104). Victorian social philosopher and art critic **John Ruskin** settled at Brantwood (see p.129) in 1872 and much of his feeling for the countryside permeated through to two later literary immigrants – **Arthur Ransome** (p.140), writer of the children's classic *Swallows and Amazons*, and Beatrix Potter, whose favourite lakeland spots feature in her timeless stories. Potter, in fact, is the only serious rival to Wordsworthian dominance, with her home at Hill Top (p.137), a gallery in Hawkshead (p.133) and a museum in Bowness (p.63) all packed with visitors throughout the year. Other well-known writers include self-appointed champion of the region Hunter Davies (born in Scotland but raised in Carlisle; diverse biographer of – among others – The Beatles, Wainwright, Wordsworth and Wayne Rooney) and his Carlisle-born wife, the biographer and novelist Margaret Forster, both long-time residents of Loweswater. Finally, there's broadcaster and writer Melvyn Bragg, born in Wigton, whose series of historical and autobiographical novels (p.274) captures the very essence of Cumbria through the ages.

Art and the Romantics

The move from classicism to the so-called Picturesque Movement gradually made the grandeur of the Lakes an acceptable subject for artists of the Romantic period. Engraved views by William Bellers and others had been popular since the 1750s, but the sheer sweep of the landscape moved to the fore only with the work of Joseph Farington in the 1770s. There was a visit by Thomas Gainsborough towards the end of his life in 1783, while J.M.W. Turner toured the Lakes in 1797, and later exhibited oils of Buttermere and Coniston at the Royal Academy. Although a young John Constable had yet to make his reputation when he visited in the autumn of 1806, he produced many lakeland sketches and watercolours in which can be seen the first strivings towards his mature style.

▲ Ruskin's Brantwood, near Coniston

▼ Swallows and Amazons boat

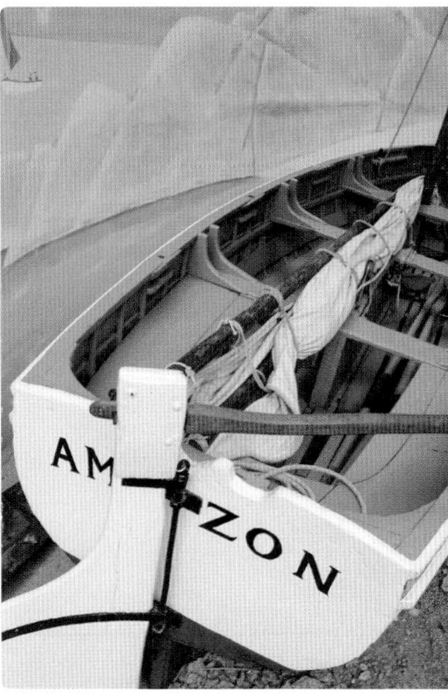

▼ *View of Skiddaw & Derwentwater*, Joseph Farington

Dove Cottage, Grasmere ▲

Ruskin's grave, Coniston ▼

Literary beginnings...

▸▸ **Wordsworth House**, Cockermouth. Where it all began – the birthplace of William and Dorothy Wordsworth has been lovingly restored by the National Trust as a living museum. See p.249.

▸▸ **Coniston Water**. The Swallows and Amazons were born from Arthur Ransome's childhood holidays here. See p.123.

▸▸ **Orrest Head**, Windermere. The very first lakeland hill climbed by fellwalker extraordinaire, Alfred Wainwright. See p.59.

▸▸ **Dove Cottage**, Grasmere. Opium-eater Thomas De Quincey started his literary career in the Wordsworths' old house. See p.104.

▸▸ **Hawkshead Grammar School**, Hawkshead. See the wooden desk at Wordsworth's first school, where he wrote his earliest surviving piece of poetry. See p.132.

... and ends

▸▸ **St Oswald's Church**, Grasmere. One of Britain's most visited literary shrines is home to the graves of William Wordsworth and his family. See p.96.

▸▸ **Haystacks, Buttermere**. Where else would you expect Wainwright's ashes to be scattered, but high in the clouds up a 1900ft mountain? See p.204.

▸▸ **Rusland Church**, near Grizedale Forest. Burial place of Arthur Ransome and his wife. See p.141.

▸▸ **Claife Heights**, Far Sawrey. Somewhere up here – and no one knows exactly where – were scattered the ashes of Beatrix Potter, at her request. See p.138.

▸▸ **St Andrew's Church**, Coniston. A magnificent carved Celtic cross marks the grave of Victorian writer, art critic and social philosopher John Ruskin. See p.124.

Keswick, Derwent Water and the north

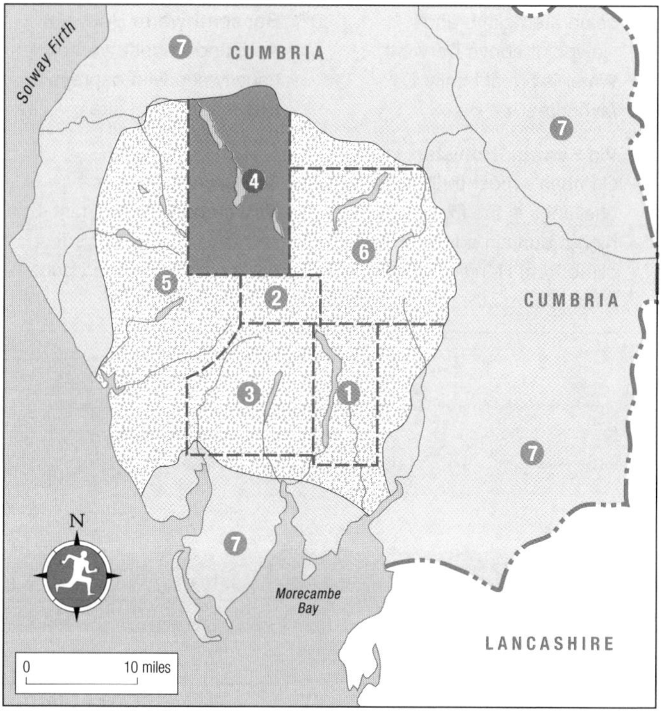

CHAPTER 4

Highlights

* **Castlerigg Stone Circle** The mysterious standing stones above Keswick are a brooding presence. See p.152

* **Evening cruise on Derwent Water** Sit back and enjoy the sunset as the shadows fall across the lake. See p.161

* **Climbing Cat Bells** This celebrated climb and viewpoint above Derwent Water is a real family favourite. See p.163

* **Via Ferrata, Honister** Cumbria's most thrilling challenge is the fixed-rope high-mountain adventure climb from Honister Slate Mine. See p.169

* **St John's in the Vale** This hidden valley has some splendid walking and you can stop for ice cream at Low Bridge End Farm. See p.170

* **Whinlatter Forest Park** Bike, hike and Go Ape in England's only mountain forest. See p.173

* **View the ospreys, Bassenthwaite** Between April and August, you can usually see wild ospreys on Bassenthwaite Lake. See p.175

* **Old Crown, Hesket Newmarket** Enjoy a pint and a curry in Britain's first co-operatively owned pub. See p.179

▲ Cat Bells

Keswick, Derwent Water and the north

Keswick – main town in north Lakeland – stands on the shores of beautiful Derwent Water, backed by the imposing heights of Skiddaw and Blencathra. Despite its long history as a market and mining town, it's now almost entirely devoted to the tourist trade, though most of Keswick's visitors are the type who like to rock-hop in the dramatic surroundings rather than clamber from tour-bus to gift shop. Consequently, there's slightly less of the themed lakeland packaging that afflicts the southern towns, and rather more of an outdoors air, with walkers steadily coming and going from the hills. The town also has solid literary connections – not with Wordsworth for a change, but with the other members of the poetical triumvirate, Samuel Taylor Coleridge and Robert Southey, who both settled in Keswick in the early years of the nineteenth century.

Derwent Water lies just a few minutes' walk from the town centre, its launch service providing easy access to long-famed beauty spots such as Ashness Bridge, Watendlath and the Lodore Falls. And even with just a day in town you should take in the charms of **Borrowdale**, the glorious meandering valley to the south of Derwent Water that's been a source of inspiration to artists and writers over the centuries. The Borrowdale settlements of Rosthwaite, Seatoller, Stonethwaite and Seathwaite are the jumping-off points for the walking routes to the peaks around **Scafell Pike**, the Lake District's (and England's) highest mountain.

Keswick also makes a good base for climbing either of its shadowing northern bulks, **Skiddaw** or **Blencathra** – the first, one of the four Lakes' mountains that clocks in at over the magic 3000-feet mark; the second, a couple of hundred feet lower but with several rather more challenging approaches. Also north of town lies **Bassenthwaite Lake**, from where minor roads and footpaths head northeast into the region known locally as **Back o' Skiddaw**, a little-visited neck of the Lakes hidden behind Skiddaw itself. This is as off the beaten track as it gets in the National Park, though handsome villages such as **Caldbeck** and the unsung heights of **Carrock Fell** make a trip worthwhile. East of Keswick, the old railway line footpath makes a fine approach to the little village of **Threlkeld**, from where some are drawn south through bucolic **St John's in the Vale** to **Thirlmere**, the Lake District's largest reservoir.

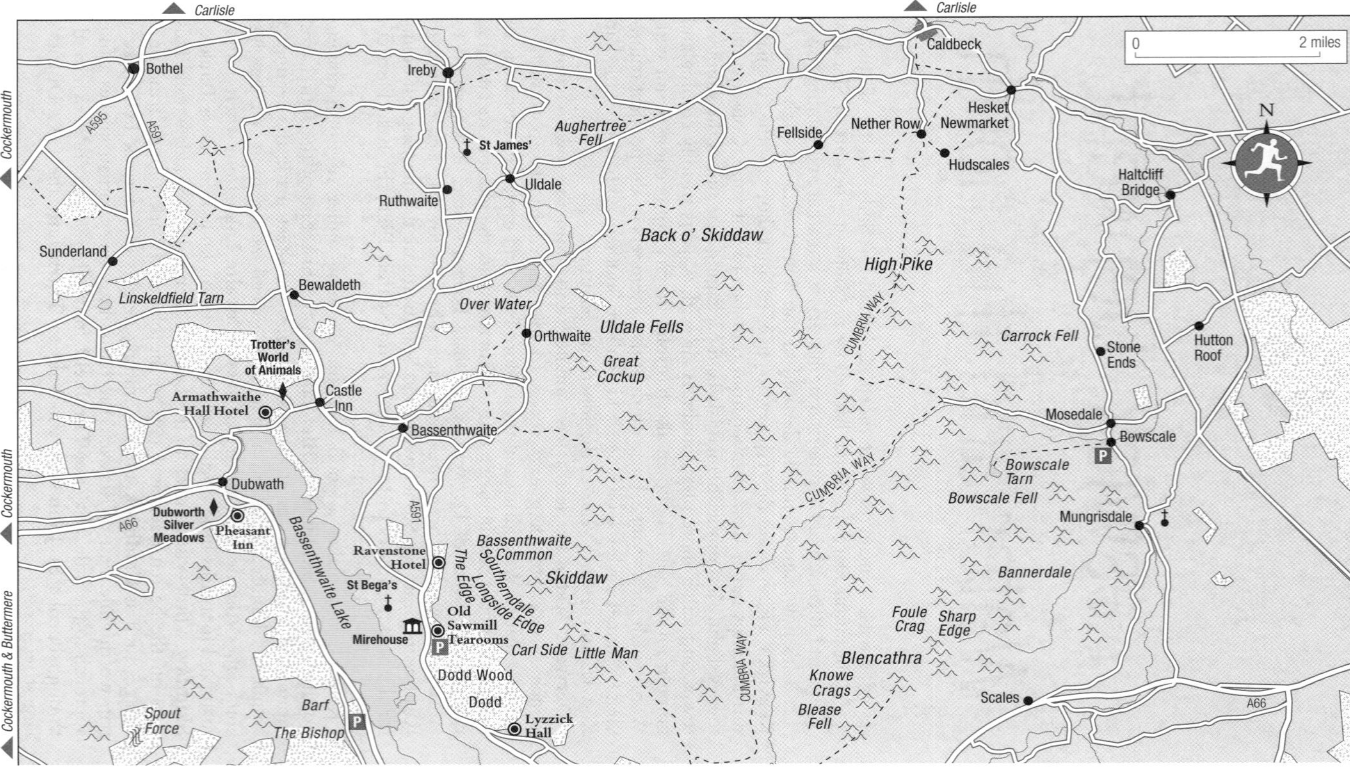
Carlisle
Carlisle
0
2 miles
N
Caldbeck
Bothel
Ireby
Hesket Newmarket
Nether Row
Fellside
Hudscales
Aughertree Fell
St James'
Uldale
Ruthwaite
Haltcliff Bridge
Back o' Skiddaw
High Pike
Sunderland
Bewaldeth
Linskeldfield Tarn
Over Water
Orthwaite
Uldale Fells
Carrock Fell
Stone Ends
Hutton Roof
Great Cockup
Trotter's World of Animals
Armathwaithe Hall Hotel
Castle Inn
Bassenthwaite
Mosedale
Bowscale
Bowscale Tarn
Bowscale Fell
CUMBRIA WAY
CUMBRIA WAY
CUMBRIA WAY
Dubwath
Dubworth Silver Meadows
Pheasant Inn
A66
A595
A591
A591
Bassenthwaite Lake
Ravenstone Hotel
Bassenthwaite Common
The Edge
Southerndale
Longside Edge
Skiddaw
Mungrisdale
Bannerdale
St Bega's
Mirehouse
Old Sawmill Tearooms
Carl Side
Little Man
Foule Crag
Sharp Edge
Blencathra
Knowe Crags
Blease Fell
Dodd Wood
Dodd
Lyzzick Hall
Barf
The Bishop
Spout Force
Scales
A66
Cockermouth
Cockermouth
Cockermouth & Buttermere
Penrith & Ullswater

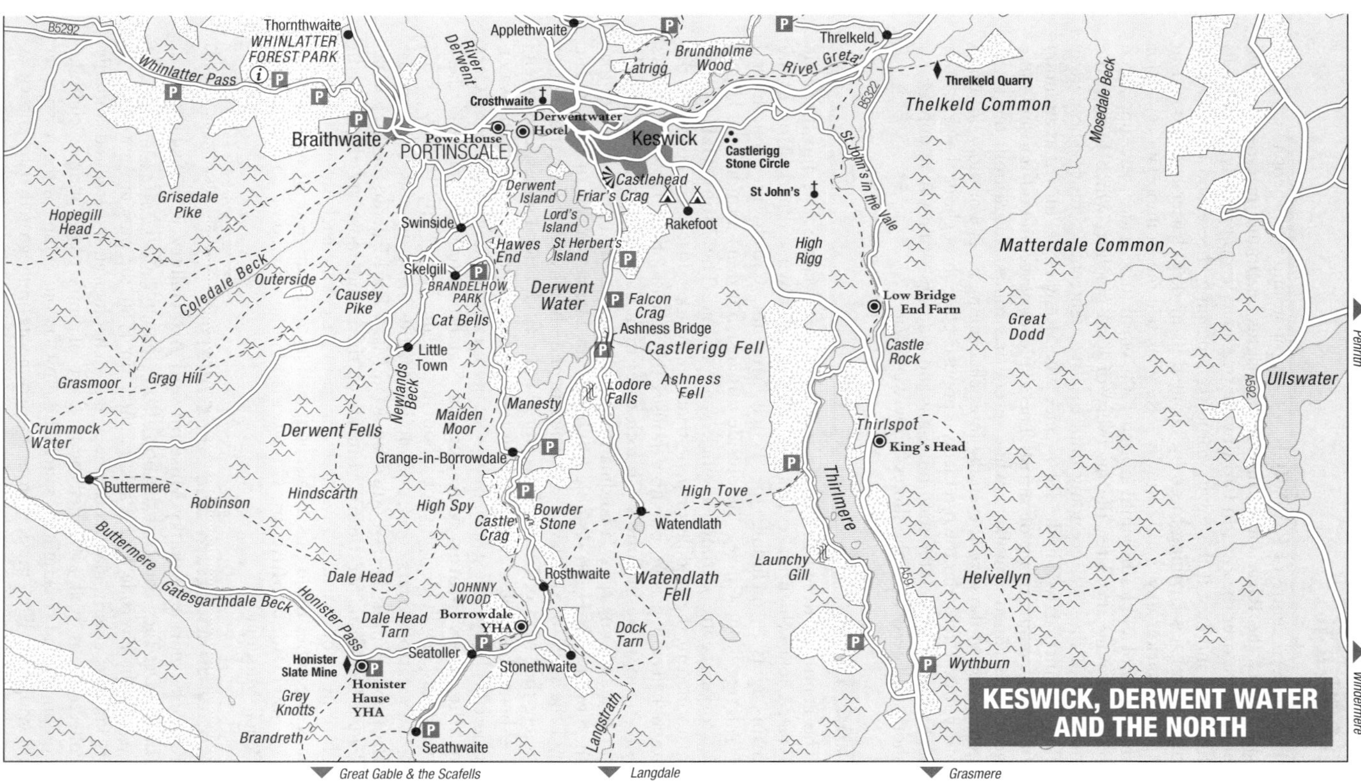

KESWICK, DERWENT WATER AND THE NORTH
B5292
Thornthwaite
WHINLATTER FOREST PARK
Whinlatter Pass
Applethwaite
River Derwent
Brundholme Wood
Latrigg
Threlkeld
River Greta
Threlkeld Quarry
B5322
Thelkeld Common
Mosedale Beck
Crosthwaite
Derwentwater Hotel
Powe House
Braithwaite
PORTINSCALE
Keswick
Castlerigg Stone Circle
St John's in the Vale
St John's
Castlehead
Friar's Crag
Rakefoot
Derwent Island
Lord's Island
St Herbert's Island
Hawes End
Grisedale Pike
Hopegill Head
Swinside
High Rigg
Matterdale Common
Skelgill
BRANDELHOW PARK
Derwent Water
Falcon Crag
Ashness Bridge
Castlerigg Fell
Outerside
Coledale Beck
Causey Pike
Cat Bells
Low Bridge End Farm
Great Dodd
Castle Rock
Little Town
Grasmoor
Grag Hill
Newlands Beck
Lodore Falls
Ashness Fell
A592
Ullswater
Penrith
Manesty
Maiden Moor
Crummock Water
Derwent Fells
Thirlspot
King's Head
Grange-in-Borrowdale
Buttermere
Robinson
Hindscarth
High Spy
Bowder Stone
Castle Crag
High Tove
Watendlath
Thirlmere
Launchy Gill
A591
Helvellyn
Buttermere
Dale Head
Rosthwaite
Watendlath Fell
JOHNNY WOOD
Gatesgarthdale Beck
Honister Pass
Dale Head Tarn
Borrowdale YHA
Dock Tarn
Seatoller
Honister Slate Mine
Honister Hause YHA
Stonethwaite
Wythburn
Windermere
Grey Knotts
Brandreth
Langstrath
Seathwaite
Great Gable & the Scafells
Langdale
Grasmere

Keswick

The modern centre of **KESWICK**, a town of around 5000 people, sits south and east of the River Greta, though its origins lie around an early medieval church just over the river in Crosthwaite. Scattered farms probably provided its first local industry, if the town's name (*kes*, meaning cheese, and *wic*, meaning dairy farm) – is anything to go by. Granted its market charter by Edward I in 1276 – **market day** is still Saturday – Keswick became an important centre for trading wool and leather until around 1500, when these trades were supplanted by ore-mining and, later, the discovery of local graphite, which formed the mainstay of the local economy until the late eighteenth century. The railway (long defunct) arrived in the 1860s, since when Keswick has turned its attention fully to the requirements of tourists. There's plenty of accommodation and some good cafés aimed at walkers, while several bus routes radiate from the town, getting you to the start of even the most challenging hikes. For those not up to a day on the fells, the town remains a popular place throughout the year, with its handsome park, interesting museums and old pubs – and you're only ever a short stroll away from the shores of Derwent Water.

The Town

The centre of Keswick fills the space between Main Street and the wide River Greta, which makes a lazy curve through town and park. Most of the main sights – including the Pencil Museum, Crosthwaite church and Castlerigg Stone Circle – lie outside this area, but don't abandon the largely Victorian centre without a quick walk around. The **Moot Hall** (1813), marooned in the middle of pedestrianized Market Place, was formerly the town hall and prison, but now houses the tourist office. Down St John's Street, sandstone **St John's Church** dates from the same year, notable only for its handsome spire (a landmark from all over town) and for the fact that the novelist Sir Hugh Walpole – who set his Herries novels in Borrowdale and the Back o' Skiddaw – is buried in the churchyard: follow the sign to where the "Man of Letters, Lover of Cumberland, Friend of his fellowmen" lies beneath a Celtic cross, looking towards the west side of Derwent Water, where his house still stands. By way of quite extraordinary contrast, the **Cars of the Stars Motor Museum**, on Standish Street (Easter–Nov daily, weekends only in Dec, plus Feb school hols, 10am–5pm; £5; ⓣ017687/73757, ⓦwww.carsofthestars.com), does no less than its name suggests. The original Batmobile, Emma Peel's Lotus Elan, Mad Max's Ford Falcon, the *Back to the Future* Delorean, Mr Bean's Mini all of these and more are displayed in glorious incongruity in a restored garage in a Keswick back-street. (Incidentally, the James Bond cars, boats, buggies and props are now all on display in the sister **Bond Museum**, ⓦwww.thebondmuseum.com, up behind the Pencil Museum.)

Keswick Museum and Art Gallery

Keswick's gloriously quirky **Museum and Art Gallery** is on Station Road (Easter–Oct Tues–Sat and bank hols 10am–4pm; free; ⓣ017687/73263), at the edge of the riverside **Fitz Park**. Founded in 1780, the museum is a classic of its kind, its elderly glass cases preserving archeological, mineral and butterfly collections, as well as stuffed birds, a set of lion's teeth, antique climbing equipment and cockfighting spurs. The most famous exhibit is the massive set of xylophone-like "musical stones" – cordierite-impregnated slate known as

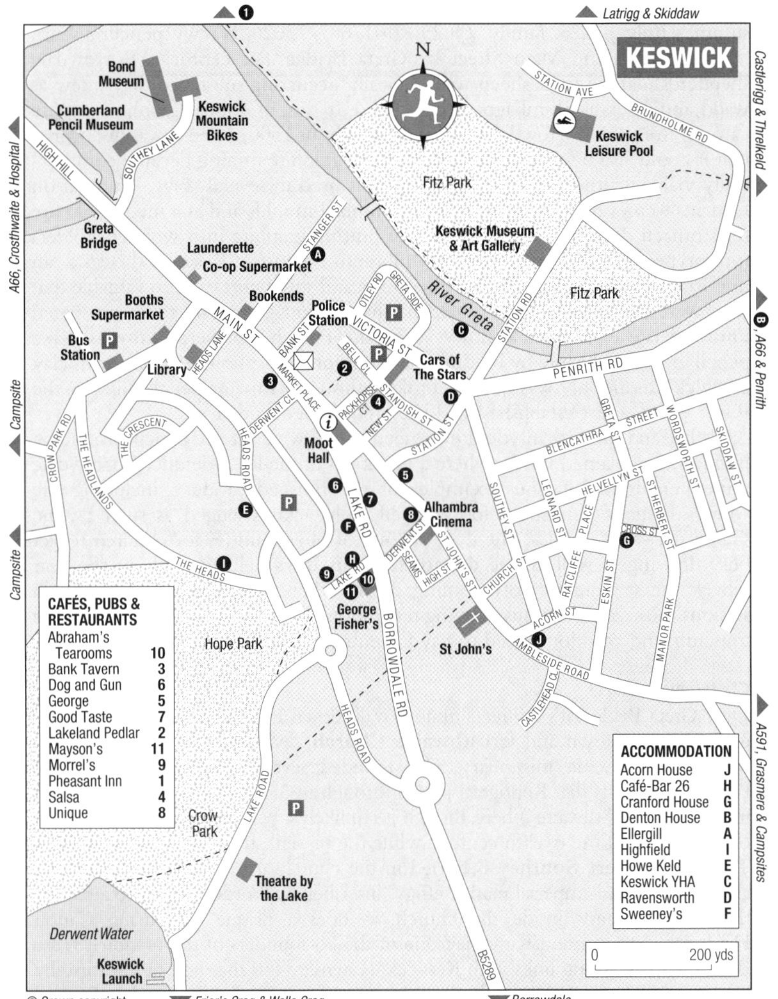

hornfels – which sound in tune when you strike them. They were collected from the Skiddaw hillsides by musical stonemason Joseph Richardson in the 1830s, who painstakingly fashioned them into instruments, added percussion and bells and then toured Victorian England with his sons as the "Rock, Bell and Steel Band". The stones came to the museum in 1917, and sometimes now go out on tour (but you can hear tunes played on them at Ⓦwww.myspace.com/musicalstones). Meanwhile, under protective covers in the literary room sits a huge array of letters, manuscripts and poems by Southey, Wordsworth, De Quincey, (Hartley) Coleridge, Walpole and Ruskin.

Cumberland Pencil Museum

For the town's industrial history, you need to head for the entertaining **Cumberland Pencil Museum** (daily 9.30am–5pm, hours extended in summer hols; £3.25, family £8.25; ⓣ017687/73626, ⓦwww.pencilmuseum.co.uk), west along Main Street by Greta Bridge. For centuries Borrowdale shepherds marked their sheep with a locally occurring substance they knew as wadd and, later, as plumbago or black lead. It was, of course, graphite (a pure carbon) from the Borrowdale fells, and after about 1500, when it was discovered that it could also be carved and cut to shape, graphite mining became commercially viable. In the early days, graphite was used in several ways – rubbed on firearms to prevent rusting, to make cannonball moulds and as a medicinal cure for stomach disorders. With the idea of putting graphite into wooden holders (prototype pencils were used by Florentine artists), Keswick became an important pencil-making town – the mines and shipments were so valuable that they were put under armed guard to thwart smugglers. The town prospered until the late eighteenth century, when the French discovered how to make pencil graphite cheaply by binding the common amorphous graphite with clay. Keswick's monopoly was quickly broken, though its major pencil mills by the River Greta – first established in 1832 – continued to thrive.

All this, and more than you'll ever need to know about the pencil-producing business, is explained inside, where a mock-up of the long-defunct Borrowdale mine heralds multifarious examples of the finished product, including the world's longest (almost 26 foot) pencil, duly acknowledged as such by the *Guinness Book of Records*. There are plenty of opportunities for children to get busy drawing as well as free **demonstration days** held throughout the year (check the website for forthcoming dates), when local artists lead hands-on sessions showcasing various drawing techniques. There's also a coffee shop at the museum, and you don't need to pay for entry to use this.

Crosthwaite

Over Greta Bridge, it's a fifteen-minute walk down High Hill and Church Lane to the edge of town and **Crosthwaite Church**, dedicated to St Kentigern (or Mungo), the Celtic missionary who founded several churches in Cumbria. Evidence suggests that Kentigern passed through in 553 AD and planted his cross in the clearing ("thwaite") here, though it's unlikely a permanent church was built on this site until the twelfth century, while the present structure dates from 1523. The poet **Robert Southey** is buried in the churchyard, alongside his wife and children; his quasi-imperial marble effigy (inscribed by Wordsworth, who attended the funeral) stands inside the church, as does a plaque honouring Canon Hardwicke Drummond Rawnsley, one of the co-founders of the National Trust. Both men had strong links with Keswick. Rawnsley was the vicar at Crosthwaite between 1883 and 1917, while Southey moved into his brother-in-law Samuel Taylor Coleridge's house in the town in 1803 and, after Coleridge moved out, continued to live there for the next forty years. Southey was Poet Laureate from 1813 until his death in 1843 and his house, a Georgian pile known as **Greta Hall**, played its part in the Lakes' literary scene: it had a library stuffed with 14,000 books, which Southey delighted in showing to his visitors – Wordsworth (who tended not to hold with libraries) laments in his memorial inscription, "Loved books, no more shall Southey feed upon your precious lore." Greta Hall is now part of Keswick School (closed to the public) whose playing fields lie across from the church.

Castlerigg Stone Circle

Keswick's most mysterious landmark, **Castlerigg Stone Circle** (always open; free), can be reached by path along the disused railway line to Threlkeld (signposted by the *Keswick Country House Hotel*, at the end of Station Road) – after half a mile, look for the signposted turning to the right. The site is a mile

Robert Southey in the Lakes

Few better or more blameless men have ever lived, than he; but he seems to lack colour, passion, warmth.

Nathaniel Hawthorne, *English Notebooks*, 1855

Robert Southey (1774–1843) – his surname, incidentally, pronounced "Sow-thee" and not "Suh-thee" – first visited the Lake District in 1801 at the request of his brother-in-law, Samuel Taylor Coleridge. The two poets already had a spiky relationship – a failed plan to form a Utopian society abroad dwindled into recriminations later as, having married Edith Fricker in 1795, Southey was accused of pushing Coleridge into an unhappy marriage with her sister, Sara. Moreover, Southey was already a published poet when Coleridge and Wordsworth produced their *Lyrical Ballads* (1798), which Southey reviewed, infamously, for the *Critical Review*. He was harsh about Wordsworth's efforts and dismissive of Coleridge's "Rime of the Ancient Mariner" ("a poem of little merit").

Reconciliation came with the deaths of Coleridge and Sara's second son Berkeley, and Southey and Edith's first child, Margaret Edith. Southey accepted an invitation to visit Coleridge, thinking it might alleviate Edith's grief. The Southeys arrived in September 1803 and Edith soon became pregnant again. Southey enjoyed the landscape and when Coleridge suggested leaving for Malta for his health, Southey agreed to stay on and pay the rent. With Sara Coleridge now effectively a lodger in her own home, Edith's other sister (and widow), Mary Lovell, also arrived to stay – soon the family joke was that Greta Hall was the "Aunt Hill". Coleridge himself never returned to live there, but with Sara Coleridge's three children at Greta Hall, Mary Lovell's son, plus the Southeys' brood, there were now up to ten children in the house at any one time, who Southey entertained with stories and poems, including his *Tale of Three Bears*.

Southey's poetry sold slowly and most of his income was derived from journalism and other works. Early visits to an uncle in Portugal had sparked an interest in the Portuguese empire and a *History of Portugal* was planned on a huge scale, though only the volumes on Brazil (1810–19) were completed. This was the work Southey considered his best, though it was his *Life of Nelson* (1813) – only moderately successful during his life – that later became the work most associated with him.

Although never in financial difficulty, Southey felt compelled to accept the Poet Laureateship in 1813 (the best of the sinecures offered to him over the years). This opened him up to attack from the likes of a young Shelley, who came to stay at Keswick and rather ungratefully belittled Southey as the "paid champion of every abuse and absurdity". At home, Edith was suffering bouts of depression, brought on by the steady loss of her children (four of the Southeys' eight children died), and she was sent to a progressive retreat in 1834 in York but never really regained full mental health. She died in November 1837 and within a year Southey had married an author, Caroline Bowles, twelve years his junior, with whom he had corresponded for almost twenty years.

Southey, ill by now, never consummated the marriage and suffered a stroke. Caroline's arrival at Greta Hall had upset everyone, especially the Southey girls, and when their father died on March 21, 1843 – a silent invalid for the last two years – the family was divided. Son Cuthbert was left in charge of the literary estate, which Wordsworth and others felt he wasn't up to – a point on which they felt vindicated following the poorly received publication of Southey's *Life and Correspondence*. And Southey's vast library – his pride and joy, catalogued by Sara Coleridge and his daughters – was broken up and sold.

further on atop a sweeping plateau, dwarfed by the encroaching fells. Thirty-eight hunks of Borrowdale volcanic stone, the largest almost eight feet tall, form a circle a hundred feet in diameter; another ten blocks delineating a rectangular enclosure within. The array probably had an astronomical or timekeeping function when it was erected four or five thousand years ago, but no one really knows. Whatever its origins, it's a magical spot – and particularly stunning in winter when frost and snow blanket the surrounding fells.

The Stone Circle is signposted off both the A66 and A591 on the way into Keswick. The "Caldbeck Rambler" bus #73/73A runs here twice a day during Easter and summer school holidays and on Saturdays all year, or town bus #86 comes this way twice a day (not Sun).

Practicalities

Buses use the terminal at The Headlands, behind Booths supermarket, off Main Street. The town is a major transport hub, with regular services to all points – see "Travel details" at the end of the chapter for full routes. Parking is easier than in many places: disc zones in town allow one or two hours' free parking, while large **car parks** down Lake Road near the lake, and on either side of Market Place, soak up most of the visiting and shopping traffic. There are no restrictions in the streets off Southey Street (where most of the B&Bs are) or on Brundholme Road behind the park.

The **National Park Information Centre** is in the Moot Hall on Market Place (daily: April–Oct 9.30am–5.30pm; Nov–March 9.30am–4.30pm; Ⓣ017687/72645, Ⓦwww.lake-district.gov.uk). They sell a series of walk leaflets for popular routes (which you can download off the National Park website for free), or you can join a **guided walk** (Easter–Oct daily 10.15am; £10, some longer walks £12). These depart from the Moot Hall, where a schedule is posted, from lakeside rambles to mountain climbs; just turn up with a packed lunch. There's **online information** for the Keswick area at Ⓦwww.dokeswick.com and www.keswick.org.

Accommodation

B&Bs and guesthouses cluster around Southey, Blencathra, Church and Eskin streets, in the grid off the A591 (Penrith road). Smarter guesthouses and hotels line The Heads, overlooking Hope Park, a couple of minutes south of the centre on the way to the lake, and there's also a clutch of guesthouses and hotels out at **Portinscale**, a small village a couple of miles west of town around the lake. If you're in the mood for an upmarket country-house-hotel experience, Keswick's rugged environs have plenty of choice. The town's riverside **youth hostel** and out-of-town **backpackers** are open all year and usually have space; hostels at nearby Derwent Water and in Borrowdale really require advance reservations in summer. The same applies to the main **campsites**, which are all very popular. For self-catering **cottages** in the area, call local specialists Keswick Cottages (Ⓣ017687/78555, Ⓦwww.keswickcottages.co.uk) or Lakeland Cottages (Ⓣ017687/76065, Ⓦwww.lakelandcottages.co.uk).

In Keswick

Acorn House Ambleside Rd Ⓣ017687/72553, Ⓦwww.acornhousehotel.co.uk. The handsome eighteenth-century house offers nine generously sized rooms with period furniture, including three with antique four-posters. Nice touches proliferate – bedside choccies, and corkscrew and wine-glasses provided – and it's a quiet, friendly base, just 5min from the centre. Breakfasts are good too. Parking. ❸

Café-Bar 26 26 Lake Rd Ⓣ017687/80863, Ⓦwww.cafebar26.co.uk. Four stylishly decorated rooms on the first floor above the café offer a chintz-free base right in the town centre. They're all nice and light, with pretty tiled shower rooms, and there's a car park just 100 yards away. Downstairs is a bright and funky café-bar with squishy sofas and good lunches (not Mon) dishing up the likes of roast veg and feta tart, or haddock fishcakes, for around £7. ❷

Cranford House 18 Eskin St Ⓣ017687/71017, Ⓦwww.cranfordhouse.co.uk. Classy town house B&B, whose appealing rooms feature large comfortable beds and decent linen and furnishings

– you're guaranteed "freedom from flowery wallpaper and doilies". The six rooms include two singles (these share a bathroom), while the two rooms at the top have rooftop views and exposed beams. Breakfast (English, vegetarian or continental) is taken in front of the open fire, and walkers and cyclists can dry clothes, store bikes and browse the books and maps. ❷

Ellergill 22 Stanger St ⓣ017687/73347, ⓦwww.ellergill.co.uk. A very friendly home-from-home, courtesy of owners Robin and Clare, who have grafted a chic European feel onto their restored Victorian house. There are five rooms with leather bedheads and chairs and a splash of deep colour, while some magnificent Lakes photography brightens the breakfast room. Street parking outside. No credit cards. ❷

Highfield The Heads ⓣ017687/72508, ⓦwww.highfieldkeswick.co.uk. Beautifully restored Victorian stone hotel whose eye-catching feature rooms include two perky turrets and a converted chapel, the latter with lots of space and a four-poster bed. Some front rooms have balconies and lake views, all have comfortable beds, and there's garden seating, a bar and a restaurant with a daily-changing menu (dinner included in the price). Parking. ❻

Howe Keld 5–7 The Heads ⓣ017687/72417, ⓦwww.howekeld.co.uk. The Fishers' boutique guesthouse puts local crafts and materials centre-stage, with furniture and floors handcrafted from Lake District trees, plus smart green-slate bathrooms and carpets of Herdwick wool. Soft browns, greens and creams create a very natural tone throughout – you're going to have no problem sleeping soundly in these designer quarters. The breakfast, too, served at handmake oak tables, has a signature style all its own, from the daily home-baked organic bread and Fair Trade coffee to pancakes and syrup, smoked salmon, veggie rissoles and other home-made specialities. Parking. ❹

Ravensworth 29 Station St ⓣ017687/72476, ⓦwww.ravensworth-hotel.co.uk. Small, friendly town-centre hotel that makes a real effort to please. The nine rooms are smartly turned out (and many have fell views), organically grown lakeland lilies adorn the lounge, while breakfast presents a choice of organic tomatoes, locally sourced meats, free-range eggs and the like. There are also maps and printed walks available, and a free parking permit provided. ❸

Sweeney's 18–20 Lake Rd ⓣ0500/600725, ⓦwww.lakedistrictinns.co.uk. Four bright en-suite rooms (including two large twin/family rooms) located above a contemporary bar-brasserie. It makes a comfortable town-centre base, with fell views from some windows, a good breakfast and the town's most spacious beer garden out back. Free parking permit provided. ❸, weekends ❹

Around Keswick

Derwentwater Portinscale, 2 miles west of town, off the A66 ⓣ017687/72538, ⓦwww.coastandcountryhotels.com. See chapter map for location. Traditional three-star lakeside retreat with nice enough rooms in the "classic" (ie standard) range and rather splendid at the "deluxe" level, which come with all sorts of little extras from separate lounge areas to complimentary sherry decanter. You also get lakeside gardens and conservatory, and free use of a nearby health spa and pool. Inclusive dinner rates offer the best deal, or there are self-catering apartments and cottages available at adjacent Derwent Manor. Parking. ❼

Lyzzick Hall Under Skiddaw, A591 ⓣ017687/72277, ⓦwww.lyzzickhall.co.uk. See chapter map for location. A couple of miles northwest of town, this relaxed country-house hotel is set in its own lovely grounds with sweeping views. It's great for an intimate, indulgent weekend away at any time – lovely indoor pool and spa, a terrace for lazy-day drinks and lounges warmed by log fires. You don't need to go anywhere else to eat either, since the restaurant is highly rated: its contemporary Cumbrian menu adds a Spanish twist to many dishes (mussels with *chorizo*, for example). Parking. ❺, superior rooms ❻

Powe House Portinscale, 2 miles west of town, off the A66 ⓣ017687/73611, ⓦwww.powehouse.com. See chapter map for location. For handsome, contemporary style on a budget, you can't beat this quiet retreat near the head of the lake. Bold, bright, light rooms overlook the gardens of this detached country house, and while some are a bit bigger than others (no. 5 is the best), most have king-sized beds and all show a keen eye for design. Parking. ❸

Youth hostels

Denton House Penrith Rd ⓣ017687/75351, ⓦwww.vividevents.co.uk. Keswick's cheapest bed is at the independent backpackers housed in a former stationmaster's house and cadet barracks, a 10min walk from the centre (by the railway bridge, just after the ambulance/fire station). A rolling refurbishment is in hand, but all the basics are in place (kitchen, washing machine, lockers, bike storage, free tea and coffee), while single-sex/mixed dorms range in size from four to twelve beds (58 in total). Breakfast is £3 (when available, usually at weekends). It's also an outdoor activity centre for kayaking, crag-climbing and abseiling (best to pre-book). Office open at least Mon–Fri 9.30am–1.30pm. Parking. No credit cards. Dorm beds £13, weekends £14.

Keswick YHA, Station Rd ⓣ0845/371 9746, ⓔkeswick@yha.org.uk. Once a riverside woollen mill, Keswick's YHA has a new, contemporary look after a major overhaul. Dorms and public areas have been completely revamped, and families, walkers and travellers all seem to approve – it's big (over 90 beds) but you're still advised to book. Facilities are bang up to date, but hostel mainstays are all present and correct (drying room, laundry, lounge, free tea and coffee on arrival), while a restaurant and bar offer good-value meals at lunch and dinner (steak pie, Cumberland sausage, veggie options, mains £7–9). Dorm beds from £17.95 (May–Sept from £21.95), breakfast included.

Campsites

Castlerigg Farm Rakefoot Lane, off A591, Castlerigg ⓣ017687/72479, ⓦwww.castlerigg farm.com. The quiet, family option, just over a mile southeast of the centre. It's mainly for tents and the facilities include a shop, laundry and hayloft café. Closed Nov–Easter.

Castlerigg Hall Rakefoot Lane, off A591, Castlerigg ⓣ017687/74499, ⓦwww .castlerigg.co.uk. Not near the lake, but with views to compensate, this award-winning tent-and-caravan site is the first one you reach up this road, just over a mile southeast of the centre. There are no advance bookings for camping, but tents and pods (standard £34, family pod £39 per night) are kept well away from the caravans and motorhomes. There's a shop, campers' kitchen, laundry, lounge and games room, plus a terrace-restaurant for cooked breakfasts, evening meals and weekly pizza nights. Closed Nov–Easter.

Derwentwater Camping and Caravan Club Site Derwent Water ⓣ017687/72392, ⓦwww .campingandcaravanningclub.co.uk. Big holiday-park site with lakeside camping, just a short walk from the centre (which means it's always busy). Closed Dec & Jan.

Eating, drinking and entertainment

Keswick is a real metropolis compared to anywhere else in the National Park, which means that there's no shortage of places to eat and drink, especially down Lake Road, which is fast becoming Keswick's "food street". Daytime **cafés** are firmly aimed at the walking and shopping crowd – you won't want for a big bowl of soup or a cream tea – and there are some decent **restaurants** and lots of **pubs**, many also serving good food. The two **supermarkets**, Booths (the biggest and best, specializing in locally sourced produce) and the smaller Co-op, are near the bus station, off Main Street.

It's always worth checking to see what's on at the **Theatre by the Lake**, whose repertoire of performances, concerts and events makes Keswick something of a cultural centre for the Lake District. Otherwise, the biggest events in town are the annual **jazz festival** and **mountain festival**, both in May, the June **beer festival**, and the traditional **Keswick Agricultural Show** (August bank holiday), which is the place to learn more about sheepshearing and other rural pursuits.

Cafés

Abraham's Tea Room George Fisher, 2 Borrowdale Rd ⓣ017687/72178. Just looking around the camping and hiking gear in the celebrated outdoors store soon works up an appetite, so all power to the top-floor tearoom – warming mugs of *glühwein*, home-made soups, big breakfasts with free-range eggs, rarebits, open sandwiches and other daily specials. Dishes £4–6.50. Daytime only.

Good Taste 19 Lake Rd ⓣ017687/75973, ⓦwww.simplygoodtaste.co.uk. Delectable deli downstairs, loft-lounge-style coffee house upstairs, serving classy snacks and meals (£3–7), from own-smoked trout to wild boar burgers. Muffins, scones, breads and gourmet sandwiches are made daily too, or you can just kick back with a coffee while the kids raid the big box of toys. And if you like the style, you can buy owner-chef Peter Sidwell's recipe book or come to his cookery classes. Daytime only; closed Sun.

Lakeland Pedlar Henderson's Yard, Bell Close Car Park ⓣ017687/74492, ⓦwww .lakelandpedlar.co.uk. Keswick's best café serves a tasty and inventive range of Mediterranean/ Tex-Mex wholefood veggie dishes, like breakfast burritos, falafel wraps or spicy chilli (£4–8). The bread's home-made and organic, the cakes are great, while a few outdoor tables soak up the sun and look up to the fells. Daytime only, but also open for dinner (Thurs–Sat until 9pm) in school holidays.

Restaurants

Mayson's 33 Lake Rd ⓣ017687/74104. A self-service restaurant under tumbling houseplants – place your order and then tuck into lasagne, moussaka, pies, curries or stir-fries, accompanied by rice and salad, with most things around £6.50–8. It's licensed as well, so you can have a beer or a glass of wine. May–Oct open until 9pm; daytime only rest of the year. No credit cards.

Morrel's 34 Lake Rd ⓣ017687/72666, ⓦwww.morrels.co.uk. Keswick's top spot is a handsome-looking restaurant where Modern British and Mediterranean styles prevail – from duck on parsnip mash to salmon and *pak choi* salad. While it's at the pricier end of Keswick dining (mains £11–17), there's a bargain Sunday *table d'hôte* menu (2/3 courses £13.95/16.50). It's also the closest restaurant to the Theatre by the Lake and opens at 5.30pm for pre-theatre meals. Dinner only, closed Mon.

Salsa 1 New St ⓣ017687/75222, ⓦwww.salsabistro.uk. Billed as a "Mexican bistro", on the right night *Salsa* can be a real buzz (it's best to book at weekends in summer) – have a drink in the downstairs bar, munch a few *nachos* and then move upstairs for hearty portions of fajitas, tacos, ribs, wraps, grilled fish or steak (mains £10–17). There's also a sister Italian bistro, *Strada*, on Lake Rd next to the George Fisher store. Dinner only.

Unique 26 St John's St ⓣ017687/73400, ⓦwww.uniquedining.co.uk. Fine dining in stylish surroundings. The modish menu takes seasonal local produce (Cumbrian veg and cheese, Borrowdale trout, fell-bred lamb) and adds a twist or two, and there's always a decent choice for veggies and fish-eaters (mains £10–16). Dinner only; closed Wed.

Pubs

Bank Tavern 47 Main St ⓣ017687/72663. Currently has a local reputation for its classic bar meals, bangers and mash to rib-eye steak (£8–13), which means that every table is often filled. The beer's good too, while a terrace at the back looks up Market Square.

Dog and Gun 2 Lake Rd ⓣ017687/73463. The best pub in town is a real-ale, open-fire, dog-friendly kind of place, which retains its old slate floor and oak beams. Good beer's a given (a changing selection of local ales, including some from the Keswick Brewing Company), while many come for the food – the house special is a deep bowl of Hungarian goulash with dumplings (£8.50), made every day to a recipe handed down over the years.

George St John St ⓣ017687/72076, ⓦwww.georgehotelkeswick.co.uk. Keswick's oldest inn has bags of character, with snug bars lined with portraits, pictures and curios, and wooden settles in front of the fire. There's a good bistro menu (mains £8–15), which you can eat in the restaurant or bar – roast ham to venison casserole, local trout to a cold fish platter, with gasps reserved for the Desperate Dan-sized "cow pie".

Pheasant Inn Crosthwaite ⓣ017687/72219. More for dining than drinking, this out-of-town Jennings pub has a classier menu than most, say posh fish pie or Moroccan-spiced swordfish (mains £9–13). It's a 10min walk from town, through Fitz Park and just up from the hospital.

Theatre and cinema

Alhambra St John's St ⓣ017687/72195, ⓦwww.lonsdalealhambrakeswick.co.uk. The town's enterprising cinema shows mainstream releases, but there are foreign-language and indie screenings most Thursdays, while Keswick Film Club (ⓦwww.keswickfilmclub.org) puts on art-house movies on Sundays (Oct–March) and hosts an annual Film Festival (in Feb) featuring the best of world cinema.

Theatre by the Lake Lake Rd ⓣ017687/74411, ⓦwww.theatrebythelake.com. England's loveliest theatre hosts a full programme of drama, concerts, exhibitions, readings and talks. "Words By The Water", a literature festival, takes place here in the spring, while the coffee shop is open daily on performance days.

Listings

Bike rental Keswick Mountain Bikes, Southey Hill (by the Bond Museum), Greta Bridge (daily 9am–5pm; ⓣ017687/75202, ⓦwww.keswickmountainbikes.co.uk). From £15–20 per day, plus tag-alongs and trailers for kids.

Bookshop Bookends, 66 Main St (ⓣ017687/75277, ⓦwww.bookscumbria.com), has a good selection of local-interest books and hiking guides, plus discounted books and novels. For secondhand books visit the big Oxfam store, 1 Museum Square, (ⓣ017687/74494).

Car rental Keswick Motor Company, ⓣ017687/72064, ⓦwww.keswickmotorcompany.co.uk.

Walks from Keswick

Keswick walks fall into three categories: strolls down by the lake or up to scenic viewpoints, and the considerably more energetic peak-bagging of Skiddaw and Blencathra. If you've got time to make only one local hike, there's a case for making it up Cat Bells (see Derwent Water, p.163), which forms the distinctive backdrop to many a Keswick view.

Around the lake

The **round-the-lake** route (8 miles; 5–6hr) is available on a leaflet at the National Park information office in Keswick, and it's an easy day out past bays filled with waterfowl and lakeshore woodland. It passes some of the prettiest highlights (Lodore, Manesty Park, Brandlehow), and the real beauty of it is that you can bail out at any point and catch the launch back to Keswick.

Latrigg

Latrigg (1203ft), north of town, gets the vote for a quick climb (45min) to a fine viewpoint – up Bassenthwaite Lake and across Derwent Water to Borrowdale and the high fells. Driving first to the Underscar car park gets you even closer, within twenty minutes of the summit, and the path from this point is now fully accessible for wheelchairs and strollers. For a circular walk (4–6 miles; 2–3hr), follow the eastern ridge to Brundholme, returning through Brundholme wood or along the railway line path.

Friar's Crag, Walla Crag and Castlehead

South of town, the best half-day walk is to **Walla Crag** (1234ft) and back (5 miles; 4hr), approaching via the Derwent Water beauty spot of **Friar's Crag**. At Calf Close Bay you cross the Borrowdale road (B5329) and climb through Great Wood to the summit, which provides terrific views of the lake, St Herbert's Island and the fells beyond. The descent back to town is via Rakefoot, with a possible diversion to **Castlehead** (530ft) for more lake views, with Scafell Pike rising in the distance.

Skiddaw

Easiest of the true mountain walks is the hike up the smooth mound of splintery slate that is **Skiddaw** (3053ft). From the Underscar car park it's a steady (and, it has to be said, boring) walk up a wide, eroded track, with a possible diversion up Skiddaw **Little Man** (2837ft), before reaching the High Man summit. Straight up and down is around five miles and takes about five hours, but there's a much better route back, descending to the southwest, along the ridge above Bassenthwaite formed by Longside Edge, **Ullock Pike** (2230ft) and The Edge, before dropping down into Dodd Wood (8 miles; 7hr). Either catch the bus along the A591 back to Keswick, or keep off the road on the signposted Keswick path from Dodd Wood.

Blencathra

Blencathra (2847ft) – also known as Saddleback – could keep hikers occupied for a fortnight. Wainwright details twelve possible ascents of its summit, and, though made of the same slate as Skiddaw, it's a far more aggressive proposition. Many use Threlkeld as the starting point: easiest route is via Blease Fell and Knowe Crags (an ascent that Wainwright pooh-poohs as too dull); the path starts from the car park by the Blencathra Centre. The more adventurous steer a course up any of the narrow ridges, whose names (Sharp Edge, Foule Crag) don't pull any punches – for most of these, the best starting point is the *White Horse* pub at Scales, another mile and a half up the A66 (towards Penrith) from Threlkeld.

See Basics, p.42, for general walking advice in the Lakes; recommended maps are detailed on p.50.

Hospital Keswick Cottage Hospital, Crosthwaite Rd, Keswick ⓣ017687/67000.
Internet access U-Compute, 48 Main St, upstairs at the post office (Mon–Sat 9am–5.30pm, Sun 9.30am–4.30pm; ⓣ017687/75127). There's also wi-fi access at lots of places around town.
Laundry Keswick Launderette, Main St, next to the Co-op (daily 7.30am–7pm; ⓣ017687/75448).
Outdoor stores George Fisher, 2 Borrowdale Rd (ⓣ017687/72178, ⓦwww.georgefisher.co.uk), is perhaps the most celebrated outdoors store in the Lakes, with a big range of gear, guides and maps, plus boot rental, a daily weather information service and café. Needle Sports, 56 Main St (ⓣ017687/72227, ⓦwww.needlesports.com), is the local climbing and mountaineering specialist. But Keswick also has a dozen other outdoors stores, most found along the western half of Main St, between the post office and the bus station.
Pharmacies Boots, 31 Main St ⓣ017687/72383; Lightfoot's, 25 Main St ⓣ017687/72108; J.N. Murray, 15–17 Station St ⓣ017687/72049.
Police station 8 Bank St ⓣ0845/330 0247, ⓦwww.cumbria.police.uk. Enquiry desk closed Thurs & Sun.
Post office 48 Main St.
Swimming pool Keswick Leisure Pool, Station Rd (Easter–Sept daily 9am–5pm; winter limited hours, call for details; ⓣ017687/72760, ⓦwww.carlisleleisure.com/keswick). It has a wave machine, waterslide, fitness centre and poolside café.
Taxis Davies Taxis ⓣ017687/72676; KLM ⓣ017687/75337, Skiddaw Taxis ⓣ017687/75600.

Derwent Water

Derwent Water may not be that big – three miles long and, at most, a mile wide – but it's a really pretty spot, only five minutes' walk south of the centre of Keswick (down Lake Road and through the pedestrian underpass). Of all the major lakes it's the easiest to get to know quickly, since you can either walk around the entire perimeter or catch the useful launch service that circles the lake at regular intervals. In fact, if you're planning on doing any of the famous walks, like Cat Bells, or visiting the local beauty spots, it's far better to take the boat to the nearest pier since parking is restricted to prevent congestion on the narrow lanes.

First thing, though, is to stand on the northern shore, headed by the grassy banks of Keswick's **Crow Park**, to look down the lake to its crags and islets. **St Herbert's Island**, in the middle of the lake, is thought to be the site of the seventh-century hermitage's cell of St Herbert, disciple and friend of St Cuthbert of Lindisfarne. Roe deer from the surrounding woods sometimes swim across to **Lord's Island**, and there's even a mysterious floating island, which appears only after sustained periods of dry weather.

During the eighteenth and early nineteenth centuries, the lake saw regular regattas, orchestrated initially by Joseph Pocklington, a wealthy banker, for whom the word eccentric seems woefully inadequate. He built himself a house, church and fortress on **Derwent Island** (the house is still there, owned by the National Trust; tours on certain days from June–Aug ⓣ017687/73780, ⓦwww.nationaltrust.org.uk) and appointed himself "Governor and Commander-in-Chief", blasting off brass cannons at the boats. The house that's now *Derwentwater YHA* was also his; he had the rocks behind it dynamited to fashion an artificial waterfall.

The most popular short walk on the lake – no more than ten minutes from the launch piers – is to **Friar's Crag**, a wooded peninsula on the northeastern shore from where medieval pilgrims left for St Herbert's Island to seek the hermit's blessing. The Friar's Crag land was acquired by the National Trust in 1922, and is held in memory of its founder Canon Rawnsley (see feature), though it's long been a beauty spot. Ruskin's childhood visit to Friar's Crag famously inspired "intense joy, mingled with awe", which is a bit over the top, but the grass banks and little rocky coves are very attractive.

The **Keswick Launch** piers are just a few minutes' walk from Keswick town centre and departures are frequent enough to combine a cruise with a walk and a picnic. You can rent **rowboats** and self-drive motorboats at the Keswick Launch piers, though for kayaking, canoeing, sailing and windsurfing you'll need to contact one of the other watersports outlets on the lake, at Portinscale or Lodore. **Bus services** to points around the lake involve

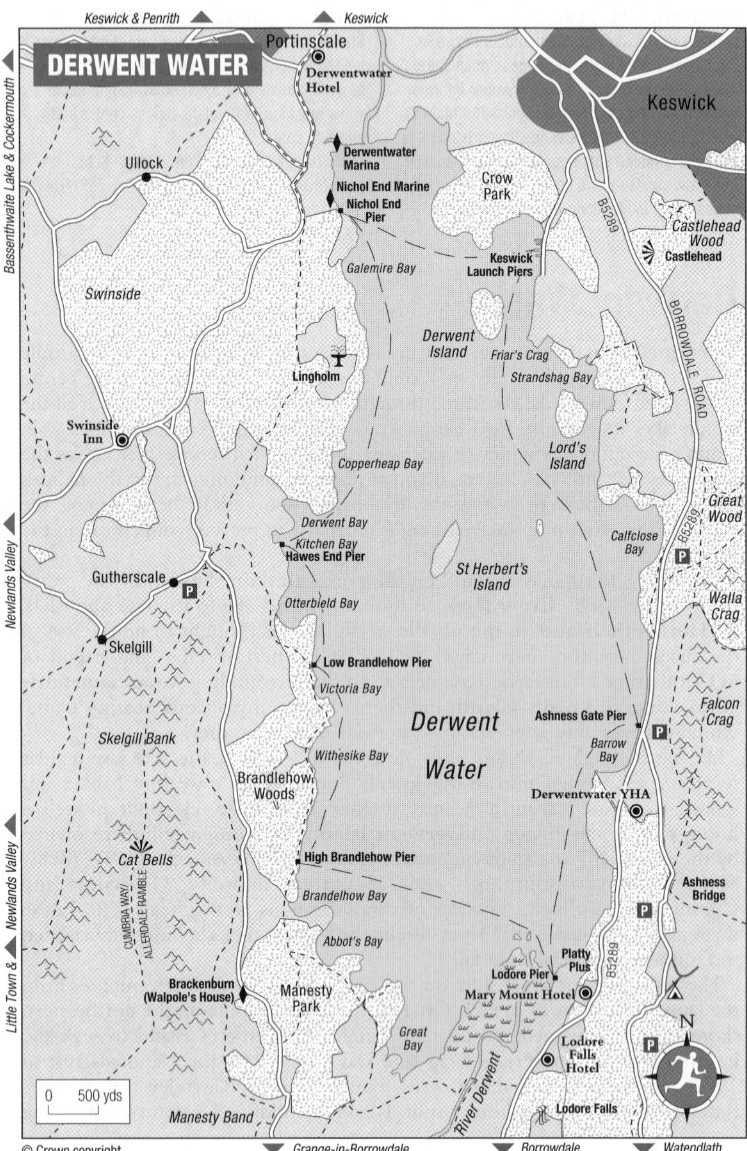

Keswick Launch

Keswick Launch (Ⓣ017687/72263, Ⓦwww.keswick-launch.co.uk) runs services right around the lake calling at six points en route (£1.85 per stage; £8.80 round trip, family £21). Between Easter and the end of November, services run hourly from 10am until 6pm, both clockwise and anticlockwise around the lake (ie, a service leaves every 30min in one direction or another). Services are extended into the early evening from the Spring bank holiday until mid-September, while from December until Easter services depart on Saturdays and Sundays only, three times daily in each direction. There's also an enjoyable one-hour **evening cruise** (£9, family £21) in school summer holidays, with anecdotal commentary and a glass of wine or soft drink included; it's best to buy a ticket earlier in the day to ensure a place.

▲ Keswick Launch

catching either the #78 "Borrowdale Rambler" (operates all year; day rider ticket from £5.60) down the B5289 from Keswick to Seatoller, or the seasonal (Easter–Oct) #77A "Honister Rambler" (day rider ticket from £6.50), which runs along the western shore via Portinscale, Cat Bells (for Newlands Valley) and Grange.

Ashness Bridge, Watendlath and Lodore

The pier at **Ashness Gate** provides access to a narrow road branching south off the B5289 that climbs a steep half-mile to the photogenic **Ashness Bridge**, an old dry-stone packhorse bridge providing marvellous Derwent Water views. The minor road past Ashness Bridge (and a well-used footpath) ends two miles further south at **Watendlath**, an isolated farmstead, tearoom and tarn which can be hopelessly overrun at times in summer. Watendlath – the Norse "end of the lake" – provided the setting for Hugh Walpole's most famous episode of his Herries Chronicles, *Judith Paris* (1931). You can buy a copy in the tearoom and lounge about for an hour or two on the grass, or rent a boat and rod from the farm for a trout-fishing trip on the tarn.

At **Lodore** landing stage there are **kayaks, rowboats and sailboats** for rent at Platty Plus (Ⓣ017687/77282, Ⓦwww.plattyplus.co.uk), and a couple of hotels

Canon Rawnsley and the National Trust

Hardwicke Drummond Rawnsley (1851–1920) was ordained in 1875, gained his first living in the Lakes (at Wray, near Ambleside) two years later, and was appointed vicar at Crosthwaite, Keswick, in 1883. It was a period of rapid industrial development and the conservation-minded Canon Rawnsley found himself opposing the proposed Braithewaite and Buttermere Railway, fighting footpath disputes and lining up with Ruskin (an old Oxford college friend) against the creation of Thirlmere reservoir – though Rawnsley later accepted the needs of the northern cities for water and even attended Thirlmere's official opening. His time served on the County Council and the newly formed Lake District Defence Society convinced him of the need for a preservation society with money and teeth. In 1893, together with Octavia Hill and Sir Robert Hunter, and the backing of the Duke of Westminster, he established the **National Trust**. This received its first piece of donated land (in Wales) the following year: the first parcel of land purchased in the Lake District was that of **Brandlehow woods and park** in 1902, and the Trust went on to acquire much of Derwent Water and Borrowdale by 1908. It's now easily the largest landowner in the Lake District.

Rawnsley remained an active part of the Trust while continuing to preach and write – he produced many collections of lakeland sonnets, poems, histories and guides, including an entertaining book of "reminiscences" of Wordsworth by the local peasantry (none of whom thought the Poet Laureate's poetry was any good). After Rawnsley's wife died in 1916 he retired to Wordsworth's old house at Allan Bank in Grasmere. He married again in 1918, but died only two years later on May 28, 1920.

for lunch or afternoon tea. The bus stops on the road nearby, from where a path heads to the **Lodore Falls**, much visited in Victorian times by the romantically inclined though only really worth the diversion after sustained wet weather. Then, you'll be able to appreciate Robert Southey's magnificent, alliterative evocation of the falls in "The Cataract of Lodore": "Collecting, projecting, receding and speeding, and shocking and rocking, and darting and parting", and so on, for line after memorable line.

Accommodation and food

Derwentwater YHA Barrow House, 2 miles south of Keswick, B5289 (Borrowdale) road ⓣ0845/371 9314, ⓔderwentwater@yha.org.uk. Based in a 200-year-old mansion with fifteen acres of grounds sloping down to the lake. It's a bit far to walk in and out for the shops and pubs, but bus #78 runs past and the Keswick Launch stops at nearby Ashness Gate pier. There are 88 beds, mostly in four- to eight-bedded rooms (the family rooms book up fast), a drying room and laundry, and evening meals available. Parking. Dorm beds from £15.95.

Lodore Falls B5289 (Borrowdale) road ⓣ017687/77285, ⓦwww.lodorefallshotel.co.uk. The most prominent accommodation at this end of Derwent Water, the three-star *Lodore Falls* is a slick, family-oriented operation with extensive lakeshore and woodland gardens, plus leisure centre, tennis court and two pools (one indoor, one outdoor). There are great lake or fell views from all rooms, daytime dining in the lounge-bar (sandwiches and meals £5–10) and a fancier dinner (£34) in the lake-view restaurant. ❻, lake-view room ❼

Mary Mount B5289 (Borrowdale) road ⓣ017687/77223, ⓦwww.marymounthotel.co.uk. Nestling under the crags in four acres of lakeside and woodland garden, this intimate family-run hotel is just a few yards from the Lodore piers. The twenty rooms are either in the main house or the lodge-style bungalow in the grounds, with half a dozen rated "superior" (room 25, for example, has bay windows and big lake views). There's a nice oak-panelled bar serving lunch (sandwich platters and mains £6–10), which you can eat outside on the terrace, a moderately priced restaurant with picture windows (mains £12–15), and they'll pack you a picnic lunch and fill a flask if you ask. ❹, weekends ❺

Cat Bells, Lingholm and Portinscale

Asked to pick a favourite Lake District walk and climb, many would plump for **Cat Bells** (1481ft), a renowned vantage point above the lake's western shore. It's not difficult (possible for all the family), the views from the top are stupendous, and it's easy to combine with the launch to or from Keswick. The name, incidentally, derives from the age-old belief that the fell once harboured a wild cat's den (*bield*, the Norse word for den, was later corrupted to "bells"). Since it featured on the BBC's "Wainwright Walks" series, the Cat Bells walk has become so popular that parking near the foot is now completely restricted and you're encouraged to come by "boat, bus or boot". Most people use the path from Hawes End launch pier, though the longer haul up from Manesty to the south (High Brandlehow launch) has its merits. Return to either launch pier along the lakeside path through Manesty Park and Brandlehow woods and park, allowing, say, two and a half hours for the entire walk. Walpole fans should note that Sir Hugh lived and worked for many years in the lee of Cat Bells, at the house he called **Brackenburn**, by Manesty Park.

The *Swinside Inn* (see "Newlands Valley" below) is only a mile from Hawes End, a welcome stop for a post Cat Bells pint, while a signposted path from Hawes End pier runs all the way back to Keswick, which is only a couple of miles away through the woods and round the top of the lake. Under a mile north of Hawes End you'll pass the entrance to **Lingholm Gardens** – now sadly closed to the public, but featuring fabulous rhododendron displays. Beatrix Potter spent many childhood holidays at the grand house at Lingholm and, hardly surprisingly, the surroundings here and in the lovely Newlands Valley to the southwest (see below) appeared in several of her later stories. Just beyond, there are refreshments at hand at the **lakeside café** (open daily until 4pm, 5.30pm in July & Aug, ⓣ017687/73082, ⓦwww.nicholendmarine.co.uk) at **Nichol End**, a marine store and boat rental place. The name is a corruption of "St Nicholas' Ending", as the site was once an embarkation point for medieval pilgrims crossing to St Herbert's Island (Saint Nicholas being the patron saint of sailors).

After Nichol End, the path joins the main road as it snakes through the village of **Portinscale**, a satellite of Keswick, where you can relax with a drink in the conservatory-bar and lakeside gardens of the *Derwentwater* hotel, before striking off over the River Derwent and through the fields to emerge by Greta Bridge in town.

Newlands Valley

A valley for connoisseurs unfolds along Newlands Beck, to the west of Cat Bells and Derwent Water. Save for the very minor road over Newlands Hause to Buttermere, there's little in the isolated farms and sparse hamlets of the **Newlands Valley** to lure touring drivers. But hikers have the choice of two fine circuits, one following the pastoral valley lowlands, the other tracing the encircling ridges and peaks. The **valley walk** (5 miles; 3hr) follows a path from Hawes End pier to **Little Town** – the main valley hamlet, with an isolated chapel – beyond which can be made out the old Goldscope lead mines. These have been long abandoned, but were a hive of activity as far back as the sixteenth century when German miners were brought here to work the seams. Better, if you (and the weather) are up to it, is the exhilarating **Newlands Horseshoe** (11 miles; 6–7hr), which begins with the ascent of Cat Bells and then links Maiden Moor (1887ft), High Spy (2143ft), Dale Head (2473ft) and Hindscarth (2385ft) in a terrific circular walk above and around the valley. The views, needless to say, are magnificent.

Either walk can be done from Keswick, via the launch to Hawes End, and should culminate in a visit to the valley's only **pub**, the excellent *Swinside Inn* (Ⓣ017687/78253, Ⓦwww.theswinsideinn.com; ❸), three miles from Keswick, whose beer garden gazes up to the encroaching fells.

Borrowdale

Beautiful **Borrowdale** stretches beyond the foot of Derwent Water, south of Keswick, and it's difficult to overstate the attraction of its river flats, forested crags, oak woods and yew trees. Early visiting writers and poets, including Thomas Gray who marvelled at the prospect in 1769, saw it as an embodiment of their Romantic fancy; Turner and Constable came to paint it; and Wordsworth praised its yews, "those fraternal Four of Borrowdale, joined in one solemn and capacious grove". But the dale's sonorous place names suggest a more prosaic heritage. The numerous "thwaites" were the site of Norse clearings, while by the thirteenth century the monks of Furness Abbey were farming the valley from their "grainge" (an outlying farmhouse), grazing sheep and smelting iron ore along the becks. The valley's higher reaches were later extensively mined and quarried, activities that impinged upon the indigenous wood cover. Borrowdale's oak woods once effectively formed part of a temperate rainforest – the surviving fragments are still known for their mosses, ferns, liverworts and lichens, and provide cover for a wide range of berries and birds, including warblers and flycatchers.

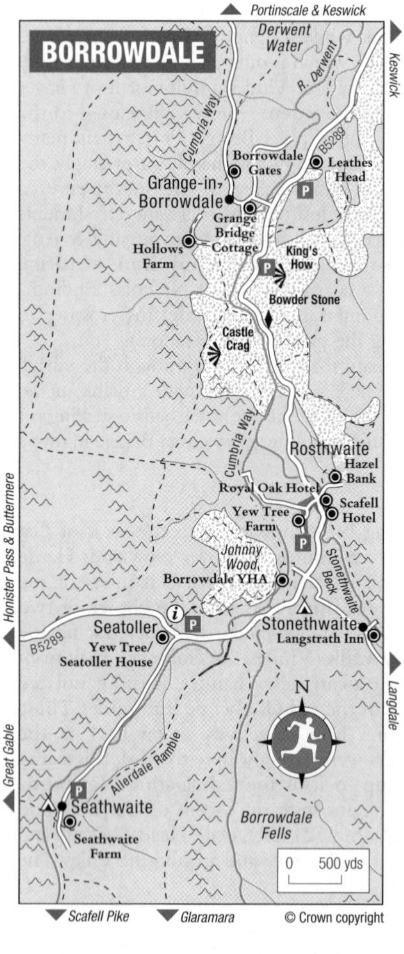

In summer there's a fairly steady stream of traffic taking hikers to the head of the valley, overshadowed by the peaks of Scafell and Scafell Pike (the two highest in the Lakes) and Great Gable, the latter one of the finest-looking mountains in England. Public transport access is by **bus** #77A (along the minor road on the west side of Derwent Water) and the highly scenic #78 "Borrowdale Rambler" (along the B5289), which runs south to Grange and Seatoller, dropping day-trippers and hikers at points of interest and walk-access points all the

▲ Bowder Stone, Borrowdale

way down. A **Borrowdale Day Rider** (from £5.60) gives a day's unlimited travel between Keswick and Seatoller on the #78 service; buy it from the driver.

Grange and around

The riverside hamlet of **GRANGE-IN-BORROWDALE**, four miles south of Keswick, sits back from an old twin-arched packhorse bridge, under which the River Derwent tumbles from the narrower confines of Borrowdale and runs across the flood plain to the lake. And flood it does on occasion, which is why the raised wooden walkways snake across the flats between here, Lodore and Manesty. It's always nice to stop for a drink at the **tearoom** at *Grange Bridge Cottage* (Ⓣ017687/77201; closed Nov–Feb, though open in school holidays), which is in a great spot, right by the bridge.

South of Grange, the valley narrows at a crag-lined gorge known as the **Jaws of Borrowdale**. Until the eighteenth century, the route beyond was considered wild and uncertain, and there was no permanent road through until the mid-nineteenth century, when travellers other than locals first began to venture into the valley. The views are famed from **Castle Crag** (985ft), possibly the site of an ancient fort and one of the western "teeth" of the Jaws, which you can reach on paths from Grange or Rosthwaite. Across the valley from the crag, also around a mile from Grange, stands the 1870-ton **Bowder Stone** (there's a car park on the B5289), a house-sized lump of rock scaled by wooden ladder and worn to a shine on top by thousands of pairs of feet. Controversy surrounds the origin of this rock, pitched precariously on its edge. Some say it came from the fells above, others contend it was brought by glacier movement during the last Ice Age. The crag behind the Bowder Stone, **King's How**, is named in memory of Edward VII. It's a fair climb to the top, but the views are worth it.

Accommodation and food

Borrowdale Gates Grange ⓣ017687/77204, ⓦwww.borrowdale-gates.com. The traditional choice hereabouts is this superbly sited country-house hotel in two acres of wooded gardens, 200 yards up the western shore road, past the church. Rooms have been upgraded, some now with doors leading out on to the lawns, others with balconies, and it has a deserved reputation for its food – dinner (included in the price, otherwise £35) is accompanied by fine views from the restaurant. Parking. Closed Jan. ❼

Hollows Farm ⓣ017687/77298, ⓦwww.hollowsfarm.co.uk. Three B&B rooms set on a working National Trust hill farm, half a mile from Grange – breakfast is from the kitchen Aga. There's also a fantastic farm field campsite with amazing views, though glampers will doubtless prefer the luxury yurts (from £285 part-week/£385 per week, school & bank hols £325/460) and bell-tents (from £225 part-week/£345 per week, school & bank hols £245/390) – for these, contact Inside Out Camping (ⓣ07884/315298 or 07813/334865, ⓦwww.insideoutcamping.co.uk). Parking. B&B closed Dec & Jan, campsite closed Nov–Easter. No credit cards. B&B ❷

Leathes Head B5289, 1 mile north of Grange ⓣ017687/77247, ⓦwww.leatheshead.co.uk. Welcoming family-run hotel with a dozen spacious rooms, all with fell views – two in particular have windows on two sides, letting the light flood in. The elegant, polished Edwardian house has three interlinked lounges, including a conservatory with telescope, while dinner (included in the price) is the main event every night – there's plenty of choice from a changing *table d'hôte* menu that always has a fish and vegetarian selection. Parking. ❻

Rosthwaite

The riverside path and the B5289 lead on to the straggling hamlet of **ROSTHWAITE**, two miles south of Grange. Its whitewashed stone buildings, backed by the encroaching fells, sustain the most concentrated batch of accommodation in the valley, while at the Rosthwaite **village shop** (open daily) – the only one in the valley – you'll be able to put together a basic picnic and buy a map or a postcard. Both hotels on the road, the *Royal Oak* and the *Scafell*, offer drinks, meals and teas to non-guests, while the *Scafell* is also the starting point of the annual **Borrowdale Fell Race** (first Sat in Aug), an eighteen-mile gut-buster that takes in the peaks of Scafell Pike and Great Gable. The winners clock in at well under three hours, their names immortalized on an honours board displayed in the hotel's *Riverside Bar*. Tortoises can reflect on these hare-like exploits while seated on the memorial bench in the hotel grounds dedicated to Walter ("W.A.") Poucher (1891–1988), author, fellwalker and photographer, whose classic *Lakeland Peaks*, first published in 1960, is the only serious rival in scope and breadth to the Wainwright guides.

Accommodation and food

Borrowdale YHA Longthwaite, 1 mile south of Rosthwaite ⓣ0845/371 9624, ⓔborrowdale@yha.org.uk. Located right on the riverside footpath to Seatoller, this has rooms available for couples and families, as well as dorms. It's a peaceful place to stay, with riverside picnic tables in the grounds, but tends to get busy with hikers so it's best to book. Dorm beds from £17.95.

Hazel Bank 200 yards from the road, over the bridge ⓣ017687/77248, ⓦwww.hazelbankhotel.co.uk. Victorian-era country house set in its own serene gardens, with magnificent fell views to all sides. There are eight elegant rooms, often full, since guests return year after year, drawn by the seclusion, the intimate atmosphere and the well-regarded food – a daily-changing four-course candlelit dinner is included in the price (otherwise £30), with coffee and chocolates served afterwards in the cosy lounge. Closed end-Nov to mid-Feb (though open Christmas and New Year). Parking. ❻

Royal Oak On the main road ⓣ017687/77214, ⓦwww.royaloakhotel.co.uk. The hikers' favourite – an expanded eighteenth-century farmhouse with barn annexe, where a hearty lakeland dinner (no choice, but vegetarian alternative available) is served promptly at 7pm, a bacon-and-eggs breakfast at 8.30am. Weather conditions are posted daily, packed lunches and filled flasks supplied, but if the rain comes down you may prefer to repair to the firelit sitting room for tea and scones, or to the stone-flagged bar. Parking. Rates include dinner. ❺

Scafell On the main road ⓣ017687/77208, ⓦwww.scafell.co.uk. Set back from a trimmed lawn, with rooms in the main building and more modern, slightly less spacious ones in the annexe. Food is traditional country-house "fayre" (prawn cocktail, silver service, meet-and-greet owner), but despite the formalities it's a friendly, relaxed place to stay. The four-course *table d'hôte* dinner is £28.50, though the attached *Riverside Bar* – the only local pub – serves cheaper bar meals, including smoked trout and grilled salmon. Special breaks, winter deals and last-minute rates are good value, as low as £55 per person including dinner. Parking. ⑤

Yew Tree Farm 200 yards up the narrow road opposite the shop ⓣ017687/77675, ⓦwww.borrowdaleherdwick.co.uk. Traditional farmhouse B&B with three rather florally decorated rooms. It has the unofficial royal seal of approval, since Prince Charles stays here occasionally on incognito walking trips. The farm also has a tearoom, the *Flock-In* (closed Wed), where you can sit in the garden over a tea or coffee (available in pints for thirsty walkers) and gaze across the valley fields – some of the farm Herdwicks end up in the tearoom's pasties, stews, sausages and burgers (meals £4–6). Parking. Closed Dec & Jan. No credit cards. ③

Stonethwaite, Seatoller and Seathwaite

STONETHWAITE, a place of some antiquity just to the southeast of Rosthwaite and half a mile up a side road, is the trailhead for those aiming to walk into Langdale via Langstrath and the watershed of Stake Pass. There's more foot traffic than you might expect, since it's on the route of both the Cumbria Way and the Coast-to-Coast walk. Pretty whitewashed stone cottages huddle around the sixteenth-century *Langstrath Country Inn* (ⓣ017687/77239, ⓦwww.thelangstrath.com; closed Sun & Mon), while the bleak Langstrath valley beyond makes for a tough day's outing.

Another mile or so up the valley from Rosthwaite, and eight miles from Keswick, lies the old farming and quarrying settlement of **SEATOLLER**, where there's a National Trust car park. A path leads from here into **Johnny Wood**, with

Scafell Pike and Great Gable

In good weather the minor road to Seathwaite is lined with cars by 9am as hikers take to the paths for the rugged climbs up some of the Lake District's major peaks, including Scafell Pike, England's highest mountain. Technically, they're not too difficult; as always, though, you should be well prepared and reasonably fit.

Scafell Pike

For England's highest peak, **Scafell Pike** (3210ft), the approach from Seathwaite is through the farmyard and up to **Styhead Tarn** via Stockley Bridge. This is as far as many get, and on those all-too-rare glorious summer days the tarn is a fine place for a picnic. From the tarn the classic ascent is up the thrilling **Corridor Route**, then descending via Esk Hause – a fairly arduous eight-mile (6hr) loop walk in all from Seathwaite.

Great and Green Gable

A direct but very steep approach to **Great Gable** (2949ft) is possible from Styhead Tarn, though most people start out from Seathwaite campsite, climb up Sourmilk Ghyll and approach the peak via **Green Gable** (2628ft), also an eight-mile (6hr) return walk. However, the easiest Great Gable climb is actually from Honister Pass, following a six-mile (4hr) route past Grey Knotts and Brandreth to Green Gable, before rounding Great Gable and returning along an almost parallel path to the west.

See Basics, p.42, for general walking advice in the Lakes; recommended maps are detailed on p.50.

its moss-covered boulders and lichen-draped trees, while thirty yards up the road a few slate-roofed houses cluster around the *Yew Tree* café, which was fashioned from seventeenth-century stone-flagged quarrymen's cottages. **Seatoller House**, a B&B next door, is owned by the family of the historian G.M. Trevelyan, who first visited a century ago as a Cambridge undergraduate and later organized "hare and hound" hunts on the fells above – stalking people rather than animals – which are still held here each year. A visitor centre (Ⓣ017687/77714, Easter–Oct daily 9am–5pm) opposite the café can help out with any other local questions.

A minor road south runs to **SEATHWAITE**, twenty minutes' walk away, where there's limited parking and a farmhouse campsite and camping barn. Seathwaite is a major departure point for walks up the likes of Great Gable and Scafell Pike, but prospective campers might like to know that it is always accused of being the wettest inhabited place in England, since it once recorded over 120 inches of rain in a single year.

Accommodation and food

Seathwaite Farm Seathwaite Ⓣ017687/77394. The hardcore hikers' favourite, at the end of the Seathwaite road and last stop before the high fells. It has a very popular campsite (open all year; shower block, toilets, and hot and cold water) as well as a refurbished camping barn that sleeps up to eighteen, with bunk beds, kitchen and lounge with pot-bellied stove. Bunk beds £6 per person – individuals welcome, though may be full at weekends with groups. No credit cards.

Seatoller House Seatoller Ⓣ017687/77218, Ⓦwww.seatollerhouse.co.uk. Stay the night in a beautifully preserved seventeenth-century Borrowdale farmhouse, which boasts plenty of original panelling, plus library, parlour and roaring fire. The cottage-style rooms are named after the wildlife hereabouts (Rabbit, Otter, Badger, Eagle etc), and in the beam-and-slate "Tea Bar" you can help yourself to drinks and cake. Communal dinners (7pm, not Tues) using local produce are served at two oak tables in the former kitchen. Closed Dec–Feb. Price includes dinner. ⑤

Yew Tree Seatoller Ⓣ017687/77634. Honister Slate Mine now runs this amiable daytime café where you can get snacks, soups and cakes (£2–4) before the climb up the pass or into the mountains. The bar's really nice too, with a riverside beer garden. Closed Nov to early March.

Honister Pass, Slate Mine and Via Ferrata

Borrowdale and Buttermere are separated by the dramatic **Honister Pass**, with the B5289 (and #77A bus) first winding its way up and then sweeping down on one of those unforgettable lakeland drives. At the top of the pass there's an isolated **youth hostel**, *Honister Hause YHA* (Ⓣ0845/371 9522, Ⓔhonister@yha.org.uk; flexible opening Nov–March; dorm beds from £13.95), superbly sited for mountain walking, while close by lie the unassuming buildings of Honister Slate Mine – an unexpectedly great place for daredevil adventurers with its deep mine tours and mountain activities. Come suitably clothed – it's either wet or windy up here at the best of times.

Slate has been quarried up here since Elizabethan times, and by the eighteenth century the local green roofing slate was much sought-after. Miners – living in wooden huts on the mountainside and working by candlelight – hand-dug eleven miles of tunnels and caverns within the bulk of Fleetwith Pike, leaving vicious scars, slate waste piles and old workings that are visible even today. Until well into the nineteenth century, the finished slate was either carried down the severe inclines in baskets on men's backs, or guided on heavy hand-pulled wooden sledges, since pit ponies couldn't get a foothold on the scree.

All this and more you can learn at England's last remaining working slate mine, **Honister Slate Mine** (daily 9am–5pm; Ⓣ017687/77230, Ⓦwww.honister-slate-mine.co.uk), rescued by local entrepreneurs in 1996 and now in full operation again as a sustainable, commercial enterprise. There's plenty of parking and it's free

People and places: That's mine

What's your journey to work like? Mark Weir flies in over Buttermere in his green Gazelle helicopter and lands outside Honister Slate Mine, which he's owned and run since the 1990s. Despite never having worked in the industry before, Mark bought the disused 300-year-old slate mine and turned it into a thriving commercial business – partly as a nod to his grandfather, who once worked at the mine, but also "to create real jobs for local people". Born and bred in Borrowdale, Mark was conscious of the mine's demise – "like the right arm of the valley being missing", he says – and is proud that the old skills have been revived and that Westmorland green slate is once again being extracted in significant volumes. The other challenge was to give visitors an experience they wouldn't forget, and there's certainly no chance of that on the high-adrenaline tours of mine and mountain. And if clinging to a steel ladder on Fleetwith Pike isn't enough excitement for one day, you can always choose to stay at the owner's nearby holiday accommodation and Mark will fly you in with him on his way to work.

For all mine details and activities, see "Honister Slate Mine" section. Holiday accommodation details on Ⓦwww.discoverparadigm.com.

to look around the visitor centre, factory trail, slate stone garden and shop, and see some of the revived skills in action, like the "docking, riving and dressing" of the slate. There's a café here too. Best of all, though, is to get an idea of what working life was really like in past centuries by donning a hard hat and lamp and joining one of the hugely entertaining 90-minute **guided mine tours** (3 or 4 daily; £9.75, family £27; advance bookings essential, by phone or online), which lead you through narrow tunnels into illuminated, echoing, dripping caverns. A more extreme version of the standard "Kimberley" tour takes you around "The Edge", a high-level shortcut into one of the most extensive mine workings.

If this wasn't thrilling enough, you also have the chance to take on England's only **Via Ferrata** ("Iron Way") climb, a system pioneered in the Italian Dolomites and used to get troops and equipment over unforgiving mountain terrain. By means of a permanently fixed cableway and clip-on harness, you follow the miners' old route up the exposed face of the mountain, clambering up and along iron rungs, ladders and supports to reach the top of **Fleetwith Pike** (2126ft), before walking back down to the visitor centre. It's terrifying and exhilarating in equal measure (you don't need any climbing experience to do it), and to see what you're in for you should definitely check out the photos and videos first on the website. There are two options (either takes around three hours), the standard **Via Ferrata "Classic" route** (1 or 2 daily; £25, family £85) or the **Via Ferrata Zip** (1 daily; £35, family £115) which basically decides that you haven't been scared silly enough and throws in a zip-wire ride across a thousand-foot chasm. **All-in day-pass tickets** are a good option if you want to do a mine tour and the Via Ferrata, with lunch in the café included in between – £37, family £125 for the Classic, £48/160 for the Zip option (advance bookings essential for Via Ferrata and all-day tickets on Ⓣ017687/77714, or online).

Threlkeld to Thirlmere

The A591 between Keswick and Grasmere runs directly past **Thirlmere**, and this is the way the buses go. But if you're in no particular hurry, it's more pleasant to detour east to **Threlkeld** first and then turn south along the minor road through **St John's in the Vale**. You can come this way entirely on foot too – it's an extremely attractive route (7 miles; 4hr) – and take the bus back up the A591 to complete the circuit back to Keswick.

Threlkeld

Keswick's disused railway path (signposted by the *Keswick Country House* hotel on Station Rd) runs straight to **THRELKELD** ("Thrall's Spring"), three miles east of Keswick; or it's a quick ride on bus #X4/X5 or the #73/73A. The riverside walk's a delight, enhanced by the promise of a drink in one of Threlkeld's charming old pubs at the end, either the *Horse & Farrier* or the *Salutation*. Threlkeld is the starting point for many of the strenuous hikes up Blencathra and there's parking at a couple of places up the signposted road to the Blencathra Centre.

A century ago Threlkeld was a busy, dirty industrial centre, with lead and copper mined in the valley and granite quarried from the hillsides for road- and railway-making. At **Threlkeld Quarry** (March–Oct daily 10am–5pm; Nov–Feb usually weekends only, call for times; museum and site £3, plus £5 for mine tour; ⓣ017687/79747, ⓦwww.threlkeldminingmuseum.co.uk), volunteers help run a fascinating open-air industrial history museum which covers all facets of the local mining industry. There's a comprehensive indoor collection of mining artefacts and minerals, but you're also welcome to roam around the site and have a look inside the locomotive shed and machine shop, where restoration work is being carried out on the impressive vintage excavators and quarry machinery. There are 45-minute guided tours down a recreated lead and copper mine – children will enjoy the underground experience and gritty anecdotes – while the relaid narrow-gauge mineral railway provides rides up into the inner quarry and back. The quarry lies across the A66 from Threlkeld; take the B5322 (St John's in the Vale road) and follow the brown signs off the road and a mile up the track, through the old quarry works.

St John's in the Vale

A bucolic walk from Threlkeld cuts south from the railway path, across Threlkeld Bridge and through the fields into **St John's in the Vale**; the B5322 shadows the same route. The old chapel of St John's and views of the Blencathra ridges behind are the draws, with the southward path hugging the base of **High Rigg** (1163ft) and eventually following the river to *Low Bridge End Farm* (ⓣ017687/79242, ⓦwww.campingbarn.com). This is a little hive of activity in a very peaceful spot, with a rustic tea garden (serving home-made cakes and local ice cream) and roaming hens, plus a woodland trail and craft workshop. The range of overnight **accommodation** options includes a small campsite, and self-catering available in the old stable and hayloft, either by the week in the flat (sleeps 2–4; £175–330, call the farm) or overnight in the camping barn (£7 per person; breakfast and packed lunches available; reservations on ⓣ01946/758198). From the farm the A591 is under a mile away – on the way, keep an eye out for climbers scaling **Castle Rock** across the river, Walter Scott's model for the fairy castle in his poem "Bridal of Triermain".

Thirlmere

Thirlmere, a five-mile-long reservoir at the southern end of St John's in the Vale, was created from two smaller lakes at the end of the nineteenth century when Manchester's booming population and industry required water. Over a hundred miles of gravity-drawn tunnels and pipes still supply the city with water from here. In an ultimately unsuccessful campaign – but one that foreshadowed the founding of the National Trust – the fight against the creation of Thirlmere was led by

Ruskin and other proto-environmentalists, outraged at a high-handed raising of the water level, which drowned the hamlet of Armboth and various small farms. No one was best pleased either by the subsequent regimental planting of thousands of conifers around the edge (to help prevent erosion), which dramatically changed the local landscape. The century since the creation of the reservoir has softened the scene – these are among the oldest planted trees in the National Park – and you'd be hard pushed now to tell that Thirlmere was man-made.

The only side served by public transport (take any bus along the A591 between Grasmere and Keswick) is the eastern one, from which some visitors choose to make the climb up Helvellyn and back – in which case, you'll be pleased at the thought of a pint in the roadside *King's Head* at **Thirlspot** (Ⓣ0500/600725, Ⓦwww.lakedistrictinns.co.uk; ❹, weekends ❺). For Thirlmere's waterside paths, forest trails and viewpoints, you need to be on the minor road that hugs the western shore. There are several small car parks, with trails leading off from each, like at **Launchy Gill**, an oak and birch woodland Site of Special Scientific Interest. Alternatively, the #555 bus can drop you at the foot of the reservoir for the six-mile walk up the western side and around to Thirlspot.

Braithwaite and Thornthwaite

Just under three miles west of Keswick, the cottage gardens of **BRAITHWAITE** ("Osprey Bus" or bus #X5 from Keswick) line the banks of Coledale Beck, with the distinctive Grisedale Pike towering above. There's some tremendous walking to be done from the village, and if you stay here rather than Keswick

Walks from Braithwaite

Grisedale Pike is the traditional climb, which can be incorporated into a much longer circular, or "horseshoe", walk. It's one of the Lakes' best one-day hikes, and dedicated Wainwright peak-baggers can knock off up to ten summits on the one circuit. The start of the route up Cat Bells is only two miles to the south of the village, as well, which means you could also walk the Newlands Valley from Braithwaite.

Grisedale Pike

From the small quarry car park on the Whinlatter road, just above the village, it's 90min to the top of **Grisedale Pike** (2593ft), along a very well-worn route. Moving on to **Hopegill Head** (2525ft) – from where the Isle of Man can be seen on the best days – you then drop to the head of the valley at Coledale Hause for the straightforward valley return to the village (total trip 5 miles; 3hr).

Coledale Horseshoe

Unless you're pushed for time, on a clear day you'd be mad not to complete the circuit since, having gained the height at Grisedale Pike and Hopegill Head, there's a relatively small amount of extra climbing involved to return to Braithwaite via **Sail** (2530ft), **Outerside** (1863ft) and **Barrow** (1494ft) – with a possible diversion to **Grasmoor** (2791ft, superb Crummock Water views) en route, and an alternative return via **Scar Crags** (2205ft) and **Causey Pike** (2035ft, Newlands Valley views). It's a hugely satisfying circuit, with changing panoramas all the way round. Depending on your peak choices, it's nine to twelve miles, six to eight hours, on clearly defined paths and ridges, with just the odd bit of scrambling.

See Basics, p.42, for general walking advice in the Lakes; recommended maps are detailed on p.50.

you could make an early start on the hills from the *Coledale Inn* (ⓣ017687/78272, ⓦwww.coledale-inn.co.uk; ❸) on the hillside above the village. Once a mill, this is now a cosy lakeland inn with a dozen (mostly upgraded, reasonably spacious) rooms, a sheltered garden and good-value bar meals (mains around £9). They'll also make you up a packed lunch and fill a flask for your day's walking.

A mile north up the minor road shadowing the A66, pretty **THORNTHWAITE** looks across the Derwent basin to the Skiddaw range. There's parking a mile or so further up the road, from where you can climb **Barf**

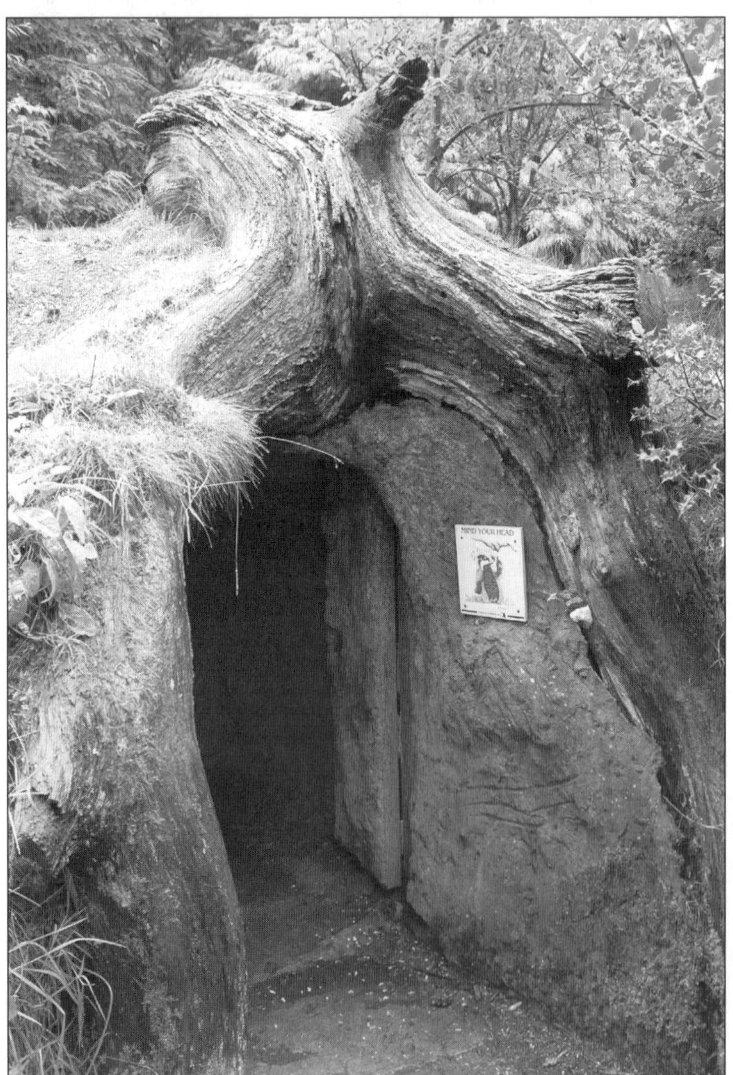

▲ Whinlatter Forest Park

(1536ft), whose distinctive craggy protuberance – usually painted white – is known as "The Bishop". Back in the village, the refined **Thornthwaite Galleries** (March–Oct daily 10am–5pm; winter hours may vary; free; ⓣ017687/78248, ⓦwww.thornthwaitegalleries.co.uk) exhibits a good range of contemporary lakeland arts and crafts – from paintings and sculpture to jewellery and fabrics – and some of the artists demonstrate their work during special sessions in the summer. The tearoom is open until 4.30pm, though muddy boots and their owners will have to give it a miss.

Whinlatter Forest Park

The B5292 climbs west past Braithwaite, en route to Buttermere or Cockermouth, through the extensive woodland plantations of **Whinlatter Forest Park**, England's only true mountain forest. It's easy to spend a day here doing all sorts of outdoor activities and the excellent visitor centre (daily: April–Oct 10am–5pm; Nov–March 10am–4pm; free; parking fee; ⓣ017687/78469, ⓦwww.forestry.gov.uk) can put you on track – in particular, the park has the Lake District's two longest purpose-built mountain bike trails, including the challenging 11-mile **Altura Trail**. Bikes and trail guides are available at the park's Cyclewise bike centre (ⓣ017687/78711, ⓦwww.cyclewise.co.uk; bikes from £20 per day) – hardcore show-offs can even rent a helmet-cam. There are also eight waymarked hiking trails (30min–3hr), plus a couple specifically for children and families, while **Go Ape** (daily Easter–Oct, Nov weekends only, closed Tues in term-time, & closed Dec & Jan; from £25; advance booking essential, online or by phone ⓣ0845/643 9215, ⓦwww.goape.co.uk) puts gung-ho visitors forty foot up in the trees on a high-ropes and zip-wire adventure course. It takes a good two hours to get around – there's a minimum age of 10 and a minimum height of 4ft 7in, but apart from that anyone can do it.

Inside the centre, seasonal exhibitions concentrate on the area's wildlife, most notably Bassenthwaite's wild **ospreys** (see p.175), which can usually be seen on the visitor centre's live video nest-cam link (Easter–Aug only). The centre's Alpine-style *Siskins Café* (ⓣ017687/78410) serves good food (meals £3–8) and proper coffee, and has an outdoor terrace that looks over the plantations and down the valley.

The regular **bus service** to Whinlatter is the #77 from Keswick, though there's also the summer-season #74 "Osprey Bus" which connects Keswick and Whinlatter with the osprey site at Bassenthwaite.

Bassenthwaite Lake

Pub-quiz fans love **Bassenthwaite Lake** as it's the only lake in the Lake District (all the others are known as waters or meres). It's also the northernmost of the major patches of water, but it doesn't receive much attention otherwise, partly because of the difficulty in actually reaching its shores. Although just three miles from Keswick, and linked by the River Derwent which flows across the broad agricultural plain between the two, most of the shoreline is privately owned with restrictions in place to preserve the lake's rich variety of plants and animals. The shoreline habitat, for example, is the best preserved in the National Park, where over seventy species of birds and wildfowl (including ospreys) winter and breed, while Bassenthwaite is one of the few places in Britain where the vendace, a nine-inch fish related to other Arctic species, is found. However, the habitats are currently under threat from increased silting and pollution and invasion by alien plants and other species, all factors that have prompted a long-term lake restoration programme to improve the water quality at Bassenthwaite.

The west shore as far as **Dubwath** and its wetland nature reserve is paralleled by the busy A66. The main attractions, though, are on the **east shore** of the lake, reached on **buses** #555 and #73/73A which stop at Mirehouse and Dodd Wood (for the ospreys). Otherwise, the summer-season #74 "Osprey Bus" (day rider ticket £5, family £11) runs on a round-Bassenthwaite circuit from Keswick, calling on the west side at Whinlatter, Dubwath Silver Meadows and Trotters World before returning down the east side.

Dubwath Silver Meadows

One of the newest nature reserves in Cumbria has been established in the water meadows of Dubwath, just west of Bassenthwaite. At **Dubwath Silver Meadows** (always open; free), a mile-long circular boardwalk runs through waist-high wildflowers and meadow plants, with some very rustic wattle, daub and thatch hides provided at various points so that you can spy on the resident deer family, butterflies and visiting birds. It's an enjoyable walk, despite the ever-present traffic noise from the A66, and the only current problem is finding the site, since they are still working on signage and other infrastructure. It's very near the *Pheasant Inn* – the easiest way to find it is to drive up the A66 from Keswick, ignore the first left signposted turn to the *Pheasant* and take the second left turn instead (opposite the Dubwath turn); the site is just on your right, through a gate by a bus stop, with the inn a bit further along.

Dodd Wood and the ospreys

The only permitted parking places close to the east shore are at the heavily planted Forestry Commission land of **Dodd Wood**. Starting from the *Old Sawmill Tearooms* (Easter–Oct daily 10am–5pm; ⓣ017687/74317) there are four marked trails of varying length. Some of the crowded pines, planted in the 1920s, are now 120ft high, which makes the climb (3 miles; 3hr return) to the heights of **Dodd** (1612ft) itself a rather disorienting experience. But native trees – including oak, ash, hawthorn and hazel – are being replanted in the wood to

Away from the lake – Linskeldfield Tarn

Sheltered in farmland just north of Bassenthwaite, **Linskeldfield Tarn** (open access; free; ⓣ01900/822136, ⓦwww.linskeldfield.co.uk) is a real hidden gem – a farm wildlife reserve, set in six acres of peat and wetland, and home to otters, red squirrels and all manner of wildfowl. There's a wooden birdwatching hide (binoculars and spotting charts provided), and though the viewing is best in winter or spring there's always something to see. Even if you don't know your widgeon from your pintail, you're going to like the farm's grazing ostriches – and you can hardly miss the 18,000 free-range hens. To find the sanctuary turn off the A591 at Bewaldeth, just north of the *Castle Inn* junction and then keep an eye out for signs for Sunderland and the farm.

prevent hillside soil erosion, while roe deer and some of the Lakes' few surviving red squirrels are occasionally seen around here.

However, the main interest in recent years has been the arrival of **wild ospreys** to nest and breed on the shores of Bassenthwaite, below the woods. A quarter-mile path (15min uphill climb) from the tearooms leads to the **lower viewpoint** (staffed Easter–Aug daily 10am–5pm; free; Ⓦwww.ospreywatch.co.uk), with an **upper viewpoint** (10.30am–4.30pm) another 30-minute climb beyond. High-powered telescopes are provided, or bring your own binoculars (visibility is best in the mornings) – on most days, you'll be able to see the ospreys fishing and feeding, hovering over the lake, then plunging feet first to catch roach, perch, pike and trout. The birds recolonized Bassenthwaite in 2001 and, although there's no guarantee, they have returned every year since – in 2006, three chicks were reared here for the first time. The ospreys usually arrive at the beginning of April; the eggs hatch in June, and the ospreys leave for Africa in August or September. For an up-close-and-personal look, don't miss the live video feed from the nests shown over at Whinlatter Forest Park.

Mirehouse

The bus stop and parking by the *Old Sawmill Tearooms* also provides access to **Mirehouse** across the road (house Easter–Oct Wed & Sun 2–5pm, plus Fri in Aug 2–5pm; gardens Easter–Oct daily 10am–5.30pm; gardens only £3, house & gardens £6.50, family £18; Ⓣ017687/72287, Ⓦwww.mirehouse.com), a fascinating manor house and extensive woodland gardens that count among the region's finest treasures. The house (built 1666) has been the home of the Spedding family since 1802 and is still lived in today, which explains the restricted opening days but also lends it a welcoming, informal air that's quite delightful. A pianist plays in the Music Room as you wind through the other rooms and corridors, while the claim that "little has been thrown away over the years" is demonstrably true – gentlemen's clay pipes, a Victorian knife-cleaner and an unexploded World War I grenade-turned-paperweight are just a few of the items displayed. Mirehouse has notable literary connections – Sir James Spedding (1808–81) was a respected biographer of Francis Bacon, and friend of Tennyson (who is supposed to have sought inspiration for his *Morte d'Arthur* here) and Thomas Carlyle among others, and the varied portraits, drawings, manuscripts, letters and books on show reveal the close relationships that many had with Carlyle's "dear hospitable Spedding". Outside are gardens, lawns, mixed woodland (with children's adventure playgrounds) and wildflower meadows, all connected by a lovely lakeside walk that takes around an hour to complete.

A short diversion from the Mirehouse grounds runs down through the fields and past two-hundred-year-old oak trees to the **church of St Bega** on the shores of Bassenthwaite. Originally Norman, and heavily restored, it's completely serene and protected by the looming flanks of Skiddaw. There's a public right of way from the road as well, so you don't need to pay for Mirehouse to visit the church.

Trotters World of Animals

Signs from the head of Bassenthwaite Lake direct you to **Trotters World of Animals** at Coalbeck Farm (daily 10am–5.30pm or dusk; £7.50, children £5.50; Ⓣ017687/76239, Ⓦwww.trottersworld.com), around the back of *Armathwaite Hall*. This is an excellent attraction, well worth an extended visit, since what started life as a simple animal farm is now a highly individual wildlife conservation project, presenting domestic, endangered and exotic animals within an educational framework. It's nothing if not all-encompassing: in spring you can help feed a newborn Cumbrian lamb, while as home to the only Canadian lynx in the UK, for example, the park highlights the plight of the related (and severely threatened) Iberian lynx. A recreated early medieval roundhouse is used to demonstrate sustainable crafts, while in the surrounding enclosures you'll come across a lively troop of gibbons, plus lemurs, meerkats, marmosets, tapirs and Asian fishing cats. Handling the animals is encouraged (even the snakes) during feeding programmes, demonstrations and other activities. There are flying displays every day with the hawks, vultures and owls, plus children's play areas, tractor and pony rides, a tearoom and picnic sites. There's always something going on, though school holidays tend to offer the pick of the child-oriented events, like the popular candlelit tours during December.

Practicalities

There's a renowned inn on the west side of Bassenthwaite Lake (the *Pheasant*) and another pub in the small village of **Bassenthwaite** (bus #73/73A), a couple of miles east of the top end of the lake. Other than that, though, the *Old Sawmill Tearooms* opposite Mirehouse is the best place for a snack or a meal.

Accommodation

Armathwaite Hall B5291, northern end of Bassenthwaite Lake ⓣ017687/76551, ⓦwww.armathwaite-hall.com. Live the noble life at one of the Lake District's most glamorous country-house hotels, a restored sixteenth-century hall set in 400 acres of deer park and woodland, with terraces overlooking rabbit-filled lawns and the lake beyond. There are obligingly attentive staff at every turn, and the oak-panelled lounges, lead windows, soaring stonework and oil paintings are just what you'd expect, while rooms, though traditional in style, are perfectly appointed in four different grades with varying outlooks. There's also a very fancy spa, plus infinity pool, outdoor hot tub, and all sorts of country pursuits available. The *Courtyard Bar and Brasserie* (mains £14–19) has a contemporary menu, or there's fine dining in the more formal restaurant (lunch £24, dinner £44). Parking. ❽

Pheasant Inn Off the A66, just before Dubwath ⓣ017687/76234, ⓦwww.the-pheasant.co.uk. An old, very upmarket coaching inn that still looks the part, especially in the carefully preserved period bar and comfortable lounges filled with flowers where superior bar lunches (£6–13) and an indulgent afternoon tea are served. Lunch (£28) and dinner (£37) in the polished restaurant are more formal affairs – the food's great, hand-dived scallops to seared duck – after which you can repair to one of the thirteen characterful rooms (two are in the Garden Lodge while three suites offer a bit more space). Parking. ❻

Ravenstone A591, 5 miles northwest of Keswick ⓣ0800/163983, ⓦwww.ravenstone-hotel.co.uk. A Victorian hotel in two acres of grounds, with terrific views over Bassenthwaite Lake and enough decorative oak to denude a small forest. "Osprey" rooms have a bit more contemporary style about them, or there's a four-poster "spa" room with whirlpool bath. Then it's a laze in the handsome firelit lounge, and a game on the full-sized snooker table before dinner (included in the price). Parking. ❻

Pub

Sun Bassenthwaite village ⓣ017687/76439. Retains its seventeenth-century air – oak beams, open fires – and serves traditional bar meals (£8–14) from noon to 2pm and 6 to 9pm. You can sit outside on a warm day too.

Back o' Skiddaw

People often complain that the Lake District is too crowded, that tourists have overwhelmed the infrastructure and transformed the villages – none of which, happily, is true of the **Back o' Skiddaw**, the local name for the arc of fells and valleys that stretches around the back of Skiddaw mountain, tucked into the northernmost section of the National Park. For the most part it's countryside that really does deserve the epithet "rolling", with farmland tumbling down from Skiddaw's gentle humps to encircle small hamlets and villages that see little tourist traffic. The only **public transport** is the seasonal #73/73A "Caldbeck Rambler" bus, which runs on a circular route from Keswick to all the places covered below.

Uldale and Ireby

From the *Castle Inn* junction, half a mile from the northern edge of Bassenthwaite Lake, the sweeping road into Uldale ends three miles further on at **ULDALE** village where the cow dung on the road announces its farming credentials. Farming in the Lakes is a precarious business at the best of times: what it must have been like in the past in "wolf's dale" doesn't bear thinking about. Walpole used the quiet village and moorland surroundings as the backdrop in the middle two Herries novels, *Judith Paris* and *The Fortress*, with the fictional Fell House as the Herries family lair. Fortified by a drink from the *Snooty Fox* pub (Ⓣ016973/71479, Ⓦwww.snootyfox-uldale.co.uk), you can press on to tiny **Over Water**, a mile and a half south – it's the northernmost splash of water in the Lake District, with the farms of Orthwaite beyond. Only bad things await, surely, on the heights of **Great Cockup** (1720ft), an easy two-mile walk east from Orthwaite.

In the other direction, Uldale's **St James church** lies a full mile from the village on the Ireby road, a pretty building with some interesting old gravestones and uninterrupted fell views. Another mile beyond is sleepy **IREBY**, with its lion's-head drinking trough. You can eat well in the venerable beam-and-nook *Sun Inn* (Ⓣ016973/71346), whose small beer garden is a restful spot on a sunny day.

Caldbeck

Prosperity came easily to **CALDBECK**, six miles east of Ireby and just twelve from Carlisle, and it remains one of the Lakes' most appealing villages. The fast-flowing "cold stream" from which it takes its name provided the power for the

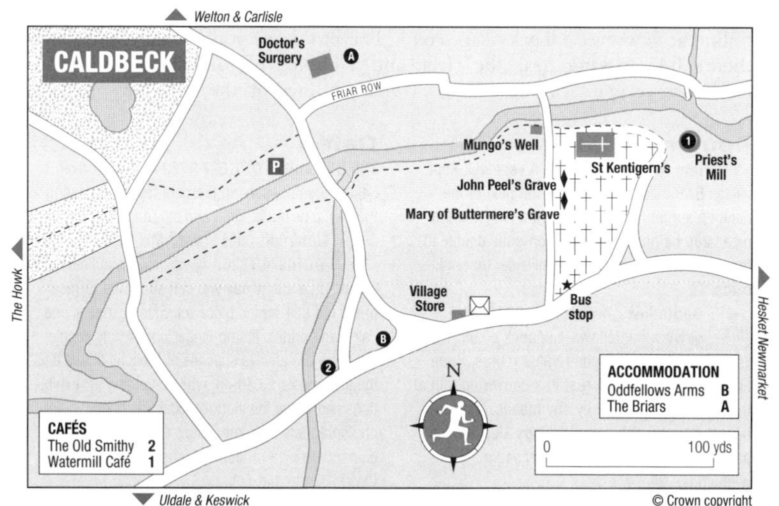

rapid expansion in the number of mills here in the seventeenth and eighteenth centuries. Corn, wool and wooden bobbins flowed out, lead and copper from the fells was carted in; and the many surviving contemporary buildings (look for the dates carved on the lintels above the doors) attest to its wealth. A signposted quarter-mile walk from the car park up to the limestone gorge known as **The Howk** shows you the river in all its rushing glory, as well as the restored ruins of one of the old bobbin mills.

The village is anchored by its **church of St Kentigern**, dedicated to the sixth-century saint better known as Mungo, who journeyed from Scotland through Cumberland to Wales to preach the gospel to the heathen Saxons and Celts. The well he is supposed to have used for baptism lies by the packhorse bridge, next to the churchyard. The first stone church here was built in the twelfth century, and although a medieval tombstone survives in the chancel, today's church bears the brunt of heavy nineteenth-century restoration. No matter, since all the interest is outside in the churchyard, where you'll easily find the ornate tombstone of **John Peel** of Ruthwaite (d.1854), emblazoned with reliefs of hunting horns and his faithful hound. Peel's is a name synonymous with fox-hunting, yet he was just one of several hardened and hard-drinking nineteenth-century hunting men of local repute; his fame today derives squarely from the song ("D'ye ken John Peel") written about him by one of his friends. Eighteen paces from his grave, walking away from the church, is the tombstone of the Harrisons of Todcrofts: Richard was a simple farmer; it's his wife Mary (d.1837) who is better known – as Mary, the Maid of Buttermere, the most celebrated beauty of her day (see p.205). These days, Caldbeck's most famous resident is mountaineer and writer Chris Bonington. **Priest's Mill** (closed Jan to mid-Feb), near the church, was a corn mill for over 200 years, but was restored in 1986 and has been turned into a little arts and business centre, with a café, jeweller and cooperative woolshop among the outlets.

For a stretch of the legs, Caldbeck's most favoured local walk is the climb up **High Pike** (2157ft), the fell to the south, mined for its minerals in the nineteenth century. The most obvious route is from Nether Row, a mile south of Caldbeck – count on five miles, three hours, there and back. Views from the cairn and bench at the summit sweep from the Solway Firth to the Yorkshire hills, with Blencathra and Bowscale Fell in the foreground.

Caldbeck makes a peaceful night's stop – you can check local information online at Ⓦwww.caldbeckvillage.co.uk. The bus drops you by the churchyard, there's free parking near the river, and a choice of local accommodation (including several farmhouse B&Bs, which are listed on the website).

Accommodation

The Briars Ⓣ016974/78633. A very well-kept village B&B, near the car park and next to the doctor's surgery. One single and a twin share a nice large bathroom, while an en-suite double at the back looks on to the local hillside. No credit cards. ❷

Oddfellows Arms Ⓣ016974/78227, Ⓦwww.oddfellows-caldbeck.co.uk. The village pub has some good-value rooms, three above the pub and the rest in a converted mill at the back. It's not flash by any means, just an honest country pub with Jennings ales and very popular bar meals (bookings advised at weekends). ❷

Cafés

The Old Smithy Ⓣ016974/78246. On the river, behind the pub, serving tearoom favourites during the day, plus crafts, gifts and ceramics.

Watermill Café Priest's Mill Ⓣ016974/78267, Ⓦwww.watermillcafe.co.uk. On a sunny day you can sit on the terrace of the old mill, a nice place for snacks, meals, and Fair Trade drinks. It's no longer completely veggie, but there are always specials of broccoli bakes and the like (meals £3.50–9), while changing art exhibitions showcase the work of local artists and photographers. In winter, once-a-month BYOB dinners are by arrangement (check the website). Closed Jan to mid-Feb.

Hesket Newmarket

There's a path from Caldbeck a mile and a half southeast through the fields to the small eighteenth-century village of **HESKET NEWMARKET**, which straddles a long village green. Markets were long held here, though the last was a century ago, and the prosperous village once supported half a dozen inns, yet the *Old Crown* (ⓣ016974/78288, ⓦwww.theoldcrownpub.co.uk) by the green is the only survivor. It's a cosy local of great charm, owned by a local cooperative (the first such in Britain), and brewing a variety of tremendous ales out the back in the Hesket Newmarket Brewery. The food is very popular, too – from local gammon and lamb to the speciality curries (mains £6.50–11.50) – and you're advised to book for dinner. There's also a tearoom at *Fellside Stores*, the local grocer's and post office, while the other way, past the pub, friendly *Denton House* (ⓣ016974/78415, ⓦwww.dentonhouseguesthouse.co.uk; no credit cards; ❷) has eight B&B rooms.

Incidentally, if Caldbeck can boast John Peel and Chris Bonington as local famous names, Hesket Newmarket is not to be outdone – road-haulage king and spotter's cult hero Eddie Stobart started out here in the family firm.

Carrock Fell, Mosedale and Mungrisdale

The road south from Caldbeck and Hesket Newmarket winds the eight miles back to the A66, effectively down the eastern boundary of the Lake District. Away to the east lie fields not fells, and beyond is the Eden Valley and Yorkshire. The bulk looming to the west, behind Blencathra and Bannerdale, is **Carrock Fell** (2174ft), best climbed from Stone Ends Farm – you can park by the road – three miles from Hesket Newmarket. The fell is riddled with abandoned mines (keep back – exploration is dangerous), while a huge tangle of fallen rocks litters the hillside: Charles Dickens and Wilkie Collins had a particularly disastrous time climbing Carrock Fell in mist, described in Dickens' *The Lazy Tours of Two Idle Apprentices* (1857).

The broad valley of **Mosedale**, another mile or so down the road, has a minor road running up to meet the Cumbria Way at the valley's head. Day walkers usually head instead for **Bowscale Tarn**, 1600ft up, scooped dramatically out of Bowscale Fell and ringed by crags. It's an easy walk (1hr) from the roadside parking at nearby Bowscale, following a clear bridleway for much of the route. The summit of **Bowscale Fell** (2306ft) itself is reached from the tarn by a further, gut-busting, 45-minute climb, and to make a circular walk of it (5 miles; 4hr) you can then drop down into **Mungrisdale**, a narrower valley whose foot embraces a few stone houses, a small church and the *Mill Inn* (ⓣ017687/79632, ⓦwww.the-millinn.co.uk; ❸), where a stone mill wheel props up the bar. The half-dozen rooms have been nicely refurbished and the inn serves local, seasonal produce (mains £9–12), including lots of fresh fish.

Travel details

All timetables can be checked on Traveline ⓣ0871/200 2233, ⓦwww.traveline.info.

From Keswick

Bus #73/73A "Caldbeck Rambler" circular route to: Castlerigg Stone Circle (6min), Mungrisdale (21min), Mosedale (26min), Hesket Newmarket (40min), Caldbeck (45min), and around to Mirehouse (1hr 20min) and back to Keswick; or to Mirehouse (14min), Bassenthwaite village (19min), Uldale (30min), Ireby (35min), Caldbeck (50min), and around to Mungrisdale (1hr 10min) and back to

Keswick. Service operates Easter & mid-July to end Aug 2–3 daily; plus Sat all year, and Sun & bank hols from end May to mid-July.

Bus #74 "Osprey Bus" circular route to: Braithwaite (7min), Whinlatter (14min), Dubwath (31min) and Trotters World (37min); and to Mirehouse/Dodd Wood (10min). Service operates 7 daily during Easter, spring bank and summer school hols, plus other Sat, Sun & bank hols between Easter and end Aug.

Bus #77/77A "Honister Rambler" circular route to: Cat Bells (11min), Grange (20min), Seatoller (30min), Honister Slate Mine (40min), Buttermere (50min), Lorton (1hr 10min) and Whinlatter Pass (1hr 20min); or to Whinlatter Pass (15min), Lorton (25min), Buttermere (45min), Honister Slate Mine (1hr), Seatoller (1hr 5min) and Grange (1hr 15min). Service operates Easter–Oct 4 daily.

Bus #78 "Borrowdale Rambler" (every 30min–1hr) to: Lodore (15min), Grange (20min), Rosthwaite (25min) and Seatoller (30min).

Bus #208 "Ullswater Connection" to: Aira Force (25min), Glenridding (35min) and Patterdale (40min). Service operates mid-July to end Aug 5 daily, plus Sat, Sun & bank hols end May to mid-July.

Bus #555 (every 30min–1hr) to: Thirlspot (10min), Grasmere (25min), Ambleside (50min), Windermere (1hr 5min) and Kendal (1hr 35min); and also (3–4 daily) to Carlisle (1hr 10min).

Bus #X4/X5 (Mon–Sat every 30–60min, Sun every 2hr) to: Threlkeld (11min), Rheged (35min) and Penrith (40min); and also to Braithwaite (7min), Bassenthwaite (13min) and Cockermouth (35min).

The western fells and valleys

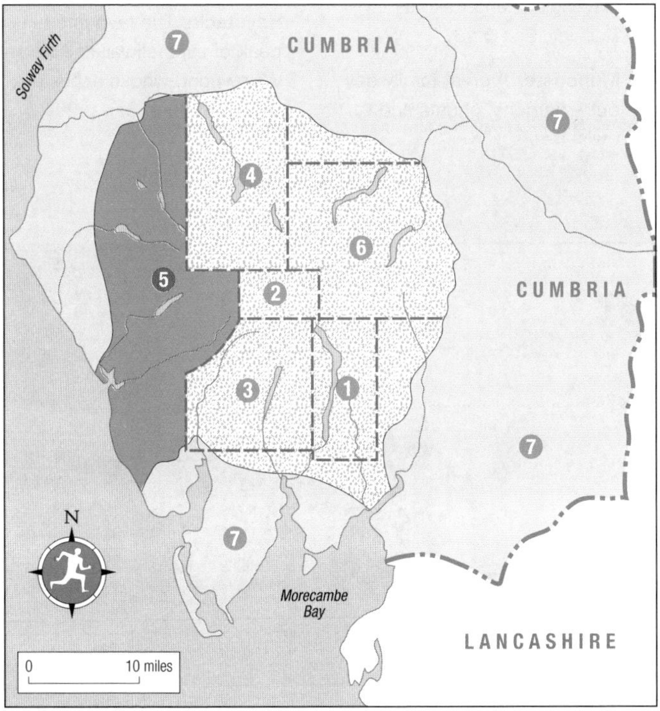

CUMBRIA

Solway Firth

CUMBRIA

LANCASHIRE

Morecambe Bay

0 10 miles

N

7 4 6 5 2 3 1 7 7 7

CHAPTER 5

Highlights

* **Silecroft beach** The only stretch of beach within the National Park extends for miles, providing wholesome walks and a habitat for wildlife. See p.186

* **Ravenglass and Eskdale Railway** The finest approach to quiet Eskdale is in the toy-town carriages of the Ravenglass and Eskdale Railway. See p.187

* **Muncaster** A great family day out – gardens, ghosts and owls. See p.188

* **Viking cross, Gosforth** This intricately carved stone cross is the finest reminder of the Norse influence on the Lakes. See p.196

* **Wasdale Head Inn** Relive the old days in the atmospheric rural inn, where walkers and climbers congregate over drinks and dinner. See p.199

* **Haystacks** The favourite peak of avid fellwalker Alfred Wainwright, whose ashes are scattered here. See p.204

▲ The Ravenglass and Eskdale Railway

The western fells and valleys

The **western fells and valleys** (Ⓦwww.western-lakedistrict.co.uk) contain some of the National Park's most dramatic scenery, from stunning lakeland vistas and isolated hamlets to deep forests and a little-visited coastline. "No part of the country is more distinguished by sublimity", claimed Wordsworth, and he had a point. Today, the region is hardly unknown, but it doesn't have anything like the visitor density of the north or south Lakes, in part because it's more difficult to reach. Public transport is limited and both the main road (A595) and Cumbria Coast railway stick to the coastal plain, meaning long circular journeys from the central tourist hot spots or painstaking climbs over the dramatic Hardknott and Honister passes into the western valleys. Emphatically, though, the region is worth the journey, whether it's for a stroll around lovely **Buttermere** or the rattling journey into **Eskdale** on the tremendous **Ravenglass & Eskdale Railway**. It's a toss-up whether **Wast Water** (England's deepest lake) or **Ennerdale Water** is the better-looking lake, though Ennerdale is, if anything, even more remote, while tiny **Loweswater** and unsung **Crummock Water** each have their fair share of stunning scenery, great hikes and hidden corners.

The **mountains** dominate all in the west, sporting names (Pillar, Great Gable, the Scafells) that are among the most resonant in the region. Certainly, there's enough great walking here to keep you occupied for weeks. The other point of interest is the **Cumbrian coast**, though this is rather less celebrated, since only a short protected section lies within the National Park boundary. It's been more brutally shaped instead by the old industrial towns between Millom and Workington, and if there's a symbol of where economic priorities lie it's the sprawling Sellafield nuclear reprocessing plant, a major local employer that lurks on the coast just north of Ravenglass.

Millom

The small, plain town of **MILLOM** lies just outside the National Park boundary, flanked to the south and east by the shifting sands of the Duddon Channel. As a product of the nineteenth-century mining industry, the town isn't an obvious target for most Lakes' tourists, but Millom's excellent

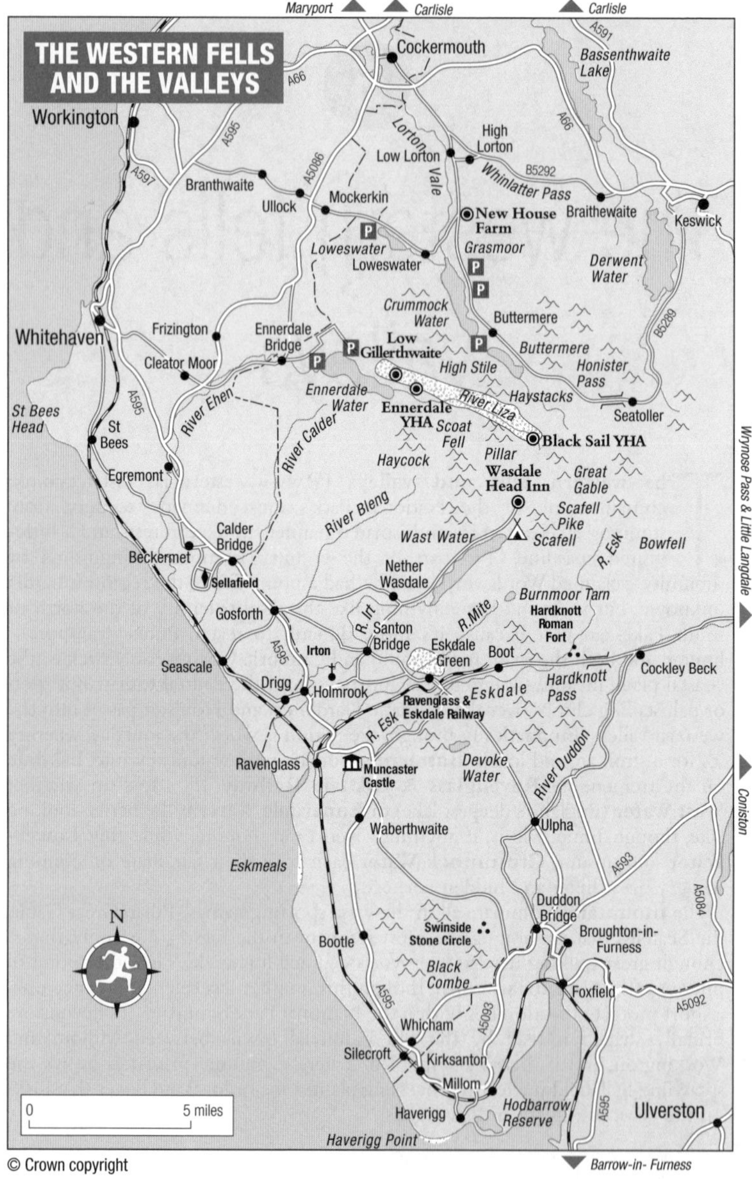

Folk Museum (daily 11am–4pm; £4, family £9; ⓣ01229/772555, ⓦwww.millomfolkmuseum.co.uk), sited at the town's train station, really is worth the short detour. This tells a graphic story of boom and bust, as the local discovery of high-grade iron ore led to the establishment of mining and ore-processing operations on the neighbouring Hodbarrow peninsula, now a nature reserve (see next section). In its day, it was a massive operation, with millions of tons of iron ore extracted by thousands of workers housed in drab, company-built streets. Their employment came to an end in 1968 when the mine finally closed, and the museum recalls their working and living conditions, alongside a re-creation of one of the old mines (using original items from the last pit to close), as well as any other number of local finds, photographs, relics and memorabilia.

The museum is also the place to discover something about Millom's famous son, the poet **Norman Nicholson** (1914–87). An only child, he contracted TB at 16 and spent two years in a Hampshire sanatorium before returning to Millom, where it was another twelve years before he was considered cured. His wide reading in convalescent isolation was one of the main factors, he considered, that made him a reflective poet; that, and his deep attachment to his Cumberland roots, whose industry, landscape, people and history informed all his work. Nicholson spent his life in Millom. His house, at 14 St George's Terrace, just off the small market square, two minutes from the train station, is marked by a blue plaque – it's now a health-food store and tearoom. In **St George's Church**, up the drive opposite the square, a beautiful contemporary stained-glass window celebrates Nicholson's life and work – ask about access at the tourist office – while he is buried with his wife in the new part of St George's churchyard. The grave lies beyond the church and down to the right, in front of a wooden bench by a wooden fence, and is inscribed with a moving line from his last published work, *Sea to the West*: "Let our eyes at the last be blinded/Not by the dark/But by dazzle."

Trains on the Cumbrian Coast line from Barrow-in-Furness (connections from Lancaster/Ulverston) stop regularly in Millom, with onward services to Ravenglass (15min) and Whitehaven (45min); it's a Monday to Saturday service, timetables available on Ⓦwww.northernrail.org. The Folk Museum can give you general visitor information and there's more local **information** on the website Ⓦwww.millom.org.uk.

Haverigg and Hodbarrow

A mile to the south of Millom, the local beach at **Haverigg** is a lengthy, duned stretch that leads a quiet existence, even in summer, despite the children's playground and beach café. The nearby **Hodbarrow RSPB Reserve**, two miles from Millom (signposted from the centre; always open; free; Ⓦwww.rspb.org.uk) – sited around a freshwater lagoon formed from flooded mine workings – is a better place for a stroll. From the parking area, a path runs all the way around the lagoon, and from either the stone beacon or the ruined windmill there are sweeping views in all directions – over the dunes and estuary, across to Barrow and up to the fells. The lagoon is of national importance for wintering waterfowl such as wigeon, goldeneye, red-breasted merganser and pintail, while in summer three species of tern nest on the reserve and can be viewed from the hide on the sea wall. The number and variety of orchids at Hodbarrow also catch the eye in summer – not just the plentiful marsh, spotted and pyramidal orchids but the largest colony of bee orchids in Cumbria. Seals are also regularly seen from the sea wall at low tide.

The National Park coast

Only a short twenty-mile section of the west Cumbrian coast – between Silecroft and Ravenglass – falls within the National Park and, in truth, it's neither particularly dramatic nor appealing, unless you simply fancy a stroll or a trot on the sands. However, it does have one unique feature, namely the bulky fell of Black Combe, which is the only Lake District mountain to fall straight to the sea.

After the dunes of Haverigg, the next decent sweep of beach is at **Silecroft**, four miles northwest of Millom; there's a train halt on the coastal line, a mile from the beach. It's a place for wildlife enthusiasts, since the coastal scrub here is a habitat for the natterjack toad, while (as elsewhere along the Cumbrian coast) terns, oystercatchers and ringed plovers nest and breed, scraping the shingle over their camouflaged eggs. It's also great for a gallop with Murthwaite Green Trekking Centre (Ⓣ01229/770876, Ⓦwww.murthwaitegreen.co.uk) which offers beach and fell **horse and pony rides** (1hr to full-day, £20–95) from the stables at Silecroft. There's another trekking option a couple of miles to the north, up the A595 in the Whicham valley at Chappels Farm, where Cumbrian Heavy Horses (Ⓣ01229/777764, Ⓦwww.cumbrianheavyhorses.co.uk) let you get up close and personal with Clydesdale and Shire horses on beach, farm and fell rides (90min to full-day, £45–140). There's a pub in Silecroft (near the station, not the beach), where you can get a lunchtime sandwich, though some prefer the *King William IV* (known to all as the "King Billy") at **Kirksanton**, a mile back down the A5093 towards Millom.

At **Bootle**, five miles up the A595, the sandstone-faced church is split from its cemetery by the road. Bootle's nearest beach is three miles to the northwest, at **Eskmeals**, which has a stony foreshore, though when the tide is out a large expanse of sand is exposed, from which you can admire the views as far north as St Bees Head. North of here, as far as Ravenglass, the coastline itself is off limits – red flags fly over an experimental firing range – while beyond lie the hard-to-miss towers and buildings of Sellafield (see feature). Whether you'd choose to swim anywhere in the vicinity of a nuclear-reprocessing plant is, of course, entirely a matter for you. Keep going to the village of **Waberthwaite**, though, just before Ravenglass, where Richard Woodall (Ⓣ01229/717237, Ⓦwww.richardwoodall.com) is a place of pilgrimage for foodies on the trail of what some say are Britain's best traditionally cured and smoked hams, bacon and Cumberland sausages.

Climbing Black Combe

The A595 makes a V-shape around the distinctive **Black Combe** massif, with the angle at the hamlet of Whicham, near Silecroft, where there's a path up to the summit (1857ft) that starts from the minor Kirkbank road, behind the church. It's not a particularly demanding climb (Wainwright reckoned you could do it in carpet slippers) and, in fine weather at least, you can certainly discount William Wordsworth's dire warnings ("Dread name derived from clouds and storms!") – it's around 3 miles there and back (2hr 30min), and the views from the top are fantastic, stretching out to sea to the Isle of Man, up the coast to St Bees Head and south to Morecambe Bay. Indeed, it's traditionally claimed that you can see up to fourteen English and Scottish counties from here, plus Snowdon and even the Irish coast, but that would require one of those all-too-rare crystal-clear days and Clark Kent-like vision.

No more nukes? The Sellafield story

The main blot on the Cumbrian coast is **Sellafield nuclear reprocessing plant**, midway between Ravenglass and Whitehaven. It's changed its name twice, from Calder Hall to Windscale and then to Sellafield, in what might seem, to a cynic, an attempt to hide its manifest dangers. It's always been controversial, since the site was first developed in the 1950s to produce plutonium for Britain's early nuclear weapons' programme. Today, Sellafield contains more than 200 separate nuclear facilities, including redundant defence work (ie, weapons) sites and Calder Hall, the world's first fully commercial nuclear power station (1957–2003). The problem is that Sellafield was developed quickly at a time when little thought was given to nuclear waste treatment, with the result that there is now a massive clean-up and decommissioning project under way at what is, in anyone's view, a dangerous industrial site. Unfortunately, returning Sellafield to a "safe, passive state" will cost billions of pounds and won't be complete until 2150 – none of which will help the government sell its current policy of promoting a new generation of "clean" British nuclear power stations, in an attempt to combat rising greenhouse gas emissions. You used to be able to make up your own mind about all this at Sellafield's remarkably even-handed visitor centre, but sadly it's become a corporate and business venue and the general public is no longer encouraged to visit. There is still a small display at the **Sellafield Centre** (Ⓣ019467/27027, Ⓦwww.sellafieldsites.com), usually open weekdays, but it's best to call first if you plan a visit since it's not the interesting, interactive experience it once was.

Ravenglass and around

The one big attraction on the coast is at **RAVENGLASS**, a sleepy village at the estuary of three syllabically challenged rivers, the Esk, Mite and Irt. The village is the starting point for the wonderful narrow-gauge Ravenglass and Eskdale Railway, but it merits a closer look anyway before you take the train or visit the other main local attraction, nearby Muncaster Castle.

The single main street in Ravenglass preserves a row of characterful nineteenth-century cottages – one with a huge profusion of tumbling flowers and shrubs, another fronted by an ancient "National" petrol pump with the pre-decimal price still showing. The cottages back on to estuarine mud flats and dunes that are accessible when the tide's out – the northern section, across the Esk, is a **nature reserve** where black-headed gulls and terns are often seen (get there by crossing over the main-line railway footbridge).

The Romans first used the estuary as a harbour, and established a supply post at Ravenglass in the first century AD for the northern legions manning Hadrian's Wall. Nothing remains of what the Romans knew as Glannaventa save the remarkably complete buildings of their **bathhouse** (always open; free), part of a fort that survived in Ravenglass until the fourth century. It's on the road out of the village, just past the station, 500 yards up a (signposted) single-track lane, past the caravan site.

Ravenglass and Eskdale Railway

You'd have to have a heart of stone not to enjoy the ride on the fabulous **Ravenglass and Eskdale Railway** (known locally as "La'al Ratty"), a narrow-gauge steam trip from the Esk estuary to the foot of the western fells. It originally opened in 1875 to carry iron ore from the Eskdale mines to the coast at Ravenglass, but now pays its way by transporting gleeful passengers on a seven-mile, forty-minute ride through two of the Lake District's prettiest valleys – first along

Train up, bike down on the Eskdale Trail

There's a great return bike route from Dalegarth station to Ravenglass (8.5 miles), which only takes around two hours, though with lunch and a visit to Muncaster en route it's also a fine day out. You'll whizz along sun-dappled wooded tracks and across open farmland, following markers all the way. For the most part it's fairly easy, either flat or downhill – aside from the hellishly steep 20-minute push uphill onto Muncaster Fell. From Dalegarth it's around 50 minutes to the start of the hill, and once you've slogged to the top be sure to see Muncaster Tarn and its huge water lilies. Descending from here, there are wonderful sea and estuary views as you freewheel down to Muncaster Castle and to the Roman bathhouse just outside Ravenglass.

A route guide to the **Eskdale Trail** is available from Ravenglass or Dalegarth stations. You'll need to call the Ravenglass and Eskdale Railway a day in advance to book your cycle on the train, leave your car at Ravenglass and then buy a one-way ticket to Dalegarth (£10, including bike carriage).

Miterdale under Muncaster Fell and then into the valley of the River Esk, where the train terminates at Dalegarth station, near Boot. You can break your journey with an "Explorer" ticket, allowing you to get off and walk from one of the half-dozen stations en route; the full return journey, without a break, takes an hour and forty minutes. At **Dalegarth**, there's a visitor centre, shop and café, and **bike rental** (half-day £8, full-day £14; printed Eskdale cycle routes available, ⓣ019467/23226) whenever the trains are running – it's best to call in advance to check availability.

Between March and October there are at least six daily **departures** from Ravenglass (and up to 15 daily in school summer holidays); there are also trains most winter weekends, plus at Christmas, New Year and February half-term holidays. An **Explorer Ticket** (£11.20, family £28.50) gives one day's unlimited travel on the line, while special days out, involving Thomas the Tank Engine and the like, are held throughout the year.

For more **information**, contact the Ravenglass and Eskdale station (ⓣ01229/717171, ⓦwww.ravenglass-railway.co.uk), adjacent to the Cumbrian Coast main-line station. There are discounted through-tickets available if you arrive on the main-line train; otherwise there's plenty of parking at Ravenglass station. There's also a small **railway museum** (same days and times as rail service), a short video showing you the route, a café on the platform and a shop, where budding engine drivers can buy that all-important driver's cap.

Muncaster Castle

A mile east of Ravenglass, on the A595, spreads the estate of **Muncaster Castle** (Feb half-term hols to first week Nov: castle Mon–Fri & Sun noon–4.30pm; gardens, owl centre and maze daily 10.30am–6pm or dusk; £11/family £32, or £8.50/£28 without castle entrance; ⓣ01229/717614, ⓦwww.muncaster.co.uk) whose house, grounds and attractions are one of the region's best days out. There's free parking at the castle, or bus #X6 runs daily from Whitehaven via Ravenglass (and on Sundays from Millom). Or you can walk here (30min) on the path from Ravenglass, up past the Roman bathhouse and across the fields. There's a good **café** in the stable yard, *Creeping Kate's Kitchen* (open daily during the season and some winter weekends), and you can even stay the night here (see "Practicalities" opposite).

The **castle** itself was built around a medieval pele tower, and has been home to the Pennington family since the thirteenth century; family members still live here today, as photographs throughout and contemporary portraits in the Drawing Room attest. An audio tour points out the family treasures (a Gainsborough here, a Reynolds there) and leads you through various rooms, notably the impressive octagonal library and the Tapestry Room, with its Flemish wall hangings and mighty Elizabethan fireplace.

The seventy-acre **grounds and gardens** are at their best in spring and autumn, but lovely to walk in at any time, with a stupendous view straight up Eskdale from the Terrace Walk, and half a dozen other marked trails, including one winding through a hilly Sino-Himalayan Garden. The plants here, all grown from seeds from Bhutan, Vietnam, and Yunnan and Sichuan provinces in China, thrive in conditions apparently similar to those 11,000 feet up a Far Eastern mountain – which doesn't say a lot for Cumbrian weather patterns.

The castle is also the headquarters of the World Owl Trust, whose excellent **Owl Centre** (Ⓣ01229/717393, Ⓦwww.owls.org) in the grounds acts as a breeding centre for endangered species (including England's own barn owl). The aviaries contain birds from forty different owl species, some of which are put through their paces on the castle lawns at the entertaining daily "Meet the Birds" display (2.30pm); the wild herons feed at 4.30pm (3.30pm in winter). Finally, the **meadowvole maze** is a light-hearted look at mole-sized life in the wildflower meadows, where escaping being eaten by an owl is the challenge for younger visitors.

The castle is closed in winter, though the grounds remain open in November and December so you can experience **Darkest Muncaster**, a sound-and-light spectacular packed with interactive surprises. There are also special Christmas tours of the castle (with mulled wine and mince pies), and **festivals** throughout the year, from summer's annual jester-fest that is the Festival of Fools to high-jinks at Halloween. Opening hours and admission prices for these events vary, but the details are all on the website.

Practicalities

Ravenglass is just half a mile off the A595 and makes a quiet night's stopover. You can also get here without a car as it's on the **Cumbrian Coast train line** (timetable on Ⓦwww.northernrail.org), with regular Monday to Saturday services from Barrow-in-Furness (45min) or Whitehaven (30min). As well as the places reviewed below, there are a couple of other B&Bs, a small shop and public bars at the two hotels.

Accommodation

Coachman's Quarters Muncaster Castle Ⓣ01229/717614, Ⓦwww.muncaster.co.uk. Live like a lord – or at least like a lord's servant – in Muncaster's smart B&B rooms in the former coachman's quarters. No meals are served other than breakfast, though guests have the use of a lounge and kitchen, and it's only a mile's walk

A night with the Muncaster spooks

Muncaster claims to be one of the most haunted houses in Britain, with tales told of spooks like the jester Tom Fool or the Muncaster Boggle. Evidence? Nothing tangible so far, though an electromagnetic "spectre-detector" has been set up to probe for poltergeists, while the castle's reputation is sufficient to attract ghost researchers and paranormal conferences. Sceptics and others can even test their nerve with an all-night **Ghost Sit** vigil in the Tapestry Room, which is supposedly the most haunted room in the castle. It's for up to six people and costs £425, or £460–495 at weekends, with breakfast included for bleary-eyed survivors.

down the path to Ravenglass and the *Ratty Arms* – or stick a bottle of bubbly in the fridge and toast yourself on the Muncaster lawns. Guests also get free access to the gardens and owl centre, and a discount on the Ravenglass and Eskdale Railway. Parking. ❸, family rooms ❹–❺

The Pennington Ravenglass ⓣ01229/717222 or 0845/450 6445, ⓦwww.penningtonhotels.com. The owners of Muncaster Castle also run this restored three-star seafront hotel, with fine rooms in a contemporary style (bold colours, pod docks, fancy bathrooms, big thick towels) set within what was once an old coaching inn. The airy, fresh feel continues in the fashionable bar and excellent restaurant, with a locally sourced menu (mains £9–15) including ingredients from Muncaster's kitchen gardens. Parking. ❺

Rosegarth Ravenglass ⓣ01229/717275, ⓦwww.rose-garth.co.uk. Hike- and bike-friendly B&B in the old doctor's house, facing the estuary. Rooms have been upgraded, most have lovely water views and there's a spacious family suite in the attic. The tearoom here (open daily Easter–Sept) is also a nice place to sit outside and enjoy the views of the water and the bobbing boats. Parking. ❸

Pub

Ratty Arms Ravenglass station ⓣ01229/717676. The main-line station house has been a popular local pub for many years – the bar is actually the old booking hall and ticket office. Real ales are on tap, and there are reasonably priced bar meals (£8–10), including specials like crab salad, lamb chops and a huge mixed grill.

Eskdale

Eskdale, accessed most easily from the Cumbrian coast, is just twelve miles long from start to finish, but what a finish it provides – in the dramatic high-fell surroundings of Hardknott Pass. The best ride in is on the Ravenglass and Eskdale Railway, though there are also minor approach roads (from Ulpha in the Duddon Valley, from Wasdale or along the River Esk itself) all meeting at the elongated hamlet of **Eskdale Green**, on a rise above the valley. From Eskdale Green, the valley road continues east, passing **Dalegarth station** (terminus of the Ravenglass and Eskdale Railway), which lies just a short walk from the valley's isolated church and from Eskdale's other hamlet, **Boot**. Here there's an old mill to explore and several more local hikes, not to mention the walk or drive up and out of the valley to the superbly sited **Hardknott Roman Fort**. There's plenty of rustic, hideaway accommodation in Eskdale, including a great selection of old inns – if you're looking for an off-the-beaten-track stay in the rural western Lakes, with walks off the doorstep, you won't find better.

Eskdale Green

First village stop on the Ravenglass and Eskdale Railway is **ESKDALE GREEN**, where you can access short walks into nearby Miterdale Forest and up to the valley head, or even plan on hiking back along the spine of Muncaster Fell to Ravenglass. This is around four miles and shouldn't take more than a couple of hours. It's a pretty sleepy village all round, only lurching into life during the annual country bash, the **Eskdale Show** (last Saturday in September), one of the biggest of the traditional rural meets in Cumbria. You can find out more at the simple village **church of St Bega** (left out of the station and past the Outward Bound centre), which doubles as an unstaffed visitor centre, with some display boards in the entrance covering the local sights and history. There's a nearby car park, by the Miterdale bridleway, and an inconspicuous sign on the bridleway, just a few yards from the road, which leads you up through Giggle Alley Wood to Eskdale Green's curious **Japanese Garden**. The series of pools, surrounded by bamboo, magnolia and maples, was originally laid out in 1913, and is now being restored by the Forestry Commission.

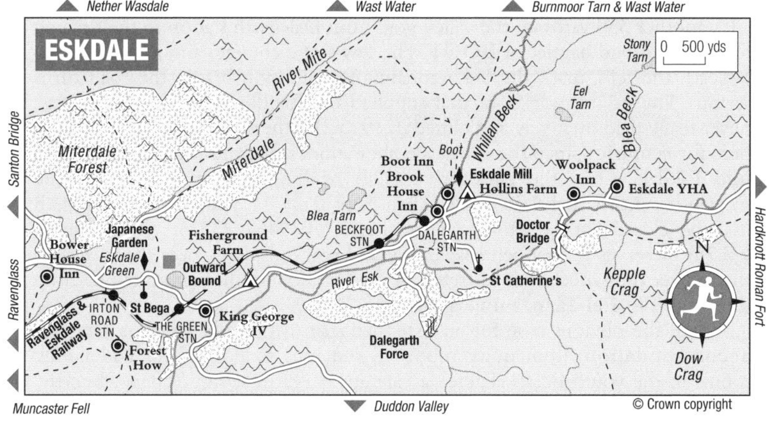

The pools fill after rain, and the encompassing shrub- and woodland is a great place for a family stroll.

Accommodation and food

Bower House Inn 1mile west, at the Santon Bridge turn-off ⓣ019467/23244, ⓦwww.bowerhouseinn.co.uk. The classiest local inn, with a good-value range of accommodation (main building, converted barn, garden rooms). The traditional bar is a beams-and-roaring-fire kind of place, and there's the usual bar menu (dishes £8–10) or a more sophisticated experience in the restaurant (say sea bass on a pesto risotto, with home-grown herbs and salad; mains from £11–14). Parking. ❸

Fisherground Farm 400 yards up the Boot road ⓣ019467/23349, ⓦwww.fishergroundcampsite.co.uk. Camping is at the peaceful, family-friendly *Fisherground*, which even has its own station on the Ravenglass and Eskdale Railway. It's great for kids (there's an adventure playground, and splashing in the nearby river), and you're only a few minutes from the *King George IV* pub. Closed Nov–Feb.

Forest How Half-mile west, near Irton Rd station ⓣ019467/23201, ⓦwww.foresthow.co.uk. Tucked under Muncaster Fell, this rural guesthouse has a lovely patio with valley views and seven country-style bedrooms (four en suite, with sparkling bathrooms) in the main house, plus an annexe with two rooms and a private bathroom, suitable for families. It's down a narrow country lane leading to Irton Rd station, and you can walk to both local pubs. No credit cards. Parking. ❷

King George IV Eskdale Green ⓣ019467/23262, ⓦwww.kinggeorge-eskdale.co.uk. Nearest pub to the station (200 yards away to the right, by the turn-off to Boot) is this traditional, ivy-strewn hostelry with three flouncy B&B rooms plus an impressive collection of real ales and malt whiskies. Parking. ❷, weekends ❸

Dalegarth station and Boot

By the time the valley road and train line reach **Dalegarth station**, two miles east of Eskdale Green, the fells beyond can be seen more clearly and eyes are drawn ever upwards to the singular skyline. Passengers pile off the train for the walk to Dalegarth Force, heading down a track opposite the station, which leads in a couple of hundred yards to Eskdale's **St Catherine's church**. Its riverside location is handsome in the extreme, and in the small cemetery you can't miss the distinctive gravestone of Thomas Dobson (d.1910), former hunt Master of the Eskdale and Ennerdale Hounds whose likeness grins from the top of the stone, above a carved fox and hound. Dobson actually died in the *Three Shires Inn* in Little Langdale, which involved his coffin being carted to Eskdale over the gruelling Wrynose and Hardknott passes. If he hadn't already been dead the bearers would probably have killed him for his thoughtlessness.

It's another 350 yards up the valley road from Dalegarth station to the turning for the dead-end hamlet of **BOOT**. The few stone cottages and pub, cowering beneath the fells, mark the last remnant of civilization before the road turns serious. The mines near Boot that supplied ore for the railway to Ravenglass never really paid their way and closed in 1913. But there's been industry of sorts here for centuries, since the Furness Abbey monks first introduced a corn mill into Eskdale. Over the packhorse bridge at the back of the hamlet, the sixteenth-century **Eskdale Mill** (April–Sept daily 11.30am–5.30pm, though may be closed Sat or Mon, call to check ⓣ019467/23335; £1.50, family £3.75) preserves its wooden machinery and you can picnic near the waterfalls that power the wheels. For a stretch of the legs, follow the signposted path up the heights to **Eel Tarn**, a mile away.

Boot is the obvious base for an extended stay in the valley, with a range of **accommodation**, from quiet rooms in old inns to dorm beds and family rooms in the youth hostel. There's a café at Dalegarth station (open when the trains are running), while a small **general store/post office** in Boot sells lakeland ice cream and even rents out hiking boots. Local **information** is available online at ⓦwww.eskdale.info and www.eskdaleweb.co.uk, while the best and most boozy day out each year is during the **Boot Beer Festival**

Walks from Eskdale

Eskdale is a great choice for a walk at any time of year: you'll rarely come across many other people on the routes outlined below, even on the shorter strolls. There's parking at Dalegarth station and in Boot, and as the train runs year-round the valley makes a fine off-season day out.

Dalegarth Force and the River Esk

Footpaths along both sides of the **River Esk** between Eskdale's St Catherine's church and Doctor Bridge (near the *Woolpack Inn*) allow an easy two-mile (1hr) riverside walk – in low water you can cross the river below the church by stepping stones, or there's a bridge further up. You can combine this with the steep climb up the wooded ravine that holds the impressive sixty-foot falls of **Dalegarth Force** (also known as Stanley Ghyll Force), in full spate for much of the year.

Hardknott and the Esk Falls

It's harder going east of Doctor Bridge, where a path to the foot of the **Hardknott Pass** keeps to the south side of the River Esk beneath Birker Fell, before cutting up, via the farm at Brotherikeld, to the Roman fort. Keeping to the Esk, you can hike on up the narrow valley between overhanging crags to **Lingcove Bridge**, beyond which tumble the **Esk Falls** – an eight-mile (5hr) round-trip that requires fine weather and good visibility, otherwise you risk getting bogged down and lost.

The Woolpack Walk

The most strenuous hike from Eskdale – and one of the most extreme in the Lakes – is the **Woolpack Walk** (18 miles; 11–12hr), a tough high-level circuit topping the two highest mountains in England (the Scafells) and several others (Bowfell, Crinkle Crags, Harter Fell) that aren't much lower. It is not easy going and a certain amount of scrambling is required, but the views and the varied terrain make this one of the finest lakeland walks. Traditional start- and finishing-point is the *Woolpack Inn*, where full route details and advice are available (*Woolpack* residents who complete the walk in under nine hours even get a free pint).

See Basics, p.42, for general walking advice in the Lakes; recommended maps are detailed on p.50.

▲ Boot

(Ⓦ www.bootbeer.co.uk), held over a June weekend and which splits its festivities between the valley's three inns.

Accommodation and food

Boot Inn Boot Ⓣ019467/23224, Ⓦwww.bootinn.co.uk. Families like the beer garden and children's areas at this cosy, traditional pub in the middle of the hamlet, and there are also nine straightforward rooms plus bar meals. Parking. ❹

Brook House Inn 350 yards east of Dalegarth station, at the Boot road junction Ⓣ019467/23288, Ⓦwww.brookhouseinn.co.uk. Cheery, family-run hotel with seven refurbished rooms with lovely rustic views. The bar's great (it's a good place for beer buffs) and the food's a real cut above ordinary pub fare – duck to seafood stew, plus some varied veggie options, with mains from £9–15. Parking. ❸

Dale View The Post Office, Boot Ⓣ019467/23236, Ⓦwww.booteskdale.co.uk. The post office has two doubles, a twin and a single, all sharing a bathroom, and can pack you a lunch for a day's walking – the *Boot Inn* is right over the road for meals. Advance reservations recommended in winter, when B&B is not always available. No credit cards. ❷

Eskdale YHA Eskdale, Hardknott Pass road, 200 yards east of *Woolpack Inn* Ⓣ0845/371 9317, Ⓔeskdale@yha.org.uk. There's an eco-feel to this secluded hostel nestling beneath Eskdale Fell, which has its own environmentally friendly heating system, plus a nature trail for bird and red-squirrel spotting. It's a family favourite, but great for walkers too (with laundry facilities and drying room), and you're only a 5min walk from the *Woolpack Inn*, though the meals here are first-rate too (wine and chestnut pâté, pan-seared chicken, red onion and goat's cheese tart, mains £7). Closed Nov–March. Dorm beds from £15.95.

Hollins Farm Eskdale, Hardknott Pass road, 200 yards east of Boot Ⓣ019467/23253, Ⓦwww.hollinsfarmcampsite.co.uk. Small campsite, beautifully sited in the Esk valley, just a short walk from the railway and the valley's pubs. For camping without canvas, they also have ten heated "pods" (from £40). It's very definitely a family-friendly place, with zero-tolerance for noise, music and large groups. Closed 2 weeks Jan, & Feb

Woolpack Inn Eskdale, Hardknott Pass road, 1 mile east of Boot Ⓣ019467/23230, Ⓦwww.woolpack.co.uk. The top choice for Eskdale dining is this friendly inn with a view, just up the road from Boot, offering a sophisticated, locally sourced menu – say home-smoked trout, followed by a fabulous ginger-and-garlic marinated Cumbrian beef fillet and the unique white chocolate and blue cheese "bomb" for

Dry-stone walls

A dry-stone wall
Is a wall and a wall,
Leaning together
(Cumberland and Westmorland
champion wrestlers),
Greening and weathering,
Flank by flank,
With filling of rubble
Between the two.

From "Wall", by Norman Nicholson

The hundreds of miles of **dry-stone walls** that crisscross the Lake District are one of the region's most characteristic sights. As early as the thirteenth century the monks of Furness Abbey were enclosing extensive tracts of moorland within stone-built walls, traces of which can still be seen in upper Eskdale. Walls provided the means of converting unproductive high land into enclosed sheep farms: separating grazing areas, providing flocks with shelter (and preventing them straying), and facilitating sheep-driving and collection (by means of stone-built "pounds").

Irregularly walled enclosures gave way to systematic patterns during the eighteenth and nineteenth centuries as the **Enclosure Acts** (1801) prevailed – basically, statutes sanctioning the grabbing of once common or wild land by the bigger, richer landowners. Behind this larceny was a rapidly increasing demand for food and wool, driven by the mushrooming population of the newly industrialized cities and the effect of the blockades during the Napoleonic War which kept food prices high. For many, the resulting walls – now an integral part of the landscape, but then a novelty – symbolized the growing hardship of the small farmer. Nineteenth-century English "peasant poet" John Clare wrote bitterly that: "Enclosure came, and trampled on the grave of labour's rights, and left the poor a slave."

The increased demand for walls outstripped the capabilities of most farmers and inspired a new trade, undertaken by bands of itinerant craftsmen (not strictly masons, but skilled nonetheless). Sleeping on the fells and using the stone they found *in situ* – which explains the homogeneous, almost organic quality of lakeland walls – these "wallers" would set about erecting what are known locally as "dykes".

As its name makes clear, a dry-stone wall has no mortar to hold it together. Instead, it's built on the cavity-wall principle – that is, as a double wall with the space between packed with small stones (guts). Ideally a two-person job (someone working alone has to keep changing sides), the wall starts off at anything up to 3ft wide, narrowing to around a foot wide at the top. Long stones (throughs) are placed at intervals through the width for stability, while the walls are topped by slanted stones (cams) so that the rain drains off. To allow sheep access from one pasture to another, a space (hogg hole) might be left in the base of a wall. The finished product is remarkably hardy: dry-stone walls might last fifty or a hundred years without shifting or collapsing, often longer.

While not exactly a growth industry these days, new dry-stone walls are still needed on modern sheep farms and existing walls require maintenance. The old skills have been kept alive by a dedicated band of wallers: you'll see them in action at annual agricultural shows, while there are also dry-stone wall-building demonstrations every summer, coordinated by the Lake District Visitor Centre at Brockhole.

dessert (mains £12–18; hearty ploughman's, casserole and stew lunches £6–10). Peaceful accommodation is in eight cosy, refurbished rooms upstairs (six en suite, one classed as "deluxe" with a double spa bath), while the bar and beer garden is the place to sample some great beers from the pub's own brewery. Parking. ❸, deluxe ❺

Hardknott Fort and Pass

Three miles beyond Boot and 800ft up the twisting road, the remains of **Hardknott Roman Fort** (always open; free access) – known as Mediobocdum to the Romans – command a strategic and panoramic position just below Hardknott Pass. If ever proof were needed of how serious the Romans were about keeping what they had conquered, then Hardknott proves the point. This full-scale fortification was built during the reign of Hadrian by a cohort of Dalmatian (Croatian) troops, who gave it walls twelve feet thick and a double-towered gateway, and endowed it with granaries, bathhouses and a plush, stone-built *praetorium* or commandant's quarters. The troops had to endure the discomforts of timber barracks, though since the *praetorium* was built along Roman lines – rooms ranged around an open courtyard – the commandant probably cursed his luck at his assignment every time the wind blew (about every ten seconds up here). Much of the lower part of the defensive wall is original Roman work; elsewhere, the foundations of the granaries and various other buildings have been re-erected to indicate their scale. Needless to say, the views back down into Eskdale and up to the Scafells are stunning.

Past the fort, after negotiating the narrow switchbacks of **Hardknott Pass**, the road drops to Cockley Beck (for the Duddon Valley), before making the equally alarming ascent of Wrynose Pass, gateway to Little Langdale.

Wasdale

Glorious **Wasdale** is all about the mountains, despite the presence of three-mile-long **Wast Water**, England's deepest lake. Awesome 1700-foot screes plunge to its eastern shore, separating Wast Water from Eskdale to the south, while the highest peaks in England – Great Gable and the Scafells – frame **Wasdale Head**, the tiny settlement at the head of the lake. As every local business and website will undoubtedly tell you, it's officially "Britain's favourite view", following a TV show public vote; and you'll have seen the panorama up the lake to Great Gable, unwittingly, countless times already since the National Park Authority uses the outline as its logo on every publication, signpost and notice board.

Apart from a few farms and cottages, and a single inn, the valley head is a remote yet starkly beautiful environment – mountain hikers know all about it, and can access some of the toughest, most rewarding lakeland peaks and circuits from here. But Wasdale has its softer side too, starting in the approach village of **Gosforth**, with its ancient cross, just off the A595. Beyond here, through forestry plantations and farmland, lie the Wasdale hamlets of **Santon Bridge** and **Nether Wasdale**, with the foot of the lake just a mile and a half east of Nether Wasdale. The drive in is a treat – bracken-covered walls hide the fields from view, while the roads cross little stone bridges and pass farm shops selling jars of bramble jelly or bags of new potatoes. Beyond Nether Wasdale the road is single-track for the most part and hugs Wast Water's western shore, with occasional parking spots by bosky groves, stony coves and little promontories.

The only public transport into Wasdale is the limited-service, pre-booked **Wasdale Taxi-Bus** from Gosforth (Thurs, Sat & Sun only; call Gosforth Taxis ⓣ019467/25308, the day before), which leaves Gosforth around 9.30am and again at 5.30pm, travelling via Nether Wasdale and the youth hostel (return from Wasdale Head around 10am and 6pm).

Gosforth and around

At the Wasdale turn-off from the A595, **GOSFORTH** ("ford of geese") – a large if unremarkable village – has one extraordinary attraction: the tall, carved **stone cross** in the churchyard of St Mary's on the eastern edge of town. Signposted as the "Viking" cross, it's a rare example in Cumbria of the clash between pagan and Christian cultures, with the four faces of the slender shaft carved with Norse figures from the Sagas, which are surmounted by a Christian cross. There's been a church on this site since at least the tenth century, though it's been rebuilt many times since: nineteenth-century restoration revealed the church's other treasures, the two Viking "hogback" **tombstones**, found buried in the foundations. If your imagination is captured by the Gosforth cross, you should really drive the three miles south back down the A595, through Holmrook, and take the left turn signposted to Santon Bridge. A mile up the ruler-straight road, a signposted track – accessible with care for cars – leads to isolated **St Paul's**, Irton, which has a worn tenth-century stone cross in its churchyard.

Practicalities

Gosforth has a couple of pubs, village shop, bakery (locally famed for its meat pies) and farm grocery shop. It's also got a post office, petrol station and an ATM, which makes it the most reliable place for services and supplies in this neck of the woods. There is village **accommodation**, but it's nicer to stay closer to the lake, either in **Nether Wasdale** (which is basically a group of inns near the green, plus a local hostel) or two miles southwest of here in **Santon Bridge**, a rustic hamlet by the River Irt.

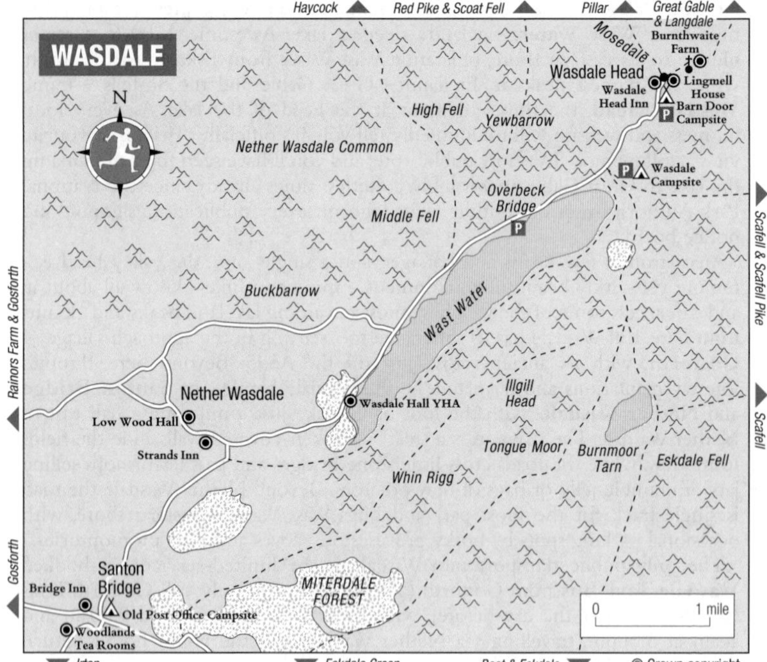

▲ Wast Water

Nether Wasdale

Low Wood Hall ⓣ019467/26100, ⓦwww.lowwoodhall.co.uk. A restored Victorian-era country house whose gardens and conservatory restaurant look toward the fells. The standard rooms are in the separate lodge, with fancier accommodation in the main house, which has kept many of its original features. Restaurant closed Sun dinner. Parking. ❸, superior rooms ❹

Rainors Farm Gosforth road, 2.5 miles west of Nether Wasdale ⓣ019467/25934, ⓦwww.rainorsfarm.co.uk. Overnighters can choose one of two B&B rooms in the very picturesque farmhouse, and the owners promise fab views without leaving your bed. Otherwise, there's a charming two-bedroom guest suite annexe (available for 3 nights from £350 or by the week from £450, no breakfast) and two cosily furnished yurts (sleep up to five, 3 nights from £385, 7 nights from £595, winter discounts available), one in the paddock, the other by the stream, with breakfast served in the house. Parking. No credit cards. ❷

Strands Inn ⓣ019467/26237, ⓦwww.strandshotel.com. The pick of the inns on the green has some nicely turned out country-style rooms above a restaurant where you can dine well on locally sourced produce, including Cumbrian air-dried ham, fell-bred lamb and Wasdale goat's cheese (most mains £10–12). The bar's a cosy bolt hole and they've got their own microbrewery too, with a beer called "Errmmm" (they couldn't decide on a name). Parking. ❸

Wasdale Hall YHA 1.5 miles east of Nether Wasdale ⓣ0845/371 9350, ⓔwastwater@yha.org.uk. Stay in a country mansion at budget rates at Wastwater's impressive YHA hostel (owned by the National Trust). It's a baronial beauty, with a half-timbered facade and wood-panelled restaurant, and there are dramatic lake views from some of the rooms. The grounds reach to the shore, while nearby Low Wood has one of the Lakes' finest displays of spring bluebells. Advance reservations essential; dorm beds from £13.95.

Santon Bridge

Bridge Inn ⓣ019467/26221, ⓦwww.santonbridgeinn.com. Bump over the little humpback bridge that crosses the River Irt to find this modest country pub, a handy Wasdale halt for rooms and food. There's great excitement and tall tales once a year (see box, p.198), but otherwise it's a peaceful overnight stop offering handsome rooms and honest-to-goodness food – with walkers' breakfasts served daily as well as very popular home-style bistro meals in the bar (£9–14). ❹

Old Post Office Campsite ⓣ019467/26286, ⓦwww.theoldpostofficecampsite.co.uk. A small, bucolic family site with babbling river on one side and *Bridge Inn* just over the bridge – the pub can even supply Jennings' beer takeaways to happy campers, and there's a handy nearby farm shop. Closed Oct–Feb.

Woodlands Tea Room ⓣ019467/26281, ⓦwww.santonbridge.co.uk. A few hundred yards away from the bridge (on the Irton road, to the A595), with teas, meals and cakes available at the café attached to a country crafts and gift shop.

Don't believe a word of it

The *Bridge Inn* at Santon Bridge is best known for hosting the annual **Biggest Liar in the World** competition every November, a tradition started in the late nineteenth century by publican **Will Ritson** (1808–90) of nearby Wasdale Head, who told famously tall tales of country life to his gullible guests. The Victorian gentleman fell-walkers and pioneer mountaineers – mostly professional men and academics from the cities – were, for example, given to believe that Wasdale turnips grew so large that farmers quarried them for food and then used the hollowed-out husks for sheep sheds. The annual contest is open to all-comers (though, for obvious reasons, lawyers and politicians are barred from entering), who have five minutes to tell the biggest lie they can. The winner gets a cup and £25, and entrants have to convince a sceptical local crowd that their tall tales of lakeland life just might have something in them, whether it's Cumbrian mermaid farms, dogs with false teeth being pursued by foxes, or flatulent sheep causing the hole in the ozone layer.

Wasdale Head

The Wast Water road ends a mile beyond the lake at Wasdale Head, a Shangri-La-like clearing between the mountain ranges, where you'll find the **Wasdale Head Inn**, one of the most celebrated of all lakeland inns. British mountain-climbing was born here in the days when the inn's landlord – and champion liar – was the famous Will Ritson: black-and-white photographs pinned to the panelled rooms inside show Victorian gents in hobnailed boots and flat caps scaling dreadful precipices with nonchalant ease (for more on the birthplace of British mountain-climbing, see p.284). The inn's gone a bit upmarket since those days, but still attracts a genuine walking and climbing crowd, not bothered in the slightest by the lack of TV or mobile phone reception in the valley.

What's reputed to be England's smallest church, **St Olaf's**, lies a couple of hundred yards from the inn, encircled by evergreens and dwarfed by the surrounding fells. The small cemetery contains graves and memorials to several of those killed while climbing them. There's been a church at Wasdale since medieval times and though no one knows quite how old this plain chapel is, its current appearance – moss-grown slate roof and all – dates from a complete overhaul in 1892. The path over Eskdale Moor, via **Burnmoor Tarn**, was the former "corpse road" along which the dead were carried for burying in Eskdale church, since St Olaf's had no consecrated churchyard until 1901.

For a true measure of your own insignificance, take a walk down to Wast Water and along the eastern lakeshore path, approaching the impassable, implacable **screes**. Thomas Wilkinson, an overawed eighteenth-century Quaker, fancied that he was gazing upon "the Pyramids of the world, built by the Architect of the Universe".

Practicalities

There's a public **car park** near the head of the lake and another close to the *Wasdale Head Inn*, but the spaces fill quickly with hill-bound hikers, even on the grottiest of days. The Wasdale Web (Ⓦwww.wasdaleweb.co.uk) is the best source of local **information**, including accommodation listings – the campsites, farm and B&B listed below are each only a short walk from the inn, while other farmhouse B&Bs lie scattered down the valley. The **Barn Door Shop** (Ⓣ019467/26384, Ⓔinfo@barndoorshop.co.uk) next to the inn has basic foodstuffs and crucial slabs of Kendal Mintcake, plus outdoor clothes, equipment and walking advice.

Accommodation and food

Burnthwaite Farm ⓣ019467/26242, ⓦwww.burnthwaitefarm.co.uk. A handsome old working sheep farm with six traditional B&B rooms available, with and without en-suite facilities. There is also a self-catering apartment (sleeps four, from £300 per week, or £50 a night when available). Parking. Closed mid-Nov to Jan. No credit cards. ❷

Lingmell House ⓣ019467/26261, ⓦwww.lingmellhouse.co.uk. This guesthouse was once the vicarage and now has three agreeable rooms sharing a couple of bathrooms, all glorying in fine fell views. Tim, the owner, can point you in the right direction for a hike and pack you a lunch. Parking. Closed Jan. No credit cards. ❸

Wasdale Head Inn ⓣ019467/26229, ⓦwww.wasdale.com. There's no finer sight at the end of a day's hiking than the famous inn at the head of the valley. The compact rooms all have supremely comfortable beds, though for more space ask for one of the "superior rooms" in the adjacent barn conversion, which have a kitchenette, lounge area and full bathroom (though breakfast is not included with these). There are also six self-catering apartments in a converted barn (sleeps two to four, from £370 per week). Local hiking information and a daily weather forecast are on hand. The inn brews its own beer, the breakfasts are legendary and, though there are hearty bistro meals in the bar (£8–11), the classy four-course dinner (£28) in the oak-panelled dining room is one of the Lake District's best buys. Parking. ❺

Campsites

Barn Door ⓣ019467/26384. The hardiest hikers of all stay at the field, tap-and-toilet campsite next to the Barn Door shop, across from the inn. There's no vehicle access (though you can park nearby), no frills and no bookings – check in on arrival at the shop or pay next morning if it's closed. Space is always available, except perhaps on bank holiday weekends. Open all year.

Wasdale Campsite ⓣ019467/26220, booking line ⓣ015394/63862, ⓦwww.ntlakescampsites.org.uk. The National Trust's Wasdale site is a mile from the pub, but you pitch your tent under the glowering mountains at the head of the lake. There's a shop, showers and a laundry room beneath the trees, and a couple of camping pods for softies (sleep 2 adults and 1 child, from £30–45). Open all year.

Walks from Wasdale Head

Wasdale Head is at the heart of some serious walking and climbing country, offering popular climbs up to Scoat Fell, Pillar, the Scafells and Great Gable, among others, and classic routes over the passes into Ennerdale or Borrowdale. It's not really beginners' country, though walks down to the lake, a scramble along its eastern shore or the hike over moorland to Burnmoor Tarn and Eskdale should be within most capabilities.

A Mosedale horseshoe

Mosedale – the valley to the northwest of Wasdale Head – is crowned by an impressive ring of high peaks and crags. A terrific horseshoe circuit starts from the **Overbeck Bridge** car park (2 miles from Wasdale Head, down the lake road) and then climbs and scrambles up via Yewbarrow (2060ft), Red Pike (1710ft) and Scoat Fell (2760ft) to **Pillar** (2927ft). The walk then continues along the ridge via Looking Stead to the top of **Black Sail Pass**, from where you descend down the old Mosedale packhorse trail right to the door of the *Wasdale Head Inn* for a welcome drink. The whole route is around 12 miles, or six to seven hours' fairly tough walking.

Scafell

Scafell (3163ft) is England's second-highest mountain, though it's actually more prominent seen from many directions than the superior Scafell Pike. The two peaks are connected by the col known as **Mickledore**, though the Broad Stand rock face – the most direct approach – presents an impassable obstacle to walkers. Meanwhile, the classic ascent of Scafell from Wasdale via **Lord's Rake** is now off-limits because of dangerous rock falls. Instead, walkers from Wasdale will need to make the long-winded ascent via **Foxes Tarn**. The easier route from Wasdale to the summit of Scafell (3hr) is the circuitous one taken since Victorian times, from Burnmoor Tarn and the old corpse road – either route starts at Brackenclose car park, at the head of Wast Water.

Ennerdale

Ennerdale, the next major valley north of Wasdale, is about as far off the beaten track as you can get in the western fells and valleys. There's only one very small village, limited public transport and no road at all around Ennerdale Water, which makes it one of the most inaccessible of the lakes – or one of the best for walkers, depending on how you look at it. Having made the effort, you'll find that Ennerdale Water is among the most alluring of the lakes, its quiet two-and-a-half-mile length (fiddle-shaped according to Coleridge) ringed by crags and dominated at the head by the dramatic heights of Pillar. If you haven't seen this peak before, you'll not recognize it from the name alone – the bulky fell takes its name instead from one of its northern crags, the devilish Pillar Rock, the proving ground of British mountaineers for over a century.

While the valley undergoes a gradual, natural transformation (see feature), the village, **ENNERDALE BRIDGE**, seems barely changed since Wordsworth's day, especially in the peaceful shaded churchyard; still "girt round with a bare ring of mossy wall", as the poet described it at the beginning of *The Brothers*. Straddling the River Ehen, and encircled by a bowl of rounded fells, the village is only ten miles from Cockermouth (from where there's a regular bus service) and seven from the coast, but seems much further from anywhere. A small post office/shop and a couple of pubs provide what few facilities there are, though the village sees a fair amount of foot traffic as it's the first overnight stop on the Coast-to-Coast walk from St Bees.

Ennerdale Water is a mile and a half to the west, where car parks provide access for walkers – two at the western end of the lake, near the village, and a third at **Bowness Knott**, midway along the northern shore. Cars aren't allowed any further than Bowness Knott, though there is a track for vehicle

Wild Ennerdale

Ennerdale was the valley most affected by the mass imposition of conifer plantations by the Forestry Commission in the 1930s. There was nothing new about planting trees for profit in the Lakes – Wordsworth was already complaining about it in his *Guide to the Lakes* (a "vegetable manufactory" he called it) – but the sheer scale in Ennerdale was unprecedented. Before 1930 the upper part of the valley was a desolate, rocky wilderness, devoid of trees. Afterwards, thousands of acres lay under a thick blanket of uniform conifer plantations – only local resistance prevented Eskdale, Wast Water and Buttermere going the same way. In England's mild climate, the rigid blocks of larch, spruce and pine grew quickly, blocking out the light and carpeting the valley floors with slow-decomposing acidic needles. Wild plants (and therefore animals) were quickly forced out of their natural habitat. More enlightened planting policies (mixing in broad-leaved trees and following the contours instead of straight lines) softened the scenery over the years, but it wasn't until the **Wild Ennerdale** (Ⓦwww.wildennerdale.co.uk) initiative that a new, holistic approach was taken. It's still a major timber provider, but Ennerdale's three main landowners (Forestry Commission, National Trust and water company United Utilities) have undertaken to "allow the evolution of Ennerdale as a wild valley" – in essence, thinning and clearing conifers, re-establishing native trees and heather and allowing the River Liza to find its own course. Free-grazing Galloway cattle have been introduced (don't be surprised to come across some on your hikes), and red deer and otters have returned to the valley. If you've steered clear of Ennerdale's brutal man-made forest swathes in the past, now's the time to come back for a look at a land reclaiming itself.

access to Low Gillerthwaite and *Ennerdale YHA* (see below) and a couple of nearby lakeside picnic areas. In past years there's been a summer-Sunday "Ennerdale Rambler" bus to Bowness Knott, from Cockermouth, Buttermere and Loweswater, but it's not a guaranteed service.

The **circuit of the lake** (8 miles; 4hr) is an enjoyable low-level walk, with the option of a scramble up **Angler's Crag** on the southwestern promontory. Sterner tests are provided by any of the peaks on the valley's southern side, though unless you're staying at either of the Ennerdale youth hostels you've got to add the valley walk-in and return to Bowness Knott car park to your day's hike. For that reason, you won't see too many others en route (most choose to climb Pillar, say, from Wasdale), which is a recommendation in itself: an **Ennerdale peaks circuit** (12 miles; 7hr) from Bowness Knott, taking in Haycock (2618ft), Scoat Fell (2760ft), Steeple (2687ft) and Pillar (2927ft), is one of the most exhilarating fell walks in the region.

Accommodation and food

Black Sail YHA 6 miles east of Bowness Knott ⓣ0845/ 371 9680, ⓔblacksail@yha.org.uk. The Lakes' most isolated and basic hostel (no vehicle access – only foot visitors) is a former shepherd's bothy with just sixteen beds, but it's stunningly set at the head of Ennerdale and the walking around here is sensational. It's not a complete back-to-basics experience – true, there's no TV, phone reception or electric sockets, but there's gas-powered central heating, and electricity from solar panels, plus a full meals service (3 courses, £11.50) and an alcohol licence. Advance reservations are essential – open daily Easter–Oct, closed for individuals from Nov–March. Dorm beds from £13.95, weekends from £15.95.

Ennerdale YHA 2.5 miles east of Bowness Knott ⓣ0845/371 9116, ⓔennerdale@yha.org.uk. Ennerdale's main YHA hostel is a fully refurbished eco-retreat converted from two old forestry cottages, providing 24 dorm beds in smart rooms for hikers and Coast-to-Coasters (and there are family rooms and a spillover bunk barn too). It has its own hydroelectric power, and there's a wood-burner in the cosy lounge-diner, while good-value meals (3 courses, £11.50) use locally sourced, organic and Fair Trade ingredients (and you can buy a Cumbrian ale or a bottle of organic wine). Open daily Easter–Oct, closed for individuals from Nov–March. Parking for up to 6 cars. Dorm beds from £13.95, weekends from £15.95.

Bradley's Riding Centre and B&B Low Cock How, Kinniside, 1.25 miles south of Ennerdale Bridge ⓣ01946/861354, ⓦwww.walk-rest-ride.co.uk. The farm is right on the Coast-to-Coast walk, and has three B&B rooms, as well as a twelve-bed bunkhouse (£17 with breakfast) with cooking and shower facilities. Evening meals, packed lunches and horseriding available. Parking. ❸

Low Gillerthwaite Field Centre 2.5 miles east of Bowness Knott ⓣ01946/861229, ⓦwww.lgfc.org.uk. Seventeenth-century Low Gillerthwaite farmhouse has been refitted as an outdoor activity centre, used by small groups but available for individual overnight stays for hikers – call in advance to check. It's bunkhouse style (bring your own sleeping bag), and there's a decent self-catering kitchen, lounge with open fire and drying room. Even if the house is full, walk-in campers can usually pitch a tent outside. Parking. Dorm beds from £13.

Shepherd's Arms Ennerdale Bridge ⓣ01946/861249, ⓦwww.shepherdsarmshotel.co.uk. Cosy old coaching inn that is a popular Coast-to-Coast stopover, hence the daily posted weather forecast. Rooms are fine for the money, though the real selling-point for weary hikers is the welcoming bar, with a winter fire, hearty bar meals (from £8) and a good choice of beers. Parking. ❸

Lorton Vale and Loweswater

Southeast of Cockermouth the B5292 rolls into the pastoral **Lorton Vale**, turning east to tackle the Whinlatter Pass on the way to Keswick. The scattered settlement of **LORTON** – divided into Low and High – has a twelfth-century church, St Cuthbert's, of minor interest, but there's also a pub and post office/general store, and some gentle walking in the fields near the River Cocker. The fiery Quaker George Fox preached to a seventeenth-century Lorton crowd under a spreading yew tree, which Wordsworth later commemorated ("pride of Lorton Vale") in his poem "Yew-trees" (1803).

Keeping south on the B5289, the fells – and Buttermere – are beckoning, but a diversion to **Loweswater**, six miles from Cockermouth, provides an opportunity to see one of the region's smallest, shallowest and least-known lakes. The water only averages a depth of sixty feet, and the reeds and lily pads that cling to the shores are a habitat for many species of insects and birds. You'll never be bothered by crowds here. There's no village to speak of, rather a collection of houses, a church and a telephone box, with a couple of signs pointing you towards the excellent *Kirkstile Inn*. Loweswater itself is a mile beyond the inn and really the only thing to do is to walk around it, on a gentle low-level route (4 miles; 1hr 30min) that stays under a woodland canopy for much of the duration. A detour in Holme Wood up to **Holme Force** adds a bit of interest after sustained rain; while the best views of the water are from Waterend, at the northern end of the lake.

The distinctive volcano-shaped peak that towers above the southern end of Loweswater is **Mellbreak** (1676ft). The view of the fell from the beer-garden of the *Kirkstile Inn* is impressive, but it's fairly easily climbed too – follow the road over the small bridge from the pub, then the obvious track up through the screes to the top (1hr). Descending, you can return to the inn either along the old drover's track along the Mosedale valley bottom, or along the Crummock Water shore path (either route, 6 miles; 3hr return), by which time you'll be ready to celebrate with a pint of their conveniently named, own-brew Mellbreak Bitter.

It's a quick, 15- or 20-minute drive to Loweswater from Cockermouth, and a longer one if you come over either pass (Whinlattter or Honister) from Keswick; there's also a back-country route on minor lanes from Ennerdale. There are a couple of small **parking** places at Waterend, and a National Trust car park (unmarked on most maps) near Watergate Farm at the southern end. If the summer-Sunday "Ennerdale Rambler" **bus** from Buttermere is running, it also passes Loweswater, following the northern shore road past Waterend. For Lorton and the Whinlatter Pass, the service is the #77A from Buttermere, which runs up the B5289 before turning east along the B5292 towards Keswick.

Accommodation and food

Kirkstile Inn Loweswater ⓣ01900/85219, ⓦwww.kirkstile.com. Best in the west? Very possibly, since the welcoming sixteenth-century riverside inn gave its rooms a contemporary makeover, retaining the beams and country furniture but adding smart bathrooms, crisp linen and very comfortable beds. There are seven rooms in the main inn and two self-contained family suites in the adjoining buildings, which can accommodate up to four adults – one also has a kitchen and lounge. On-the-ball staff deliver quality bar meals (smoked chicken salad, local trout, slow-cooked lamb shoulder, fell-bred steak, mains £9–12) and you can take in the sunsets in the beer garden and sink one of their own-brew beers. Parking. ❹, suites ❺

New House Farm B5289, 1 mile south of Low Lorton ⓣ0784/1159818, ⓦwww.newhouse-farm.co.uk. This is a gem of a place with five hugely attractive rooms, either in the meticulously restored seventeenth-century farmhouse or its period outbuildings – the Old Dairy room (the largest), for example, has an extraordinary carved four-poster bed and a stunning bathroom with freestanding bath and hanging tapestry. Outside, 15 surrounding acres include mown grass walkways, ponds, gardens and an outdoor hot tub, while the barn tearoom (closed Nov to mid-Feb, though open some weekends) provides all-day meals and snacks – a three- or five-course dinner (£28/37) is available too, usually based around a proper English roast or casserole. Parking. ❻

Old Vicarage Church Lane, Low Lorton ⓣ01900/85656, ⓦwww.oldvicarage.co.uk. Wooded grounds surround this impressive Victorian property, where a mahogany staircase ascends to

People and places: Meet the brewers

There must be something in the water in the west – how else to explain the sheer number of microbreweries that have sprung up here in the last few years, even in the most isolated valleys, from Eskdale to Ennerdale. For some, like Roger Humphreys at Loweswater's **Kirkstile Inn** (Ⓦwww-kirkstile.com), it was a logical extension of the business, given that they were already selling other people's real ale – "and, of course, we thought it would be an enjoyable venture". Successful too, as visitors increasingly seek out locally made products, so much so that production of the original Kirkstile beers has now shifted to bigger premises in Hawkshead, having taken over Cumbrian Legendary Ales (Ⓦwww.cumbrianlegendaryales.com). Other brewers have stayed resolutely in-house, including the **Great Gable Brewing Company** (Ⓦwww.greatgablebrewing.co.uk) at the *Wasdale Head Inn* where, as owner Howard Christie points out, you can buy the beer they make just ten yards away in the pub. That was the attraction too for Dave Bailey and his **Hardknott Brewery** (Ⓦwww.woolpack.co.uk), tucked away at the back end of Eskdale at his *Woolpack Inn*. "Now, when people ask, 'What's the most local brew?'", says Dave, "we can say, 'this one, brewed the other side of that wall!'" Of course, you've got to name your beers once you've made them, and you can either be inspired by the names of the local mountains (as at the *Wasdale Head*) or come up with something a bit different. "Tenacity" seemed to sum up both beer and effort involved in the first brew that Dave Bailey made, but "Dickie Doodle" (at the *Kirkstile*), "T'Errmmminator" (*Strands Inn*, Nether Wasdale) and "Grasp the Nettle" (from the *Bitter End* in Cockermouth)? There's a story behind every one, and a brewer to tell it to you.

the rooms. There's also a family suite in an old coach house. Afternoon tea is served in the garden in good weather and the pub is only 5min walk away (they'll lend you a torch for evening visits). Dinner is available (£25) if you prefer to stay put. Parking. ❺

Wheatsheaf Inn Low Lorton ⓣ01900/85199, Ⓦwww.wheatsheafinnlorton.co.uk. Lorton's local pub has a pleasant beer garden, substantial bar meals (mains £9–13) and Jennings ales. Out the back, there's a camping and caravan site (closed Dec–Feb) with shower, toilet block and drying facilities (enquiries at the inn).

Winder Hall Low Lorton ⓣ01900/85107, Ⓦwww.winderhall.co.uk. There's been a grand manor house here on the banks of the River Cocker since the fifteenth century, but there are no airs and graces in this fabulously welcoming home from home. Where else are you invited to collect your own breakfast eggs and feed the pigs that supply the bacon? Seven spacious rooms have antique beds, window seats and original fireplaces, although "Fellbarrow" is more contemporary in style. Books, maps, jigsaws and games are provided, and children are positively welcomed, while a summerhouse overlooking the river meadow contains a smashing hot tub and sauna. Dinner (£39, open to non-residents) is an informal treat, hot on locally grown, organic and free-range ingredients and flavours. Parking. ❺, weekends ❻

Crummock Water and Buttermere

A simple glance at the map shows that **Crummock Water** and **Buttermere** – separated by only a half-mile of slightly elevated flood-prone farmland – were once joined as one lake. In the main, they're visited as one, with nearly all the day-traffic concentrated in and around **BUTTERMERE** village, a small settlement in the middle of the two lakes with an outlying church, two inns and the rest of the local facilities.

The two lakes, however, have entirely different aspects: small Buttermere ("Boethar's lake") is ringed by crags and peaks, culminating in the desolate heights of Gatesgarthdale; more expansive Crummock Water ("crooked lake") is almost twice as long (at two and a half miles) and half as deep again, yet peters out in the gentle flat lands of Lorton Vale. It's a contrasting beauty that brought back that most obsessive of fell walkers, Alfred Wainwright, again and again. A plaque in the small parish **church of St James**, on a hillock above Buttermere village, asks you to pause and remember him and then lift your eyes to Haystacks, his favourite peak, where his ashes are scattered. In *Fellwanderer*, his account of the writing of his famous *Pictorial Guides*, he's typically and playfully brusque: "If, dear reader, you should get a bit of grit in your boot as you are crossing Haystacks in the years to come, please treat it with respect. It might be me."

The grandeur of the locality was well known even before Wainwright gave it his seal of approval. With the Lakes in vogue amongst travelling men in the late eighteenth century, many made their way over the passes to what was then a remote hamlet with a reputation for good fishing in the twin lakes. A certain

Walks from Crummock Water and Buttermere

Many hikers have their fondest memories of the fells around Buttermere and Crummock Water, and one – Haystacks – is the final resting place of the greatest walker of them all, **Alfred Wainwright**. It's easy to gain height quickly around here for some terrific views, though the low-level circuits of the two lakes are also very rewarding.

Crummock Water and Scale Force

Any circuit of **Crummock Water** should include the diversion to the 170ft drop of **Scale Force**, among the most spectacular of Lake District waterfalls. You can then either regain the western shore and stick close to the lake for the rest of the circuit (8 miles; 4hr), or climb past the falls and follow the Mosedale valley path to Loweswater (where there's a pub, the *Kirkstile Inn*) before completing the circuit (10 miles; 5–6hr).

Around Buttermere

The four-mile stroll circling **Buttermere** shouldn't take more than a couple of hours – in wet weather, the waters tumbling a thousand feet down Sour Milk Ghyll are amazing. And you can always detour up **Scarth Gap** to Haystacks (see below) if you want more of a climb and some views. It's worth knowing that, in summer, there's usually an ice-cream van parked by Gatesgarth Farm at the southern end of the lake.

Red Pike to Haystacks

The classic Buttermere circuit (8 miles; 6hr 30min) climbs from the village up **Red Pike** (2479ft) and then runs along the ridge, via **High Stile** (2644ft), **High Crag** (2443ft) and **Haystacks** (1900ft), before descending to the lake – either by backtracking and heading down Scarth Gap or by picking your way down off Haystacks, rounding Inominate Tarn and descending via **Warnscale Bottom**. For a fuller experience, add another hour to the beginning of the hike by first climbing up Scale Force from Buttermere and working your way across to Red Pike from there.

Robinson

The quickest ascent from Buttermere (2.5 miles; 1hr 30min) for some top-drawer views is the climb up **Robinson** (2417ft) – the path is signposted a little way up the Newlands valley road, past the church. You'll get a bit wet at any time of year crossing the wide marsh of Buttermere Moss (the only way water can escape from here, opines Wainwright, is by being carried away in the boots of pedestrians), but then it's up to the rocky plateau summit for majestic mountain views.

See Basics, p.42, for general walking advice in the Lakes; recommended maps are detailed on p.50.

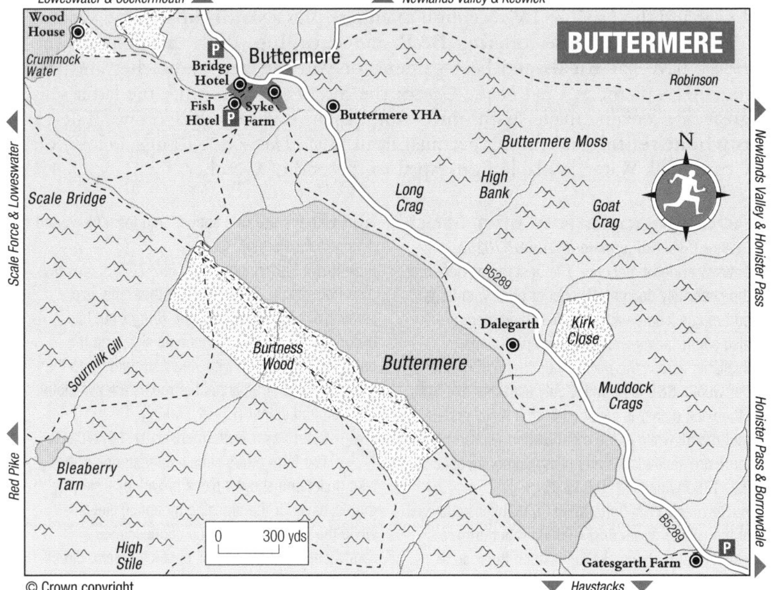

Captain Budworth – resident at the *Fish Inn*, the only inn in those days – waxed lyrical about the beauty of the landlord's daughter in his bestseller, *A Fortnight's Ramble in the Lakes*. Within a couple of years, curious sightseers – Wordsworth and Coleridge included – were turning up to view **Mary Robinson, the Maid of Buttermere**. One such visitor was Alexander Augustus Colonel Hope, Member of Parliament and brother to an earl. Flush with money and manners, he wooed and married Mary – only to be revealed as the bigamous impostor John Hatfield, whose whole life had been one of deception and fraud. Arrested and tried for forgery (franking letters as an MP without authority was a capital offence), Hatfield was hanged at Carlisle in 1802 – the entire scandal recorded for the *Morning Post* by Coleridge in investigative journalist mode. Mary became a cause célèbre, the subject of ballads, books and plays, before retiring from the public gaze at the *Fish* to become wife to a Caldbeck farmer. She died there, as Mary Harrison, in 1837.

Practicalities

There's an official pay-and-display **car park** behind the *Fish Hotel* and another 300 yards up the road to Crummock Water; free parking places can be found on the Crummock Water lakeshore road or up the minor Newlands valley road, past the church, though it gets very busy everywhere in holidays and good weather. The direct **bus** service is the #77, which runs between April and October on a circular route from Keswick, via Whinlatter Pass and Lorton and then back through Borrowdale; the #77A comes the other way round, through Borrowdale first. Buy a **Honister Day Rider** ticket (from £6.50) from the driver and you can use both services all day.

There's no tourist office in Buttermere, though Ⓦwww.buttermereweb.co.uk and www.buttermere-lorton.com gather together some useful local listings and **information**. The village has no shops either, but it does have two **hotels**, the

Bridge and the *Fish* (no TV reception in either), plus a **youth hostel** and various local farms and houses offering **B&B** and **camping**. Both the *Fish* and the *Bridge* have bar **meals** and beer gardens, or you can get sandwiches and put together a picnic at *Croft House Café* or the *Syke Farm* tearoom – the latter sells great ice cream, made with milk from their own Ayrshire cows. There's **rowboat rental** (and fishing permits) from *Wood House* (see listings below) on Crummock Water, available from April to the end of October.

Accommodation and food

Bridge Hotel Buttermere ⓣ017687/70252, ⓦwww.bridge-hotel.com. The best rooms here are the cheerfully decorated superior ones with large bathrooms, some with balconies; and there are also south-facing, self-catering apartments available across the beck (sleep 2–4, £400–800 per week). B&B is normally only available midweek, otherwise dinner is included from a fancy restaurant menu, while in the oak-beamed Walkers' Bar there are sandwiches and filling Cumbrian specials (£7–12). Parking. ⑤, D,B&B ⑥

Buttermere YHA Buttermere, 0.25 miles southeast of the village ⓣ0845/371 9508, ⓔbuttermere@yha.org.uk. Overlooks the lake on the road to Honister Pass – not surprisingly, the views from this quiet lakeland slate house are supreme, which makes it one of the more popular hostels in the Lakes. The pubs are close by, but the hostel also has local beers and organic wines available and the restaurant serves good food (Borrowdale trout to goat's cheese salad, mains £7–8). Dorm beds from £17.95, includes breakfast.

Dalegarth Buttermere, 1.5 miles southeast of the village ⓣ017687/70233, ⓦwww.dalegarthguesthouse.co.uk. The grounds at Dalegarth extend to the lakeside and you can walk off the property and on to the fells. The house has a Swiss-chalet look, with nine B&B rooms (not all en suite), plus all-year camping (weather permitting) on a grassy lawn, with the use of a shower and toilet block and drying room. Parking. ②

Fish Hotel Buttermere ⓣ017687/70253, ⓦwww.fish-hotel.co.uk. Buttermere's other hotel is a smaller, simpler place than the *Bridge*, but has history, romance and price on its side, and the better beer garden – with views straight up to the Red Pike ridge. Traditional bar meals are available at lunch and dinner (£7–9). Parking. ④

Syke Farm Buttermere ⓣ017687/70222. The farm offers simple camping near the lake (toilet and shower block provided) – simple, that is, save for the amazing mountain views – while the tearoom dishes up cappuccinos, sandwiches and the Lakes' best ice cream, direct (well, almost) from cow to customer. No credit cards. Tearoom closed Jan, and might also be closed winter weekdays.

Wood House Crummock Water ⓣ017687/70208, ⓦwww.wdhse.co.uk. Quite the nicest local choice is this attractive house in a serene setting on Crummock Water, just a few hundred yards from Buttermere village. Three elegant bedrooms and the drawing room enjoy marvellous views, while the gardens and surrounding woodland harbour red squirrels and woodpeckers. You can take a boat out on Crummock Water, and then settle in at night for a good dinner (£29). Closed Nov–March. Parking. No credit cards. ④

Travel details

All timetables can be checked on Traveline ⓣ0871/200 2233, ⓦwww.traveline.info. For Ravenglass & Eskdale Railway services to Dalegarth, Boot, see p.188.

From Keswick

Bus #77 circular route to: Whinlatter Pass (15min), Lorton (25min), Buttermere (45min), Honister Pass (1hr) and through Borrowdale. Service operates April–Oct 4 daily.

Bus #77A circular route: through Borrowdale to Honister Pass (40min), Buttermere (50min), Lorton (1hr 10min), Whinlatter Pass (1hr 20min). Service operates April–Oct 4 daily.

From Buttermere

Bus #263 "Ennerdale Rambler" to: Loweswater Waterend (25min), Ennerdale Bridge (45min) and Bowness Knott (50min); and to Lorton (15min) and Cockermouth (30min). Service operates July & Aug Sun & bank hol Mon 3 daily.

6

Ullswater

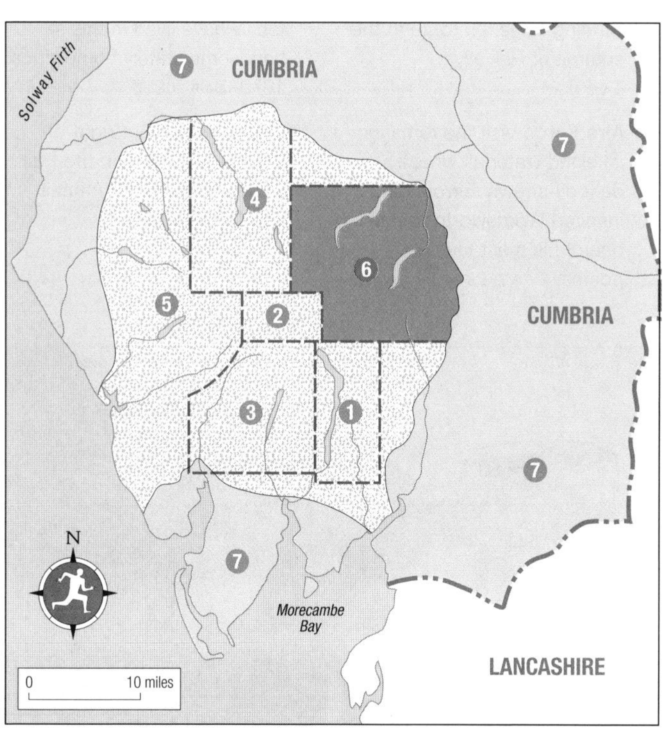

CUMBRIA
Solway Firth
7
4
6
5
2
3
1
CUMBRIA
7
7
7
Morecambe Bay
LANCASHIRE
N
0
10 miles

CHAPTER 6 Highlights

* **A steamer ride on Ullswater** Get off for some marvellous local walks or stay aboard for the round-the-lake cruise. See p.213
* **Striding Edge** There's no more exciting mountain walk than inching your way along Striding Edge, en route to the summit of Helvellyn. See p.214
* **Aira Force** Visit the romantic lakeland waterfall whose daffodil-strewn surroundings inspired Wordsworth to pen one of his most famous poems. See p.215
* **Pooley Bridge** Ullswater's prettiest village has a popular farmers' market and some excellent country-house accommodation and cafés nearby. See p.216
* **Dalemain** Successive generations of the same family have lived in this handsome stately home since 1679. See p.218
* **Haweswater** Get right off the beaten track on the trail of golden eagles, Withnail and Uncle Monty. See p.222

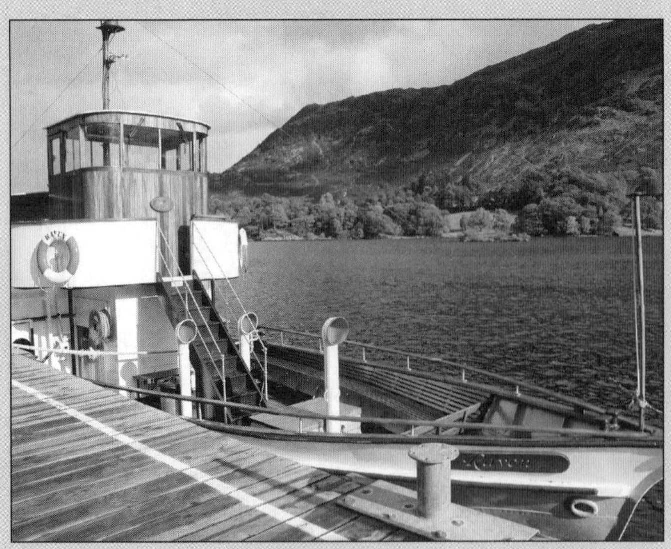

▲ Ullswater steamer

6

Ullswater

Wordsworth declared **Ullswater** "the happiest combination of beauty and grandeur, which any of the Lakes affords", a judgement that still holds good. At almost eight miles, it's the second longest lake in the national park, with a dramatic serpentine shape that's overlooked by soaring fells, none higher than the challenging reaches of **Helvellyn** (one of the Lakes' celebrated three-thousand-footers). The shores meanwhile are stippled with woods of native oak, birch and hazel – one of the best surviving examples of pre-plantation lakeland scenery. Ullswater has been a tourist magnet for a couple of centuries, and **steamer services** started as far back as 1859, carrying both passengers and cargo around the lake. The same two vessels, *Lady of the Lake* and *Raven*, have been in operation for almost as long: both were converted to diesel in the 1930s, and have since been joined by two other vessels, *Lady Dorothy* and *Lady Wakefield*, which between them run a year-round ferry and cruise service on Ullswater.

On spring and summer days the A592 up the western side of the lake is packed with traffic, everyone looking for space in one of the few designated car parks. Twin lakeside settlements, **Patterdale** and **Glenridding**, less than a mile apart at the southern tip of Ullswater, soak up most of the visitors intent upon the local attractions: namely **cruises** from Glenridding, the tumbling waterfalls of **Aira Force** and the Wordsworthian daffodils of **Gowbarrow Park**. From Glenridding, boats run across to **Howtown** on the eastern side, where walking routes run up glorious hidden valleys such as Fusedale and Martindale and along the High Street range. Last stop is at **Pooley Bridge** at the head of Ullswater, where you're close to the historic house at **Dalemain** and the attractive village of **Askham**, gateway to the rolling Lowther parklands.

The northeastern lakes finish with a flourish in the crinkled valleys between the southern foot of Ullswater and the desolate Shap Fells at the eastern edge of the National Park. The A592, heading south from Ullswater for the Kirkstone Pass and Ambleside, passes **Brothers Water**. Otherwise the only roads are the minor lanes south from Askham and west of Shap, which meet at **Haweswater**, easternmost and very possibly the least visited of all the lakes (and, with Thirlmere, the Lake District's other main reservoir).

Glenridding

A fast-flowing beck, flanked by stone buildings and cottages, tumbles through the centre of **GLENRIDDING**, which was formerly a mining village and is now the busiest of Ullswater's lakeside settlements. Although the village itself consists of little more than a couple of rows of cottages set back from the lake,

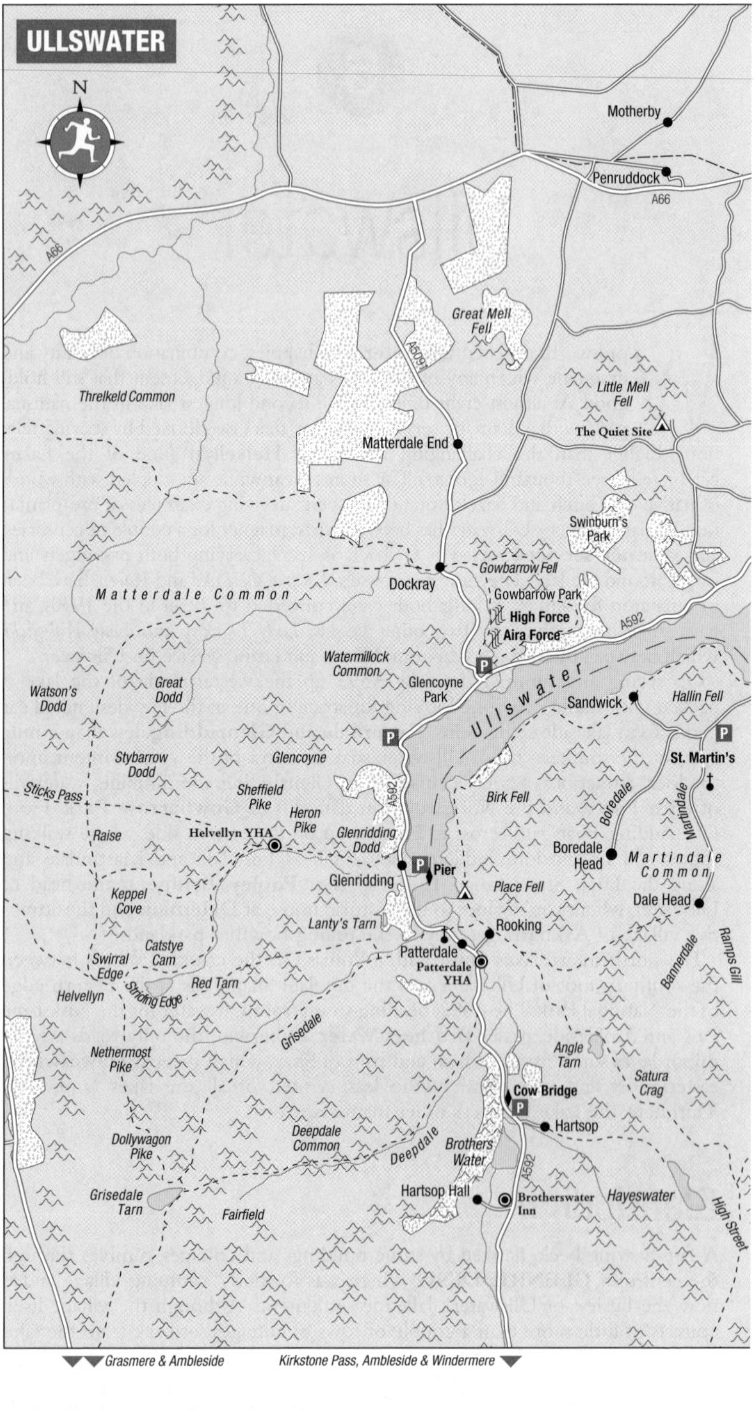

ULLSWATER

N
Motherby
Penruddock
A66
A66
Keswick
Great Mell Fell
A5091
Little Mell Fell
Threlkeld Common
The Quiet Site
Matterdale End
Swinburn's Park
Gowbarrow Fell
Dockray
Matterdale Common
Gowbarrow Park
High Force
Aira Force
A592
Watermillock Common
Glencoyne Park
Ullswater
Great Dodd
Watson's Dodd
Sandwick
Hallin Fell
Stybarrow Dodd
Glencoyne
St. Martin's
Sticks Pass
Sheffield Pike
A592
Birk Fell
Boredale
Martindale
Heron Pike
Raise
Helvellyn YHA
Glenridding Dodd
Boredale Head
Martindale Common
Thirlmere
Pier
Glenridding
Place Fell
Dale Head
Keppel Cove
Lanty's Tarn
Rooking
Ramps Gill
Catstye Cam
Patterdale
Swirral Edge
Patterdale YHA
Bannerdale
Red Tarn
Helvellyn
Striding Edge
Grisedale
Nethermost Pike
Angle Tarn
Satura Crag
Cow Bridge
Hartsop
Dollywagon Pike
Deepdale Common
Deepdale
Brothers Water
A592
Hayeswater
Grisedale Tarn
Hartsop Hall
Brotherswater Inn
Fairfield
High Street
Grasmere & Ambleside
Kirkstone Pass, Ambleside & Windermere

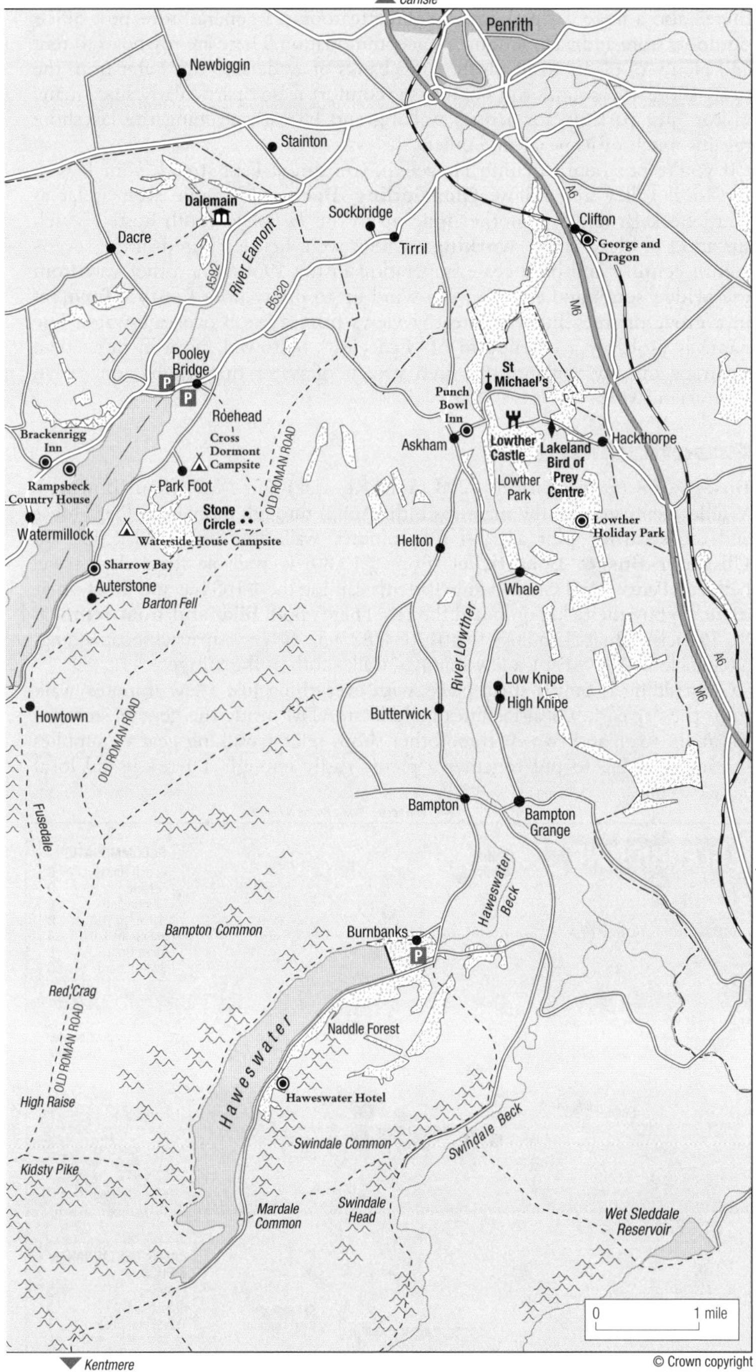

Carlisle
Penrith
Newbiggin
Stainton
Dalemain
Sockbridge
Clifton
George and Dragon
Dacre
Tirril
River Eamont
A592
B5320
A6
M6
Pooley Bridge
St Michael's
Punch Bowl Inn
Roehead
Askham
Lowther Castle
Lakeland Bird of Prey Centre
Hackthorpe
Brackenrigg Inn
Cross Dormont Campsite
Rampsbeck Country House
Park Foot
OLD ROMAN ROAD
Lowther Park
Stone Circle
Watermillock
Waterside House Campsite
Lowther Holiday Park
Helton
Sharrow Bay
Auterstone
Whale
Barton Fell
River Lowther
Low Knipe
High Knipe
Howtown
Butterwick
Kendal & Lancaster
Bampton
Bampton Grange
Fusedale
Haweswater Beck
Shap
Bampton Common
Burnbanks
Oxenholme
Red Crag
Naddle Forest
Haweswater
Haweswater Hotel
High Raise
Swindale Beck
Swindale Common
Kidsty Pike
Mardale Common
Swindale Head
Wet Sleddale Reservoir
0
1 mile
Kentmere

there's also a huge car park, two or three tearooms, a general store, post office, outdoors store and a fair amount of accommodation. There are rowboats to rent and plenty of places to sit on the grass banks or wade into the water from the stony shore. If it sounds too popular for comfort it isn't particularly, since many visitors just park up for a day's walking and by early evening the lakeshore regains much of its peace and quiet.

If you're not here to climb Helvellyn, you can at least stretch your legs in the local valley and follow **Glenridding Beck** half a mile west as far as Rattlebeck Bridge. It's another mile up to the *Helvellyn* youth hostel, which sits amid old lead **mine workings**, which were first exploited in the seventeenth century and only ceased operation in the 1960s. The other way from the bridge, south and east, you can wind up to pretty little **Lanty's Tarn**, set in a grove of trees and with nearby views from a knoll over Ullswater. The name is probably a corruption of "Lancelot", bestowed more in hope than accuracy on any romantically sited stretch of water that might conceal an Arthurian sword.

Practicalities

Buses #108 (from Penrith), #208 (from Keswick) and #517 (from Bowness/Windermere) stop on the main road (the A592) through the village. Pier House and the **steamer pier** are just five minutes' walk away on the lakeside. An **Ullswater Bus & Boat ticket** (from £13.80) is available for a day's travel between Penrith and Glenridding/Patterdale, using the #108 bus and the steamer service – buy the ticket on board the bus. There's both **bike and boat rental** at St Patrick's Boat Landings (Ⓣ017684/82393, Ⓦwww.stpatricksboatlandings.co.uk; closed Nov–Feb), a few minutes' walk south of the village.

Glenridding is only a small place, with everything just a few minutes' walk from the car park. Local facilities include an ATM inside the general store on the main road, and two or three other shops selling walking gear or supplies – you'll be able to put together a picnic easily enough. There's useful local

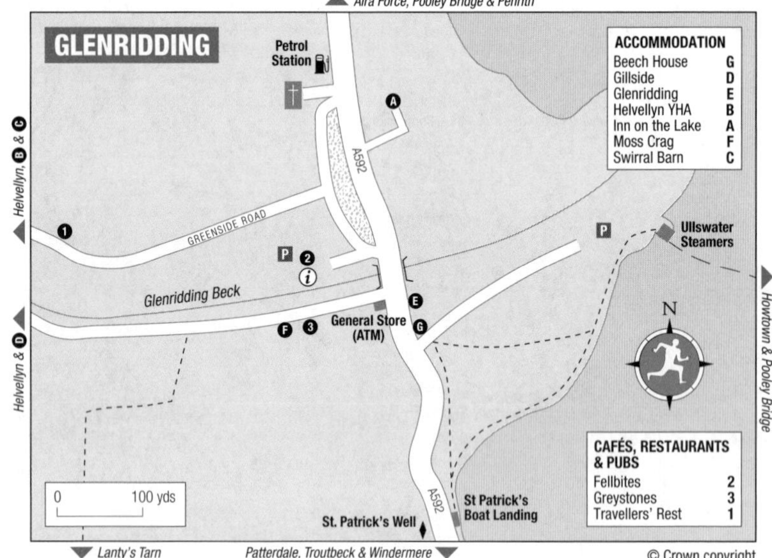

Ullswater lake services

The **Ullswater Navigation & Transit Company** (ⓣ017684/82229, ⓦwww.ullswater-steamers.co.uk) has four vessels operating from Glenridding to Howtown (40min) and on to Pooley Bridge (20min), and back again. Any one stage costs £5.60 one-way, £9 return, family return £24, though there's also a one-day "Round the Lake Pass" (£12.30, family £29.95) as well as a "Walker's Ticket" (£10.70) that lets you travel three separate stages.

In school and summer holidays there are up to nine **daily departures** from Glenridding (basically an hourly service), down to between three and six a day at other times of the year – only Christmas Eve and Christmas Day have no sailings. There are also special cruises and activity weekends (like Halloween's "Ghostly Galleons" and Santa Specials), with current details posted on the website.

There's a bar on board the steamers, plus parking, a café and picnic area at Glenridding's Pier House. At Pooley Bridge, a staffed café operates during the summer season.

information on ⓦwww.ullswater.com, while the **National Park Information Centre** (daily 9.30am–5.30pm; ⓣ017684/82414, ⓦwww.lake-district.gov.uk) is sited on the edge of the **car park** and posts a daily weather report for walkers – you can buy all-day parking tickets inside the centre. Two big traditional slate **hotels** dominate the village, the *Inn on the Lake* and the *Glenridding Hotel*, and there are several cheaper **B&Bs**. Hikers make a beeline for the out-of-village youth hostel, campsite, bunkhouse and camping barn, all lying en route to the area's major peak, Helvellyn.

Hotels and B&Bs

Beech House On the main road ⓣ017684/82037, ⓦwww.beechhouse.com. A spick-and-span B&B base for local walks and excursions. Eight rooms (half share a bathroom), though small, are prettily furnished, and a couple sport lake inlet and fell views. Packed lunches available. Parking. ❷, en suite ❸

Glenridding On the main road ⓣ017684/82228, ⓦwww.bw-glenriddinghotel.co.uk. The traditional hotel choice is this three-star Best Western, with standard and lake-view rooms available (supplement charged for the latter), while family rooms and suites provide a bit more space. It's decidedly unglamorous, but you get an impressive indoor pool and sauna for your money, plus the associated *Kilner's Coffee House* (with internet access) as well as dining at *Ratcher's*, which is both pub and pizza-grill restaurant combined (dishes £8–14). Parking. ❺

Inn on the Lake Ullswater lakeside ⓣ017684/82444, ⓦwww.lakedistricthotels.net/innonthelake. Rooms and public areas at this three-star hotel have been upgraded and decked in flowers, there are some splendid views, and fifteen acres of gardens stretching down to Ullswater. The *Ramblers' Bar* is the place for a beer, a bar meal and a game of pool, but there's also a more sophisticated lounge bar and lake-view restaurant (*table d'hôte* menu £35), plus gym, sauna, jacuzzi, croquet lawn and tennis court. Parking. ❻

Moss Crag On the south side of the beck near the shops ⓣ017684/82500, ⓦwww.mosscrag.co.uk. A genial B&B with half a dozen cottage-style rooms (four of them en suite, including a superior four-poster room) and an attached tearoom. Dinner available (£16). Parking. ❸, four-poster ❹

Campsite, hostel and camping barn

Gillside Caravan & Camping ⓣ017684/82346, ⓦwww.gillsidecaravanandcampingsite.co.uk. In a beautiful spot, en route to Helvellyn, a quarter of a mile up the valley behind the village – follow the path along the beck. There are also caravans for rent (from £50 a night, minimum two nights), a good bunkhouse with a modern kitchen (£10 a bed), though you need your own sleeping and cooking equipment, and a laundry. Milk and eggs are available from the family farm. No credit cards. Closed Nov–Feb.

Helvellyn YHA Greenside ⓣ0845/371 9742, ⓔhelvellyn@yha.org.uk. Walkers wanting an early start on Helvellyn stay at this dramatically

Helvellyn walks

The climb to the summit of **Helvellyn** (3114ft) is among the region's most challenging. You are unlikely to be alone on the yard-wide approaches – on summer weekends and bank holidays the car parks below and paths above are full by 9am – but the variety of routes up and down at least offers a chance of escaping the crowds. The most direct route from Glenridding, via Striding Edge, returning via Swirral Edge and Red Tarn, is a good seven-mile (5–6hr) walk, while for any of the other variations you can count on being out all day.

Striding Edge

The most frequently chosen route to the summit is via the infamous **Striding Edge**. Purists negotiate the undulating ridge top of Striding Edge; slightly safer, but no less precipitous tracks follow the line of the ridge, just off the crest. However you get across (and some refuse to go any further when push comes to shove), there's a final, sheer, hands-and-feet scramble to the flat **summit** (2hr 30min from Glenridding). People do get into trouble on Striding Edge: if you're at all nervous of heights you'll find it a challenge to say the least, your mood probably not improved by the occasionally hovering rescue helicopters.

Swirral Edge and Red Tarn

The classic return from the summit is via the less demanding **Swirral Edge**, from where a straightforward route leads down to stunning **Red Tarn** – the highest Lake District tarn – then follows the beck down to Glenridding past the Helvellyn youth hostel. This is the best route *up* Helvellyn if you don't fancy Striding Edge, as Swirral Edge is far less exposed an approach (though there is still some hands-and-feet climbing). If you come up this way, then you can make your return circuit to the north instead (see next walk).

Raise and Sticks Pass

North from the Helvellyn summit there's an obvious cairned route heading towards **Raise** (2897ft), with stupendous views away to the east over Red Tarn and down the valleys. The path then drops down to **Sticks Pass** for an interesting descent alongside Sticks Gill and through the scars of the old mine workings. The route runs right past *Helvellyn YHA* for the final mile into Glenridding. Depending on the time and weather conditions, peak-baggers might make the decision at Sticks Pass first to tick off **Stybarrow Dodd** (2766ft), an easy twenty-minute diversion, and even **Watson's Dodd** (2589ft) beyond.

Grisedale

South from the Helvellyn summit, you can follow the flat ridge past **Nethermost Pike** (2920ft) and **Dollywagon Pike** (2810ft), after which there's a long scree scramble down to **Grisedale Tarn** and then the gentlest of descents down **Grisedale** valley, alongside the beck, emerging on the Patterdale–Glenridding road. This really is a fantastic walk, with a fine mix of terrain, a good six hours all told for the entire circuit.

See Basics, p.42, for general walking advice in the Lakes; recommended maps are detailed on p.50.

sited hostel, 900ft and a mile and a half up the valley road from Glenridding (the last half unmetalled, but suitable for vehicles if taken with care). There are lots of beds (and private rooms available), plus a full meals service and alcohol licence, while the nearest pub, the *Travellers Rest*, is only a mile away. The hostel is closed on occasional nights, and advance bookings are advised – call for availability. Closed Dec. Dorm beds from £11.95.

Swirral Barn ⓣ01946/758198, ⓦwww.lakelandcampingbarns.co.uk. A hundred yards beyond the YHA, there's self-catering bunk-barn space in accommodation converted from former mine buildings. There are only eight beds and it's pretty basic (eg unheated, toilet in a separate building), but the hiking routes to Helvellyn go right past the door. Beds £7.

Eating and drinking

Fellbites ⓣ017684/82781, ⓦwww.fellbites.co.uk. The café in the car park is a handsomely converted lakeland barn with a few picnic benches outside. Daytime food is the usual café menu (snacks £3–5, mains £8–9) though dinner promises more choice and a hint of sophistication, from fresh fish to Cumbrian venison sausages (mains £10–12). Dinner is usually Fri to Tues only, and not in winter, when the café also might only be open at weekends.

Greystones Gallery and Coffee House ⓣ017684/82392, ⓦwww.greystonesgallery.co.uk. Alongside the beck, cheery *Greystones* dishes up teas, cappuccinos and tasty hiker-fuel such as ciabatta sandwiches or beans on toast (dishes £4–6). There's a "boots welcome" policy inside, while a few outdoor tables catch the sun in summer. It's also a gallery space for contemporary art and sculpture and there's wi-fi access. Daytime only. Nov–Jan open weekends and selected days only.

Travellers' Rest ⓣ017684/82298. It's worth the 500-yard tramp up the hill from the village centre to this unpretentious pub, tucked under the fells. Returning hikers fall in on the way back down from the fells for a pick-me-up, and there are filling bar meals, cask ales and an outdoor terrace.

Patterdale

PATTERDALE, less than a mile south of Glenridding down the A592 (a path avoids the road for much of the way), lies at the foot of **Grisedale**, which provides access to a stunning valley hike up to Grisedale Tarn. St Patrick is supposed to have preached here (Patterdale is "Patrick's Dale") and the water in St Patrick's Well, on the road between Glenridding and Patterdale, was once thought to have miraculous powers. The saint's church, at the northern end of the village, is a nineteenth-century replacement of the medieval original, known for the locally made embroidered tapestries that hang inside.

The #108, #208 and #517 **bus** services stop in Patterdale. You're just off the lake in the village – though never very far away – but there's some reasonable **accommodation** strung along the road. Patterdale's only pub, the *White Lion* (ⓣ017684/82214; ❷), has seven rooms available; sizzling steak platters are the house speciality, or try the trout with almonds. There's also a public bar at the large *Patterdale Hotel* up the road – it's no great shakes as a hotel, but the front beer garden fills up quickly on a summer's day. South, past the pub, on the bend in the road, *Old Water View* (ⓣ017684/82175, ⓦwww.oldwaterview.co.uk; ❸) is an attractive guesthouse with half a dozen rustic rooms, private gardens and parking. They're used to walkers – even Alfred Wainwright stayed here on occasion. Just beyond lies Patterdale's quirky **youth hostel**, *Patterdale YHA* (ⓣ0845/371 9337, ⓔpatterdale@yha.org.uk; dorm beds from £11.95; restricted opening Nov–March), looking like a retro 1970s ski lodge – it's popular with families and big on outdoor activities. There's **camping** at *Side Farm* (ⓣ017684/82337, ⓔandrea@sidefarm.fsnet.co.uk; closed Nov–Easter) – the track to the farm is across from the church, with the campsite on the eastern shore of the lake – and the only other service is a small **village shop/post office** opposite the pub.

Aira Force, Dockray and Gowbarrow

To avoid the crowds trailing up the needle-carpeted woodland paths to **Aira Force**, three miles north of Glenridding (where the A5091 meets the A592), get there first thing in the morning or last thing in the evening. This is one of the prettiest, most romantic, of lakeland forces – a seventy-foot waterfall that's spectacular in spate and can be viewed from stone bridges spanning the top and bottom of the drop. It's only a thirty- to forty-minute round-trip from the car park, though you'll soon leave most of the visitors behind if you extend your walk further up the valley to High Force and on to **Dockray** (where there's a pub with a beer garden, the *Royal*) and back – a three-mile, two-hour, circuit. Keep an eye out for red squirrels in the woods on the way. Back at the Aira Force car park there's an attractive **tearoom** (closed Nov–Easter) with an outdoor terrace; buses #108 and #208 stop nearby.

The falls flank the western side of **Gowbarrow Park**, whose hillside still blazes green and gold in spring, as it was doing when the Wordsworths visited in April 1802. Dorothy's sprightly recollections of the visit in her journal inspired William to write his "Daffodils" poem, though it was not until two years later that he first composed the famous lines (borrowing many of Dorothy's exact phrases). Despite its fame now, nothing much was thought of the poem at the time; it didn't even have a title on first publication in 1807 (in *Poems in Two Volumes*).

The walking is tougher going on adjacent **Gowbarrow Fell** (1579ft), which you can climb in an hour from Aira Force car park. The route runs via the viewpoint of Yew Crag and then up the boggy slopes to the cairn at the summit. From here you can descend to Dockray and the pub or, more directly, over the top to Green Hill and thence to Aira Force (2hr return). The National Park Authority is trying to cut the number of sheep grazing the fell in an attempt to lure back some of the wildlife, while every spring there's a battle of wits with visitors intent on picking the famous daffs.

Pooley Bridge and around

POOLEY BRIDGE, at the head of the lake, has a boulder-speckled shore with wonderful views south. The bridge itself is the sturdy example that crosses the River Eamont on the way into the village, evidence – along with the old village square, once used for markets – that this was a substantial settlement in past times. Its market charter was granted by King John in the twelfth century, the modern equivalent being the thriving **farmers' market** (last Sun of month, April–Sept, 10.30am–2.30pm) held behind the *Sun Inn*. Pooley Bridge itself is a cute retreat, rendered less so once the car parks on either side of the bridge are full, but it's still not a bad lunch or overnight stop, with a couple of tearooms, three pubs and some excellent nearby country cafés. Apart from the **steamer** (whose jetty is a couple of hundred yards from the bridge), there's a daily, year-round **bus service** (the #108) from Penrith to Pooley Bridge (and on to Glenridding/Patterdale), as well as a limited postbus from Penrith (not Sun), which continues on to Howtown and Martindale.

One of the shops on the square contains an informal visitor **information point** (Easter–Oct daily 9am–5pm). The best **accommodation** is listed below; in addition, a few local B&Bs advertise vacancies. Plenty of **campsites** on both sides of the lake make the Pooley Bridge area popular with families looking for a quiet place to stay.

Accommodation

Brackenrigg Inn Watermillock, A592, 2 miles southwest of Pooley Bridge ⓣ017684/86206, ⓦwww.brackenrigginn.co.uk. See chapter map for location. Best place for a lake view without spending a fortune is this traditional roadside inn, with water views both from the best rooms at the front and from the outside terrace. It's good for families too as some rooms can be linked together. Food's another high point, with an

▲ Pooley Bridge

emphasis on locally sourced produce, fish and seafood, lamb hot pot to lake char (mains £10–18), and it's very easy-going – you can eat from the same menu in the bar, the family dining area, the more formal dining room, or even outside. Parking. ❸

Pooley Bridge Inn ⓣ017684/86215, ⓦwww.pooleybridgeinn.co.uk. Just by the village square, this Alpine-style hotel seems to have been plucked out of a *Heidi* story. Breakfast in the wicker chairs on your own balcony is tempting, though there are also cheaper standard rooms without a balcony. Meals are available in the rustic bar *Stables* courtyard and restaurant. Parking. ❸ , balcony room ❹

Rampsbeck Country House Hotel Watermillock, A592, 2 miles southwest of Pooley Bridge ⓣ017684/86442, ⓦwww.rampsbeck.co.uk. See chapter map for location. Victorian-era house with a magnificent lakeside location on the western shore – gardens run right down to the water's edge, and the terrace has sweeping views. There's a rather comforting, old-fashioned feel within, abetted by hands-on family management. The twenty rooms vary in size but the best are very spacious and have uninterrupted lake views. The food is a hit, with a four-course contemporary Cumbrian dinner (£50) served nightly in the candlelit dining room overlooking Ullswater. Parking. ❻, deluxe rooms ❼

Sharrow Bay 2 miles south of Pooley Bridge, on the Howtown road ⓣ017684/86301, ⓦwww.sharrowbay.co.uk. See chapter map for location. The special-occasion place *par excellence*, England's first country-house hotel (in business since 1948) offers a breathtaking setting, personal service and highly refined Michelin-starred food. Needless to say, it's London prices in the country (rooms from £200–440 a night, suites up to £700) but there are few places anywhere in England that compare. You can choose from a variety of lovely, antique-filled rooms in the main Victorian house, a garden annexe, the Edwardian gatehouse or in a converted, elevated Elizabethan farmhouse a mile away. Lake and fell views abound, there are acres of gardens and woods to wander in, and books and games in the rooms to pass the time when it pours. The dining room is open to nonresidents (reservations essential); afternoon tea here is famous, while lunch (£43) and dinner (£70) are classy, formal affairs – desserts are renowned, notably the sticky-toffee pudding, which the hotel claims as its own invention. Parking. ❽

Sun Inn ⓣ017684/86205, ⓦwww.suninnpooleybridge.co.uk. The best of the village pubs (100 yards up the road from the square) is the eighteenth-century *Sun*, with a carved, panelled bar and a beer garden to catch the rays. There are nine good-value rooms, plus Jennings beers and bar meals (mains £6–12). Parking. ❸

Campsites

Cross Dormont On the Howtown road ⓣ017684/86537, ⓦwww.crossdormont.co.uk. Simple family-run site on a working farm (raising

Herdwick sheep on the local fells). You can launch dinghies and kayaks from the lakeside fields, or walk right off the farm on to the fells.

The Quiet Site Watermillock ⓣ07768/727016, ⓦwww.thequietsite.co.uk. The eco-friendly choice for cool campers is this charming site with sweeping views a mile and half up past the *Brackenrigg Inn*. It's open all year and thoughtfully designed all round, from family bathrooms to a great bar-in-a-barn, while a dozen cosy camping pods (£35–50 per night) keep the rain off anyone without a tent. Pick-ups from Penrith station are also available.

Waterside House On the Howtown road ⓣ017684/86332, ⓦwww.watersidefarm-campsite.co.uk. Right on the water, on another working farm, this is a tent- and motorhome-only site just a mile from Pooley Bridge. It has a separate family field and is pretty well equipped, with canoes, rowboats and bikes for rent plus laundry, shop and children's playground. Closed Nov–Feb.

Eating and drinking

Alpaca Centre Snuff Mill Lane, Stainton, A592 ⓣ01768/891440, ⓦwww.thealpacacentre.co.uk. A tearoom with a difference, sited on a working alpaca farm a couple of miles north of Pooley Bridge (just past Dalemain). Think llamas, and you're not far off – you can see the alpacas from the paddock or tearoom, and there's a craft shop and gallery selling clothes made from alpaca fibre, South American artefacts and jewellery, and handcrafted furniture and ornamental wood. Daytime only.

Granny Dowbekin's ⓣ017684/86453. Terraced riverside tea garden, by the bridge, serving home-made cakes inspired by the recipes of the owner's great-great Lancastrian granny. There are also locally sourced meats and free-range eggs in the all-day brekkies, and mains (around £8) from veggie pie to Cumbrian lamb casserole. Daytime only. Closed Jan.

Greystone House Stainton ⓣ01768/866952, ⓦwww.greystonehousefarm.co.uk. Top choice hereabouts for lunch and teas is this enterprising farm's handsome oak-beamed tearoom. The family has farmed here since the eighteenth century, and went organic in 2001 – they now produce their own beef, lamb, pork, fruit and vegetables, with lots more besides (handmade butter to damson gin) also available in the excellent farm shop. You'll find the farm up past Dalemain and the Alpaca Centre, or it's just a very short drive off the A66. Daytime only.

Dalemain

Two miles north of Pooley Bridge, up the A592, the grand stately home of **Dalemain** (Easter–Sept Mon–Thurs & Sun 11.15am–4pm, gardens & tearoom same days 10.30am–5pm, and also open Feb half-term; Oct same days and hours, though house closes at 3pm, gardens 4pm; Nov to mid-Dec & Feb–Easter gardens & tearoom only Mon–Thurs & Sun 11am–4pm; £9; gardens only £6, under-16s free; ⓣ017684/86450, ⓦwww.dalemain.com) sits back from the road amid close-cropped lawns. Residence to the same family since 1679, it started life in the twelfth century as a fortified tower, but has subsequently been added to by every generation, culminating with a Georgian facade grafted on to a largely Elizabethan house. Its grounds are gorgeous – pristine terraces, radiant roses and Tudor gardens provide the main interest, best in late May and June – while the estate stretches west to encompass the fourteenth-century keep of Dacre Castle (no public access), which you can reach on a mile-long footpath from the house (there's also a nice old pub in Dacre village).

There are **guided tours** of the house in the mornings (the first at 11.15am), while in the afternoon it's self-guided. Rather remarkably, you're given the run of the public rooms, which the Hasell family still uses – hence the photographs and contemporary portraits alongside those of the ancestors. The house is heavy with oak, hewn from the estate's plantations, though lightened by unusual touches such as the eighteenth-century hand-painted wallpaper in the Chinese Room. The servants' corridors and pantries offer a glimpse of life "below stairs", commanded from the Housekeeper's Room – at the rear of which was discovered a priest's hole. Outside, the medieval courtyard and Elizabethan great barn doubled as the schoolroom and dormitory of Lowood School in a TV adaptation of Charlotte Brontë's *Jane Eyre*. There's an agricultural and countryside collection in the great barn, and plenty of other displays and exhibits throughout the house, from dolls' houses and old toys to Gillows and Chippendale furniture and the family glassware. The **Medieval Hall** provides drinks, lunches and afternoon teas – you don't need a ticket to visit this – while every February the house hosts the "world's original" **Marmalade Festival**, a great day out of competitions, tastings, garden visits and children's games (with, naturally, Paddington Bear in attendance).

Askham and Lowther Park

Three miles east of Pooley Bridge, and five south of Penrith, the serene little village of **Askham** lies across the River Lowther from the rolling lands of **Lowther Park**, seat of the eighteenth-century coal-mining and shipping magnates, the Lowthers, creators of the Georgian port of Whitehaven. The most notorious family member, Sir James, employed Wordsworth's father as his agent but, when John Wordsworth died, refused to pay his back-salary to the Wordsworth children. Not that there was any shortage of Lowther money in those days, as attested to by an extravagantly built Gothic Revival castle in the estate grounds, though eventually its ruinous upkeep was too much, even for the Lowthers, and it was allowed to fall into disrepair. For years, all that you could see were the ruins from the road, though a new generation of Lowthers (and a generous dollop of funding) has started an ambitious restoration project. Eventually (by 2012, it's hoped) there will be a panoramic viewing tower within the castle ruins, plus restored gardens and a visitor centre – you can follow developments on Ⓦwww.transforminglowther.co.uk. Until this all comes to fruition, there's another glimpse of the Lowther heritage at **St Michael's church**, just outside Askham, on a ridge above the river. Effectively the family chapel, this is filled with memorials to one Lowther or another – whose scions took the title Earl of Lonsdale – including a fine brass portraying a splendidly bewhiskered Henry Lowther. A later Lowther, the fifth Earl, Sir Hugh, was a keen sportsman, whose title at least is remembered in boxing's Lonsdale Belt, while the estate's **horse trials**, held here every August, are one of the region's biggest sporting events. The estate is also a major local food producer, not only selling its produce in shops and restaurants but also showcasing it at its own restaurant-with-rooms operation at nearby Clifton (see p.220).

You'll drive through rolling Lowther estate land – which includes two small villages, various farms and plantations and a deer park – en route to the **Lakeland Bird of Prey Centre** (Easter–Oct daily 11am–5pm; £8, family £22; Ⓣ01931/712746), just outside Askham. Here eagles, hawks, falcons and owls are put through their paces daily at 2pm, though they are also all on show in the aviaries set in the walled garden. There's a tearoom here, too.

Public transport to Askham is limited to the #111 "Haweswater Rambler" **bus** from Penrith, which runs year-round on Tuesdays and Saturdays; however, there's no bus out to the Bird of Prey Centre. Askham itself has a couple of local B&Bs, and two village shops at the top of the sloping village green.

People and places: From estate to plate

The French call it "terroir", a sense of place that influences local produce, and Charles Lowther – youngest son of the late seventh Earl of Lonsdale – knows a thing or two about it. His family, the Lowthers, have lived on their estate near Penrith since at least the eleventh century and have a long history of food production. Lowther Park itself has been a working farm since 1283 and the same principles of local, sustainable production underpin the venture today. "We have a real affinity with what comes off our land", says Charles, who runs the farm, including 3000 acres that are currently farmed organically. That means fish from estate rivers, free-range beef, pork, lamb and chicken, game from the Lowther woods and moors, and seasonal vegetables from a traditional kitchen garden. All of this finds its way on to the menu at the estate's inn, the *George and Dragon*, which Charles also oversees. Food miles, accordingly, are kept to a minimum (most produce is from only two or three miles away), while more local skills and crafts were drawn upon to help with the inn's meticulous restoration, from stone-wallers and joiners to artists and photographers. If you want to know exactly what's on your plate and where it came from, then it's hard to resist the Lowther lure in this part of the Lake District – "basically, our family home for the last thousand years", says Charles; "we hope everyone else loves it as much as we do".

Accommodation and food

George and Dragon Clifton, A6, 3 miles northeast of Askham ⓣ01768/865381, ⓦwww.georgeanddragonclifton.co.uk. An immediate hit, this revamped eighteenth-century inn is a class act. Country-chic rooms feature woollen carpets, Roman blinds, big beds with brocade headboards and slate-floor bathrooms (some with claw-foot baths), while the informal downstairs bar and restaurant (around £25 for 3 courses) takes local sourcing to a new level. Pretty much everything is from the adjacent Lowther Estate, whether it's organic meat, farmhouse cheese, kitchen-garden veg and herbs or wild fish – seasonally changing dishes from the open-to-view kitchen might include char-grilled vegetables or shorthorn beef burger, though the twice-baked cheese soufflé signature dish is ever-present. Parking. ❹, superior rooms ❺

Lowther Holiday Park Lowther Estate ⓣ01768/863631, ⓦwww.lowther-holidaypark.co.uk. There's a well-equipped site for camping and caravans in the estate grounds (closed Nov–March), with pub, shop, laundry facilities and children's activities; it's signposted within the estate and from the A6 nearby. The estate also rents out two superior holiday cottages (see ⓦwww.lowther.co.uk), one in Askham village and one just to the south in the hamlet of Whale.

Punch Bowl Inn Askham ⓣ01931/712443, ⓦwww.punchbowlaskham.co.uk. The old inn at the bottom of Askham green has half a dozen upgraded B&B rooms and a certain bygone charm downstairs in its ancient public bar – or you can eat and drink outside on the patio. ❸

Howtown and Martindale

HOWTOWN – best reached by regular steamer services in summer from Glenridding – is tucked behind a little indented harbour, four miles south of Pooley Bridge. It's a popular spot that lies at the start of several fine walks. Many people cross to Howtown by boat and then walk back (6 miles; 3hr), following the shore of Ullswater around Hallin Fell to **Sandwick** and then through the woods and on around the bottom of the lake to Patterdale.

There are only a few houses in Howtown, huddled around the resolutely old-fashioned *Howtown Hotel* (ⓣ017684/86514, ⓦwww.howtown-hotel.com; no credit cards; closed Nov–March; ❺), which has a cosy wood-panelled and stained-glass snug bar around the back where hikers can revive themselves with

Walks from Howtown

For some of the nicest but least-vaunted walking in the Lake District, cross Ullswater on the steamer from Glenridding. Various routes radiate from Howtown, including the two described below.

Fusedale

A strenuous route (8 miles; 4–5hr) cuts past the *Howtown Hotel* and heads up lovely **Fusedale**, at the head of which there's an unrelenting climb up to the **High Street**, a broad-backed ridge that was once a Roman road. The path is clearly visible for miles and following the ridge south you meet the highest point, **High Raise** (2632ft) – two hours from Howtown – where there's a cairn and glorious views. The route then runs south and west, via the stone outcrops of **Satura Crag**, past **Angle Tarn** and finally down to the A592, just shy of Patterdale's pub and post office.

To Pooley Bridge

Time the steamer services from Glenridding right and you can cross to Howtown, walk to Pooley Bridge and catch the boat back. The most direct route (5 miles; 3hr) leaves Howtown pier and runs northeast under Auterstone Crag before cutting up to the **Stone Circle** on the Roman road, south of Roehead, a couple of miles from Pooley Bridge. But for the best views and most exhilarating walk climb up to High Street from Fusedale (see above) and then charge straight along the ridge to the Stone Circle (7 miles; 3–4hr).

See Basics, p.42, for general walking advice in the Lakes; recommended maps are detailed on p.50.

a beer or a cup of coffee. Dinner is included in the room rate, though non-guests can also take advantage of the moderately priced cold-table lunch or *table d'hôte* menu available in the hotel dining room.

The minor road from Pooley Bridge runs south through Howtown and climbs up in switchbacks to a car park at the foot of **Martindale**. The road, in fact, continues another couple of miles up to Dale Head, but it's best to abandon the car and walk the ten minutes along to **St Martin's**, the most beautifully sited of all the Lake District's isolated churches. An Elizabethan stone chapel of great simplicity, all there is inside is a stone-flagged floor, a seventeenth-century altar table and lectern and rows of plain wooden benches. It's barely changed in centuries and, outside, the feeling of time immemorial is emphasized by the vast spreading yew tree, thought to be a thousand years old, whose gnarled branches shroud the tomb of Martindale's nineteenth-century curate George Woodley.

Brothers Water, Hartsop and Hayeswater

The car park at **Cow Bridge**, two miles south of Patterdale, is the jumping-off point for the short stroll along a quiet stretch of Goldrill Beck to **Brothers Water**. The Water itself (possibly taking its name from a corruption of the Norse name "Brothir") is a mere liquid scoop, but the path along the western shore takes you under the canopy of some of the Lakes' oldest oak woodlands. This was the way Dorothy Wordsworth came on Good Friday in April 1802, after her daffodil-spotting excursion of the previous day, and it's easy to trace her exact route from her journal: "I left William sitting on the bridge, and went along the path on the right side of the lake through the wood. I was delighted with what I saw. The water under the boughs of the bare old trees, the simplicity of the mountains, and the exquisite beauty of the path." When she got back to Cow Bridge, William was busy writing a poem, which he later entitled (mistakenly) "Written in March".

The path alongside Brothers Water runs a mile or so up to the 500-year-old **Hartsop Hall Farm**, standing on land which experts reckon has been farmed since the Bronze Age. You can press further on if you're in the mood for a decent hike – there are routes up Dovedale, for Dove Crag, Hart Crag and Fairfield – while local climbers and walkers all know about the beautifully sited *Brotherswater Inn* (Ⓣ017684/82239, Ⓦwww.sykeside.co.uk; ❸) and associated *Sykeside Camping Park*, just to the east over by the A592. There are six straightforward rooms in the inn, plus food available all day, while campers have their own shop and *Barn End* bar (open all summer and winter holiday weekends): there are also beds available in the bunkhouse (from £14).

Back at the Cow Bridge car park, you cross the main road for the tiny hamlet of **Hartsop**, from where it's a mile-and-a-bit walk east up the valley to **Hayeswater**, a limpid little lake sitting under the High Street range. It's hard to believe now, but Hartsop was once a thriving mining and quarrying centre, the biggest in the region, and the track up to Hayeswater sits beneath crags riddled with old workings.

Haweswater

With the example of Thirlmere already set, there was less opposition when **Haweswater** was dammed in the 1930s to provide more water for the industrial northwest. The Lake District's easternmost lake became almost twice as long as a result (now four miles in length), while the water level rose by 100 feet, completely drowning the village of Mardale. (It was visible in the hot summers of 1976, 1984 and 1995, when its deluged buildings emerged briefly from the depleted reservoir.) Such brutal dealings seem a long way off nowadays: the water company manages the valley and lake as a nature reserve, where woodpeckers and sparrowhawks inhabit Naddle Forest, and buzzards, peregrine falcons and the only golden eagles in England (see below) swoop to the fells.

You can park at **Burnbanks**, at the northern end, near the dam wall, which is the best place to start the moderately strenuous **round-the-lake walk** (10 miles; 5hr), perhaps the best lakeside walk in the entire region – you'll usually be completely on your own on the way round. The path meanders above the water and through the woods on both sides of the lake, and if you walk anticlockwise you can reward yourself near the end with a drink at the *Haweswater Hotel* (see below).

The road ends at the southern foot of the lake where there's an official car park at **Mardale Head**: from here, walkers can climb south over the passes to Kentmere (Nan Bield Pass) and Longsleddale (Gatsegarth Pass) or west up to High Street for Troutbeck, Patterdale or Howtown. The traditional **circular day walk** from Mardale Head (7 miles; 5hr) is up via Kidsty Pike to High Street (2719ft) and then south and east along the ridge to Mardale Ill Bell (2496ft) and Harter Fell (2539ft) before dropping down Gatescarth Pass back to the car park. On a clear day, the views for most of the way around are magnificent.

There's a shorter walk from Mardale Head car park a mile and a half into Riggindale (signposted as the "Bampton shore" path) to the RSPB's

golden eagle viewpoint (always open, but staffed April–Aug, weekends & bank hols 11am–4pm; Ⓦwww.rspb.org.uk). Outside the Scottish Highlands, this is the only place in the UK you'll get the chance to see the soaring bird – there's currently a single male bird at Haweswater, still looking for a mate.

Public transport is limited to the #111 "Haweswater Rambler" **bus** which runs from Penrith to Bampton, Bampton Grange and Burnbanks (all year, Tues & Sat only). Apart from the *Haweswater Hotel* on the reservoir, the only other local facilities are in the small village of **Bampton** (a couple of miles before the water) and neighbouring **Bampton Grange**, less than a mile beyond and approached over a sandstone bridge; both are very cute and each has a really good pub. There's also a bend-over-backwards-to-be-helpful post office, store, tearoom, B&B and book exchange in Bampton (Ⓦwww.bamptonvillagestore.co.uk), not to mention a yesteryear cottage garage with retro Texaco petrol pumps.

Accommodation and food

Crown & Mitre Bampton Grange Ⓣ01931/713225, Ⓦwww.crown-and-mitre.co.uk. The local inn glows after a sympathetic refurbishment and now features eight lovely rooms with curvy, comfy beds, moody Lake District photography and modern bathrooms with deep roll-top baths. Good food is served downstairs in a cosy space that's more lounge-bar than pub – gastropub stalwarts like lamb shank, steak pie, sea bass and stir-fries cost from around £10 and (with a nod to the hiker and cyclist crowd) portions are immense. ❸

Haweswater Hotel Haweswater Ⓣ01931/713235, Ⓦwww.haweswaterhotel.com. The only place to stay by the water is this extremely peaceful old hotel, built in 1937 to replace the inn at Mardale, lost when the valley was drowned. Rooms (not all en suite) have been given a modern makeover, and there's no TV to distract you – just magnificent views from all points. The walker-friendly bar is open for home-made cakes, drinks and bistro-style lunches (around £10); otherwise, for dinner there's a classier two- or three-course *table d'hôte* menu (£25/30). ❸, en suite ❹, superior rooms ❺

Mardale Inn Bampton Ⓣ01931/713244, Ⓦwww.mardaleinn.co.uk. Another beaut of a refurbished pub, with handcrafted tables, slate floors and a peaceful green interior, and some charming, cosy rooms upstairs. Food's just the ticket too, with a five-quid weekday lunch, or dinner mains from £10 that range from a Herdwick lamb burger to chicken-and-ham pie. It's also a great place for beer, with Cumbrian ales on tap and bottles from three dozen countries. ❸

Withnail and I: a location guide

"We've gone on holiday by mistake", bleats Withnail (Richard E. Grant) in cult film classic *Withnail and I* (1987), about two booze-and-pill-ridden unemployed actors who leave London for a trip to the country. The holiday in question is a disastrous stay in a bleak, freezing, rain-sodden cottage belonging to Withnail's lecherous Uncle Monty. While the location is never specified, the "country" parts of the film are largely set on the eastern fringes of the Lake District between Shap and Haweswater. Uncle Monty's cottage was, in fact, the delapidated **Sleddale Hall** overlooking **Wet Sleddale Reservoir**, two miles south of Shap, off the A6 (and 12 miles south of Penrith). In the past you could park at the reservoir and walk up to see the building, though things may change now that it's been sold to a private buyer for conversion into a home. If all else fails, fans can still can track down some of the other locations. The lake shown in the film isn't the Wet Sleddale reservoir but the far larger **Haweswater** to the west. Sadly, the **Penrith Tea Rooms** – scene of a desperate search for alcohol ("We want the finest wines available to humanity") – doesn't exist, or at least, not in Penrith. This and the Penrith pub scene were actually filmed in Stony Stratford, near Milton Keynes, though the old red telephone box used by Withnail to call his agent is the one in **Bampton** village, near Haweswater.

Travel details

All timetables can be checked on Traveline ⓣ0871/200 2233, ⓦwww.traveline.info. For Ullswater Steamers see box on p.213.

From Penrith

Bus #108, "Patterdale Bus" (4–5 daily) to: Pooley Bridge (18min), Aira Force (32min), Glenridding (40min), Patterdale (45min).
Bus #110 postbus to: Pooley Bridge (quickest journey time 25min), Howtown (40min) and Martindale (45min). Service operates Mon–Sat 2 daily. Of the two, the much quicker afternoon service (shown here, not Sat) is the only realistic option.
Bus #111, "Haweswater Rambler" (2–3 daily) to: Askham (12min), Bampton (26min), Bampton Grange (33min) and Burnbanks (40min). Service operates Tues & Sat all year.

From Glenridding/Patterdale

Bus #208, "Ullswater Connection" (5 daily) to: Aira Force (12min) and Keswick (38min). Service operates late May to mid-July, Sat, Sun and bank hols; mid-July to Aug daily.
Bus #517, "Kirkstone Rambler" to: Brothers Water (10min), *Kirkstone Pass Inn* (25min), Troutbeck *Queen's Head* (35min), Windermere (47min) and Bowness (55min). Service operates Easter to mid-July & Sept–Oct Sat, Sun & bank hols 3 daily; mid-July to early Sept 3 daily.

From Bowness/Windermere

Bus #517, "Kirkstone Rambler" to: Brothers Water (45min), Patterdale (50min) and Glenridding (55min). Service operates Easter to mid-July & Sept–Oct Sat, Sun & bank hols 3 daily; mid-July to early Sept 3 daily.

7

Out of the National Park

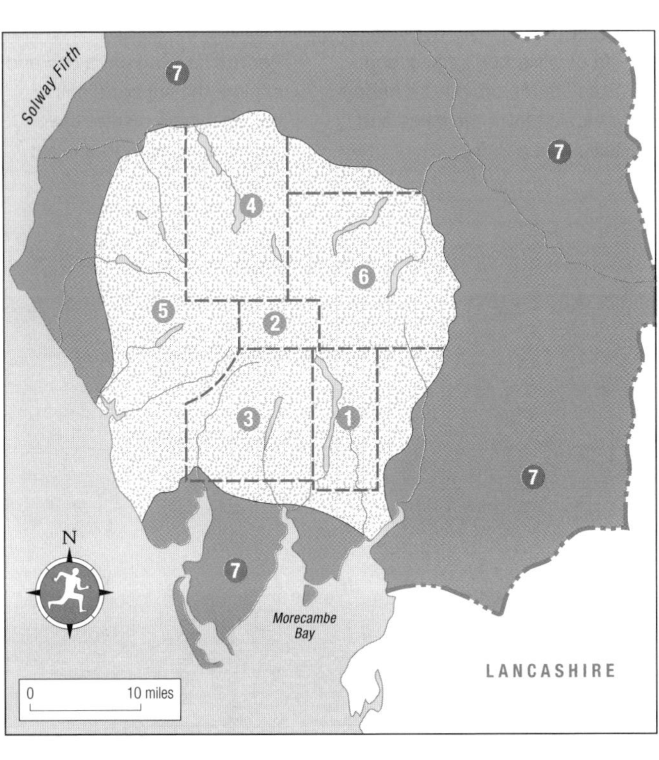

CHAPTER 7 **Highlights**

* **Cartmel** A cutting-edge gastronomic retreat in one of the region's prettiest medieval villages. See p.236

* **Holker Hall** The gardens and grounds of this stately pile make a fine family day out. See p.237

* **Laurel and Hardy Museum, Ulverston** Picking over the life of Ulverston's finest son, Stan Laurel, provides a happy diversion from the lakes and fells. See p.240

* **Whitehaven** West Cumbria's most captivating town has a Georgian centre and revitalized harbour. See p.244

* **Wordsworth House, Cockermouth** Wordsworth's childhood home has been enterprisingly restored as a working Georgian household. See p.249

* **Penrith** Take an extra day and explore the surroundings of this enjoyable market town from ostrich farm to ancient stones. See p.254

▲ Whitehaven harbour

7

Out of the National Park

When the Lake District National Park boundary was drawn around the lakes and fells, it excluded several peripheral Cumbrian towns, nearly all of the west Cumbrian coast and the southern Furness peninsulas. Most visitors to the Lakes will pass through at least one of these areas – indeed, the usual approaches to the Lake District make it hard to avoid Kendal or Penrith. And there's a case for aiming to see several other destinations not strictly within the National Park on any trip to the region. The distances help: it's not much more than thirty miles between Penrith and Cockermouth, and about the same around the west coast, making it easy to nip from lakeland valley to outlying town.

En route to Windermere, **Kendal**, in the southeast, was once the county town of Westmorland and is still an enjoyable market town, with a fine riverside location and plenty of local attractions. **Penrith**, to the north, is also an ancient commercial centre and, like Kendal, retains the ruins of the castle that defended it during the turbulent medieval border wars. It's not far from Ullswater and the northern Lakes, and many combine a visit with nearby **Rheged**, the Cumbrian visitor centre and 3D film experience. Religious foundations established in the south at **Cartmel** and **Furness Abbey** had a lasting regional significance; the enterprising Furness monks could be said to have made early Cumbria an economic powerhouse well before the Industrial Revolution. Of the Cumbrian ports and towns that boomed in the eighteenth and nineteenth centuries, **Ulverston** still thrives as a market town (and claims comedian Stan Laurel as its best-known son), while **Whitehaven**, on the west Cumbrian coast, has been rejuvenated by investment in its fine harbour and quayside. Here, and at nearby **Cockermouth** – yet another handsome market town – the Georgian well-to-do (including the young Wordsworth family) lived out their comfortable lives.

All the places covered in this chapter are accessible by public transport and details are given where necessary. Cumbria's **Traveline** (Ⓣ0871/200 2233, Ⓦwww.traveline.info) can provide specific routes and timetables.

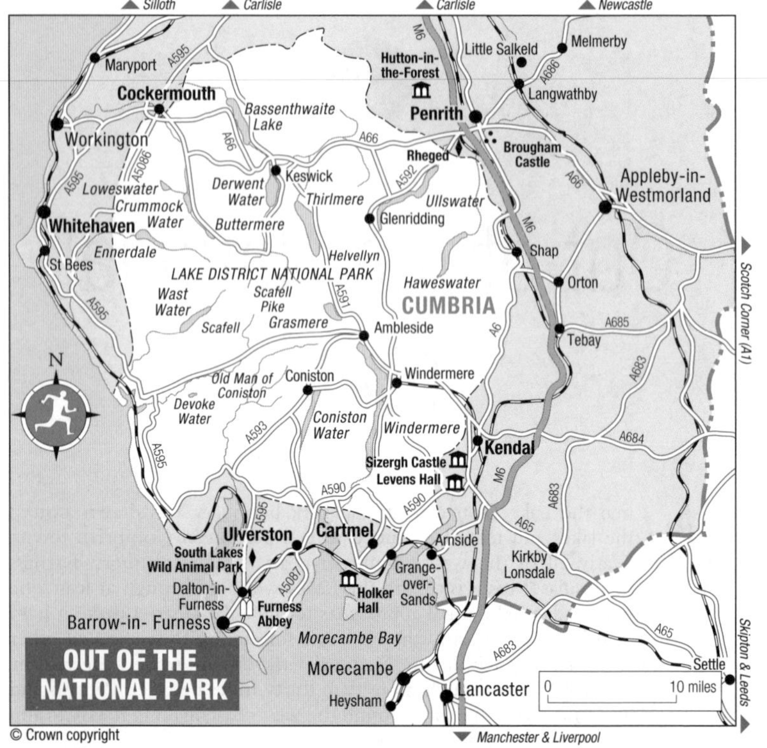

Kendal

The self-billed "Gateway to the Lakes" (though nearly ten miles from Windermere), limestone-grey **KENDAL** is the largest of the southern Cumbrian towns, with a population of 25,000. Upwardly mobile Norman barons created a medieval market town on the banks of the fast-flowing River Kent and built a castle here. They also bequeathed to the town its most characteristic feature by establishing uniform building plots along a single main street in an attempt to increase their rents. This resulted in the layout visible today on both sides of Highgate and Stricklandgate: houses and shops to the fore, stables and workshops to the rear in the numerous "yards" and "ginnels". The town became known for its archers – who fought at Crécy and Poitiers in the Hundred Years War with France – and for its cloth, particularly the "Kendal green" (plant-dyed wool), which earned the town a mention in Shakespeare's *Henry IV*. No wonder that the town motto became the no-nonsense "Cloth is my bread". By the eighteenth century Kendal was a major European cloth distribution centre, while its tanneries laid the foundation for today's most important industry, shoe-making. However, you could be forgiven for thinking that **Kendal Mintcake** is what keeps the contemporary coffers filled. This solid, energy-giving block of sugar and peppermint oil, invented by accident in the mid-nineteenth century, has been hoisted to the top of the world's highest mountains and is on sale throughout the Lakes.

The Town and around

The old **Market Place** has long since succumbed to development, with the market hall now converted to the Westmorland Shopping Centre (off Stricklandgate), but traditional stalls still do business outside every Wednesday and Saturday and there's a well-established farmers' market on the last Friday of the month. The long main street – Stricklandgate and then Highgate – is backed by historic yards and alleys, many now tidily renovated and containing stores, businesses and shopping centres. Strolling along here will eventually take you down to the riverside, past restored almshouses, mullioned shopfronts and old trade signs, among them the pipe-smoking Turk outside the snuff factory on Lowther Street.

At Kirkland, by the river at the bottom of Highgate, the wide aisles of the Early English **Parish Church** house a number of family chapels, including that of the Parr family, who once owned the ruined **Kendal Castle** (free access) on a hillock to the east across the river. First erected in the early thirteenth century, it's claimed as the birthplace of Catherine Parr, Henry VIII's sixth wife, but the story is apocryphal – she was born in 1512, at which time the building was in an advanced state of decay. It's a stiff climb to the grassy top for some breezy views from the ruined walls; to get there, cross the footbridge just north of the church and follow the footpath from the end of Parr Street.

Kendal Museum

The **Kendal Museum** on Station Road (hours may vary, but currently Thurs–Sat noon–5pm; £2.80; Ⓣ01539/721374, Ⓦwww.kendalmuseum.org.uk) contains the district's natural history and archeological finds. Founded as early as 1796, what was essentially a gentleman's private collection was later given to the town and moved into an old wool warehouse in 1913, where it's been stationed ever since. It's highly entertaining, since as well as the usual flints, stuffed birds and Roman and Viking finds there are plenty of well-presented displays relating to the town's history and many unclassifiable curiosities – from the original key to the town castle to a stuffed grizzly bear, shot by the Earl of Lonsdale. There are exhibitions, events and family crafts and activities, especially in school holidays, while the museum also makes a big fuss of famous fell-walker **Alfred Wainwright**, which is fair enough seeing as he was honorary clerk at the museum between 1945 and 1974. There's a reconstruction of his office here, together with various original pen-and-ink drawings and some of his personal effects (including his socks and pipe) – many of the museum artefact labels are also written in Wainwright's distinctive hand.

Quaker Tapestry

Just off the river, between New Road and Stramongate, one of Britain's largest Quaker Meeting Houses (built 1816) contains the 77 beautifully embroidered panels of the **Quaker Tapestry** (April–Oct Mon–Fri 10am–5pm, last admission at 4pm, plus some Sats 11am–3pm; £6, family £12; Ⓣ01539/722975, Ⓦwww.quaker-tapestry.co.uk). This area of the southern Lakes was a hotbed of early Quakerism, beginning with the travelling ministry of George Fox (1652), a seeker after truth, whose followers were dubbed Quakers "because we bid them tremble at the Word of the Lord". The tapestry – produced by almost four thousand people gathered in embroidery groups between 1981 and 1996 – forms a narrative history of Quaker experience through the ages, with the delicately worked panels portraying historical subjects such as Elizabeth Fry's work in Newgate prison and the anti-slavery "underground railroad" in the USA, as well as contemporary Quaker campaigns for peace, relief work and reconciliation. Embroidery workshops and demonstrations are held throughout the year, and there's also a vegetarian tearoom, which is open weekdays in winter, too, when the exhibition is closed. You can enter the Meeting House from either New Road or Stramongate.

Abbot Hall Art Gallery and Museum of Lakeland Life and Industry

The town's other two attractions – the Art Gallery and Museum of Lakeland Life and Industry – are found at the Georgian **Abbot Hall** (Mon–Sat 10.30am–5pm, Nov – March 10.30am–4pm; closed 2 weeks in Dec; ⓣ01539/722464, ⓦwww.abbothall.org.uk), by the river near the parish church. The main hall, painstakingly restored to its 1760s town house origins,

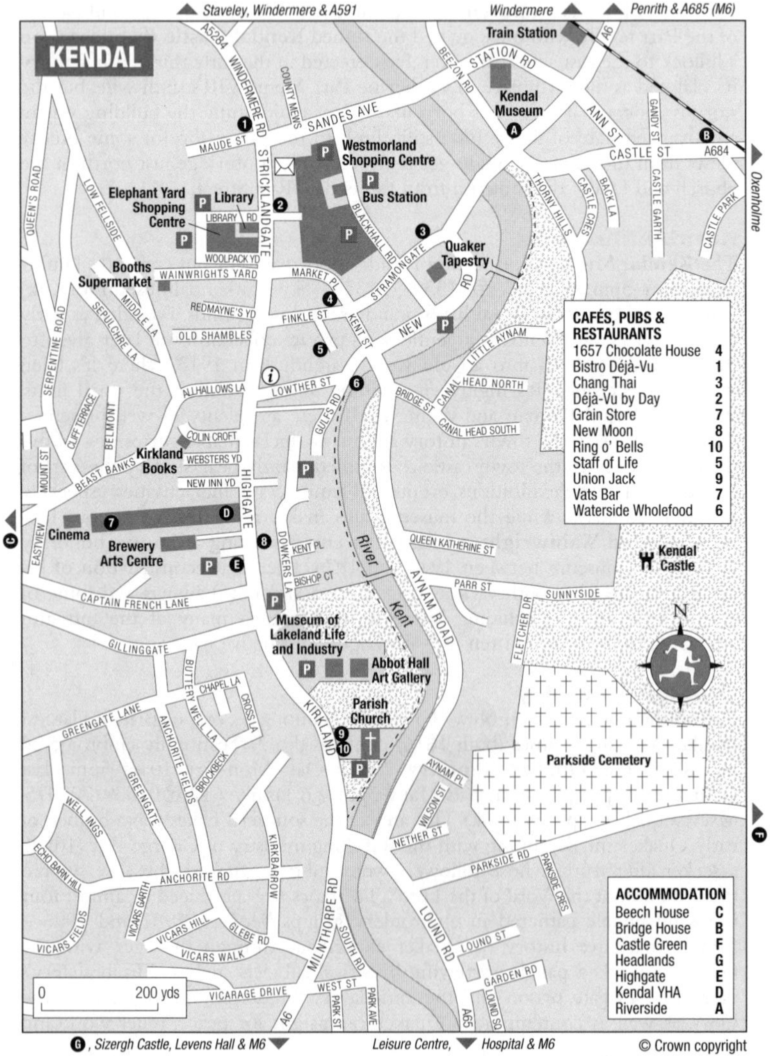

Fellwalker extraordinaire – Alfred Wainwright

If ever a person has changed the way others look at the Lake District hills it's **Alfred Wainwright** (1907–91), whose famous handwritten walking guides are studied with the intensity normally reserved for religious texts. Wainwright was born in Blackburn in Lancashire, left school at 13 and worked his way up through the Borough Treasurer's office, qualifying as an accountant in 1933. After a first visit to the Lake District in 1930 he became a keen walker and returned to the Lakes at every possible opportunity. So taken was he with the fells that he engineered a move to Kendal in 1941; he was Borough Treasurer from 1948 until his retirement in 1967.

Wainwright was nothing if not obsessional, setting off alone at the crack of dawn every weekend to tackle distant lakeland fells and valleys. In 1952, dissatisfied with the accuracy of existing maps, he started work on a series of seven walking guides, each painstakingly handwritten with mapped routes and delicately drawn views. These **Pictorial Guides** to the Lake District were a remarkable undertaking, especially since the original idea was only for his own amusement. The first book, *The Eastern Fells*, was published in 1955 and was an unexpected success; six others followed by 1966, thus completing the task he had set himself of recording in detail 214 separate lakeland fells. The seven volumes have subsequently sold over two million copies. Many other titles followed: a *Pennine Way Companion* (1968), the *Coast-to-Coast* route he devised from St Bees to Robin Hood's Bay (1973), endless sketchbooks and guides to the Lake District, Scotland, Wales, the Yorkshire Dales and the Lancashire hills; fifty-odd books in all. His first wife, Ruth, left him in 1966, and in 1970 Wainwright married Betty McNally, with whom he'd corresponded (and secretly met on his walking trips) for years. He died in 1991, having given away most of his considerable earnings to animal rescue charities, and his **ashes were scattered** on Haystacks in Buttermere.

The effect his books have had is plain to see. People who don't normally consider themselves walkers are happy to tick off the routes and peaks in his guides, though others point to the problems this has caused in terms of visitor numbers to certain areas. The BBC's recent "Wainwright Walks" and "Coast to Coast" series have also had a significant effect on traffic at popular targets like Cat Bells. It's tempting but wrong to treat Wainwright as gospel, as many do in their attempts to "bag" his 214 recorded fells. The number was an entirely arbitrary figure – most of the Wainwright fells are over 1400ft high, but there are plenty of other crags and fells lower than that but just as spectacular, not to mention the lakes, tarns and valleys which he covered only in passing.

Wainwright allowed no revision of the *Pictorial Guides* to be made during his lifetime, but with the agreement of the Wainwright Estate revised editions of all seven guides have now been completed by cartographer and Wainwright disciple Chris Jesty. Up-to-date news and views about this and other related subjects are observed by the **Wainwright Society** (Ⓦwww.wainwright.org.uk), dedicated to the "Master Fellwalker" and his works.

houses the splendid **Art Gallery** (£5.75, 1-year season ticket £16.55, under-18s free), whose upper floors host well-regarded exhibitions on various artists and themes. The lower-floor galleries are more locally focused, concentrating on the works of the eighteenth-century "Kendal School" of portrait painters, notably Daniel Gardner and, most famously, George Romney. Born in Dalton-in-Furness (and buried there), Romney set himself up as a portrait painter in Kendal in 1757, where he stayed for five years before moving to London to further his career. His society portraits are the pick of the gallery's collection, though you'll also find changing displays of works by those who came to the Lakes to paint, such as Constable, Ruskin, Turner and Edward Lear, and a growing collection of contemporary British art. In addition, eighteenth-century chairs, writing desks and games tables designed and built by famed furniture-makers Gillows of Lancaster have all survived in Abbot Hall in excellent condition.

There's a good **café** at the gallery (with outdoor seating on the riverside lawn in summer), while over in the hall's former stables is the excellent **Museum of Lakeland Life and Industry** (£4.75, family £13.60, Ⓦwww.lakelandmuseum.org.uk, ticket valid for a year), which explores Cumbria's social history and traditional heritage. Reconstructed house interiors from the seventeenth, eighteenth and nineteenth centuries stand alongside artisans' workshops to create a vivid presentation of rural trades and crafts, from mining, spinning and weaving to shoe-making and tanning. You can trace Cumbrian fashion through the ages, or investigate the Arts and Crafts movement, while the museum also contains a room devoted to the life and work of the children's writer Arthur Ransome, whose widow donated his pipes, typewriter and other memorabilia to the collection after his death.

Sizergh Castle and Levens Hall

Three miles south of Kendal stands **Sizergh Castle**, tucked away off the A591 (Easter–Oct Mon–Thurs & Sun noon–5pm, gardens open same days from 11am; £7.15, family £17.90, gardens only £4.65; Ⓣ015395/60951, Ⓦwww.nationaltrust.org.uk); take bus #555. Home of the Strickland family for eight centuries, the stately home owes its "castle" epithet to the fourteenth-century pele tower at its core – one of the best examples of these towers, which were built as safe havens during the region's protracted medieval border raids. The Great Hall underwent significant changes in Elizabethan times, when most of its rooms were panelled in oak with their ceilings layered in elaborate plaster-work. There are guided tours between noon and 1pm; thereafter you can

▲ Milking parlour at Low Sizergh Barn

Walks from Kendal

Although Kendal isn't the most obvious hiking centre, you can in fact walk straight out of town and on to the nearby hills. There are no particularly dramatic heights to gain, but it's pretty countryside. The two moderate walks below offer a variety of scenery, while you're also only a short drive or train ride away from Staveley, the access point for Kentmere and its walks.

The River Kent to Staveley

Follow the path along the **River Kent** north out of Kendal (or jump the train one stop) to Burneside (the *Jolly Anglers* is a good pub), where you cut northeast up minor roads and farm tracks before climbing to **Gurnal Dubs** and **Potter Tarn**, two prettily sited tarns. The path skirts both before descending to Staveley (and its Mill Yard craft shops and cafés), where you pick up the signposted Dales Way, which then meanders back down the River Kent through pastoral country to Burneside. From Burneside, this is a 7.5-mile (4hr) circular walk, though if you walk in and out of Kendal you can add another three miles (1hr) to this.

Scout Scar

The high limestone ridge known as **Scout Scar** is 3 miles southwest of Kendal and, on a clear day, provides some scintillating views. Again, you can walk out of Kendal if you want to make a day of it, though it's more usually climbed from either the Underbarrow road (north) or from Brigsteer (south) – there's parking at both places and a pub in Brigsteer.

See Basics, p.42, for general walking advice in the Lakes; recommended maps are detailed on p.50.

wander around at will. At nearby **Low Sizergh Barn** (daily 9.30am–5pm; ⓣ015395/60426, ⓦwww.lowsizerghbarn.co.uk), four miles south of Kendal on the A591, there's a really good farm shop and craft gallery, while the tearoom has a viewing window onto the organic dairy herd's milking parlour (cows milked daily around 3.45pm).

Two miles south of Sizergh, **Levens Hall** (April to mid-Oct Mon–Thurs & Sun noon–5pm; gardens same days from 10am; £11, family £27; gardens only £8, family £20; ⓣ015395/60321, ⓦwww.levenshall.co.uk), also built around a medieval tower (1250–1300), is more uniform in style than Sizergh, since the bulk of it was built or refurbished in classic Elizabethan style between 1570 and 1640. House stewards are on hand to answer any questions and point out the oddities and curios – for example, the dining room is panelled not with oak but with goat's leather, printed with a deep-green floral design. Upstairs, the bedrooms offer glimpses of the beautifully trimmed topiary gardens, where yews in the shape of pyramids, peacocks, top hats, spirals and crowns stand adjacent to blooming bedding plants and apple orchards. The oldest ha-ha (sunken ditch and wall) in England allows views across the fields beyond, while on Sundays and bank holiday Mondays a showman's steam engine is put to work. You don't have to pay the admission charge just to visit the plant centre and tearoom; the #555 bus stops outside the hall.

Practicalities

Kendal's **train station** is the first stop on the Windermere branch line, just three minutes from the Oxenholme main-line station. It's a ten-minute walk into town, or you can catch bus #41 or #41A (to the Town Hall) direct from

Oxenholme station (Mon–Sat every hour). The **bus station** is on Blackhall Road (off Stramongate), with main routes including the #599 (to Windermere, Bowness, Ambleside and Grasmere) and #555 (towards Keswick, or to Lancaster or Carlisle). Driving in from the M6, take junction 38 (north) or 36 (south). There are signposted **car parks** all over town, including one at the Westmorland Shopping Centre (Blackhall Road) and several off Highgate, plus free unlimited parking on New Road by the river (though this is always busy). The **tourist office** (Mon–Sat 10am–5pm, Nov–Feb until 4pm; ⓣ01539/797516, ⓦwww.kendaltowncouncil.gov.uk) is in the Town Hall on Highgate (at the junction with Lowther Street).

Accommodation

Kendal makes a reasonable overnight stop on the way to or from the Lakes, and can be a useful base for the southern region – though walkers should note that the central fells and valleys are all a good drive or bus ride away. Most of the local **B&Bs** lie along Windermere Road, north of the centre, and on Milnthorpe Road, to the south, while the celebrated *Punch Bowl Inn* at Crosthwaite is only five miles to the west.

Beech House 40 Greenside ⓣ01539/720385, ⓦwww.beechhouse-kendal.co.uk. Boutique B&B with a keen sense of decorative design – think swagged curtains, plump pillows, richly coloured fabrics and black-and-white bathrooms with gleaming roll-top baths. Some rooms are classed deluxe, and for space and views look no further than the top-floor "Penthouse". It's a short, steep climb up the hill from the town centre (on the green, just past the *Riflemans' Arms* pub), and there's parking outside. ❸, deluxe rooms ❹

Bridge House 65 Castle St ⓣ01539/722041, ⓦwww.bridgehouse-kendal.co.uk. Georgian family house, not far from the station (it was once the station master's residence), with a couple of pretty B&B rooms available. No credit cards. ❷

Castle Green Castle Green Lane ⓣ01539/734000, ⓦwww.castlegreen.co.uk. Kendal's biggest hotel is a large, efficiently run resort-style development a mile or so out of the centre. There's plenty of space in the modern rooms, and a touch more style in the executive ones, while facilities range from pool, steam room and spa to its own pub in the grounds. There's a steakhouse menu in the pub, and locally sourced, modern Brit food with a view in the hotel restaurant (dinner from £24). Parking. ❺, family rooms ❻

Headlands 53 Milnthorpe Rd ⓣ01539/732464, ⓦwww.headlandskendal.co.uk. The pick of the bunch on a popular road for guesthouses is this traditional stone house, 5min walk south of the centre. Rooms are small but smart – the one at the top of the house, a family room with a couple of bunks, is the most spacious. Parking. ❷

Highgate 128 Highgate ⓣ01539/724229, ⓦwww.highgatehotel.co.uk. Right in the centre and originally built for the town's first doctor, the rambling Georgian house now conceals a variety of traditionally furnished rooms, plus a small garden and patio. Parking. ❷

Kendal YHA 118 Highgate ⓣ0845/371 9641, ⓔkendal@yha.org.uk. Straightforward hostel accommodation in a building attached to The Brewery Arts Centre. The multi-bunked rooms are a bit barrack-like (though a few double-bedded rooms are available) and the hostel's tight on space, but the location's great and there's a lively arts centre bar next door. Dorm beds from £17.95, includes breakfast.

Riverside Stramongate Bridge ⓣ01539/734861, ⓦwww.riversidekendal.co.uk. One of Kendal's old riverside tanneries has proved to be a perfect building for a hotel restoration. The long rows of riverside windows let light into the spacious rooms, while a decent restaurant makes the most of the riverside setting – ingredients are sourced from the hotel group's own kitchen garden and farm. Also a leisure club on site with heated pool, spa, sauna and gym. Best deals are on the website. Parking. ❹

Eating, drinking and entertainment

Kendal has the best selection of places to **eat and drink** in the south Lakes, so if you're moving on to the fells you'll want to get your cappuccinos and veggie specials while you can. There are sandwich bars and cafés down Finkle Street especially, as well as a huge Booths **supermarket** in Wainwrights Yard. Many of the town-centre **pubs** have had unsympathetic makeovers, but there are still one or two traditional boozers left plus a few more stylish bars and coffee lounges ranged up and down the main street. Apart from the regular programme at the **Brewery Arts Centre** (see listings below), there's also a special season of Christmas events and a renowned annual **jazz and blues festival** every November. Other annual events in Kendal include the town's **Torchlight Procession** and **Westmorland County Show** (both Sept) and the **Mountain Film Festival** (Nov), which presents climbing and mountain-related films, events and speakers from around the world.

Cafés and bakery

1657 Chocolate House 54 Branthwaite Brow, Finkle St ⓣ01539/740702, ⓦwww.chocolatehouse1657.co.uk. Olde-worlde spot that sells divine hot chocolate in dozens of guises, plus a belt-threatening selection of home-made cakes and filled croissants. Up in the Chocolate Loft you can find out how the stuff is made, and don't miss a browse in the lovely choccie shop. Daytime only; closed Sun Jan–Easter.

Déjà-Vu By Day Blackhall Yard ⓣ01539/724407. The daytime outpost for Kendal's bistro (see opposite) is this little French-style café with a nice line in rustic baguettes, salads and light lunches (like smoked salmon and asparagus roulade), all between £4 and £5.50. There's a small outdoor terrace, while upstairs is a late-opening bar (Thurs, Fri & Sat from 7pm). Daytime only; closed Sun.

Staff of Life 2 Berry's Yard, off Finkle St ⓣ01539/738606, ⓦwww.artisanbreadmakers.co.uk. Marvellous hand-made bread, gingerbread and chocolate brownies, great for picnics – it's hidden down an alley off Finkle St, with a deli opposite.

Union Jack 15 Kirkland ⓣ01539/722458. If you want veggie food but also crave chips and beans, this is the spot – a family-run diner where full breakfasts and mixed grills take their place on the menu alongside veggie grills, spicy bean burgers and other non-meat treats. You're hard-pushed to spend a fiver. Daytime only; closed Sun.

Waterside Wholefood Gulfs Rd, bottom of Lowther St ⓣ01539/729743, ⓦwww.watersidewholefood.co.uk. A great place by the river for veggie and vegan wholefood snacks or meals (from £3.50 to £7) – you can eat outside or grab a table in one of the homely little interior rooms. Soups, salads, bakes and cakes form the mainstay of the menu, but stuffed tortillas, wraps and other specials provide daily variation, and organic and Fair Trade ingredients are used where possible. Daytime only; closed Sun.

Restaurants

Bistro Déjà-Vu 124 Stricklandgate ⓣ01539/724843, ⓦwww.dejavukendal.co.uk. The pitch? Classic bistro dishes (Toulouse sausage on garlic mash, Moroccan couscous, warm smoked mackerel salad) at pretty unbeatable prices (three courses for a tenner, Sun–Thurs all night, Fri & Sat before 7.30pm). The verdict? A reliable, laid-back place to dine on a budget. Dinner only; closed Tues.

Chang Thai 54 Stramongate ⓣ01539/720387. Northern Thai dishes are the speciality in this intimate restaurant – such as *laab*, a spicy, minced-meat salad – but all the usual stir-fries are available, alongside fragrant "mussaman" curries (with coconut, pineapple and peanuts) and lots of veggie and fish choices. Mains are in the £8–12 range, though a whole steamed sea bass will set you back £16. Dinner only.

Grain Store Brewery Arts Centre, 122 Highgate ⓣ01539/725133, ⓦwww.breweryarts.co.uk. The easy-going arts centre café/restaurant opens from 10am for coffee and cake, and then switches to a lunch menu of sandwiches, salads, classic dishes like bangers and mash, and the famous gourmet pizzas. Dinner keeps the pizzas but also combines seasonal local produce with world flavours – goat's cheese salad to crayfish cocktail, fell-bred beef to swordfish. Last orders are usually at 9pm, or 9.30pm for pizzas, and prices range from £7–8 for pizzas and £10–15 for other dishes.

New Moon 129 Highgate ⓣ01539/729254, ⓦwww.newmoonrestaurant.co.uk. Kendal's longest-serving foodie choice is a contemporary bistro with a seasonally changing menu. Lunch sticks to things like panini, risottos, pastas and salads (£5–7), but at dinner (most mains £11–16) there's a modish take on locally sourced ingredients, like a rack of Cumbrian lamb served on garlic mash. There's always a good choice for fish-eaters and vegetarians too. Closed Sun & Mon.

Pubs and bars

Ring o' Bells 37 Kirkland ⓣ01539/720326. This pub, uniquely, stands on consecrated ground by the parish church, making it the bell-ringers' local. Does its holy location make the beer taste better? You decide.

Vats Bar Brewery Arts Centre, 122 Highgate ⓣ01539/725133. Best bar in town is the Arts Centre hangout – the huge "vats" provide circular booth seating and there's a great summer terrace which turns into a real social hub. When you get the munchies it's good to know that the menu (lunch and dinner) is the same as in the adjacent *Grain Store* (see "Restaurants", above).

Arts Centre

Brewery Arts Centre Brewery Arts Centre, 122 Highgate, information line ⓣ01539/795090, box office ⓣ01539/725133, ⓦwww.breweryarts.co.uk. Hub of everything that's happening in town, with its cinema, theatre, galleries and concert hall, not to mention café/bar, restaurant and pub. There's live music here throughout the year (including live outdoor concerts on summer Sundays).

Listings

Bookshop Kirkland Books, 11 Collin Croft ⓣ01539/733220, ⓦwww.kirklandbooks.biz (only open Thurs–Sat). Offers an excellent selection of secondhand and antique books, and is especially strong on local authors, walking and the mountains.
Car rental Westmorland Vehicle Hire ⓣ01539/728532, ⓦwww.carhirecumbria.co.uk.
Emergencies Westmorland General Hospital, Burton Rd, Kendal ⓣ01539/732288, ⓦwww.mbht.nhs.uk.
Internet access Kendal Library, Stricklandgate (Mon & Wed 9.30am–7pm, Tues & Fri 9.30am–5pm, Thurs 9.30am–noon, Sat 9.30am–3.30pm, Sun noon–4pm; ⓣ01539/713520).
Pharmacies Boots, 10 Elephant Yard ⓣ01539/720180; Highgate Pharmacy, 41 Highgate ⓣ01539/720461; Lloyd's, Station Yard ⓣ01539/723988.
Police station Busher Walk ⓣ0845/330 0247, ⓦwww.cumbria.police.uk.
Post office 75 Stricklandgate.
Swimming pool Lakes Leisure, Burton Rd ⓣ01539/729777, ⓦwww.lakesleisure.org.uk/kendal. Public admission usually lunchtime and evenings only during school term-time, otherwise all day, but call or check the website for specific times; there's also a sauna, gym and squash court.
Taxis There's a rank near the Town Hall, or call Blue Star Taxis ⓣ01539/723670.

Cartmel and around

The pretty village of **CARTMEL** is something of an upmarket getaway, with its Michelin-starred restaurant, winding country lanes and cobbled market square brimming with inns and antique shops. You're in luck if you're looking to buy a handmade dolls' house or embroidered footstool, while in the **Cartmel Village Shop** (open daily; ⓦwww.stickytoffeepudding.co.uk) on the square they sell the finest sticky-toffee pudding known to humanity. In keeping with this rather genteel air is the delightful **Cartmel Racecourse** (ⓦwww.cartmel-racecourse.co.uk), home of fashionable race days for the county set each May and August bank holiday weekend. Quite what the original monks of Cartmel would have made of all this is anyone's guess – the village first grew up around its twelfth-century Augustinian priory and is still dominated by the proud **Church of St Mary and St Michael** (daily: Easter–Oct 9am–5.30pm, Nov–Easter 9am–3.30pm; church entrance free, tours Easter–Oct Wed at 11am & 2pm, £2.50; ⓦwww.cartmelpriory.org.uk). The fine interior is illuminated by a 45-foot-high East Window and features immaculate misericords, carved with entwined branches, bunches of grapes, tools, leaves and crosses. A patron of the church, one Rowland Briggs, paid for a shelf on a pier near the north door and for a supply of bread to be

Time, tide and guide

It's only three miles by road from Cartmel to the coast at **Grange-over-Sands**, whose grand yesteryear hotels and floral gardens are fronted by a mile-long esplanade with fine views of the sands and salt marsh of **Morecambe Bay**. It may look benign, but the sands of Britain's second largest bay are treacherous and many lives have been lost here over the centuries (including, notoriously, a gang of Chinese cockle-pickers caught by the racing tide in 2004). Monks from Cartmel who knew the slip sands and hidden channels once led intrepid travellers safely across the bay, but from the sixteenth century onwards the route was considered so dangerous that an official guide was appointed by royal command. The tradition continues today with cross-bay walks in the company of the Queen's Guide, Cedric Robinson, who takes groups out at least weekly (conditions permitting) between May and September. Many of the walks are charity ventures, though anyone is welcome (as are donations). You have to book in advance by calling Cedric Robinson, and you can usually check the walk schedule at Grange-over-Sands tourist office (Ⓣ015395/34026, Ⓦwww.grange-over-sands.com).

distributed from it every Sunday in perpetuity "to the most indigent housekeepers of this Parish".

A couple of miles west of Cartmel, **Holker Hall** (Easter–Oct Mon–Fri & Sun, house open 11am–4pm, gardens 10.30am–5.30pm; hall and gardens closed Sat; £10, family £27.50, gardens only £6.50, family £16.50; Ⓣ015395/58328, Ⓦwww.holker.co.uk) is one of Cumbria's finest stately homes, still in use by the Cavendish family which has owned it since the late seventeenth century. The impressive 25-acre **gardens** are the real highlight, featuring sweeping views from the surrounding meadows to the fells and estuary beyond. There's plenty to seek out – sunken garden, grotto, stone labyrinth and massive slate sundial – while a water cascade tumbles from a seventeenth-century marble Neptune down through the rhododendrons and oak trees. There's also a celebrated annual **garden festival** (May/June), and spring (April) and winter (November) markets held here, while you don't have to pay for entrance to visit the food hall deli and café (see p.238), both of which are also open on Saturdays and in winter when Holker Hall is otherwise closed.

Practicalities

Cartmel lies a few miles inland of Morecambe Bay and just five miles south of Lakeside, the southern tip of Windermere. **Trains** stop at Cark-in-Cartmel, two miles southwest of the village (the station is a mile from Holker Hall); **buses** (not Sun) from here or from Grange-over-Sands run to the village. The turn-off from the M6 is junction 36; the **car park** is by the racecourse.

There's no **information** office in Cartmel, but the local website Ⓦwww.cartmelvillage.com is useful. Save for race meeting weekends, accommodation is generally easy to find, and there are also several cafés and old pubs – the *King's Arms*, with tables outside on the square, is the best bet for real ales and good-value bar meals. If you're coming on the gourmet trail it's wise to book ahead for the stellar experience of *L'Enclume*, though there are several other local foodie destinations, from organic farm shop to country-house café and food hall, that welcome visits.

Accommodation and food

Cavendish Arms Cavendish St ⓣ015395/36240, ⓦwww.thecavendisharms.co.uk. The oldest of Cartmel's inns – on the road through the gatehouse – retains many of its original sixteenth-century features and has an open fire in the public bar. Other than that, there are few surprises – various traditional rooms (some a bit on the small side, some with four-posters, etc) and standard pub meals (£8–14), but it's pretty good value and three-for-two-night deals (midweek, low season) are a bargain. Parking. ❸

L'Enclume Cavendish St ⓣ015395/36362, ⓦwww.lenclume.co.uk. Cartmel's medieval blacksmiths (*enclume* is French for anvil) could only have dreamed of food so fine. Chef Simon Rogan's ideas are simply extraordinary, with artfully constructed dishes presented in a bewildering succession of courses, up to 17 in number, depending on the menu – a single seared sea scallop on bacon polenta, or a dainty beef fillet with a fennel coulis, are typical examples, while other dishes are accompanied by intensely flavoured jellied cubes, mousses or foams, or suffused with wild herbs, hedgerow flowers and exotic roots. It's one of England's most critically acclaimed, Michelin-starred experiences, with menus at £55, £75 and £95 (or there's a 3-course lunch for £25). Meanwhile, a dozen smallish but highly individual rooms mix French antique furniture, designer fabrics and excellent bathrooms – there's an attic Art Deco suite and a couple of rooms overlook gardens and priory. Dinner daily, lunch Wed–Sun, closed first two weeks Jan. Parking. ❺, deluxe rooms ❻

Howbarrow Farm 2 miles west of Cartmel ⓣ015395/35746, ⓔpaul.h@howbarrowfarm.co.uk. Very peaceful and appealing B&B with one double and one twin room, with a shared bathroom down the hall (bathrobes provided). It's a fully certified organic farm and a really nice place to kick back and relax – there's a cosy lounge and farmhouse kitchen, and a walking trail around the farm, while breakfast, from milk to bacon, is local and organic. Dinner is also available with advance notice (£22.50), while a farm shop (open Tues–Fri; ⓦwww.howbarroworganic.co.uk) sells fruit, veg, meat and dairy products. From Cartmel, take the road out alongside the racecourse, turn left at the signpost and follow the country lane for another mile. No credit cards. Parking. ❷

Market Cross Cottage Market Square ⓣ015395/36143, ⓔdburgess@marketcross.freeserve.co.uk. Seventeenth-century cottage with flouncy, floral B&B rooms upstairs and oak-beamed tearoom downstairs, where you can sample Morecambe Bay potted shrimps and other traditional dishes. Tearoom closed Mon & Tues. No credit cards. ❷

Cafés and restaurants

Courtyard Café Holker Hall, 2 miles west of Cartmel ⓣ015395/58328, ⓦwww.holker.co.uk. The café at the stately home (opens daily 10.30am; closed Jan) is an excellent place for breakfast (until noon), lunch or tea, especially on nice days when you can sit outside in the courtyard. Much of the produce is from the estate, and there's a huge array sold in the adjacent Holker Food Hall (same opening times, ⓣ015395/59084, ⓦwww.holkerfoodhall.co.uk), from shorthorn beef, oak-smoked farm cheese and the local salt-marsh lamb to gourmet sausages and damson gin. Regional producers' markets are also held here, usually on the first Sunday of each month.

Hat Trick Café Yew Tree Barn, Low Newton, 3 miles northeast ⓣ015395/30577, ⓦwww.hattrickcafe.co.uk. Worth the drive out for a glass of home-made lemonade and out-of-the-ordinary café food, from hash-brown-and-pancake breakfasts to smoked-fish chowder and ranch-style eggs. It's set within Yew Tree Barn (ⓦwww.yewtreebarn.co.uk), always good for a browse around the artists' studios, craft gallery and architectural salvage business. Open daily, usually Mon–Thurs from 8am, Fri–Sun from 9 or 10am.

Hazelmere Café Yewbarrow Terrace, Grange-over-Sands, 3 miles east ⓣ015395/32972, ⓦwww.hazelmerecafe.co.uk. For the finest local cuppa head over to the seaside at Grange, where the award-winning *Hazelmere* dishes up single-estate teas in bone china cups alongside traditional meals and cakes and bread from its own bakery. Café open daily all year, bakery closed Sun.

Rogan & Company Devonshire Square ⓣ015395/35917, ⓦwww.roganandcompany.co.uk. Simon Rogan's casual dining Cartmel offshoot is in no sense a substitute for eating at *L'Enclume*, but it's just as essential a stop for anyone with good food in mind. The gastro-bistro menu (slow-cooked pork, moules marinière, smoked meat platter, fish and chips) is beautifully presented and impeccably sourced (the local butcher and milkman get a salute on the blackboard), while prices are positively encouraging – most dishes £6–15, lunch and dinner. It's also open for breakfast if you fancy starting the day in style.

Ulverston and around

The railway line winds westwards from Cartmel to **ULVERSTON** – eleven miles by road – a close-knit market town on the Furness peninsula that formerly prospered on the cotton, tanning and iron ore industries. The cutting of Britain's shortest, widest and deepest canal in 1796 allowed direct shipping access into town and boosted trade with the Americas and West Indies, while exports from the heart of the Lake District (from wooden bobbins and linen to copper and slate) passed out through Ulverston and made it wealthy. It's still an attractive place today, with dappled grey limestone cottages and a jumble of cobbled alleys and traditional shops zigzagging off the central Market Place. There are plenty of family attractions in the surrounding area, while walkers know the town as the start of the **Cumbria Way** (Ⓦwww.thecumbriaway.info), the 70-mile footpath from Ulverston to Carlisle – a waymarker spire signals the start from The Gill, at the top of Upper Brook Street. There's also an increasingly popular annual **walking festival** held each spring, with ten days of outdoor events, from one-mile strolls to all-day hikes.

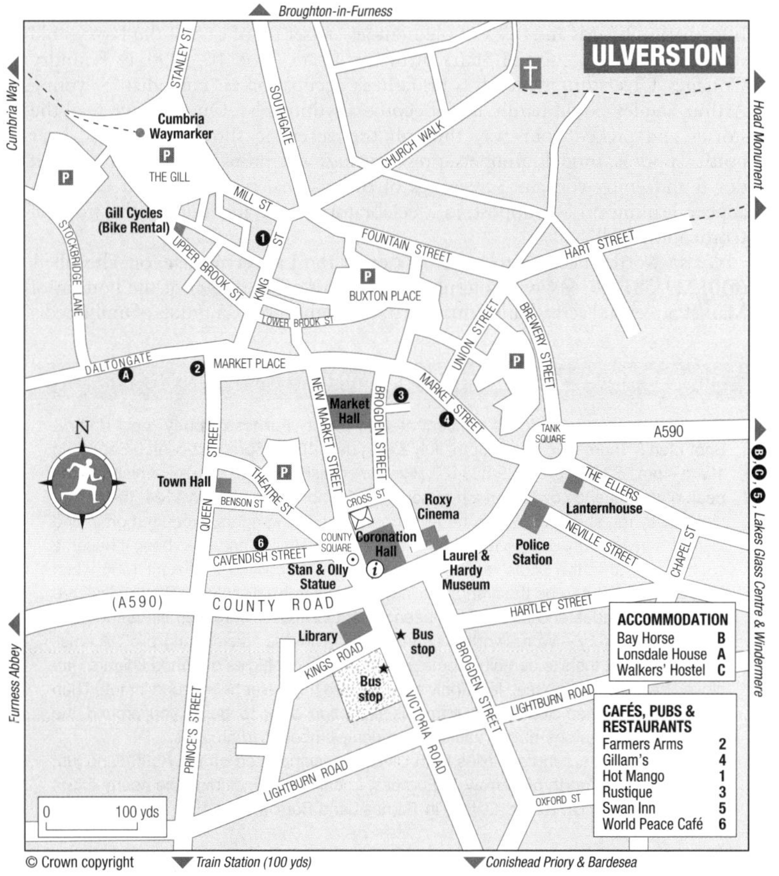

The Town

What looks like a lighthouse high on a hill to the north of town is the **Hoad Monument**, built in 1850 to honour locally born Sir John Barrow, a former Secretary of the Admiralty. It's open on summer Sundays and public holidays (if the flag's flying) and the walk to the top grants fine views of Morecambe Bay, the town and – to the north – the lakeland fells. To get there, follow Church Walk from the end of King Street, past the parish church.

The **Market Hall** on New Market Street (9am–5pm; closed Wed & Sun) is the centre of commercial life, while stalls set up in **Market Place** and surrounding streets every Thursday and Saturday for the busy outdoor market, held since the thirteenth century – the granting of the town charter, by Edward I, is still celebrated here every autumn during Ulverston's Charter Festival. There's also a good **food fair** and farmers' market on the third Saturday of every month.

Ulverston's most famous son is Stan Laurel (born Arthur Stanley Jefferson), the whimpering, head-scratching half of Laurel and Hardy. The duo are celebrated in an endearing collection of memorabilia at the **Laurel and Hardy Museum** (daily 10am–4.30pm; £4; closed Jan; ⓣ01229/582292, ⓦwww.laurel-and-hardy-museum.co.uk), which you'll find behind Coronation Hall; you enter through a rear entrance of the Roxy Cinema, formerly a theatre and music hall. Information boards and cases of mementoes are set up of one of the Roxy's old stages, including a copy of Stan's birth certificate (June 16, 1890, in Foundry Cottages, Ulverston), which lists his father's occupation as "comedian" – young Arthur Stanley could hardly have become anything else. Once you've read the stories and picked your way through the eccentric showcase of hats, beer bottles, photos, models, puppets, press-cuttings and props, you can sit yourself down and enjoy constant screenings of the original films. Stan and Olly also appear, leaning on a lamppost, in a celebratory statue just outside the front of Coronation Hall.

It's also worth checking to see what's on at the **Lanternhouse**, on The Ellers (ⓣ01229/581127, ⓦwww.lanternhouse.org), just off the A590, at the bottom of Market Street and across Tank Square (a traffic roundabout). A group of multimedia

Furness Abbey: a medieval powerhouse

Cumbria's wealth used to be concentrated at mighty **Furness Abbey** (April–June & Sept Mon & Thurs–Sun 10am–5pm; July & Aug daily 10am–5pm; Oct–March Sat & Sun 10am–4pm; £3.50; ⓣ01229/823420, ⓦwww.english-heritage.org.uk), which at the peak of its influence owned much of southern Cumbria. Founded in 1124, the Cistercian abbey ran sheep farms on the fells, controlled fishing rights, produced grain and leather, smelted iron, dug peat for fuel and manufactured salt and even beer. It became such a prize that the Scots raided it twice, though it survived until April 1536 when Henry VIII chose it to be the first of the large abbeys to be dissolved. The roofless red sandstone arcades and pillars have been a popular tourist attraction since the early nineteenth century – Wordsworth was very taken with the "mouldering pile". A small visitor centre at the site contains some rare examples of effigies of armed knights with closed helmets and crossed legs (only seven others have ever been found intact). Then you can borrow an audioguide from the reception desk to guide you around the massive slabs of stone-ribbed vaulting and richly embellished arcades.

The abbey lies around six miles from Ulverston (signposted off the A590), and just a mile and a half north of Barrow-in-Furness. Local buses (including the hourly #X35) between Kendal, Ulverston, Dalton-in-Furness and Barrow pass by.

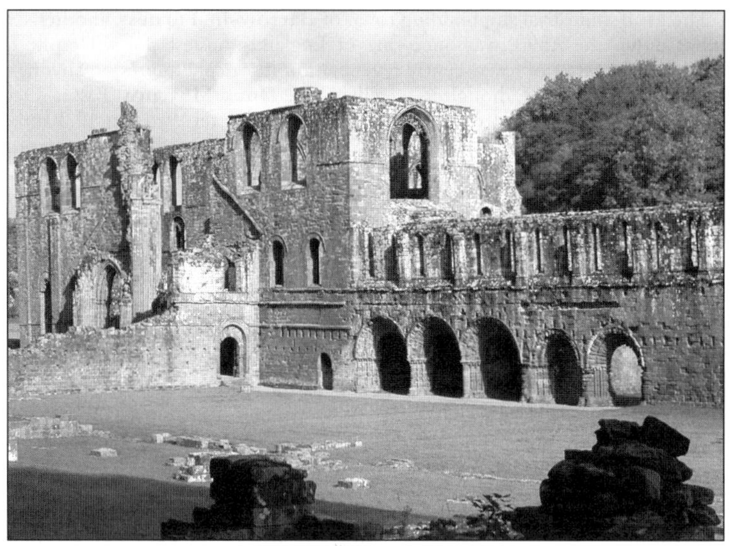

▲ Furness Abbey

artists known as Lanternhouse International occupies this award-winning conversion of an old school, presenting imaginative exhibitions, installations, concerts and community events relating to the "participatory arts".

Around Ulverston

Ulverston makes a good base for a few days' exploration as there's plenty to see and do in the local area known rather optimistically as the Lake District peninsulas (Ⓦwww.lake-district-peninsulas.co.uk). Just outside town, the dramatic Victorian Gothic mansion that is **Conishead Priory** stands on a site originally occupied by a twelfth-century Augustinian priory. It's now a residential Buddhist centre, and the house and specially built **World Peace Temple** are open for visits (Mon–Fri 2–5pm, Sat, Sun & bank hols noon–5pm; closed last 2 weeks in May and mid-July to mid-Aug; admission free, weekend guided tours £2.50; Ⓣ01229/584029, Ⓦwww.conisheadpriory.org), while several acres of woodland grounds (dawn to dusk; free) provide a peaceful place for a stroll. A conservatory café is also open at weekends. It's a couple of miles out of town on the A5087 coast road, or there's access from the Cumbria coastal footpath. Just beyond, at **Bardsea**, there's paddling when the tide is in, scenic views across Morecambe Bay, and a pub in the village for refreshments.

Whatever you feel about zoos, you're likely to be positively surprised by the **South Lakes Wild Animal Park** (daily 10am–5pm; £11.50, Nov–March £8; Ⓣ01229/466086, Ⓦwww.wildanimalpark.co.uk), three miles down the A590 Barrow road, just outside Dalton-in-Furness (bus #618 or #X35). An award-winning conservation zoo, it relies for the most part on ditches and trenches (not cages) and is split into separate habitat areas, from Australian bush to tropical rainforest. It's quite something to encounter free-roaming kangaroos or hand-feed a giraffe in rural Cumbria, while the Sumatran tiger-feeding (encouraging them to climb and jump for their meal) is unique in Europe.

The gruff, industrial shipbuilding town of **Barrow-in-Furness**, another six miles down the A590, was once one of England's busiest ports. Despite a significant amount of town-centre regeneration it scarcely figures on anyone's Lake District itinerary, though its excellent, free **Dock Museum** (Easter–Oct Tues–Fri 10am–5pm, Sat & Sun 11am–5pm; Nov–Easter Wed–Fri 10.30am–4pm, Sat & Sun 11am–4.30pm; ⓣ01229/876400, ⓦwww.dockmuseum.org.uk) is definitely worth a visit. Located in the dried-out graving dock where ships were once repaired, the striking-looking museum tells the history of Barrow, which is also the history of modern shipbuilding, while popular family events are held here every summer. It's signposted throughout town, and from the train station.

Practicalities

The turn-off from the M6 for Ulverston is junction 36; there are **car parks** off Market Street and at The Gill. Ulverston **train station**, serving the Furness and Cumbrian coast railway, is only a few minutes' walk from the town centre – walk up Prince's Street and turn right at the main road for County Square. **Buses** arrive on nearby Victoria Road from Cartmel, Grange-over-Sands, Barrow, Bowness, Windermere and Kendal. The **tourist office** is in Coronation Hall on County Square (Mon–Sat 10am–4pm; ⓣ01229/587120, ⓦwww.ulverston.net, ⓦwww.goulverston.co.uk), and has a leaflet detailing a good 11-mile **circular walk** from town taking in the Hoad Monument, the canal, Conishead Priory and the local coast.

Accommodation

Ulverston is certainly worth a night of anyone's time and though there are town-centre B&Bs you might want to make a real night of it at the celebrated out-of-town restaurant-with-rooms.

Bay Horse Canal Foot, 1.5 miles east of town ⓣ01229/583972, ⓦwww.thebayhorsehotel.co.uk. This cosy old inn on the Leven estuary lulls you with gorgeous views and jolly good Cumbrian cuisine. Cream-and-fawn rooms are comfortable rather than cutting edge, but most open out onto a terrace and you don't even need to get out of bed to see the water. There's a traditional bar for drinks and light meals, while dinner (open to non-guests; reservations advised) is served in the candlelit conservatory – proper steaks, lakeland lamb, game in season and fresh fish, book-ended by home-made bread and truffles. There's either a monthly changing à la carte menu (mains around £23) or a more bistro-style two/three-course *table d'hôte* (£22/28). From town, follow the A590 and turn off at the signpost for Canal Foot, running through an industrial estate to reach the inn, by the last lock on the Ulverston canal (or a 30min walk). Parking. ❹, April–Oct ❺

Lonsdale House Hotel 11 Daltongate ⓣ01229/582598, ⓦwww.lonsdalehousehotel.co.uk. Businesslike rooms in a Georgian town house (no surprise that each has a trouser-press and some have the regulation four-poster), but the best part is the private walled garden at the back. Overlook this and you'll escape any street noise. Afternoon tea and sundowner drinks are available in the garden, and there's also a cellar bistro and bar, *Eleven*, with mains from around £7. Parking. ❹

Walkers' Hostel Oubas Hill, Canal Head ⓣ01229/480511 or 07767/882943, ⓦwww.walkershostel.co.uk. The main choice for Cumbria Way walkers, backpackers, cyclists and outdoor types of all kinds. Beds are in small shared rooms sleeping two to eight people (one's a family room with double beds and bunks), with packed lunches, laundry, kitchen and internet available, plus plenty of local walking info, including details of Ulverston's annual walking festival. The house is near the canal basin, east on the A590, at the foot of the Hoad Monument, a 15min walk from the centre (look for the "big boots" painted on the house). Parking. Beds £17.50, including breakfast.

Eating, drinking and entertainment

As befits a market town there's plenty of choice when it comes to eating and drinking, from traditional cafés to stylish restaurants. Ulverston is also trumpeted as a "Festival Town" and there's a celebration of one kind or another almost every month. The local cultural centre – for theatre, opera, concerts and other events, including the annual beer festival – is **Coronation Hall** in County Square (Ⓣ01229/587140, Ⓦwww.corohall.co.uk).

Farmer's Arms 3 Market Place Ⓣ01229/584469. More wine bar and restaurant than pub these days (with wicker chairs, sofas and newspapers), but still the best place in town for a convivial drink and a bar meal. Food ranges from sandwich lunches and traditional bar meals to pricier blackboard specials (£10–15), with fish always a good choice – expect things like a big bowl of mussels, clams and langoustines, or grilled plaice with a prawn and sweet chilli sauce.

Gillam's 64 Market St Ⓣ01229/587654. A tearooms (with summer terrace garden) that's wholly organic, Fair Trade and veggie, and has no truck with the microwave. They're serious about their drinks, whether you want a single-estate oolong or pot of Ethiopian Yirgacheffe, while food (mushrooms on toast, veggie quiche and the like, £5–7) is locally sourced. Daytime only, though there are food-and-music nights most months.

Hot Mango 27 King St Ⓣ01229/584866. The town's funkiest café is the place for cappuccinos, breakfasts, big ciabatta sandwiches and home-made soups (£4–8). Daytime only; closed Sun & Mon.

Rustique Off Brogden St Ⓣ01229/587373, Ⓦwww.eatatrustique.co.uk. Classy dinner-only restaurant with a Modern European menu that changes every couple of weeks. Fish is a speciality, perhaps served with a basil mash or crab risotto (mains around £20, plus midweek two/three-course set menu at £15.50/19.50). There's also lunch to go (salads, soups and fancy sandwiches) from their next-door deli. Closed Sun & Mon.

Swan Inn Swan St Ⓣ01229/582519. The real-ale choice – nine cask ales served at any one time, in a refurbished old pub on the edge of town. It's just off our map, 300 yards down the A590, on the left. Mon–Thurs from 3.30pm, otherwise from noon.

World Peace Café 5 Cavendish St Ⓣ01229/587793, Ⓦwww.worldpeacecafe.org. An outlet of the Buddhist temple at nearby Conishead Priory, this relaxed veggie organic café serves bagel or rice-cake sandwiches and a short list of hot daily dishes (£4.50–5.50). Also cosy armchairs, wireless internet access and a meditation centre for lunchtime and evening classes. Café open daytime only; closed Sun & Mon.

Listings

Bookshop Best independent bookshop is the Tinners' Rabbit, 48 Market St (closed Sun; Ⓣ01229/588858, Ⓦwww.ulverstonbookshops.co.uk), a real treasure trove specializing in children's books, local history and walking guides, and promoting book signings, talks and reading groups.

Bike rental Gill Cycles, The Gill (Mon–Sat 9am–5pm; Ⓣ01229/581116, Ⓦwww.gillcycles.co.uk). From £25 per day (and £10 per day thereafter) – they have info on local cycle routes, including the 72-mile Cumbria Way Cycle Route (Ⓦwww.cumbriawaycycleroute.co.uk) which shadows the hiking route to Carlisle.

Car rental Alan Myerscough (Ford), Ⓣ01229/581058, Ⓦwww.alanmyerscough-ford.co.uk.

Emergencies Local doctors are based at the Community Health Centre, Victoria Rd Ⓣ01229/484045. Otherwise, the nearest full hospital is in Barrow-in-Furness (Furness General Hospital, Dalton Lane; Ⓣ01229/870870, Ⓦwww.mbht.nhs.uk).

Internet access At Ulverston Library, King's Rd (Mon & Thurs 9am–6pm, Tues & Fri 9am–5pm, Wed & Sat 9am–1pm; Ⓣ01229/404151), and at the *World Peace Café*, 5 Cavendish St.

Pharmacies Boots, Market St Ⓣ01229/582049; J. Hewitt, 10 Market Place Ⓣ01229/582003.

Police station Neville St Ⓣ0845/330 0247, Ⓦwww.cumbria.police.uk.

Post office County Square.

Swimming pool Lakes Leisure Ulverston, Priory Rd Ⓣ01229/584110, Ⓦwww.lakesleisure.org.uk/ulverston. Public admission usually morning and evenings during term-time, otherwise all day, but call or check the website for specific times. There's also a gym, bowling green, astroturf pitch and Cumbria's biggest tennis centre.

Taxis McKenna's Ⓣ01229/582180.

Whitehaven and around

Some fine Georgian houses and an impressively restored harbour mark out the centre of **WHITEHAVEN**, one of the few grid-planned towns in England and easily the most interesting destination on Cumbria's west coast. A mere fishing village of 250 people in the early seventeenth century, within a hundred years Whitehaven had boomed fifty-fold as the Lowther family exploited the local coal seams and expanded the harbour. Later economic expansion was as much due to the slave trade and the town spent a brief period during the eighteenth century as one of Britain's busiest ports, importing sugar, rum, spices, tea, timber and tobacco. Town and harbour regeneration has wrought handsome changes in Whitehaven and it makes a good day out these days, with three excellent museums and some coastal stretches north and south that might just persuade you to stay longer.

The Town

Best place for the local history is **The Beacon** (Tues–Sun 10am–4.30pm; £5; ⓣ01946/592302, ⓦwww.thebeacon-whitehaven.co.uk), an enterprising museum on the harbour that resembles a squat lighthouse. There are interactive exhibitions on all floors, covering themes from slaving to smuggling, with a special emphasis on the local characters who have shaped the town, from the iron ore miners known as the "Red Men" (after the colour of the dust they were covered in) to the nineteenth-century ship rescue company, the "Rocket Brigade". You can easily spend a couple of hours here, teaching yourself how to build a ship, tie a knot or dress like a Roman centurion.

The **harbour** itself sits at the heart of a renaissance project that has spruced up the quayside with promenades, sculptures and heritage trails. The **Crow's Nest**, a 130-foot-high tower, lit at night, is the dramatic centrepiece of the marina, while the whole waterfront becomes the focus of the annual **summer festival** (usually June, details from the tourist office) which has a maritime bent (including visiting tall ships), but also features things like street theatre and celebrity chef cook-offs.

For all the changes round the harbour, it's Whitehaven's Georgian streets and neatly painted houses that make it one of Cumbria's most distinguished

Hero or pirate?

That's the question the Whitehaven Beacon poses about **John Paul Jones**, so-called "Father of the American Navy", who attacked Whitehaven in 1778. A couple of centuries ago, the answer would have very much depended on which side you stood during the American War of Independence (or, as Americans know it, the Revolutionary War). Jones had been born in Scotland and first sailed as an apprentice out of Whitehaven, where he served on merchant and slaving ships. Later, in America, he joined the revolutionary Continental Navy and, while harrying British shipping, conceived a plan to assault the port of his apprenticeship. It would have been a mighty coup against one of Britain's biggest ports, but, let down by a drunk and mutinous crew, he damaged only one of the two hundred boats in dock, though he did spike Whitehaven's defensive guns. In the United States his reputation ebbed and flowed with the years after his death in 1792, and not until 1913 was he granted full honours as a naval hero; in Britain, for most of that time, he was always viewed as a mere pirate. To chase down the story in Whitehaven – and decide which side you're on – visit the exhibit at the Beacon.

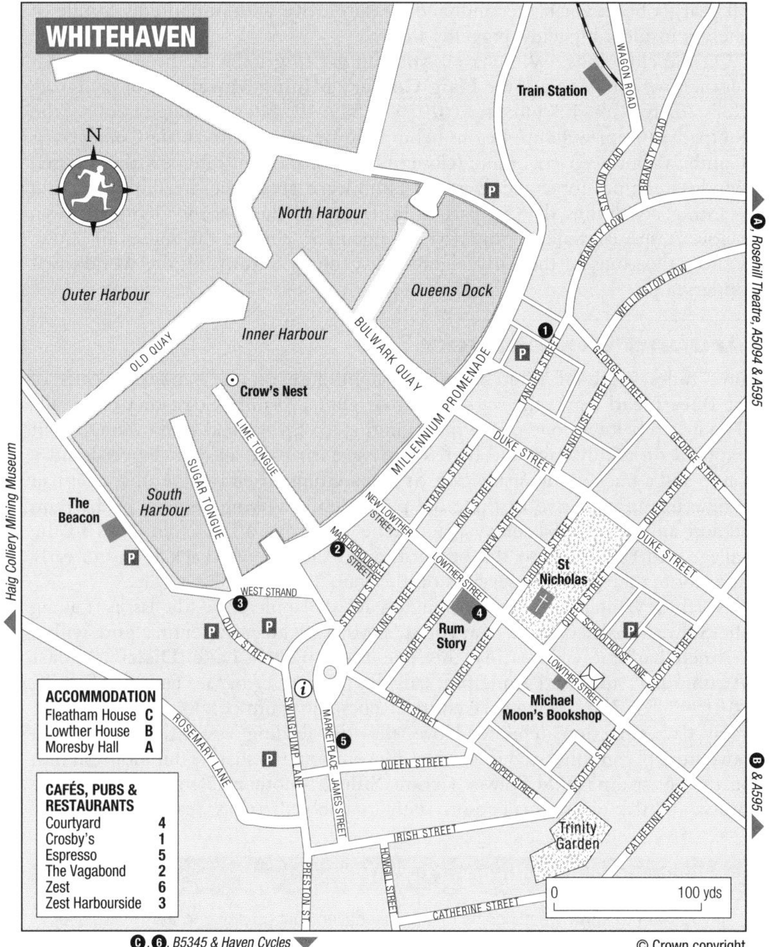

towns. Market Place hosts the **market** every Thursday and Saturday, which adds a bit of colour. Otherwise, stroll up Lowther Street to **The Rum Story** (daily 10am–4.30pm; £5.45, family £16.45; ⓣ01946/592933, ⓦwww.rumstory.co.uk), housed in the eighteenth-century shop, courtyard and warehouses of the Jefferson rum family. This is another place you could happily spend an hour or so, discovering Whitehaven's links with the Caribbean and learning all about rum, the Navy, temperance and the hideousness of the slaves' Middle Passage.

Across Lowther Street is the seventeenth-century church of **St Nicholas**, though all that stands today is its tower (containing a café). The rest succumbed to a fire in 1971, but there's a lovely garden surrounding the former nave – a further American connection with the town is that **George Washington's grandmother**, Mildred Gale, wife of a Whitehaven merchant, lies buried here. Also on Lowther Street, don't miss **Michael Moon's bookshop** at no. 19 (ⓣ01946/599010; closed Wed Jan–Easter, & closed Sun all year), a bookworm's secondhand treasure trove with, supposedly, a mile of shelves inside a higgeldy-piggeldy house.

On the cliffs above Whitehaven, you can get to grips with the industry that set the town on its way at the **Haig Colliery Mining Museum**, Solway Road, Kells (daily 9am–4.30pm; free; ⓣ01946/599949, ⓦwww.haigpit.com) – the footpath (10min walk up) begins behind the Beacon Centre. Haig Colliery was Cumbria's last deep-coal mine (closed in 1986), and you can view the restored winding engines (operated every day) and learn about the dreadful living and working conditions that, in part at least, funded the elegant Georgian town below. A special walking tour (by arrangement, contact the museum) shows visitors the ruins of the early eighteenth-century Saltom Pit, the world's first undersea pit.

Around Whitehaven

Five miles south of Whitehaven, the lighthouse on the sandstone cliffs of **St Bees Head** marks the start of Wainwright's 190-mile Coast-to-Coast walk. The beach below is one of the finest on the coast, wide and sandy, though a bit exposed on windy days, and there's a massive car park, an even-bigger holiday camp and a bucket-and-spade café. **St Bees village** itself is rather nicer, set half a mile inland with two or three old pubs within walking distance of the train station and a twelfth-century priory. The bus from Whitehaven stops in the village and runs right to the beach, though the last one back is in the early afternoon; there are later services on the train.

North of Whitehaven, past Workington, it's a 14-mile drive (the last part along the Solway Firth coast) to **Maryport**, another eighteenth-century port with a restored harbour and marina, this one featuring the **Lake District Coast Aquarium** (daily 10am–5pm; all-day ticket £6.75, family £18.75; ⓣ01900/817760, ⓦwww.lakedistrict-coastaquarium.co.uk). It's a handy rainy-day attraction (children love the fish-feeding sessions and nautical adventure playground) and there's also free entry to the shark exhibition and film in the aquarium's Wild Solway Centre. **Silloth**, another 13 miles north, is the Solway Firth's nicest small resort with its cobbled streets, seafront green and

People and places: I'll cry if I want to

If you want to know what's going on in Whitehaven, just go along to the Thursday or Saturday market and keep an ear out for official Town Crier, Rob Romano. The weekly "Town Shout" is just one of the Town Crier's duties, along with welcoming dignitaries, opening fairs and fetes, talking to local schools and, once a year, reading out the Lammas Fair Proclamation in the marketplace – something that's been done since 1672, when Charles II first granted the market charter to the town. How did Rob get to be Town Crier in the first place? "Well, I don't mind dressing up and I don't mind shouting," admits Rob, though just as important to him is the chance to promote the joys of Whitehaven to the wider world. Although London-born, Rob married a Whitehaven girl and has lived here since 1974, becoming Town Crier in 2001. "I'll get involved in anything that helps put a bit of polish on a cracking little town," he says, and to that end in his official capacity he welcomed the Queen and Prince Philip on their visit in 2008. Ask this most indefatigable booster of Whitehaven if there's any downside at all to being Town Crier and he'll only admit to one thing – apparently, the costume gets a bit too hot at times.

Contact Whitehaven tourist office on ⓣ01946/598914 for the latest appearance details of the Whitehaven Town Crier.

promenade, salt marshes and dunes. The **Solway Coast Discovery Centre** (Mon–Thurs 10am–4pm, Fri–Sun 10am–1pm & 2–4pm; £3.50; ⓣ016973/33055, ⓦwww.solwaycoastaonb.org.uk) here is another good family-friendly attraction, delving into the history and environment of this area of outstanding natural beauty. You can reach Maryport easily on the scenic Cumbrian coastal train line; for Silloth, there are daily buses (not Sun) from Maryport.

Practicalities

From Whitehaven's **train station** (services to St Bees, Ravenglass, Millom and Barrow, or north via Maryport to Carlisle) you can walk around the harbour to The Beacon in less than ten minutes. **Buses** use a variety of stops around town – catch services going south from Duke Street, including to St Bees (#20, not Sun) and Ravenglass and Muncaster (#6/X6); or north from Lowther Street, including to Cockermouth and Carlisle (#600, not Sun). There's limited-time disc zone **parking** in town (pick up a disc from local shops); for longer stays you're better off following signs to a central car park. The helpful **tourist office** is in the Market Hall on Market Place (daily 9.30am–4.30pm, plus Sun 11am–3pm in July & Aug; ⓣ01946/598914, ⓦwww.rediscoverwhitehaven.com, www.western-lakedistrict.co.uk), just back from the harbour.

The Coast-to-Coast walk aside, Whitehaven itself is the start of the 140-mile **C2C cycle route** to Sunderland/Newcastle. A metal cut-out, protruding from the harbour slipway, marks the spot – it's traditional for C2C cyclists to dip their front wheel in the water before starting.

Accommodation

Fleatham House High House Rd, St Bees ⓣ01946/822341, ⓦwww.fleathamhouse.com. Just 5min from St Bees station (first left off Main St), this lovely house is set in its own secluded grounds. It's very informal, with tea and cakes offered on arrival – politicians looking for a quiet retreat have often stayed here down the years, including Tony Blair. There are six large rooms (three of them singles, two overlooking the gardens) and a good breakfast. Parking. ❸

Lowther House 13 Inkerman Terrace ⓣ01946/63169, ⓦwww.lowtherhouse-whitehaven.com. A highly personal, period restoration of an old Whitehaven house brings boutique B&B style to town. Three charming, high-ceilinged rooms contrast cream carpets and crisp white linen with antique French beds and padded window seats, while big bathrooms feature schooner-print wallpaper, walk-in showers and Molton Brown toiletries. One room has harbour and sea views. You're welcomed with tea and cake, while breakfast is a chatty affair around your host's kitchen table. It's a 10min walk from the centre (keep on up Lowther St, past the Esso garage, to find Inkerman Terrace) or it's on the way in to town from the A595. Street parking outside. ❸

Moresby Hall Moresby, 2 miles north of Whitehaven ⓣ01946/696317, ⓦwww.moresbyhall.co.uk. Quality accommodation in a very attractive Grade I listed manor house, where you can stroll the lawns and walled gardens, or sit in the orangerie and enjoy the views. There's residents' dining from Monday to Thursday (£25), and glam restaurant nights on Friday and Saturday nights (open to nonresidents, £27.50), choosing from a monthly changing menu (advance booking required for either). Parking. ❺

Cafés and restaurants

Courtyard Café In The Rum Story, Lowther St ⓣ01946/592933. The museum café is an interesting place, set under a glass roof and furled sailcloth in the old Jefferson stables. Serves wraps, sandwiches, baked potatoes and meals (£3–6) during the day, while the Rum Story is open.

Crosby's Tangier St ⓣ01946/62622. Cumbria's best fish and chips? Many would make the claim – it's been a family-run fixture in town for more than forty years, and all the fish is now sourced from sustainable fishing grounds. Around £6 if you eat in, or cheaper if you get a takeaway and walk down to the harbour front for a marina view.

Espresso 22 Market Place ⓣ01946/591548. Whitehaven's classic old-school espresso bar (in business since the 1960s) has had a bit of a spruce up, but the basics are still the same – sassy service, frothy coffees, plus fry-ups and grills, with most things well under a fiver. Daytime only.

Zest Low Rd, B5349 ⓣ01946/692848, ⓦwww.zestwhitehaven.com. The town's classiest night out, and its only real gastro destination, is this stylish stop for Modern British cuisine (mains £14–17), three-quarters of a mile out of the centre on the St Bees road. It's only open for dinner, Wed–Sat (bookings recommended), but the rest of the time you can visit the sister café-bar, *Zest Harbourside*, open daily for superior sarnies, wraps, salads and bistro meals (£6–8). This is right on the harbourfront, but the only drawback is that, despite the tables for drinks, you can't eat outside.

Pub

The Vagabond 9 Marlborough St ⓣ01946/693671, ⓦwww.thevagabondwhitehaven.co.uk. Most of Whitehaven's pubs are a bit on the boisterous side, to put it diplomatically, so the stripped wood, real-ale, family-friendly, food-and-music *Vagabond* stands out from the crowd. Bar meals are out of the ordinary (fish straight from the harbour boats, chicken with *chorizo* and butter bean ragout, Cumberland goat's cheese tart, most mains £8–12), and the muso vibe is strong, from acoustic sets to concert photos and posters. And kudos to anyone who recognizes which album cover is used for the pub sign.

Arts, theatre and music

Rosehill Theatre 1 mile north of Whitehaven, signposted off A595 ⓣ01946/692422, ⓦwww.rosehilltheatre.co.uk. Enterprising local theatre venue for classical and contemporary music, drama and art-house films. It was founded by a Hungarian émigré, arts enthusiast and textile designer, Sir Nicholas Sekers – where else in Cumbria can boast a silk-lined theatre?

Cockermouth

COCKERMOUTH, midway between the industrial coast and Keswick at the confluence of the Cocker and Derwent rivers, dominates the flat vales that leach out of the northwestern fells. There's a lot to admire about the town – impressive Georgian facades, tree-lined streets and riverside setting – and there's no shortage of local attractions, not least the logical first stop on the Wordsworth trail, namely

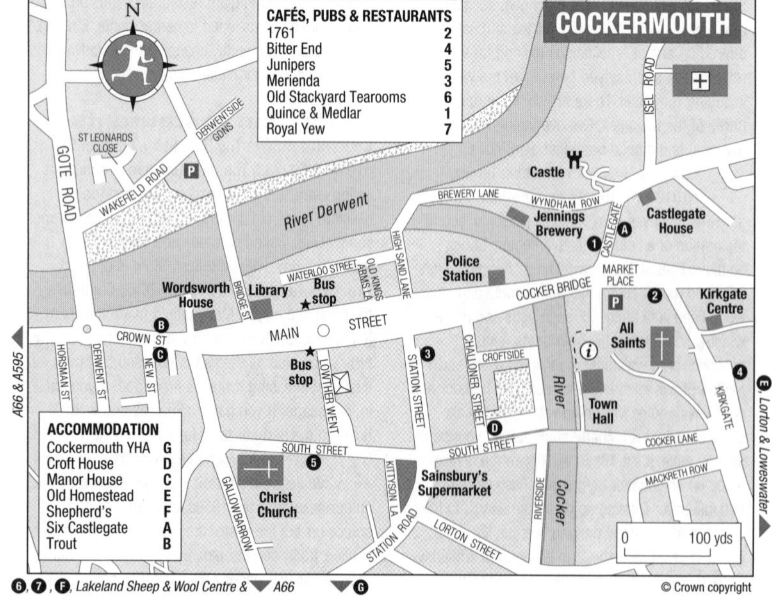

Herdwick sheep

The hardiest of indigenous British sheep breeds is the **Herdwick**, its name derived from the "herdwyck" (or sheep pasture) on which it was raised in medieval times. Other sheep breeds are more numerous but it's the grey-fleeced (black when young), white-faced Herdwick that's most characteristic of the Lake District – and which, in many ways, echoes the enduring struggle of lakeland hill farmers. The sheep live out on the inhospitable fells for almost the whole year – most are so good at foraging they never require additional feed. They are territorial, knowing their own "heafs" or particular grazing areas on the fells, and are historically concentrated in the central and western fells. The National Trust has been instrumental in maintaining the breed on its own farms by obliging tenants to keep Herdwicks. Beatrix Potter was also a keen sheep farmer and encouraged the breed on the farms she left to the Trust on her death. Partly, the emphasis on maintaining the numbers of Herdwicks is to do with heritage: much of the existing lakeland landscape has been created for and around them, from the intensively grazed fields of the valley bottoms to the dry-stone walls further up the fells. But there's also an economic imperative not to let upland sheep farmers (guardians of much of the landscape) go to the wall without a fight. Despite low wool prices, there's a renewed interest in locally sourced Herdwick wool products (from carpets to thermal insulation) while many farmers sell on their flocks to restaurants and suppliers as high-quality meat. During the Lake District's summer agricultural shows, the **Herdwick Sheep Breeders' Association** hands out prizes to the healthiest and best-looking sheep – there's plenty more information on their website Ⓦwww.herdwick-sheep.com, including a list of working Herdwick farms with B&B accommodation.

the house where the future poet was born. The disastrous flooding in winter 2009 made the national news and badly affected Cockermouth, particularly along main street and market place. Most businesses and attractions should be operating again by now – the local tourist office has all the latest details.

The Town

Cross the River Cocker from Market Place and walk along Main Street and Cockermouth immediately reveals its quirky, traditional charms and independent shops. In the space of a few hundred yards you could as easily buy a rack of lamb as an antique sherry barrel. The whiff of hops in the air from Jennings brewery is ever-present, while down Old Kings Arms Lane (60 Main St) modern businesses are now housed in the former stables and lodgings of an old coaching inn. In **Market Place** (now with monthly farmers' markets) there are more reminders of bygone days, from the pavement plaque teaching you the basics of talking Cumbrian to the unchanged facade and mahogany counter inside J.B. Banks, ironmongers in the town since 1836.

At the western end of Main Street is the **Wordsworth House** (March weekends plus Easter–Oct daily except Fri 11am–5pm, admission by timed ticket; £6.20, family £15.50; Ⓣ01900/820884, Ⓦwww.wordsworthhouse.org.uk), a handsome Georgian building that was the birthplace of all five Wordsworth children, including William (1770) and Dorothy (1771). It's a house suitable for the professional man that Wordsworth's father was, though he only rented it from his employer, Sir James Lowther, for whom he spent much of his time away on business. The children, too, though happy in the house, were often sent to their grandparents in Penrith, and when Wordsworth's father died in

1783 – with the children already either away at school or living with relations – the family link with Cockermouth was broken. The building has been beautifully restored, but rather than a pure period piece it's presented as a functioning eighteenth-century home – with a costumed cook willing to share recipes in the kitchen and a clerk completing the ledger with quill and ink. In around half the rooms you're encouraged to touch the items on display – children can dress up in one of the bedrooms – or lend the servants a hand, while the walled kitchen garden beside the river has been planted with fruit, vegetables and herbs that would have been familiar to the Wordsworths. It's an education, in the best sense, and a really excellent visit.

Back along the Main Street, if you follow your nose you're likely to stumble upon **Jennings Brewery** on Brewery Lane by the river confluence. Jennings have been brewers in the town since 1874 and you don't have to step far to sample their product, available in any local pub. Or you can take the hour-and-a-half-long **brewery tour** (July & Aug 2 daily; March–June, Sept & Oct Mon–Sat 2 daily; Nov–Feb Mon–Fri 1 daily, Sat 2 daily; £5.50; Ⓣ0845/129 7190, Ⓦwww.jenningsbrewery.co.uk), which ends with a free tasting in the bar. It's also always worth checking to see what's on at **Castlegate House** (Mon & Fri–Sat 10.30am–5pm; free; Ⓣ01900/822149, Ⓦwww.castlegatehouse.co.uk), a Georgian mansion on Castlegate, opposite the entrance to Cockermouth Castle – itself a private residence and closed to the public. The house and sculpture garden supports a changing programme of contemporary art displays, specializing in the work of accomplished regional artists.

Less rarefied lakeland affairs are dealt with in the **Lakeland Sheep and Wool Centre** (daily 9.30am–5.30pm; closed for 2 weeks in Jan; Ⓣ01900/822673, Ⓦwww.sheep-woolcentre.co.uk), a mile south of town on the Egremont road (A66/A5086 roundabout), which introduces visitors to the complexities of country life. In particular, don't miss the brilliant indoor **sheep show** (March–Oct; 4 shows daily Mon–Thurs & Sun; £5), when 19 breeds of sheep (including the characteristic lakeland Herdwick) present themselves proudly podium style, while super-smart sheepdogs handle a flock of unruly geese. Afterwards, you're encouraged on to the stage to meet the animals. When there's no show you can view the video introduction to the region and browse for sheep and wool gifts in the shop – access to visitor centre, video show, shop and café is free.

Practicalities

All **buses** stop on Main Street, from where you follow the signs east to the **tourist office** in the Town Hall, off Market Place (April–Oct Mon–Sat 9.30am–4.30/5pm; July–Sept also Sun 10am–2pm; Nov–March Mon–Fri 9.30am–4pm, Sat 10am–2pm; Ⓣ01900/822634, Ⓦwww.cockermouth.org.uk). Driving in, the A66 (from Keswick or Workington) bypasses the town to the south; turn in on either the B5292 (Whinlatter Pass road) or A5086 (from Loweswater and Ennerdale). The **car park** in front of the tourist office is the best place to park, since parking on Main Street is limited to an hour (and you need to display a disc in your car, available from local shops).

Accommodation

Cockermouth makes a handy base for exploring the western Lakes – not far from Loweswater, Ennerdale Water and Buttermere – and has a good range of accommodation.

In Cockermouth

Cockermouth YHA Double Mills ⓣ0845/371 9313, ⓔcockermouth@yha.org.uk. The local hostel is housed in a seventeenth-century watermill down a track by a bend in the River Cocker: the double wheels (that lend the mill its name) and grindstones are still *in situ* and it's in a very peaceful spot – 15min walk south from Main Street, along Station Rd and then Fern Bank. It's self-catering only, and there's limited parking. Usually closed for individuals Nov–March, though call for availability. Dorm beds from £13.95.

Croft House 6–8 Challoner St ⓣ01900/827533, ⓦwww.croft-guesthouse.com. A stylish revamp of a Georgian town house on a quiet residential street. It's decidedly chintz-free – contemporary furnishings and maplewood floors throughout – while the owners offer daily specials, veggie and vegan alternatives for breakfast as well as Fair Trade coffee and tea. Six rooms available, one (with bunks in a separate alcove) suitable for families. Parking. Closed 3 weeks Feb. ❷

Manor House Crown St ⓣ01900/828663, ⓦwww.manorcockermouth.co.uk. A favourite mid-range choice, the small family-run hotel spreads thirteen cosy rooms across several floors of a Georgian-style detached house, complete with rotunda and spiral staircase. Parking. ❹

Six Castlegate 6 Castlegate ⓣ01900/826786, ⓦwww.sixcastlegate.co.uk. This period-piece house has been completely refurbished – the lofty Georgian proportions, impressive carved staircase and oak panelling remain, but the half-dozen rooms are contemporary country in style with coordinated fabrics in soft colours, good bathrooms with walk-in power-showers and rooftop views. There's also a neat single in the "Butler's Pantry". Permit available for nearby parking. ❸

Trout Crown St ⓣ01900/823591, ⓦwww.trouthotel.co.uk. On the banks of the Derwent, this is the top choice in Cockermouth, well known among the fishing fraternity. It retains something of a traditional aspect with its ornate staircase, panelled bar and silver-service restaurant, but the rooms are large and modern, and there's a contemporary bar and bistro, *The Terrace*, with courtyard seating. Rates vary – river and garden views are pricier – but two-night weekend deals (including dinner) and other special offers can be a real bargain. Parking. ❺

Around Cockermouth

Old Homestead Byresteads Farm, Hundrith Hill Rd, off B5292, 2 miles southeast ⓣ01900/822223 or 07795/823385, ⓦwww.byresteads.co.uk. Wake to the sight of pedigree sheep grazing outside your window on this 180-acre farm, whose original farmhouse (from 1624) has been authentically restored using traditional lime plaster, cobbles, oak and stone. It's serious country-chic – spacious rooms (some are king-sized) feature underfloor heating, walk-in showers, carved pine beds, leather chairs and sofas, and sweeping views down the Lorton valley. The breakfast room was where the animals were once kept, and there's a huge inglenook fireplace in the lounge. It's a short drive into town, though there are bar meals a couple of hundred yards' walk away at the *Hundrith Hill Hotel*. Parking. ❸, king/4-poster rooms ❹

Shepherd's At the Lakeland Sheep and Wool Centre, Egremont Rd, A66/A5086 roundabout, 1 mile south ⓣ01900/822673, ⓦwww.shepherdshotel.co.uk. Big, bright motel-style rooms on the edge of town (including four family rooms), some with fell views – and it's definitely the only hotel in Britain with its own "live sheep show". There's a bar and restaurant. Parking. ❹, family room ❺

Eating, drinking and entertainment

You'll find most of the **cafés and restaurants** in town spread along Main Street and up Market Place. There are lots of **pubs**, too – this is the home ground of Jennings brewery, remember – and if you're in the mood, Cockermouth provides the hostelries for one of the more bizarre **pub-crawls-of-the-rich-and-famous**. Soccer manager Sir Matt Busby, cricketer Ian Botham and (strange but true) crooner and fisherman Bing Crosby have all had a drink in the bar of the *Trout Hotel*, while Robert Louis Stevenson plus local lad (and father of atomic theory) John Dalton frequented the front bar (now the *Outback*) of the *Globe Hotel* on Main Street.

Cafés and restaurants

Junipers 11 South St ⓣ01900/822892, ⓦwww.junipersrestaurant.co.uk. An easy-going joint that's great during the day (from 10.30am) for café stuff, tapas and lunches (£3–8). There's tapas at night too, or a classic bistro dinner menu (salmon, rack of lamb, steaks, £10–18) in the upstairs restaurant. Closed Tues, & open evening only on Sun.

Merienda 7a Station St ⓣ01900/822790, ⓦwww.merienda.co.uk. Bright and breezy café-bar – it's Spanish for "snack" – with an arty feel, offering breakfasts, soup and sandwiches, and *meze* plates (£3–6), with the emphasis on locally sourced and Fair Trade products. Also open Friday nights for tapas and music. Daytime only, though Fri until 10.30pm; closed Sun.

Old Stackyard Tearooms Wellington Farm, off A66/A5086 roundabout, 1 mile southwest of town ⓣ01900/822777, ⓦwww.wellingtonjerseys.co.uk. The Stamper family farm on the edge of town has a great tearoom and farm shop – not only are there fine views from the terrace and tasty home-made food, but there's also award-winning ice cream made with the milk from the farm's pedigree Jerseys. Dubbs Moss wetland and woodland reserve is only a short walk away, so you can park up for a stroll (bring wellies or boots). At the roundabout, take the exit signposted for "Mitchell's" agricultural market and the farm. Daytime only.

Quince & Medlar 13 Castlegate ⓣ01900/823579, ⓦwww.quinceandmedlar.co.uk. Gourmet veggies have long made a beeline for this elegant Georgian house where dinner is a romantic, candlelit affair. The menu offers creative meat-free cuisine – fancied-up nut roasts, cassoulet, smoked cheese roulade, stuffed filo parcels and the like, with mains at £13.95. Reservations advised. Dinner only; closed Sun & Mon.

Pubs

1761 1 Market Place ⓣ01900/829282, ⓦwww.bar1761.co.uk. Eighteenth-century building given a re-boot as a chintz-free contemporary pub, keeping the slate and tile floors and old fireplace but adding padded bar seats, great beers, a range of wines by the glass and snacky tapas for when you get the munchies (£2.50–3.50).

Bitter End 15 Kirkgate ⓣ01900/828993, ⓦwww.bitterend.co.uk. The nicest, cosiest pub in town also contains Cumbria's smallest brewery, producing ales like "Farmers'", "Cockersnoot" and "Cuddy Lugs". The food is really popular – get here early if you want to eat – ranging from bistro favourites (bangers and mash, rack of lamb) to a daily specials list that could include guinea fowl or peppered tuna. The meat is all sourced from Cumbrian farms, and most mains are £9–15.

Royal Yew Dean, 5 miles south of Cockermouth ⓣ01946/861342, ⓦwww.royalyew.co.uk. The *Bitter End* people are also behind this handsome-looking gastropub, a short drive out into the country. The beer's good, of course (including their own Yew Tree Ale), and the bistro-style menu is a similar mix of classics and specials, chargrilled steaks to a Mediterranean veg-and-polenta stack (most mains £9–15). It's best to book if you want to eat.

Arts centre

Kirkgate Centre Kirkgate ⓣ01900/826448, ⓦwww.thekirkgate.com. The converted Victorian school offers a wide-ranging programme of theatre, cinema, music and the arts.

Listings

Emergencies Cockermouth Cottage Hospital, Isel Rd ⓣ01900/822226.

Internet access Cockermouth Library, Main St (Mon & Wed 10am–7pm, Tues & Fri 10am–5pm, Thurs 10am–12.30pm, Sat 10am–1pm; ⓣ01900/325990).

Laundry DIY Wash & Dry, Meadow Bank, Windmill Lane (daily 8.30am–6.30pm; ⓣ01900/827219).

Pharmacies Allison, 31 Main St ⓣ01900/822292; Boots, 56–58 Main St ⓣ01900/823160.

Police station Main St ⓣ0845/330 0247, ⓦwww.cumbria.police.uk.

Post office Lowther Went, Main St.

Swimming pool Cockermouth Leisure Centre, Castlegate Drive ⓣ01900/823596, ⓦwww.carlisleleisure.com/cockermouth. There's a gym and climbing wall, as well as a pool; public admission hours vary; check the website or call for exact times.

Taxis A. & K. Taxis ⓣ01900/823665.

Penrith and around

PENRITH – four miles from Ullswater and sixteen east of Keswick – is a handsome, bustling market town, paved and built in red sandstone, and with a beguiling kernel of winding alleys, open squares and traditional shops. It's pretty unbeatable if you've got any shopping to do, while out in the nearby rolling countryside are any number of offbeat attractions, from ostrich farm to prehistoric stone circle. The town also has a long pedigree and an historic significance greater than anywhere else in the Lakes. Probably Celtic in origin, it was the capital of the independent kingdom of Cumbria until 1070, and from the thirteenth century onwards was a thriving market town on the main north–south trading route. Its major historic relic, the castle, was built as a bastion against Scottish raids from the north, and served as one of the northern headquarters of Richard III. Penrith is actually in the Eden Valley, and has far more in common with the brisk towns of the North Pennines than the stone villages of south Cumbria, but that hasn't stopped it positioning itself as one of the main gateways to the Lake District; reasonable enough given that it's a stop on the London–Scotland train route and lies just off the M6 motorway and A66 to Keswick.

The Town

Come on market day, Tuesday, if you want to get to grips with the local economy. The narrow streets, arcades and alleys off **Market Square**, the old **Corn Market** and the open space of **Great Dockray** provide traditional shopping for stalwart Cumbrian families, in the butchers' shops, fishmongers, outfitters, tobacconists and agricultural feed merchants. There's a really good **farmers' market**, too, held in Market Square on the third Tuesday of every month.

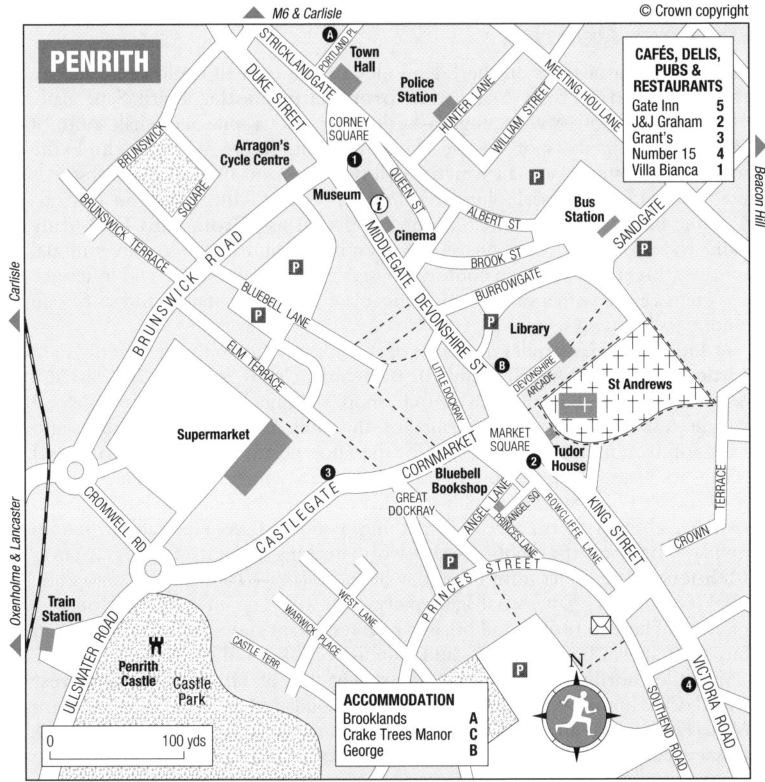

St Andrew's Church (possibly designed by Nicholas Hawkmoor) sits back from the square in a spacious churchyard surrounded by Georgian houses. The so-called "Giant's Grave" is actually a collection of pre-Norman crosses and "hogsback" tombstones. If you walk back round to the square and up Devonshire Street to the *George Hotel* – where Bonnie Prince Charlie spent the night in 1745 – you'll pass **Arnison's**, the drapers and milliners. The shop stands on the site of the town's old Moot Hall, owned in the eighteenth century by Wordsworth's grandparents. The young William and Dorothy often stayed here and their mother died in the house in 1778 (she's buried in St Andrew's churchyard, though the grave isn't marked).

At the far end of Middlegate, the tourist office shares its seventeenth-century schoolhouse premises with a small local **museum** (Mon–Sat 10am–5pm, plus April–Oct Sun 10am–4pm; free). After a quick review of the town's history, climb up to the immaculately kept sandstone ruin of **Penrith Castle** (daily: Easter–Sept 7.30am–9pm; Oct–Easter 7.30am–4.30pm; free), whose warm colour is at its best at sunset. Traditionally, warnings of attack or – in Napoleonic times – of possible invasion came from the north side of town, from **Beacon Hill**. To get there, head up Sandgate and Fell Lane to Beacon Edge (15min), turn left and follow the signposted right turn up through the woods. It takes about an hour, there and back, though the best views of Penrith and the fells beyond are on the way up rather than from the tree-shrouded summit.

Around Penrith

Lots of local attractions on the Eden Valley side of Penrith could easily add up to an extra day's tour. Start with **Brougham Castle** (April–Sept daily 10am–5pm; £3.50; Ⓦwww.english-heritage.org.uk), a mile and a half south of Penrith in a pretty spot by the River Eamont, where you can climb the towering sandstone keep, in which you'll find remnants of Roman tombstones used as building material, plundered from an earlier Roman fort on this site. Coming back (follow the B6262), you can detour past **Brougham Hall** (daily 9am to dusk; Ⓣ01768/868184, Ⓦwww.broughamhall.co.uk), an unusual fourteenth-century fortified country house, slowly being restored and in service as a crafts centre with a smokehouse, chocolate and truffle-maker, and small café among its businesses.

At Little Salkeld, six miles northeast of Penrith (off the A686), the prettily sited **Little Salkeld Watermill** (daily 10.30am–5pm; closed Jan; Ⓣ01768/881523, Ⓦwww.organicmill.co.uk) has a mill shop, organic bakery and wholefood veggie tearoom, plus guided tours of the mill. You can also detour into Langwathby, a mile and a half away, for the idiosyncratic **Eden Ostrich World** (daily 10.30am–3.30pm, closed Mon & Tues in winter; £5.95, family £21; Ⓣ01768/881771, Ⓦwww.ostrich-world.com); chick-hatching season is May to October, though there's always something to do and see, especially in school holidays. Back on the A686, it's also worth making a point of going as far as **Melmerby**, nine miles from Penrith, where the *Village Bakery* (daily until 5pm; Ⓣ01768/881811, Ⓦwww.village-bakery.com) was one of England's organic pioneers. There's a really good organic café-restaurant and a shop where you can buy their artisan breads, wheat- and gluten-free cakes and chocolate brownies.

Six miles northwest of Penrith, the stately pile of **Hutton-in-the-Forest** (April–Oct: house Wed, Thurs, Sun & bank holiday Mon 12.30–4pm; gardens Mon–Fri & Sun 11am–5pm; £7, family £17, gardens only £4; Ⓣ017684/84449, Ⓦwww.hutton-in-the-forest.co.uk) is open for house tours and strolls in the

Round tables and stone circles

Devoted stone-chasers and druid-fanciers can have a whale of a time around Penrith, tracking down mysterious standing stones and earthworks. Nearest to town, just south of Eamont Bridge, by the A6, **King Arthur's Round Table** is actually a prehistoric circular earthwork with a wide ditch – another, **Mayburgh**, just a few hundred yards away, still has a standing stone in the middle. Both are at least 3000 years old and point to the presence of a significant prehistoric population in these parts. Most impressive of all, though, is the site of **Long Meg and her Daughters**, six miles northeast of Penrith, just outside Little Salkeld, off the A686. Standing outside the "daughters" (a ring of stones almost 400 feet in diameter, the largest stone circle in Cumbria), Long Meg herself is the tallest stone at 12 feet high and has a profile like the face of an old lady.

magnificent gardens, grounds and woodland. There's also a seasonal calendar of "meet the gardener" tours and guided gamekeeper walks, plus plant and food fairs, garden shows and open-air theatre.

Practicalities

Trains from Manchester, London, Glasgow and Edinburgh pull into Penrith station, five minutes' walk south of Market Square and Middlegate. The bus station is on Albert Street, behind Middlegate, and has regular services to Patterdale, Keswick, Cockermouth and Carlisle. Driving in off the M6, take junction 40 – there's disc parking on town-centre streets (discs available from the tourist office and elsewhere), a large **car park** off Brunswick Road and others signposted around town, though spaces are hard to come by on Tuesdays (market day). The **tourist office** is on Middlegate (Mon–Sat 9.30am–5pm, plus April–Oct Sun 10am–4pm; ⓣ01768/867466, ⓦwww.visiteden.co.uk).

Accommodation

If you're aiming for the Lakes themselves it doesn't make much sense to stay in Penrith, with Ullswater and Keswick both under half an hour away. But there's a good enough choice if you fancy a night in town, and some very nice options in the surrounding countryside – the Lowther Estate's *George and Dragon* gastro-inn at Clifton (see p.220) is also close to town. The bulk of the standard B&Bs line noisy Victoria Road, the continuation of King Street, two minutes' walk south of Market Square. Portland Place has a rather more refined row of guesthouses.

Brooklands 2 Portland Place St ⓣ01768/863395, ⓦwww.brooklandsguesthouse.com. A very handsome 1870s town house that's been lovingly restored. Seven colour-coordinated rooms have country pine furniture and small but snazzy bathrooms: a couple are rated superior, one with a four-poster, the other with Victorian bedstead and leather sofa. Rooms at the rear overlooking the churchyard are the quietest. On-street parking outside. ③

Crake Trees Manor Crosby Ravensworth, 15 miles southeast of Penrith, A6 via Shap or M6 junction 39 ⓣ01931/715205, ⓦwww.craketreesmanor.co.uk. It takes more effort to reach than most, but this gorgeous barn conversion B&B in the nearby Eden Valley is emphatically worth it. There's one room in the stylish, galleried family home, three round the courtyard, all with slate floors, antique beds, serious showers and fluffy wrap-me-up towels. It's a working farm set in beautiful surroundings, and there are self-guided walks available right off the property. Help yourself to hot drinks and home-made biscuits in the house, where a fantastic breakfast (and evening meals by arrangement) are taken around an enormous oak table. There's a local pub or it's a 10min drive to Shap (on the A6) and the excellent bar meals at

Potty Penrith

Potfest (Ⓦwww.potfest.co.uk), Europe's biggest ceramics show, takes place in Penrith over two consecutive weekends (late July/early August). First up is **Potfest in the Park**, with ceramics on display in marquees in front of Hutton-in-the-Forest country house, as well as larger sculptural works laid out in the lovely grounds. This is followed by the highly unusual **Potfest in the Pens**, which sees potters displaying their creations in the unlikely setting of the covered pens at Penrith's cattle market, just outside town on the A66. Here, the public can talk to the artists, learn about what inspires them and even sign up for free classes.

the *Greyhound*, or 25min to Penrith. Closed Jan & Feb. Parking. ④

George Devonshire St ⓣ01768/862696, Ⓦwww.lakedistricthotels.net/georgehotel. The traditional choice in Penrith is this atmospheric old coaching inn right in the centre. Refurbishment has brought most of the rooms up to three-star standard and, though some can be a bit of a squeeze, the gloriously old-fashioned public areas compensate – there are cosy wood-panelled lounges with roaring fires, rustic bric-a-brac and armchairs you could hibernate in. Also a decent bar and restaurant (mains £10–17) – the sort of place where Cumbrian ladies-who-lunch come to take tea and sip sherry. Parking. ⑤

Eating, drinking and entertainment

Penrith is a solid country **dining** kind of place, though nearby village gastropubs have raised the bar a bit. The town is the regional arts and music hub, with **Eden Arts** (ⓣ01768/899444, Ⓦwww.edenarts.co.uk) the place to find out about concerts, events, exhibitions and festivals. These include performances hosted by the venerable **Penrith Music Club** (Ⓦwww.penrithmusicclub.com), with classical concerts and recitals held monthly (Sept–April) in Penrith Methodist Church. The local **cinema**, the Alhambra, is on Middlegate (ⓣ01768/862400, Ⓦwww.penrith-alhambra.co.uk), next to the tourist office – they usually show art-house and indie films on Sunday nights.

Cafés, delis and restaurants

Gate Inn Yanwath, B5320, 2 miles south of Penrith ⓣ01768/862386, Ⓦwww.yanwathgate.com. A gastropub *par excellence* offering the best informal dining for many miles around in a handsome old inn that really looks the part. Lunch (mains £9–12) might be a wild venison burger or a bowl of seafood chowder, while dinner (mains from £14) combines locally sourced ingredients with a dash of imagination – say native oysters dressed with soy and spring onion, or Herdwick lamb in a smoked paprika and garlic marinade. Beers and wines are spot on too – a great find.

J.& J. Graham Market Square ⓣ01768/862281, Ⓦwww.jjgraham.co.uk. Penrith's famous grocer's-cum-deli has been supplying the good folk for more than 200 years. There's pretty much anything you could want here, all beautifully presented – don't go anywhere else for superior picnic supplies. Closed Sun.

Grant's of Castlegate 54 Castlegate ⓣ01768/895444. Wine bar-bistro that attracts a loyal local following for its casual ambience and range-the-world menu (home-made fishcakes to Thai-style prawns). There's a shorter, simpler, cheaper menu at lunch (mains £6–8), otherwise dinner dishes average £11–15. Closed Mon & Tues.

Number 15 15 Victoria Rd ⓣ01768/867453. A corker of a café with art shows and music nights on the side. The veggie-friendly, Mediterranean-style menu (most dishes £5–8) boasts things like *meze* platters, stuffed peppers and big sandwiches and there's always home-made soup and a tart or quiche of the day, all using local organic produce where possible. Daytime only.

Villa Bianca Corney Square ⓣ01768/862221. Cheery Italian restaurant in characterful cottage surroundings. Friendly service and decent prices (£6–8) for pizza (the "Villa Bianca" comes with rocket and Parma ham) and pasta make this a good choice for fill-me-up dining, though meat and fish mains are pricier.

Theatre and music

Penrith Playhouse Auction Mart Lane, at the top of Castlegate ⓣ01768/865557, ⓦwww.penrithplayers.co.uk. Puts on theatrical productions throughout the year and also hosts regular rock, folk and blues gigs sponsored by Plug & Play (usually first Sun on month, ⓦwww.plug-play.co.uk).

Listings

Bookshops Bluebell Bookshop, Angel Square (ⓣ01768/866660) is a great local bookshop with coffee and cakes upstairs.
Bike rental Arragon's Cycle Centre, Brunswick Rd (Mon–Sat 9am–5.30pm; ⓣ01768/890344, ⓦwww.arragonscycles.com) has bikes for £20 a day.
Car rental Westmorland Vehicle Hire ⓣ01768/864546, ⓦwww.carhirecumbria.co.uk.
Emergencies Penrith New Hospital, Bridge Lane, Penrith ⓣ01768/245300.
Internet access At Penrith Library, Devonshire Arcade ⓣ01768/242100 (Mon, Tues & Fri 10am–7pm, Wed 10am–1pm, Thurs 10am–5pm, Sat 10am–4pm, Sun noon–4pm).
Pharmacies Boots, 3 Grahams Lane ⓣ01768/862735; Lightfoot's, 8 Middlegate ⓣ01768/862695.
Police station Hunter Lane ⓣ0845/330 0247, ⓦwww.cumbria.police.uk.
Post office Crown Square.
Swimming pool Penrith Leisure Centre, Southend Rd ⓣ01768/863450, ⓦwww.leisurecentre.com. Also has a climbing wall, gym, bowling and café. Public admission hours vary; check the website or call for details.
Taxis Town Taxis ⓣ01768/868268; Eden Taxis ⓣ01768/865432.

Rheged

Rheged (daily 10am–5.30pm; general admission and parking free; ⓣ01768/868000, ⓦwww.rheged.com) – a Cumbrian "visitor experience", just outside Penrith – is a good place to bring children, especially if it's pouring down outside. Sited in a disused limestone quarry, and billed as Europe's largest

▲ Rheged visitor centre

earth-covered building, it's designed to blend in with the surrounding fells, which it does admirably – from the main road you wouldn't know it was there. It's at Redhills, on the A66, half a mile west of the M6 (junction 40); bus #X4/ X5 (between Penrith and Keswick/Cockermouth) calls at the centre.

The names comes from the ancient kingdom of Cumbria, which once stretched from Strathclyde in Scotland as far south as Cheshire. Inside, an impressive atrium-lit underground visitor centre fills you in on the region's history, while you'll also find souvenir shops, galleries displaying arts and crafts, seasonal exhibitions and events, workshops, demonstrations and play areas. There's a farmers' market here, too, held on the last Sunday of the month throughout winter. The staple visit, though, is for the big-screen **3D cinema**, showing family-friendly 50-minute movies (like "Wild Ocean" or "Dinosaurs Alive"); **admission** to one film costs £4.95 (family £14), while each extra film costs £4 (family £8.50).

There's also an atrium **café** for soups, sandwiches, pizza and grills, though the finer dining is at the horseshoe bar of the contemporary "food hall" known as *Taste*, which specializes in regional Cumbrian foods and dishes. If you can't find something here to take home (sticky-toffee pudding, smoked venison, Cumbrian cheese, damson gin), you're not trying.

Contexts

Contexts

History

The Lake District remained a land apart for centuries, its features – rugged and isolated – mirrored in the characteristics of its inhabitants. Daniel Defoe thought it "eminent only for being the wildest, most barren and frightful of any that I have passed over" – and, as he went on to point out, he'd been to Wales so he knew what he was talking about. Two factors spurred the first waves of tourism: the reappraisal of landscape brought about by such painters as John Constable and the writings of William Wordsworth and his contemporaries, and the outbreak of the French Revolution and its subsequent turmoil, which put paid to the idea of the continental Grand Tour. Later, as tourism to the Lakes was cemented by the arrival of the railway, Wordsworth – while bemoaning mass travel – wrote in his *Guide to the Lakes* that he desired "a sort of national property, in which every man has a right and interest who has an eye to perceive and a heart to enjoy". His wish finally came to fruition in 1951 when the government established the Lake District as England's largest national park. It's subsequently become one of the most visited parts of England.

Early times

Geologically speaking, the Lake District is extremely old. The rocks which make up the Skiddaw and Blencathra massif consist of 500-million-year-old slate, while 100 million years later occurred the immense volcanic activity which shaped the high central mountains. The granite outcrops visible at Ennerdale and Eskdale were formed 350 million years ago. Later still, a tropical sea covered the region (320 million years ago) whose shell remains formed the ubiquitous limestone and sandstone.

At the heart of the region is Scafell, the remnant of a volcanic dome that had already been weathered into its present craggy shape before the last **Ice Age**, when glaciers flowed off its flanks to gouge their characteristic U-shaped valleys. As the ice withdrew, moraines of sediment dammed the meltwater, creating the main lakes, all of which radiate from Scafell's hub – Wordsworth, in a famous image, described them as immense spokes. The gentler terrain to the south was formed after this main burst of activity, with subsequent mini ice ages (the last around 12,000 years ago) gouging out smaller tarns, flattening the valley bottoms and modifying the shape and scale of the mountains. Consequently, the Lake District as it appears today comprises a huge variety of terrains and geological material within a compact region.

The first humans

Before **Neolithic peoples** began to colonize the region around 5000 years ago, most of the now bare uplands were forested with pine and birch, while the valleys were blanketed with thickets of oak, alder, ash and elm. As these first settlers learned to shape flints into axes, they began to clear the upland forests for farmland – remnants of shaped stone axes have been found in so-called "factory" sites on Pike of Stickle (in Langdale) and on the slopes of Scafell. During the later **Stone and Bronze ages**, the subsistence existence of Lake District settlers is unlikely to have changed much. Their hunter-gatherer lifestyle was augmented by early stock-rearing and planting, though evidence of their lives is sketchy. Bronze tools and weapons have been found (around Ambleside, Keswick and St John's in the Vale), though few burial or settlement sites have been pinpointed. The **stone circles** at Castlerigg (near Keswick), Little Salkeld (near Penrith) and at Swinside (near Duddon Bridge) are the region's most important sites and even the purpose of these is unclear. Some have suggested they had a time-keeping function or were used for religious purposes; others that the circles were a commercial focus or meeting place. What's clear is the high degree of cooperation between people required to erect the stones in the first place.

By the third century BC, **Celtic peoples** from the south and east were pushing into the region. From their hillfort settlements (like that on Carrock Fell) they exploited the local metal deposits and employed advanced farming techniques. Sophisticated religious practices (including burial) and basic systems of law and communal defence (against raiders from the north) were established features of their lives by the time the Romans arrived in Britain in 55 BC.

The Romans and Celts

The **arrival of the Romans** in the north of England after 69 AD led to the first large-scale alteration of the region's landscape. **Hadrian's Wall**, from the Tyne to the Solway Firth – marking the northern limit of the Roman Empire – was completed by 130 AD. Associated with the wall were roads, forts and supply routes which cut through the heart of the Lakes. There are the remains of fortresses still to be seen at Hardknott Pass and at Waterhead, near Ambleside, while Roman roads can be traced between Kendal and Ravenglass and, most obviously, from Troutbeck to Brougham (near Penrith) along the ridge known as High Street.

Throughout the Roman period the Lake District was essentially a **military zone**, policed by auxiliaries (recruited from all parts of the Roman Empire) rather than true legionnaires. However, around the bases grew **civilian settlements** as at Ambleside – which formed the basis of later towns and villages. Lead-mining was first practised during Roman times, while upland forests continued to be replaced by agricultural land as cereal crops were planted to supply the various permanent settlements. At Ravenglass, on the Cumbrian coast, are the extant remains of a bathhouse, part of a fort which survived in Ravenglass until the fourth century.

In the face of constant raids and harassment, England had become irrevocably detached from what remained of the Roman Empire by the start of the fifth century AD. The original **Celtic inhabitants** of the northwest had never fully abandoned their traditions in the face of Roman might, and surviving Celtic place names (Derwent, Blencathra) indicate strong local ties. Indeed, from the Celts comes the word they used to describe themselves – *Cymry* – from which derives the modern place name Cumbria. **Christianity** secured an enduring toehold in the region too. St Kentigern (or Mungo), the Celtic missionary, founded several churches in the region, passing through Crosthwaite in Keswick in 553 AD.

The Saxon and Norse invasions

The **Saxon invasion** of England's south and east during the sixth century initially had little impact on the Lake District, which slowly fell under the control of the newly established **kingdom of Northumbria**. However, place-name evidence does suggest that Saxon farmers later settled on the lakeland fringes – names ending in "ham" and "ton" betray a Saxon influence, as does the suffix "-mere" attached to a lake.

A greater impact was made by **Norse (ie Norwegian) Vikings** during the ninth and tenth centuries. Although they eventually supplanted much of the native lakeland population, it would be wrong to see the Norse arrival as a violent invasion. Unlike the Danes, who had sacked Lindisfarne on the east coast in 793, the Norse invasion was less brutal, with Viking settlers (rather than warriors) gradually filtering into the Lake District from their established bases in Scotland, Ireland and the Isle of Man. They farmed the land extensively and left their indelible mark on the northern dialect – dale, fell, force, beck, tarn and the suffix "-thwaite" (a clearing) all have Norse origins. Physical remains are scarce, the finest example being the splendid Norse cross in the churchyard at Gosforth, which combines pagan and Christian elements in a style reminiscent of similar crosses in Ireland and the Isle of Man. By the end of the eleventh century, wherever they originated, lakelanders were living in small farming communities in recognized shires, or administrative districts, whose names survived for the next nine hundred years: Cumberland and Westmorland.

However, the region began to be disputed in a burgeoning number of turf wars between rival kingdoms. **Dunmail**, a Cumbrian warlord, was defeated in battle in 945 by the Saxon **King Edmund**, who granted control of the region to the kings of Scotland. This heralded six hundred years of political manoeuvring, between Scottish kings keen to push the border south and, after the Conquest, Norman rulers intent upon holding the line at Carlisle. The Lakes themselves, and their farming communities, were largely left alone as the opposing armies marched north and south, but the northern and western lowlands became a cross-border battleground. Castles at Cockermouth, Penrith and Kendal attest to the constant political threat, while raiding "**reivers**" or local clans made the borderlands ungovernable.

Medieval and Elizabethan times

By medieval times, most of the Lake District's **traditional industries** had been firmly established. The native breed of sheep, the Herdwick, had proved itself a hardy species since at least Roman times, surviving harsh winters on the fells, while in summer cropping the hills of their wild flowers and preventing the regeneration of the woodland. **Religious houses** bordering the Lake District, such as Furness Abbey in the south, Carlisle in the north and St Bees in the west, came to hold large rural areas, establishing outlying farms – or "grainges" – which further exploited the land. The **wool** produced found its way into markets throughout Europe and beyond, with **packhorse routes** meandering across the region to and from market towns such as Kendal, Keswick, Penrith and Cockermouth. The monks also maintained woods, or **coppices**, whose timber they used to produce charcoal (for iron-smelting) and bark (used in tanneries). The **Dissolution of the Monasteries** in 1536 had little effect on these industries. The new crown tenants and the emerging "**statesman" farmers**, who bought their own smallholdings, merely continued the age-old practices, denuding the uplands further with every passing year.

Mining was also altering the contours of the land. Plumbago, or graphite, had been discovered in Borrowdale and in 1564 Elizabeth I gave royal assent to an Anglo-German venture to exploit the ore – invaluable for pencil-making, glazing, black-leading iron weapons (to stop them rusting) and making casting moulds for cannon bore and shot. German miners settled in Keswick, while locals found employment in providing lodging, transport and charcoal. Later, copper mining took hold in the Keswick and Coniston areas, while slate quarrying in Borrowdale had always taken place on a local basis and was to boom in later centuries. For most people, though, **domestic life** probably altered very little for three hundred years – clothes were still produced locally, while primitive agricultural methods and poor land kept yields relatively low. The general diet was largely unchanged since Viking times, based around oatmeal cakes or porridge, bread and cheese – potatoes weren't widely cultivated until the eighteenth century. Increasingly, however, houses were being built of durable stone (rather than turf and timber) and many of the Lake District's farms and cottages – including notable examples such as Townend at Troutbeck – can trace their origins back as far as the seventeenth century.

The Picturesque and the Romantic

Until the eighteenth century, it was difficult to persuade the wider world – or at least fashionable England – that the Lake District had anything to offer. Indeed, the old county of Cumberland (containing the northern part of the Lake District) was viewed as a dangerous, unstable corner of the kingdom, too close to lawless Scotland for comfort. William, Duke of Cumberland, the "butcher" son of George II, put down the Jacobite rebellion of 1745, and the fortified towers and castles on the lakeland periphery tell their own story of border raids and skirmishes.

A sea change occurred with the advent of the so-called **Picturesque Movement** in the late eighteenth century, when received notions of beauty shifted from the classical to the natural. Vivid, irregular landscapes were the fashion amongst writers and artists, and it was with a palpable sense of excitement that the era's style arbiters discovered such landscapes on their doorstep. The poet **Thomas Gray** made the first of two visits in 1767 and recorded his favourable impressions in his journal (published in 1775), while in 1778 **Thomas West** produced the first guidebook dedicated solely to the region, waxing lyrical about the "Alpine views and pastoral scenes in a sublime style". These, and a dozen other books or treatises touching on the Lake District published during the 1770s, merely reinforced the contemporary Romantic view that contact with nature promoted artistic endeavour and human development. **Thomas Gainsborough**, **J.M.W. Turner** and, later, **John Constable** were all eager visitors to the Lakes, and all drew inspiration from what they saw. The first visitors were encouraged to view the mountains and lakes in a methodical manner – from particular "stations" (ie viewpoints) and through a "claude glass" (or convex mirror) to frame the views.

The pre-eminent Romantic, **William Wordsworth**, was born in Cockermouth in 1770, moving to Dove Cottage outside Grasmere in 1799 and, in 1813, to nearby Rydal Mount. He became the centre of a famous, if fluctuating, literary circle – not only one of the so-called **Lake Poets** with **Samuel Taylor**

Coleridge and **Robert Southey**, but also friend of the critic, essayist and opium eater **Thomas De Quincey** and of the writer **John Wilson** ("Christopher North" of *Blackwood's Magazine*). Wordsworth's own *Guide to the Lakes* – a mature distillation of all his thoughts on nature and beauty – was first published in 1810 and had gone through four further editions by 1835.

The eighteenth and nineteenth centuries

The **Industrial Revolution** didn't so much pass the Lake District by as touch its periphery. Carlisle was a cotton manufacturing town of some repute, while the coastal ports became important shipping centres and depots for nearby coal and iron industries. Georgian Whitehaven was one of Britain's busiest ports for a time in the late eighteenth century; Barrow-in-Furness is still an important shipbuilding town.

Within the Lakes themselves, sheep farming remained the mainstay of the economy. Textile production still tended to take the form of homespun wool, as it had for centuries. However, the manufacture of wooden **bobbins** for the northwest's cotton mills later became an important local industry. There were also improvements in farming as turnips were introduced widely as a crop, which meant that cattle and sheep could be kept alive throughout the winter. Meanwhile, the French Revolution and the ensuing **Napoleonic Wars** (1803–15) not only precluded European travel (in part explaining the growing popularity of the Lakes with the English gentry) but also pushed food prices higher. As a consequence, farmers began to reclaim the once-common land of the hillsides, a tendency sanctioned by the General Enclosure Act of 1801. Most of the region's characteristic dry-stone walls were built at this time.

Copper mining at Coniston became increasingly important, as did **slate quarrying** at Honister Pass and around Elterwater. The still-visible scars, shafts and debris on the Old Man of Coniston and at Honister Pass are evidence of these booming trades.

Transport and communications improved slowly. Roads and packhorse routes that had been barely altered since Roman times saw improvement following the passing of the Turnpike Acts in the 1750s. High passes opened up to the passage of stagecoaches, while England's burgeoning canal system reached Kendal in 1819. The **railway age** arrived late, with early railway lines associated with the mining and quarrying industries. The first passenger line, in 1847, connected Kendal with Windermere – and prompted a furious battle with the elderly Wordsworth who, having spent years inviting appreciation of the Lake District by outsiders, now raged against the folly of making the region easier to visit. Not only was it easier to visit, but after 1869 the Lake District even had its very own indigenous candy to sweeten the tooth of visitors – **Kendal Mintcake**, a peppermint candy that's been the mainstay of climbing expeditions ever since. It's still made in Kendal today.

With the passing of Southey (1843) and Wordsworth (1850), the mantle of local literary endeavour passed to writer **Harriet Martineau**, who lived at Ambleside between 1845 and 1876, and to social philosopher and critic **John Ruskin**, who settled at Brantwood near Coniston in 1872. Meanwhile, a seemingly endless succession of men and women of letters continued to visit or take a house, pronounce upon and then write about the region – **Sir Walter Scott**, **Percy Bysshe Shelley**, **Matthew Arnold**, **Alfred (Lord) Tennyson**,

Thomas Carlyle, George Eliot, Charlotte Brontë, Ralph Waldo Emerson and **Nathaniel Hawthorne** all spent various periods in the Lake District. **Charles Dickens** and **Wilkie Collins** came together and climbed Carrock Fell, a trip recounted in Dickens' *Lazy Tour of Two Idle Apprentices* (1857).

The twentieth century: protecting the Lake District

Two thousand years of farming and two hundred years of industrialization began to take their toll on the region. John Ruskin's unsuccessful campaign to prevent the damming of Thirlmere was just one example of an increased **environmental awareness** which manifested itself most obviously in the **creation of the National Trust** in 1895. Ruskin's disciple, Octavia Hill, and a Keswick clergyman, Canon Rawnsley, were the Trust's co-founders (with Rawnsley its first secretary) – Brandlehow Woods on Derwent Water's western shore was the Trust's first purchase in the Lakes (1902). The Trust is now the largest landholder in the Lake District, gaining early impetus from the generous bequests of **Beatrix Potter**, who has probably done more than anyone – after Wordsworth – to popularize the region through her children's stories.

The **formation of the Forestry Commission** in 1919 presented another threat to the natural landscape as afforestation gathered pace, turning previously bare valleys and fellsides into thick conifer plantations. Successful environmental battles in the 1930s limited the scope of the plantations, but afforestation is still an emotive subject today.

Similarly, **water extraction** had long fuelled fears for the landscape. The Lake District has been used as a water source for northwestern England since Thirlmere was dammed in 1892. Construction at Haweswater in the 1930s raised the water level there by ninety feet – and drowned a village in the process. (Ennerdale Water still supplies the coastal towns and as late as 1980 there were serious proposals to raise levels there and at Wast Water in an attempt to drain more water for industrial use.)

Legal protection of the Lake District was, therefore, long overdue by the time of the establishment in 1951 of the **Lake District National Park**, spreading over 885 square miles. For the first time, there was to be direct control over planning, building and development within the Lake District, as well as systematic maintenance of the footpaths, bridleways, dry-stone walls, open land and historic monuments. The widely recognized National Park emblem – the outline of Great Gable – was adopted in 1953, and the Queen made the first royal visit to the park in 1956.

The National Park: the first fifty years

The establishment of the National Park didn't, of course, end the threats to the social and natural environment of the Lake District, but it did provide the framework to defend the region from mass commercialism and development. Even so, many of the current problems facing the National Park were signalled in its earliest years.

As the privations of the postwar years were reduced, the number of leisure visitors increased dramatically. The first dedicated car park, at Tarn Hows, was established in 1954, while traffic in the National Park doubled in the five years until 1959. The number of caravan sites increased and there were early worries about litter on the fells and other obtrusive irritants. In the 1960s, speed restrictions were imposed on Derwent Water, Ullswater and Coniston for the first time and the first full-time park warden was employed as tourism to the Lakes became a year-round phenomenon. The house at **Brockhole**, near Windermere, was acquired in 1966 and opened in 1969 as the country's first National Park Visitor Centre. Meanwhile, in 1974, centuries of tradition were abandoned when local government reorganization resulted in the scrapping or reduction of the old counties of Cumberland, Westmorland and Lancashire: the Lake District became part of the new county of **Cumbria**.

During the 1970s and 1980s, **conservation** became the new watchword as visitor numbers steadily increased. Car park charges were introduced for the first time, to provide revenue and deter drivers; meanwhile, footpath erosion had become a major problem in many areas. Attempts were made to educate visitors about the impact of their presence on the lakes and landscape – information centres were opened at Keswick, Bowness Bay and Seatoller among others, while 10mph limits were imposed on craft using Derwent Water, Ullswater and Coniston. Cars were kept out of ancient villages such as Hawkshead, whose centre became pedestrianized, and the centre of Ambleside became the Lakes' first formal conservation area.

However, the underlying fragility of the park's ecosystem was exposed in 1986, after the accident at the nuclear power station at Chernobyl in the Soviet Union. Radioactive fallout contaminated Cumbrian soil, acting as a reminder – if one were needed – of the danger on the Lakes' own doorstep presented by the presence of the **Sellafield nuclear-reprocessing plant**, near Ravenglass, symbol of all that threatens the local environment.

Great strides were made during the 1990s to address some of the most fundamental problems facing the National Park. Coordinated traffic management and erosion control schemes were formulated, which began to have a significant effect on the environment. In 1993, Bassenthwaite became the first lake in Britain to be declared a National Nature Reserve and, in the same year, the **Lake District Environmentally Sensitive Area** (ESA) was established to protect traditional buildings and landscapes. Upland farmers – struggling with the downturn in their industry, and affected by the BSE crisis and other health scares – were given grants to maintain dry-stone walls and hedgerows, renovate traditional buildings and stock wildflower meadows.

The Lakes today

The National Park celebrated its half-centenary in 2001, with its successes balanced equally against its numerous challenges. There's no doubt that it's been a force for good – for example, defending the lakes from over-exploitive water extraction and preventing mass development in scenic areas. But, at times, it seems as if it's fighting a battle with the wider problems facing rural England as a whole.

In the Lake District, the unproductive nature of much of the land means that **hill farming** is basically undertaken at subsistence level, and would hardly be possible at all without European Union and central government subsidies.

Cumbria was also hardest hit of all the English counties by the **foot and mouth crisis** of 2001, which badly affected tourism as visitors were asked to keep away from infected areas. Although many Cumbrian farms subsequently restocked, replacing the thousands of animals slaughtered in the government's programme to contain the disease, not all businesses survived. The truth is, there were probably too many farms trying to make a living in inauspicious economic circumstances (a deep-rooted problem for British farming as a whole) and no amount of diversification – from camping barns to pony rides – could save some businesses from going under.

In a region where **hunting with hounds** dates back to Norman times, local concern about the fate of agriculture also manifested itself in solid support for the pro-hunting "Countryside Alliance" cause. The government's 2005 ban on hunting foxes and other wildlife with dogs caused much anger in Cumbria though, despite dire warnings at the time, none of the local hunts has closed. The hunts instead now meet – within the law – for trail-hunting, though as they generally use fox urine as the trail scent (rather than aniseed), it's clear that hounds in England are being kept accustomed to fox scent in the event of the ban being overturned (either by the European Court of Human Rights or a future change of government). Hardly surprisingly, there are constant reports of foxes being "accidentally" killed by hunts that flush them out in the course of their trail-hunt.

Another flash point is the necessary **development restrictions** imposed by the National Park Authority, the National Trust (which owns a quarter of the land) and the district councils. At the same time, second-homers from the towns and cities ("off-comers" in the local parlance) push up **housing** prices, thus forcing the lakeland youth away from home and from the land – in line with other rural British holiday regions, it's estimated that up to a fifth of all Lake District houses are second or holiday homes. However, **employment** initiatives are working to provide more opportunities for local people, not just in tourism and hospitality, but also in the retail, small business and technology industries. The establishment of the **University of Cumbria** in 2007 (with campuses in Carlisle, Penrith, Ambleside and elsewhere) also means more sustainable educational and training opportunities for the region.

In some ways, the National Park is simply too successful for its own good. At its first meeting in 1951, the authority dealt with fifteen planning applications. Today, it deals with over 1200 a year. A local population of just 42,000 is swamped by annual **visitor numbers** topping eight million to the Lakes (fifteen million to Cumbria), with all the traffic and environmental pressure that that entails – it's estimated that 89 percent of visitors currently arrive in the National Park in a private motor vehicle. Expanded bus services, the promotion of cycling and water-bus routes around Windermere, and an integrated **transport strategy** are starting to have some effect, but it's a long haul to persuade people to leave their cars at home.

Around 350 **voluntary rangers** help manage the environment (patrolling lakeshores, maintaining footpaths, planting trees, restoring hedgerows and rebuilding stone walls), but they are faced with an exponential increase in leisure activities which impinge directly upon the Park's habitats – such as mountain biking, ghyll scrambling, four-wheel-drive safaris and watersports. The long-running saga of **speed restrictions** on Windermere presented the park authorities with the classic dilemma of balancing business needs with those of the environment. Watersports companies and related businesses fought a long campaign against the restriction but since 2005 powered craft on England's largest lake have been restricted to 10mph. Other initiatives point the way to a greener future for the lakes, including the solar-powered Coniston Launch and the projects currently under way to improve the **water catchment** areas at Bassenthwaite and Windermere. However, the disastrous **floods** that hit Cumbria in the winter of 2009 – badly affecting places like Cockermouth and Workington – were a salutory reminder that nature cannot always be controlled.

On the land, the 2005 CRoW Act, giving a statutory "right to roam" across open countryside, has provided new rights for the public while safeguarding the landscape and wildlife. Over fifty percent of the National Park area is open for public access: more than two thousand miles of **paths and bridleways** are virtually all clear of obstructions and many have been made suitable for wheelchair users and pushchairs. **Erosion control** is well in hand on all the most popular walking routes under the "Fix the Fells" initiative, which is a partnership of interested parties including the National Park Authority.

The Lake District Environmentally Sensitive Area (ESA), set up in 1993 and covering almost the entire National Park, provides the supportive framework for traditional farm buildings to be restored, hedges and orchards replanted, and moorland and riverbanks protected. Over one hundred Sites of Special Scientific Interest (SSSIs) cover another sixteen percent of the Park, and there are eight National Nature Reserves (NNRs), and another eighty-odd Regionally Important Geological Sites. Projects designed to preserve some of the Lake District's most **threatened species** (such as the red squirrel, otter and the water vole) are increasingly successful and new native woodlands are being established. The **Wild Ennerdale** project (returning parts of the valley to a more "natural", pre-plantation state) is an excellent example of contemporary conservation in action, while the presence of ospreys at Bassenthwaite and golden eagles at Haweswater are further evidence of success.

Conservation is now seen as fundamental to the National Park's wellbeing; the future challenge is to extend the same protection to lakeland traditions and the way of life, which is partly the idea behind the current bid to secure **World Heritage Site** status for the Lake District, possibly by 2012.

Books

We've highlighted a selection of books below which will give you a flavour of Lake District life, past and present, as well as the impressions of the visitors, writers and poets who have toured and settled in the region. As a glance in any bookshop will show you, there are hundreds of Lake District titles available. We've concentrated on titles of interest to the general reader (which discounts most of the academic literary criticism of the Lake Poets) and those most useful to the non-specialist visitor – for rare historical monographs, mountain-climbing guides, lavish limited-edition pop-up Beatrix Potter books and other arcana, consult a specialist bookshop or Amazon (@www.amazon.co.uk, www.amazon.com). **Books Cumbria** (@www.bookscumbria.com) is a very handy source for locally published, out-of-print, rare or otherwise esoteric books about the Lake District and Cumbria. Two useful **publishers** are Frances Lincoln (@www.franceslincoln.com), now responsible for all the Wainwright walking guides, plus many other lakeland titles, and Cicerone (@www.cicerone.co.uk), who specialize in walking, climbing, scrambling and cycling guides.

Lakeland life, history and nature

Richard Askwith *Feet in the Clouds.* If you've ever been passed on a mountain by wiry people running uphill, very quickly, and wondered quite how barmy they must be – here's your answer. Askwith's painful and obsessive quest to join the ranks of the hardest-of-the-hard fell runners manages to be both insightful and funny at the same time. It's a sports book, certainly, but only in the same way as *Fever Pitch* or *Touching the Void*.

Hunter Davies *A Walk Around the Lakes*; *London to Loweswater*; *Strong Lad Wanted for Strong Lass*. The journalist, biographer and author Davies takes every opportunity to plug the Lakes in print. His account of a walk around the region is an entertaining mix of anecdote, history and reportage, while in *London to Loweswater* (and inspired by J.B. Priestley's *English Journey* of 1934) Davies spends a year travelling from London to his Lake District home, reflecting on his own past and the state of the nation. *Strong Lad Wanted for Strong Lass*, meanwhile, is his wry account of growing up in Carlisle in the 1950s.

A.H. Griffin *A Lifetime of Mountains*; *The High Places*; *The Coniston Tigers*; and others. The veteran lakelander climber, writer, journalist and *Guardian* newspaper country diarist, Harry Griffin (1911–2004) produced a dozen volumes that range around the fells with a keen eye for nature and tradition. Although the early books, written in the 1960s and 1970s, are mostly out of print (*Inside the Real Lakeland*, *In Mountain Lakeland*, *Pageant of Lakeland* etc), the best of his *Guardian* diary pieces are collected in *A Lifetime of Mountains*, his weekly features for the *Lancashire Evening Post* are included in *The High Places*, while *The Coniston Tigers* is a climbing and walking memoir recalling seventy years of mountain adventure.

Tom Holman *A Lake District Miscellany*. A stocking-filler Christmas present for any Lake District lover – a list-heavy, anecdote-filled, information-packed pocket book of facts, from how to make a Cumberland sausage to counting in dialect.

Grevel Lindop *A Literary Guide to the Lake District*. Poet and critic

Lindop's well-received guide to the Lakes presents five routes for walkers and drivers, covering places associated not just with the Lake Poets, Beatrix Potter and the rest but literary visitors from Hardy to Lawrence. First published in 1993 but a revised edition appeared in 2005.

Norman Nicholson *The Lakers; Portrait of the Lakes; The Lake District: An Anthology*. Cumbria's best-known poet turned to prose with his informed, sympathetic studies of lakeland life, history, geology and people. The comprehensive *Anthology* is a joy, with extracts from writings of every period since the first visitors, and incorporating dialect verse, legends, letters and journals.

John Pepper *Cockley Beck*. Pepper happened upon a farm cottage in the Duddon Valley in the early 1980s, and spent several winters there, later writing a lyrical tribute to the countryside and local community which was first published in 1984 (with a new edition in 2006). Inspired in parts by Henry David Thoreau's account of a solitary rural retreat in *Walden*, it's a reflective, philosophical book that soon attracted the epithet "classic".

Nikolaus Pevsner *Cumberland and Westmorland*. The regional edition of Pevsner's renowned architectural guide to the old counties of England. First published in 1967 (when there was still a Cumberland and Westmorland, rather than Cumbria) and detailing every church, hall, house and cross worth looking at.

William Wordsworth *Guide to the Lakes*. The old curmudgeon's guide to the Lakes went through five editions between 1810 and 1835. This facsimile of the last, and definitive, edition is full of his prejudices (on the "colouring" of buildings, the shape of chimneys, forestation, the railway, the great unwashed) and timeless scenic observations.

John Wyatt *The Shining Levels*. Billed as "the story of a man who went back to nature", this was originally published in 1973 (and later reissued in 1993). John Waytt was brought up in industrial Lancashire but disowned city life to become a forest-worker, living in a woodsman's hut in the Lakes (he was later Head Warden for the National Park). Sleeping by the fire, coppicing, rabbit-hunting, searching for wild berries and nuts, adopting a roe deer – three decades later it reads as a heartfelt rural lament.

Landscape and photography

Bill Birkett *A Year in the Life of...the Langdale Valleys; Buttermere; Borrowdale; the Duddon Valley*. Birkett is well known as a climber and walker, but he's also a respected mountain writer and photographer. Here he turns his camera on the lakeland valleys in his own backyard to provide stunning photographic essays of the seasonal landscapes, interspersed with features on local history, heritage, farming and nature.

Gilly Cameron Cooper *Beatrix Potter's Lake District*. A beautifully produced coffee-table book, presenting Potter as naturalist, farmer and conservationist, as well as seeking out the places that inspired her stories. The excellent photography is from the National Trust (with map references to help you track down the locations), and there are also reproduced Potter watercolours and illustrations, plus images from the 2007 *Miss Potter* film about her life.

Jim Watson *Lakeland Towns; Lakeland Villages; Lakeland Panoramas.* The first two titles are coffee-table format books covering all the lakes and towns and villages in chatty, anecdotal fashion, with the text accompanied by black-and-white pen-and-ink drawings and detailed hand-drawn maps. Not guidebooks as such (though walks and viewpoints are included), more background information and observations by the Penrith-born artist and cartoonist. His *Lakeland Panoramas* are Wainwright-style drawings presenting the widescreen view from the top of 49 easy-to-get-to viewpoints.

Walking guides

Bill Birkett *Complete Lakeland Fells; Lakeland Fells Almanac; Exploring the Lakes and Low Fells.* The *Complete* edition is the definitive, modern fell-walking reference guide from a leading Cumbrian mountain writer and photographer; classic walks to the top of 541 separate fells for all levels of walker. The *Almanac* distils the *Complete* fells into 129 circular walks taking in the tops, with maps, times and route details. Less adventurous walkers can tour the lake perimeters, tarns, valley bottoms, viewpoints and low fells in his company, too, using eighty easy-to-follow, half-day circular routes laid out clearly over two small-format hardback volumes of *Exploring the Lakes and Low Fells.*

Ian and Krysia Brodie *The Cumbria Coastal Way.* The first available guidebook to the 150-mile Cumbria Coastal Way (Morecambe Bay to the Solway Firth), which runs around the southern lakeland peninsulas and up the west Cumbrian coast to the Scottish border. Essential for day-walkers (the route can be walked in sections) and long-distance hikers alike.

Anthony Burton *The Cumbria Way.* This is the best guide to pack for the 72-mile Cumbria Way (Ulverston to Carlisle), which cuts right through the heart of the Lake District National Park. Durable format, clear walking instructions, Ordnance Survey map extracts, plus history and anecdotes.

Frank Duerden *Best Walks in the Lake District.* First published in 1986, but thoroughly revised in 2006, the forty well-conceived walks in this hefty pocket guide range from easy strolls to major full-day hikes in every area of the Lakes, complete with historical and descriptive background notes. Only sketch maps are included, but the walking instructions are very detailed, and it's particularly good on the dozen or so strenuous "horseshoe" routes that are among the Lake District's finest walks.

Eileen and Brian Evans *Short Walks in…North Lakeland; South Lakeland; West Lakeland.* A three-volume series of pocket-sized walking guides which cover fifty half-day (four- to eight-mile) walks in each lakeland region, concentrating on the lower fells, valleys and woodlands. Some classic routes are included, but the emphasis is more on out-of-the-way tracks and secluded areas.

John and Anne Nuttall *The Tarns of Lakeland, Vol. 1 (West)* and *Vol. 2 (East).* Wainwright walked fells, the Nuttalls tackle tarns (mountain lakes), the little specks of blue in their own words – hundreds of them, across the Lake District, linked by forty walks in each volume that range from easy to hard. Obsessive? Clearly so, but you'll soon be seduced by the clear, hand-drawn route maps and walk details, handsome line drawings and interesting asides and anecdotes.

Pathfinder Guide *Lake District Walks; More Lake District Walks*. The best general guides for the day-pack: two slim volumes of walks, graded from short-and-easy to challenging, with useful accompanying text and clear Ordnance Survey map extracts.

W.A. Poucher *The Lakeland Peaks*. First published in 1960 and updated intermittently, Walter Poucher's classic guide for fell-walkers and peak-baggers has almost as many fans as the Wainwright volumes. The pocket-sized guide details 142 routes up fourteen separate mountain groups, accompanied by Poucher's impressive black-and-white landscape photographs (on which are superimposed the various summit routes).

Jim Reid *Tour of the Lake District*. A unique trekking guide to the Lakes that proposes a one- or two-week circular tour taking in the region's scenic valleys, passes and bridleways, rather than conquering peaks for their own sake.

Colin Shelbourn *Rocky Rambler's Wild Walks*. Put the children in charge of the route with this delightful ring-bound family walking guide, aimed at 6- to 14-year-olds. It contains ten colourfully illustrated short walks concentrated in the main tourist areas between Windermere, Coniston, the Ravenglass and Eskdale Railway, and Keswick. There are rhymes and riddles, and things to spot, and "grown ups can help but don't let them become a nuisance".

Graham Thompson *The Backpacker's Guide to the Lake District*. Covers forty two-day walks in the Lake District, an ideal companion for weekend hikers who want to experience the high fells. The walks are either circular or point-to-point, backed up by useful planning information and some fine photography.

A. Wainwright *A Pictorial Guide to the Lakeland Fells (7 vols); The Outlying Fells of Lakeland; Lakeland Sketchbooks (5 vols)*. Wainwright's *Pictorial Guide* is his masterpiece: seven beautifully produced small-format volumes of handwritten notes and sketches (written between 1952 and 1966) guiding generations of walkers up the mountains of the Lake District. Wainwright refused any revision during his lifetime and the originals still stand as remarkable works, though all seven volumes have now been revised and updated by Chris Jesty (between 2005 and 2009) to take account of changing routes and landscapes. The *Outlying Fells* scooped up lower, lesser fells on the perimeter of the Lakes, and there are also five volumes of pen-and-ink lakeland sketchbooks from the late 1960s and early 1970s. New interest has seen all sorts of spin-off publications, from *Twelve Favourite Mountains* to *Wainwright's TV Walks*, while Wainwright himself produced other large-format titles (most with superb photography by Derry Brabbs) holding forth on the majesty of lakeland mountains, passes and valleys.

Wainwright, on the box and in your ear

A new generation of walkers has been introduced to the Lake District fells by the BBC's **Wainwright Walks** series, presented by Julia Bradbury (available on DVD in 2 volumes). Ten of his favourite fells are featured, from Haystacks to Helvellyn, including some fantastic aerial photography. The gravelly voice of Wainwright in the series was actor Nik Wood-Jones, who also narrates **Wainwright: The Podcasts**, a book and audioguide (MP3 format) to eight classic Wainwright walks – one of the podcast walks, Helm Crag, is currently available for free download from the Cumbria Tourism website (Ⓦwww.golakes.co.uk).

Lakeland novels

Melvyn Bragg *Without A City Wall; The Silken Net; The Second Inheritance; For Want of a Nail; The Maid of Buttermere; The Cumbrian Trilogy; The Soldier's Return; A Son At War; Crossing the Lines.* The writer, broadcaster, professional Cumbrian (born in Wigton) and butt of Dame Edna Everage – "don't write any more, Melvyn dear, or we'll never catch up" – Bragg is at his best in *The Maid of Buttermere*, a fictionalized romantic tragedy involving one of the Lakes' most enduring heroines. *The Soldier's Return* and its sequels, *A Son At War* and *Crossing the Lines*, all very moving portraits of small-town life in the years after World War II, draw heavily on the experiences of his own family in Wigton. Other novels also lovingly explore the Cumbrian past and present, notably *The Cumbrian Trilogy* (comprising *The Hired Man, A Place in England* and *Kingdom Come*), which traces the lives of four generations of a Cumbrian family through the twentieth century.

Sarah Hall *Haweswater; The Carhullan Army; How to Paint a Dead Man.* Hall's lyrical first novel, *Haweswater*, delves graphically into the lives of a simple farming community in the 1930s, as the remote village of Mardale is destined to be flooded to create Haweswater reservoir. Different kinds of passions run high in *The Carhullan Army*, an extraordinary near-future novel about female freedom fighters set in a dystopian Cumbria, with Penrith and the bleak northern fells a backdrop to violence and betrayal. Meanwhile, in *How to Paint a Dead Man*, a Cumbrian artist is one of four connected voices that make up an intriguing novel exploring art and illusion.

Reginald Hill *The Stranger House.* Prolific crime-writer Hill – creator of book and TV detective duo Dalziel and Pascoe – goes back to his native Cumbria in a hugely entertaining thriller. Two strangers arrive in the remote village of "Illthwaite" in "Skaddale", pursuing personal histories but soon becoming enmeshed in a web of past religious intrigue, child abuse, ghosts and murder. Hill claims the inn at the heart of the novel, the Stranger House, isn't based on any particular hostelry, but the setting is clearly the western valleys of Eskdale and Wasdale, with their isolated churches, old halls, mountain tarns and Viking crosses.

Val McDermid *The Grave Tattoo.* What if Bounty mutineer Fletcher Christian didn't die on Pitcairn Island, but returned in secret to his native Lake District? And what if he told his tale to his childhood friend William Wordsworth – both were born in Cockermouth – who produced an epic poem on the subject, never yet found but potentially worth millions? Psychological thriller writer McDermid takes a few literary and historical facts and mixes them up with a dollop of speculation, intrigue and forensic science to produce a contemporary Lake District mystery that never quite shifts into top gear.

Magnus Mills *All Quiet on the Orient Express.* Strange goings-on in an unnamed lakeland community as the outsider-narrator is slowly sucked into the confused relationships of the hard-to-fathom locals. Great, and increasingly sinister, fun.

Hugh Walpole *Rogue Herries; Judith Paris; The Fortress; Vanessa.* Largely forgotten now, Walpole was a successful writer by the time he moved to the Lake District in 1923.

Classic guidebooks

The first guidebook to the Lake District was written in the late eighteenth century and dozens more followed as the region opened up to people of leisure. Most of the earliest guides are long out of print, but a trawl through the stock in any local second-hand/antiquarian bookshop throws up old copies of other classic publications. They make interesting souvenirs, while you'll often find that the landscapes described have hardly changed in more than a century.

The earliest lakeland writings were contained in the journal of the poet **Thomas Gray**, first published as part of **Thomas West**'s *Guide to the Lakes in Cumberland, Westmorland and Lancashire* (1778). In 1810, **William Wordsworth** wrote down his own observations, appearing in the most complete form as his *Guide to the Lakes* (1835), which, alone of all the historic guides, is still in print. His friend in later life, the writer and political observer **Harriet Martineau** of Ambleside, produced her own *Complete Guide to the English Lakes* (1855). Fifty years later, **W.G. Collingwood**'s *The Lake Counties* (1902) set new standards of erudition, while **Canon H.D. Rawnsley** (founder of the National Trust) also found time to produce a multitude of lakeland volumes: *Round the Lake Country* (1909) is typical. Between 1904 and 1925, in the days before cheaply available colour photography, landscape watercolourist **Alfred Heaton Cooper** illustrated guidebooks for A. & C. Black; the Lake District titles are fairly easy to come by, as are the four lakeland books illustrated by his son **William Heaton Cooper**, starting with *The Hills of Lakeland* (1938). *The Lake Counties* (1937) volume in **Arthur Mee**'s classic "King's England" series is widely available too.

He immersed himself in the local history to produce these four volumes covering two hundred years of the rip-roaring lives and loves of the Herries clan – too flowery for today's tastes but full of lakeland lore and life.

Children's books

Beatrix Potter *The Tale of Peter Rabbit*; *The Tale of Jemima Puddle-duck*; *The Tale of Squirrel Nutkin*; and many more. Rabbits, pigs, hedgehogs, mice and ducks in lakeland stories of valour, betrayal, adventure and romance. The original 23 titles (available individually or as *The Complete Tales* box set) have been ruthlessly merchandised since Potter's day – as colouring books, pop-up books, foam-filled fabric books, wallpaper, board games, diaries, calendars, etc – while the Renee Zellweger–Ewan McGregor biopic *Miss Potter* (about her life and the writing of the first book, *The Tale of Peter Rabbit*) spawned even more spin-offs, from commemorative movie editions to audio CDs.

Arthur Ransome *Swallows and Amazons*; *Swallowdale*; *Winter Holiday*; *Pigeon Post*; *The Picts and the Martyrs*. Ransome's innocent childhood stories of pirates and treasure, secret harbours and outdoor camps, summer holidays and winter freezes still possess the power to entrance. The series starts with *Swallows and Amazons* (first published in 1930), and there's no better evocation of the drawn-out halcyon days of childhood. Read the books alongside Christina Hardyment's *Arthur Ransome & Captain Flint's Trunk*, a companion guide and "voyage" in search of the people, places, boats and other influences behind the stories.

People

Juliet Barker *Wordsworth: A Life.* Gets right to the emotional heart of her subject's life and loves. Barker manages to make the irascible man of letters seem more human, even more likeable, as a consequence, and the evenly paced account of his quiet death, which came in 1850, is a moving read.

John Batchelor *John Ruskin: No Wealth But Life.* This book provides the best background material yet on Ruskin's life for the non-academic reader. The subtitle is Ruskin's own evaluation of "wealth" and Batchelor conveys well Ruskin's journey from precocious child to visionary and moralist.

A.S. Byatt *Unruly Times.* Authoritative, insightful study of Wordsworth and Coleridge "in their times", which charts their relationship, ideas, work and family situation against a lively backdrop of contemporary politics, society and culture.

Roland Chambers *The Last Englishman.* Recent interest in children's author Arthur Ransome stems largely from the gradually revealed evidence that, long before he wrote the books that made his name, he had spent years in Russia (1917–24) as a foreign correspondent, Bolshevik apologist and, ultimately, spy. This new biography, subtitled *The Double Life of…*, is a spirited investigation of the complexities of this "simplest of men".

Hunter Davies *Wainwright: The Biography*; *William Wordsworth.* Davies turns his informal, chatty style upon two of the Lake District's biggest enigmas. Hard biographical detail aside, there's not much to learn about the character of either man that a close reading of their respective works won't tell you already – but then that's not Davies's fault.

Richard Holmes *Coleridge: Early Visions*; *Coleridge: Darker Reflections.* The supreme account of the troubled genius of Coleridge, who emerges from Holmes's acclaimed two-volume biography as an animated intellectual and creative poet in his own right as well as the catalyst for Wordsworth's poetic development.

Kenneth R. Johnston *The Hidden Wordsworth.* For "hidden" read "young", as Johnston's controversial book focuses on the creation of the poet by examining his early life and work in exhaustively researched detail. The book ends in 1807 with more than half of Wordsworth's life yet to run, but the argument is that "his young life was his most important life". And along the way are sprinkled the controversies, with Wordsworth variously touted as lover, rebel and – most contentiously – spy.

Kathleen Jones *A Passionate Sisterhood.* Welcome feminist take on the lives of the sisters, wives and daughters of the Lake Poets, whose letters and journals reveal not quite the rustic idyll we've been led to expect by the poetry.

Linda Lear *Beatrix Potter: The Extraordinary Life of a Victorian Genius.* Potter's is a life that's been largely overlooked by serious biographers, possibly down to snobbery about the perceived literary value of her works. But as this definitive biography makes abundantly clear, not only was she a pioneer children's writer (one of the first to see the potential in tie-in merchandising) but also an accomplished scientist, innovative farmer, businesswoman and conservationist.

Thomas De Quincey *Confessions of an English Opium-Eater*; *Recollections of the Lakes and the Lake Poets.* Tripping out with the best-known literary drug-taker after Coleridge

– "Fear and Loathing in Grasmere" it isn't, but neither is the *Confessions* a simple cautionary tale. The famous *Recollections* collected together magazine features De Quincey wrote in the 1830s, providing a highly readable, often catty, account of life in the Lakes with the Wordsworths, the Coleridges and Southey.

Mark Storey *Robert Southey: A Life*. Although he's little known now, in his day Southey was a major man of letters, author of 45 books, and expert on Brazil, Portugal and Spain. He was thought of primarily as a poet, his reputation established by *Joan of Arc* and subsequent epics and by his appointment as Poet Laureate. Despite his poetry, however, what has endured most is his clear, plain prose style – thought "perfect" by Byron – and his biographical history of Nelson.

Andrew Wilson *An American President's Love Affair with the English Lake District*. The president in question is Woodrow Wilson (1865–1924), whose mother was born in Carlisle. He visited the Lake District five times between 1896 and 1908, cycling along Ullswater, staying in local inns and hotels, paying his respects at the literary shrines and discovering his Cumbrian roots. This definitive account traces Wilson's Cumbrian heritage and records his local tours and friendships, and is a handy companion if you want to retrace the presidential steps.

Frances Wilson *The Ballad of Dorothy Wordsworth*. Dorothy is put centre-stage in this excellent, gripping biography of the often-overlooked sister of the sage. It's extremely perceptive, especially on the deep emotional ties between poet brother and supportive sister that led from affection via "strange fit of passion" to breakdown, depression and death.

Dorothy Wordsworth *The Grasmere Journals*; *Home at Grasmere*. Was she a poet in her own right? Judge for yourself from the sharply observed descriptions of nature and day-to-day Grasmere life contained in the *Journals*. *Home at Grasmere* lets you see the debt Wordsworth owed his sister by placing journal entries and completed poetry side by side.

Poetry

Samuel Taylor Coleridge *Selected Poems*; *The Complete Poems*; *Critical Edition of the Major Works*. Final texts of all the poems in varying editions: the Penguin *Selected* (edited by his biographer Richard Holmes) also includes extracts from Coleridge's verse plays and prefaces; the Penguin *Complete* edition includes unfinished verses.

Norman Nicholson *Collected Poems*. The bard of Cumbria – who lived all his life in Millom, on the coast – produced five books of verse by the time of his death in 1987, collected here. He writes beautifully and movingly of his country, its trades, its past and its people.

William Wordsworth *The Prelude*; *Lyrical Ballads*; *Poetical Works*; *Selected Poems*. There are dozens of editions of the works of Wordsworth on the market, but these are the current pick. The major poems, sonnets and odes are all collected in *Selected Poems* (Penguin), which has the advantage of being a cheap, pocket-sized edition. For the full text of major works, you'll need *Lyrical Ballads* and *The Prelude* (both Penguin) – the latter presenting the four separate texts of 1798, 1799, 1805 and 1850. (Wordsworth revised his original, 1798, text three times, the last published after his death.) *Poetical Works* (OUP) contains every piece of verse ever published by Wordsworth.

Habitats of the Lake District

The **Lake District National Park** covers 880 square miles, or half a million acres – approximately one percent of Britain's land area. For such a relatively small region it has a highly varied landscape, geology and climate, and possesses a unique combination of spectacular mountains, rugged fells, pastoral and wooded valleys, and tarns, lakes and rivers. This section gives a general introduction to the region's various habitats, including a rundown of the threats posed by modern agricultural methods and human encroachment. Each habitat description includes brief details of the flora and fauna found there, while some of the more prominent nature reserves in the National Park are also covered. For more information about local habitats and wildlife, don't miss the exhibits at the Lake District Visitor Centre at Brockhole (see p.70).

Today's landscape and habitats within the National Park are heavily protected and maintained for future generations. There are currently eight **National Nature Reserves** (NNR), over a hundred **Sites of Special Scientific Interest** (SSSI), three **RAMSAR** sites (an internationally important wetland designation), two **European Special Protection Areas** (SPA) and 23 candidate **Special Areas of Conservation** (cSAC). In addition, in an attempt to combat the threat of agricultural intensification the Lake District National Park was designated an **Environmentally Sensitive Area** (ESA) in 1993. By providing them with financial incentives, farmers are encouraged to reduce chemical inputs such as fertilizers and pesticides; to safeguard and restore hedges, dry-stone walls, traditional farm buildings and archeological remains; and to take care of wildlife habitats such as flower-rich hay meadows, heather moor, wetlands and native woodland. At the same time, the National Park Authority works closely with organizations such as the **Cumbria Wildlife Trust** (Ⓦwww.cumbriawildlifetrust.org.uk), **Friends of the Lake District**(Ⓦwww.fld.org.uk), **Natural England** (Ⓦwww.naturalengland.org.uk), the **National Trust** (Ⓦwww.nationaltrust.org.uk) and the **Royal Society for the Protection of Birds** (Ⓦwww.rspb.org.uk) to monitor important habitats and ensure they are protected and maintained for future generations.

Woodland and forest

There is more **native woodland** in the Lake District than in any other upland National Park in Britain. The most widespread type, sessile-oak woodland, occurs on the acid rocks that make up most of the Lake District, with birch, rowan, hazel and holly also present alongside the dominant oaks. On limestone it's ash woodland that dominates, though elm, hazel, silver birch, yew and rowan might also be present. The woodlands provide food, shelter and breeding sites for many different birds and animals, from the buzzard to the wood mouse, while common plants include bluebell, primrose, wood anemone, cowslip and wild daffodil. Shrubs such as blackthorn and buckthorn are typical. In more acidic soil, bilberry, wavy hair and other grasses, ferns and bracken are common, shrubs less so. Woodlands in **Borrowdale** are particularly important for their lichens and their rich moss and liverwort communities, which depend upon high rainfall and humidity.

Five thousand years ago, nearly all of Britain was covered in woodland but over time it was cleared for settlement and agriculture. Indeed, there's little, if any, true natural forest, or "wildwood", remaining in the Lakes – clearances were well under way by Roman times, and the process gained speed during the Norse settlement of the Lake District (place names ending in "thwaite", signifying a clearing in the forest, are a clue to the changing landscape) and again during monastic times, with the rapid development of sheep farming. However, there are sites that have been continually wooded for at least the past four hundred years, which are known as **ancient semi-natural woodland**. The continuity of woodland cover over such a long period of time has allowed a rich flora and fauna to develop. **Roudsea Wood NNR**, on the southern fringes of the National Park (a mile southwest of Haverthwaite village), is a good example of this kind of habitat, featuring a large variety of trees, ferns and woodland birds. East of Windermere, near Staveley, **Dorothy Farrer's Spring Wood** shows the continuing benefit of coppicing (cutting trees, often hazel, back to a stump) in ancient semi-natural woodland. The tree canopy is periodically opened up, allowing more light to reach the woodland floor and encouraging the growth of plants and fungi. The National Park also contains the highest-altitude woodland in England and Wales, including the **Eskdale and Birkrigg woods** in the Newlands Valley, which are both thought to be descended from original wildwood.

Conifer plantations occupy large areas of the Lake District. They often contain fast-growing, non-indigenous, tree species such as spruce and pine, which are favoured by commercial timber growers but support only a limited range of wildlife. They are, however, used by several birds of prey, including the sparrowhawk, goshawk and merlin, and provide refuge, feeding and nesting areas for the native red squirrel. Recent moves towards more varied planting and felling patterns are producing a mosaic of smaller stands of different-aged trees, seen for example in plantations at **Thirlmere** and in **Grizedale Forest**. These are more botanically diverse and of much greater value to wildlife. For example, young plantations often harbour small mammals such as voles and mice which, in turn, are a food source for kestrels and owls. Other coniferous plantations worth visiting include **Dodd Wood**, four miles north of Keswick (harbouring red squirrel and various birds of prey, including the Lake District ospreys) and **Thornethwaite Forest** (buzzard and sparrowhawk), while in **Ennerdale** the "Wild Ennerdale" project is encouraging a more natural approach to the evolution of valley and forest – alongside the resident roe deer, red squirrel and badger, wild cattle have been introduced to some of the cleared plantation land.

Overgrazing by stock and deer is the greatest cause of decline in the natural regeneration of broad-leaved woodlands, so in some areas woodland management schemes (providing stock-proof fencing or undertaking coppicing and so on) are being practised. Other threats are posed by the **ornamental species** introduced by the Victorians, such as rhododendron and laurel, which have escaped from the private gardens for which they were originally intended. Their dense canopy prevents light from reaching the woodland floor, while the roots produce toxic chemicals that prevent other plants from growing.

Grassland

Before people began to clear the forests for agriculture and settlement, open grassland was a rare feature below the tree line. Most grasslands have been created by humans and grazing animals. Some areas have been drained, ploughed and re-seeded with "improved" grass mixtures for agriculture and so have limited wildlife value. Others remain as unimproved pasture, which supports a greater diversity of plants and animals.

Acid grassland is common on upland sheep pasture where high rainfall, coupled with a long history of burning and grazing, has favoured this relatively species-poor habitat. However, the invertebrate species associated with grasslands provide a vital food source for birds such as skylark and meadow pipit, along with small mammals such as mouse and vole. Acid grasslands often contain small areas of richer habitat in the form of wet flushes, springs and mires where many interesting plants, such as the insectivorous sundew and butterwort, can be found.

Calcareous grassland occurs on the limestone outcrops in the Lake District, which were formed during the last Ice Age when huge glaciers scoured the bedrock. In limestone areas this created a smooth, flattened surface, which is characteristic of **limestone pavements**. Weathering and runoff from rainwater widened and deepened any cracks in the rock, giving rise to a complex pattern of solid blocks called **clints**, separated by fissures (sometimes several feet deep) known as **grikes**. These habitats form distinctive niches for a range of plants and animals. For instance, rare ferns thrive in the deep grikes, while above you may catch a glimpse of the Duke of Burgundy or other rare butterflies.

The flattened area of limestone known as limestone pavement is a nationally rare habitat of international importance and, outside Britain, it's found in only a few other areas of Europe. However, commercial exploitation of limestone pavement (to build walls, gateposts and decorative rockeries) has led to large-scale destruction of this fragile habitat and, today, most pavement in England is protected. Cumbria holds 36 percent of Britain's limestone pavement and examples at **Whitbarrow NNR** are some of the finest in Britain. Here, just to the southeast of Cartmel Fell and Bowland Bridge in the Winster Valley, the limestone ridge of Whitbarrow Scar is dominated by the rare blue moor grass, but also contains the hart's tongue fern, dog's mercury, yellow rockrose and limestone bedstraw, as well as the rarer dropwort, dark-red helleborine and rigid buckler fern. Uncommon orchids and distinctive plants, such as crested hair-grass, can also be seen, along with four species of fritillary butterfly, plus the grayling, northern brown argus and common blue butterfly.

Further south, near Witherslack village, a very different mix of grassland flora occupies the small reserve of **Latterbarrow**. Grazing has cleared much of the ancient woodland here, allowing over 150 flowering plant species to be recorded, including numerous orchids.

Hay meadows support a rich variety of wild flowers and tall-growing grasses, and provide nectar for invertebrates. Their richness is maintained by the fact that plants can flower and set seed before mowing, enabling them to be dispersed during summer hay-making. Unfortunately, many hay meadows have been lost over the years with the intensification of agriculture. The move away from hay-making towards silage production (which requires an earlier cut and often relies on the input of artificial fertilizer) has led to a considerable loss of species diversity. However, farmers are now being encouraged to take care of traditional hay meadows, which can sometimes support more than a hundred different species of flowering plants.

Upland heath

Heathland is an open habitat dominated by dwarf shrubs like heather. Such areas were originally cleared for agriculture but their poor acidic soils made them unsuitable for farming – the acid-tolerant heather, therefore, was able to colonize the land. These open habitats are particularly important for insects, and over 170 species of butterfly and moth have been identified at **Rusland Moss NNR** in the south of the National Park (three miles north of Haverthwaite village), along with numerous spiders, flies, beetles, birds and reptiles.

Large areas of upland heath have traditionally been managed as shooting estates. A diverse age structure of vegetation is maintained through systematically burning strips of heather to promote seed germination and encourage the growth of new shoots. This practice ensures a constant food supply for birds, such as the red grouse (found only in Britain), and provides an important breeding ground for the short-eared owl as well as Britain's smallest bird of prey, the merlin.

Heathland needs careful management to prevent it reverting to woodland. This is commonly achieved through stock grazing. However, if stocking densities are too high, the regeneration of heather cannot keep pace with the consumption of young shoots by the sheep, and the heather dies back.

Mires

The cool, wet climate of the Lake District provides ideal conditions for the development of peat, and the area is considered to be of national importance for both the extent and quality of its **mires**. Peat is characteristic of waterlogged conditions and consists of partially decomposed plant material. In areas where soil micro-organisms cannot complete their natural breakdown processes due to highly acidic conditions and a lack of oxygen, organic remains accumulate as peat. Many mires are nutrient-poor ecosystems, unsuitable for farming. The vegetation depends almost entirely on dilute nutrient supplies present in rainwater and atmospheric dust. Mosses and liverworts flourish, along with many species of lichen and dwarfed forms of heathers and sedges.

Blanket mire (ie where there's a blanket covering of peat) is a scarce habitat, particularly important for breeding moorland birds such as red grouse, golden plover and merlin. Extensive areas remain on some of the flatter fell tops within the National Park, where you'll find cross-leaved heath, purple moor grass, cotton grass, bog asphodel, sundew and sphagnum mosses. Small fragments of **raised mire** (flattish, boggy areas of deep peat) also occur within the National Park, such as **Meathop Moss SSSI**, which supports a wide range of plants, over two hundred species of moth and butterfly (including the large heath butterfly), and several species of dragonfly and damselfly. At **Roudsea Mosses NNR** (a mile southwest of Haverthwaite village), a raised mire provides a breeding site for over fifty species of bird including woodcock, curlew, greater spotted woodpecker and reed bunting. **Dubbs Moss**, a small reserve just to the southwest of Cockermouth, is a mostly wet mixture of mire, fen, meadow and woodland, with plenty of mosses and ferns in evidence.

Unfortunately, artificial drainage of sites, coupled with the increased demand for peat by gardeners, has led to a widespread decline of this wetland habitat. However, attempts are being made to raise gardeners' awareness of alternatives for soil conditioning (such as home-made compost), and steps are being taken to protect and manage existing mires more sympathetically. In areas where rare plants such as the bog orchid have been found, grazing has been controlled.

Lakes, tarns and rivers

The iconic **lakes and tarns** were formed in the last Ice Age by huge glaciers gouging out depressions, which were later filled by meltwater and rain. They vary considerably in size, depth and nutrient status, but between them support an exceptional variety of aquatic plants and animals. However, the lakeshore habitat is a fragile "soft shore" environment that is highly susceptible to erosion. Trampling feet, livestock grazing and waves from passing boats can lead to soil and organic material being washed away. Over time a reedy shoreline may begin to resemble a pebble beach, which contains only a fraction of the invertebrate species and little or no aquatic vegetation.

The deep, cold, clear lakes of **Buttermere**, **Ennerdale** and **Wast Water** only have a restricted range of plants and animals, but these include some rare crustaceans specifically adapted to nutrient-poor environments. In contrast, lakes such as **Windermere** and **Bassenthwaite** – with their wooded shorelines, shallow bays and reedbeds – provide valuable nesting haunts for swans, grebes, ducks, geese and other birds. **Esthwaite Water** is the most nutrient-rich of the lakes, supporting white and yellow water lilies and rare pondweeds as well as nesting grebes, plus wild rainbow and brown trout. Windermere is of national importance for wintering wildfowl, while Bassenthwaite Lake is very rich in aquatic plants (including the scarce floating water plantain) and is one of only two lakes in Britain known to support the rare fish, vendace – the other, **Derwent Water**, also attracts various wintering wildfowl, including the pochard and tufted duck. In 2001, the first pair of ospreys to nest in northern England for 150 years bred near the shores of Bassenthwaite Lake, and ospreys continue to return – three chicks were reared for the first time in 2006.

Many of the **rivers** within the National Park are of considerable ecological importance. The significant populations of fish, together with other species such as native crayfish, freshwater pearl mussel, water vole and otter, reflect the generally high standards of water quality. The fast-flowing upland **streams** provide ideal conditions for birds such as dippers and yellow and grey wagtail.

Rock and scree

Glacial activity has produced a wide variety of crags, knolls, ledges and other rock features. In some places, steep-sided **gills** cut deeply into the fellsides. These ravines provide a damp, sheltered environment and are largely inaccessible to grazing animals, which enables them to support many unusual plants. Steep rocky cliffs, known locally as **crags**, support a mixture of lowland plant species and the more distinctive arctic-alpine flora (including yellow, purple and mossy saxifrage and alpine lady's mantle). Sheltered **rock ledges** and **screes** provide a habitat for tall herbs and ferns (including the parsley fern, common in the Lake District, but fairly rare elsewhere) along with many mosses, liverworts and flowering plants.

Crags and ledges also provide a habitat for a varied range of bird species, including stonechat, wheatear and ring ouzel, and nest sites for the buzzard, raven, peregrine falcon and golden eagle. The population of peregrine falcons, in particular, suffered a huge decline during the 1950s and 1960s due to widespread use of pesticides and illegal persecution. Their numbers dropped to just six pairs in Cumbria, though over the last twenty years they have made a considerable recovery and the Lake District today supports the highest density of peregrines anywhere in Europe. Golden eagles are far less numerous; in fact, the only ones in England have been seen on the outcrops and open fells above **Haweswater**, along with buzzards and peregrine falcons. The very high fells (particularly in Langdale) are also the only place you'll spot the mountain ringlet butterfly, Britain's only true alpine butterfly.

Cliff, rock and scree habitats are, of course, highly vulnerable to the activities of climbers, walkers and scramblers. Seasonal access restrictions to crags with nesting birds are negotiated annually, and walkers should always keep to marked paths and trails, since going "off trail" – even just stepping off a marked path – can spoil a fragile habitat.

Coastal environments

Five sites of international importance for nature conservation are located on the coast of the National Park, while on its southern boundary the National Park encompasses small parts of the **Duddon Estuary** and **Morecambe Bay**. These extensive areas support huge numbers of breeding and wintering birds for which they are awarded special European protection – RAMSAR status. Depending on the time of year, you're likely to see flocks of knot, dunlin and oystercatcher, plus grey and ringed plover, curlew, greenshank, spotted redshank, mallard, shelduck and wigeon.

In the west, the National Park's coast stretches from **Drigg Local Nature Reserve** (SSSI) for twelve miles south to **Silecroft**. Large numbers of the natterjack toad are found here along with the palmate, great crested and smooth newt, and the common lizard, while other important species include the adder and the slowworm. Over two hundred plant species are found in the coastal habitats, from sea campion, sea beet and sea kale established on the shingle beaches to typical salt-marsh plants such as glasswort and sea arrowgrass. On the dunes, marram grass and lyme grass help stabilize the sand, while in the hollows, or "slacks", of the dune systems (sometimes filled with fresh or sea water) rarer species such as creeping willow, marsh pennywort and various other marsh orchids can often be found. Shingle and dune habitats also provide breeding areas for five species of tern and large colonies of gulls. The **Hodbarrow** nature reserve, near Millom – a habitat fashioned from a former iron-ore mining site – sees a huge variety of coastal bird species, including great crested grebe, tufted duck, shelduck, oystercatcher and ringed plover, as well as birds of prey such as the kestrel, sparrowhawk and barn owl.

This feature is based on literature kindly provided by the Lake District National Park Authority.

Climbing in the Lake District

Two centuries ago, no one climbed rocks for fun. That's not to say that people didn't go up mountains, but they would never have thought of themselves as climbers or what they were doing as a sport. Shepherds, soldiers and traders ventured onto high ground, but only with good reason. Mountains were the stuff of myth and legend – useless to farmers, dangerous to travellers, largely unknown and often feared. Daniel Defoe, writing of the Lake District in the 1720s, thought the region's mountains "had a kind of inhospitable terror in them"; and Dr Johnson, some fifty years later, was "astonished and repelled by this wide extent of hopeless sterility". But revolution was afoot in the late eighteenth century, as much in man's perception of the natural world as in politics, and two new influences were making themselves felt upon the landscapes of Europe: Romanticism and the urge for scientific discovery.

Early steps

In August 1786, Mont Blanc in the French Alps (the highest summit in Western Europe) was climbed for the first time by a young Chamonix doctor, **Michel-Gabriel Paccard** and his porter **Jacques Balmat**. The pair made notes and collected botanical and geological specimens as they went – and picked up a substantial prize in addition, offered by the Swiss scientist and explorer Horace-Benedict de Saussure for the first successful ascent. Given that only eighty years previously a serious attempt had been made to seek out and classify "alpine dragons", Paccard's climb was both a mountaineering *tour de force* and a triumph of scientific rationalism over superstition.

In England it was the artistic, rather than the scientific, community which began to influence the general attitude towards the Lake District's own, lesser, mountain range. **The Picturesque Movement**, precursor of Romanticism, had made the depiction of landscape fashionable and, by the 1760s, various English artists were making good money out of the developing public taste for mountainous scenery. Idealized prints of Derwent Water by Thomas Smith and William Bellers proved both popular and profitable, while in 1783 the renowned artist Thomas Gainsborough visited the Lakes and produced three well-received works (including one of the Langdale Pikes).

Capturing the prevailing Romantic spirit, other visitors published successful accounts of their lakeland expeditions, and in the writings of **William Gilpin**, **Thomas West** and novelist **Mrs Ann Radcliffe** are found the first descriptions of mountains as objects to be climbed (primarily for the "picturesque" views from the top). But the relatively easy ascent of Skiddaw aside (which could be conquered on horseback), most Lake District mountain tops were still well off-limits. It took the energy and vision of an opium-riddled, rheumatic poet to transform the way people regarded lakeland crags and cliffs.

Coleridge and the birth of rock climbing

If Wordsworth was the great walker in the Lake District, then **Samuel Taylor Coleridge** was the pioneer of rock climbing. In August 1802, setting off from his home in Keswick, he made a nine-day solo tour – which he dubbed his "circumcursion" – taking in the peaks and valleys of the central and western Lakes in a hundred-mile circuit. Coleridge was escaping a troubled marriage and an ebbing literary career and, recording his travels in his journal and in a series of letters to his beloved "Asra" (Wordsworth's sister-in-law, Sara Hutchinson), he became the sport's first great writer.

Coleridge's was a wild spirit and it was with a real sense of exhilaration that he found himself on the top of Scafell on the fifth day of his tour. In a famous passage from his journal he records his hair-raising descent, dropping down the successive ledges of **Broad Stand** by hanging over them from his fingertips. In this manner, he soon found himself in a position where: "... every Drop increased the Palsy of my Limbs…and now I had only two more to drop down, to return was impossible – but of these two the first was tremendous, it was twice my own height, and the Ledge at the bottom was so exceedingly narrow, that if I dropt down upon it I must of necessity have fallen backwards and of course killed myself". A moment's reflection brought respite: "I know not how to proceed, how to return, but I am calm and fearless and confident."

This ability to overcome the body's response to fear is a quality all climbers must possess, and Coleridge's breathless account marks him out as a true mountaineer. He revelled in the activity for its own sake and in his "stretched and anxious state of mind" he discovered calm and an escape from the cares of home.

Others followed Coleridge onto the fells. The description of Ennerdale's **Pillar Rock** as "unclimbable" by a guidebook writer, John Otley, in 1825, led to a competition among local dalesmen to ascend the only sizeable summit in the area that could not be gained by walking alone. It was duly scaled in 1826 by a shepherd, **John Atkinson**. By 1875, some fifty annual ascents were being recorded, amongst them that of the first woman, a Miss Barker of Gosforth, and a 14-year-old boy, Lawrence Pilkington, later a pioneering Alpine climber (and the founder of the famous glass company).

Wasdale and the Victorian climbers

For the most part, the Lake District crags were largely ignored by daring English gentlemen climbers and their professional guides. Mountaineering meant Alpine glaciers and snow ridges, and most Alpinists regarded lakeland rock climbers as mere "chimney sweeps" and "rock gymnasts". But change was in the air. A handful of more broad-minded climbers began to gather for winter practice at **Wasdale Head**, from where Coleridge had set off for Scafell in 1802. On the whole they were professional men from the industrial cities or academics, with the time and energy to indulge their passion for the mountains. From their ranks came the Cambridge classicist and unlikely sporting revolutionary **Walter Parry Haskett Smith**. Having been introduced to the high fells at Wasdale in 1881, Haskett Smith returned the following year and set out to discover challenging routes up the gullies and chimneys that cleave their way through the rocks. Climbing for the sheer thrill of it, Haskett Smith began to record his routes, guiding those who might choose to follow his footsteps and handholds. The visitor's book at the **Wastwater Hotel** (now the *Wasdale Head Inn*) became the lakeland climber's bible, and the hotel doubled as the rock climbers' clubhouse.

An almost chivalrous code developed amongst the climbers: comradeship tempered the excesses of competition and bar-room bragging was not tolerated. These men found in climbing an escape from the demands of their professions, families and society, and a few days spent at Wasdale each year was an excuse for the sort of behaviour not usually associated with the staid lives of Victorian gentlemen. After a hard day on the crag, there were often evening gymnastic revelries: the "billiard room traverse" – circling and leaving the room without touching the floor – or the "passage of the billiard table leg", completed by climbing beneath the table and around a table leg.

In 1886, Haskett Smith made the first ascent of **Napes Needle**, that slender pillar of rock that rises on the southern flank of Great Gable. This was no simple gully scramble, nor could it be rationalized as merely an alternative route to a fell top. This was climbing pure and simple, and climbing for its own sake at that. If one climb set the standard for a new sport, this was it. The route is short, but exposed, and is still many a novice's first lakeland climb. Haskett Smith did it alone, unroped and in nailed boots, at the end of a full day in the hills. (He later repeated this pioneering climb on its fiftieth anniversary, when he was a sprightly 76-year-old.)

Haskett Smith's exploits didn't go unnoticed. **Owen Glynne Jones**, the son of a Welsh carpenter, was teaching at the City of London School when, in 1891, he saw a photograph of Napes Needle in a shop on the Strand and within a fortnight had climbed it during his Easter holidays. He was a bold, brash man ("The Only Genuine Jones", as he called himself), who climbed ferociously well and pioneered several physically demanding routes, eagerly taking up the right of first ascenders to name new climbs (a tradition that remains to this day) – "Jones's Route Direct" on Scafell owes its name to him.

Jones came to dominate lakeland climbing in the 1890s, doing much to publicize the new sport in the process. In 1897, his book, *Rock Climbing in* the English Lake District, was published, including thirty magnificent full-page photographs by Keswick brothers and photographers **George** and **Ashley Abraham**. Jones's accompanying descriptions of the routes included **grades** allocated according to the difficulty of the climb – from Easy to Severe. This was the first attempt to put some order into what had been, until now, a sport without classification, and Jones's basic grading framework still stands, although there are now some twenty intermediate and additional grades.

Danger and progress on the fells

Jones was killed in a fall in the Alps in 1899 and his death highlighted the dangers facing the early climbers. Their **specialist equipment** was basically limited to nails arranged in varying patterns on the sole or around the edge of the boot to help grip the rock. Heavy hemp ropes (as used when crossing crevasse-strewn Alpine glaciers) were of dubious benefit on lakeland crags. Two or more climbers might rope themselves together but, as the rope itself was not attached to the rock (as it is today), the chances of surviving a fall were slim. Put bluntly, it was "one off, all off" and the tragic results can be seen in

St Olaf's graveyard at Wasdale Head, where three headstones mark the graves of a roped party who fell together from the Pinnacle Face of Scafell in 1906.

Some measure of organization came to lakeland rock climbing with the establishment in 1907 of the **Fell and Rock Climbing Club (FRCC)** of the English Lake District. Ashley Abraham became its president, with honorary memberships granted to Haskett Smith, Cecil Slingsby (a great lakeland climber on Scafell and Gable, and probably the first Englishman to learn the art of skiing) and Norman Collie (an experienced climber in Skye, the Alps, the Rockies and the Himalayas, who also found time to discover the gas neon and develop the first practical application of the X-ray). The Fell and Rock, as the club came to be known, not only promoted safer climbing techniques but helped usher the sport out of the Victorian age with its revolutionary acceptance of women members (something the more established Alpine Club didn't do until after World War II).

Meanwhile, lakeland climbers continued to push at the boundaries of possibility. **Siegfried Herford** (Welsh-born but with a German mother) began climbing in 1907, and his eventual ascent of **Central Buttress** on Scafell in the spring of 1914 was a landmark climb, requiring a new grade to be added to the grading framework – it was so tough, no one else repeated the climb for seven years.

A democratic sport

By the **mid-1930s**, climbing had become a popular, rather than a specialist, pastime. Partly, this was because it was now a safer sport than it had been: rubber-soled gym shoes were worn in dry weather rather than nailed boots, and rope techniques had improved markedly. But, more importantly, what had once been the preserve of daring gentlemen was now open to all – better road access, more holiday time and the establishment of youth hostels and rambling clubs all brought new faces (known as "crag rats") onto the crags.

Jim Birkett, a quarryman from Langdale, and **Bill Peascod**, a Workington coal miner, were typical of the new breed of climber. Birkett was a reserved man and a traditionalist, who kept climbing in nailed boots long after his contemporaries had abandoned them. On May 1, 1938, he pioneered his first classic route on **Scafell East Buttress**, calling it "May Day". This was followed by "Gremlin's Groove" on the same face and two other classics on **Esk Buttress** ("Afterthought" and "Frustration"), before Birkett turned his attention to **Castle Rock** in Thirlmere, climbing what was then known as the Lakeland Everest in April 1939 by a route he called "Overhanging Bastion". Meanwhile, the more extrovert Peascod was making similar advances in **Buttermere**, with routes such as "Eagle Front", climbed in June 1940, followed by nine other new routes of a similarly severe standard in 1941.

Popularity and professionalism

By **the 1960s**, thanks to the conquest of Everest, climbing rode high in the public conscience. Men like **Joe Brown** and **Chris Bonington** became household names – although they were better known for their achievements in the Alps and Himalayas than for any of the notable lakeland routes they had also created. Other British climbers were also branching out from the Lakes, not only to Scotland and Wales but to the warmer rocks of France, Spain and

Morocco. However, fashions come and go and the Lake District has always attracted climbers back, drawn by the huge variety of rock faces crammed into such a tightly packed mountain range.

By **the 1970s**, an increasing number of professional climbers were taking a new approach to their sport, training as hard as any top athlete in order to push the boundaries still further. Typical of this single-minded athleticism were the exploits of the Yorkshireman **Pete Livesey**, whose great lakeland season came in 1974. In **Borrowdale** alone he put up four routes of such a magnitude that many at first thought them impossible without using "aid" (pitons, ropes or other artificial help on the rock). But Livesey maintained the tradition of so-called "free climbing" (whereby equipment is used only to provide safety in the event of a fall), thus proving it was simply another psychological barrier that had to be broken. Soon others were climbing even more "impossible" routes than Livesey. **Bill Birkett** – son of the Langdale climber, Jim – undertook some audacious climbing in the Patterdale area, most notably on **Dove Crag**, in the 1970s and 1980s. And today, **Dave Birkett**, Bill's nephew, has a reputation as one of the world's finest adventure climbers, creating new standards right back in the heart of the Lakes, where many of his routes (graded Extreme 9, about as tough as it gets) have been unrepeated by other climbers.

Modern equipment and challenges

Climbing equipment has developed alongside the athletic professionalism. Nailed boots and gym shoes have given way to specialized climbing shoes, first developed in the 1950s by the French climber Pierre Allain (and known by his initials as PAs). Where Haskett Smith would have climbed in tweeds, modern climbers don multicoloured Lycra leggings: chalk bags hang from belts, ready to dry sweat-dampened fingers, along with a battery of safety chocks and slings, placed in the rock to give the nylon rope a secure anchor point in the event of a fall. Despite the severity of today's climbing, accidents are few and far between, since a securely placed sling or "runner" (through which the rope is clipped) holds anyone whose ambition out-runs their ability. There was a move towards "**aid climbing**" in the Lakes in the 1960s, when pitons and screws were used to assist an ascent, but it was largely frowned upon and today nearly all lakeland climbers climb "**free**"; that is, by their own efforts alone. It's a technique championed by Cumbria's latest young gun, adventure climber and BASE jumper Leo Houlding – one of a bunch of young British climbers (including Ian Parnell, Andy Kirkpatrick and Airlie Anderson) scaling crags and peaks from Yosemite to Patagonia.

The number of climbers on the Lake District's crags has increased to such an extent that queues now form on popular routes in the summer. But there are still **challenging routes** to be discovered alongside the classics on Gable and Scafell. Hikers, meanwhile, have the history of climbing all around them. Take a walk up from the *Wasdale Head Inn* and the very names of the features around the Great Napes on Great Gable – Sphinx Ridge, Needle Gulley and Napes Needle itself – are all attributable to the pioneer climbers. You may not know it, and it will not be listed by the Ordnance Survey, but on Scafell Crag you could pass by "Botterill's Slab" (1903, F.W. Botterill), "Pegasus" (1952, A. Dolphin & P. Greenwood) or "The White Wizard" (1976, C.J.S. Bonington & N. Estcourt), and find climbers on each. All are finding something different in the challenge of hand and foot on rock, and all are, in their own way, conquering the impossible. In that, nothing has changed.

William Wordsworth: A Life

Wordsworth was of a good height, just five feet ten, and not a slender man... Meantime his face...was certainly the noblest for intellectual effects that, in actual life, I have seen.

Thomas De Quincey, *Recollections of the Lake and Lake Poets*

William Wordsworth and the Lake District are inextricably linked, and in the streets of Grasmere, Hawkshead and Cockermouth, and the fells surrounding Ullswater, Borrowdale and the Duddon Valley you're never very far away from a house or a sight associated with the poet and his circle. His birthplace, houses, favourite spots and final resting place are all covered in the Guide, together with anecdotes about, and analysis of, his day-to-day life, his poetry and personal relationships. Below, a general biographical account of Wordsworth's life is provided to place the various sites and accounts in context.

Childhood, school and university

William Wordsworth was **born in Cockermouth** (April 7, 1770), the second eldest of four brothers and a sister, Dorothy. His father, John, was agent and lawyer for a local landowner, Sir James Lowther, and the family was comfortably off, as the surviving Wordsworth home in Cockermouth attests. The children spent much time with their grandparents in Penrith – William even attended a school there – and when their mother Ann died (she was only 30) in 1778, the family was split up: Dorothy was sent to live with relations in Halifax in Yorkshire, while William and his older brother Richard began life at the respected **grammar school in Hawkshead**, lodging with **Ann Tyson** and going back to Penrith or Cockermouth in the holidays. On his father's death in 1783, William and the other children were left in relative poverty as the Lowthers refused to pay John Wordsworth's long-owed salary (indeed, it was almost twenty years before the debt was honoured).

At school in Hawkshead, Wordsworth (now supported by his uncles) flourished, storing up childhood experiences of ice-skating, climbing, fishing and dancing that would later emerge in his most celebrated poetry. In 1787, finished with school and clutching new clothes made for him by Ann Tyson and the already devoted Dorothy, Wordsworth went up to **St John's College, Cambridge**, where his uncles intended that he should study to become a clergyman. His academic promise soon fizzled out. Despite a bright start – to his evident amusement, De Quincey later recalled that Wordsworth briefly became a "dandy", sporting silk stockings and powdered hair – he abandoned his formal studies and left in 1790 without distinction and with no prospect of being ordained. His uncles were furious, but Wordsworth had other plans for his future.

In France

A walking tour through **France and the Alps** in the summer of 1790 excited the young, idealistic Wordsworth who had grand thoughts of being a poet. His interest was fired by the contemporary revolutionary movements of Europe.

The Bastille had fallen the previous year and Wordsworth's early republicanism flowered. ("Bliss was it in that dawn to be alive, but to be young was very Heaven!") He returned to France in 1791 where he met one **Annette Vallon**, with whom he fell in love – she became pregnant, giving birth to their child, Caroline, in December 1792. But by this time, Wordsworth had returned to England, to oversee the publication, in 1793, of his first works, *Descriptive Sketches* (inspired by his revolutionary travels) and the lakeland reverie *An Evening Walk*. When war broke out between England and France in 1793 Wordsworth was unable to return to France or to Annette; they didn't meet again until 1802.

Depressed by the events of the Terror in France, which rather dented his revolutionary enthusiasm, Wordsworth alternated between fretting and idling in London and making walking tours around England. He thought he might become a teacher and shared Dorothy's oft-expressed dream of setting up home together and devoting his life to poetry – something that at last seemed possible when a small, but unexpected, bequest from the dying **Raisley Calvert**, the brother of an old schoolfriend, gave him just enough to live on.

Becoming a poet: the Lyrical Ballads and Germany

William and Dorothy moved to **Dorset** in 1795 (where they'd been offered a house), and William became acquainted with a fiery, widely read, passionate young critic and writer. **Samuel Taylor Coleridge** had read and admired Wordsworth's two published works and, on meeting Wordsworth himself, was almost overcome with enthusiasm for his ideas and passions. There's no doubt that they inspired each other and the Wordsworths moved to **Somerset** to be near Coleridge – "three people, but one soul", as Coleridge later had it. Here they collaborated on what became the **Lyrical Ballads** (1798), a work which could be said to mark the onset of English Romantic poetry and which contained some of Wordsworth's finest early writing (quite apart from Coleridge's "The Rime of the Ancient Mariner"): not just the famous "Lines Written above Tintern Abbey", but also snatches later incorporated into *The Prelude* (Wordsworth's great autobiographical work, unpublished during his lifetime – Wordsworth only ever knew it as the "Poem on my own Life"). It's hard to see today quite how unusual the *Lyrical Ballads* were for their time: conceived as "experiments", the mixture of simple poems with a rustic, natural content and longer narrative works flew right in the face of contemporary classicism. Sales and reviews were universally poor.

Wordsworth, Dorothy and Coleridge went to **Germany** in 1798, during which time their joint idea for a long autobiographical, philosophical work began to gel in Wordsworth's mind. He produced a first version of *The Prelude* in Germany, along with the affecting "Lucy" poems (including "Strange fits of passion have I known"), which some say pointed to an unnatural passion for his sister. It was certainly an unusual relationship: Dorothy devoted herself entirely to William (her favourite brother since childhood) and his work; she kept house for him, walked with him, listened to his poems, transcribed and made copies of them, and he wrote passionate poems about nameless women who could be no one else but Dorothy. But there's no evidence – to be blunt – that she slept with him, despite the claims of some critics.

Grasmere

In 1799 William and Dorothy moved to **Grasmere** (and Coleridge followed), in the search both for conducive natural surroundings in which Wordsworth's work could flourish and for somewhere they could survive on a restricted budget. William was to spend the last two-thirds of his life in and around the village.

Brother and sister first moved into **Dove Cottage** where they remained until 1808, a period in which Wordsworth established himself as a major poet. A new edition of the *Lyrical Ballads* (1801) appeared, including some of the poems he'd written in Germany together with his first major Grasmere poems, such as "The Brothers" and "Michael", based on local stories and characters. This edition also included its famous **preface** expounding his theories of poetry (against "inane phraseology"; for simple, natural, emotive language), which many critics found arrogant. Wordsworth was at his most productive in the years to 1805, resulting in the publication of *Poems in Two Volumes* (1807), containing the celebrated odes to "Duty" and "Immortality", the Westminster Bridge sonnet, the "Daffodils" poem (untitled when first published) and a hundred other new poems and sonnets. A third edition of *Lyrical Ballads* appeared, and he had also found time to expand and complete a second version of *The Prelude*. All this early work set new standards in poetry: questioning the nature of perception, challenging contemporary prejudices and orchestrating a highly original vision of the human soul within nature.

Dorothy, meanwhile, kept a **journal** recording life at Dove Cottage which has become a classic in its own right. Her skilled observations of the local people and landscape prompted some of William's best-known work, most famously the "Daffodils" stanzas – Wordsworth relied heavily on her journal for the famous images of the flowers dancing and reeling in the breeze.

Marriage and money

Wordsworth's dire financial position slowly improved. His sales and reviews weren't getting any better (Byron trashed most of *Poems in Two Volumes*) but the Lowthers finally stumped up the debt owed to William's long-dead father. This allowed him to marry an old childhood friend from Penrith, **Mary Hutchinson**, in 1802, having first travelled with Dorothy to France to make amends with his first love Annette; Wordsworth later provided an annuity for Annette and their young daughter. Outwardly, the **marriage to Mary** seemed precipitous and passionless and scholars have speculated about Wordsworth's motives, though letters between William and his wife (discovered in the 1970s) tend to scotch the myth that he was marrying out of duty. **Children** followed – John, Dorothy (always known as Dora), Thomas, Catherine and William – though Catherine and then Thomas, both infants, succumbed to mortal illnesses in the same tragic year of 1812.

Dove Cottage became too small for comfort as the family grew. His wife's sister, Sara Hutchinson, was a permanent fixture, as was Coleridge (by now separated from his wife) and his visiting children. The Wordsworths moved to other houses in Grasmere (Allan Bank and the Old Rectory), and then in 1813 finally settled on **Rydal Mount**, a gracious house two miles south of the village. Here William lived out the rest of his life, supported for some years by his salaried position as **Distributor of Stamps for Westmorland** (good fortune, caused, as De Quincey noted, by the current incumbent distributing "himself and his office into two different places"). It was hardly a sinecure – he had to travel through the county, collecting dues and granting licences, work which he undertook assiduously – but it brought him in £200 a year.

The Rydal years

Wordsworth may have already written his finest poetry, but after the move to Rydal he was at the peak of his fame. Over the years, the literary world made its way to his door, a procession recorded in detail by the critic and essayist **Thomas De Quincey** who first made the pilgrimage to Grasmere to meet his hero in 1807. After a long friendship interrupted by disagreements, De Quincey's frank series of articles on Wordsworth and his family in 1839 (later published as *Recollections of the Lakes and the Lake Poets*) caused an irreparable rift. **Coleridge**, too, was *persona non grata* after a falling-out in 1810, though the two old friends did come to some kind of an accommodation in later life, and *The Prelude* remained dedicated to him.

There were family setbacks. The death of William's brother, John, in 1805 had affected him deeply (and led later to a burgeoning religious faith); after 1828, his beloved sister Dorothy suffered a series of depressive illnesses, which incapacitated her mind for most of the rest of her long life; and his wife's sister, Sara Hutchinson – who had so besotted Coleridge and who had lived with them for thirty years – died of the flu in 1835.

Wordsworth continued to be productive, at least in the early Rydal years. The *Excursion* (1814), long enough in itself, was conceived as part of an even longer philosophical work to be called "The Recluse", which he never completed. His first *Collected Poems* appeared the following year, together with *The White Doe of Rylstone*; but it wasn't until *Peter Bell* (1819) and *The River Duddon sonnets* (1820) that sales and reviews finally flourished. His *Vaudracour and Julia* (1819) also had deep significance: a tale of seduction, it was a fictionalized account of his affair with Annette.

As Wordsworth grew older he lost the radicalism of his youth, becoming a loud opponent of democracy, liberalism and progress. Political developments in France and the threat of the mob and the Reform Bill at home appalled him. His views on nature and the picturesque had led him to produce his own descriptive **Guide to the Lakes** ("for the minds of persons of taste"), at first published anonymously (1810) to accompany a book of drawings; its later popularity (a final, fifth edition, appeared in 1835) did much to advertise the very charms of the region he was keen to preserve. In the end, fulminating against the whitewashed houses and fir plantations he thought were disfiguring the Lakes, Wordsworth retreated to his beloved garden at Rydal Mount.

Apart from the rare crafted sonnet or couplet, Wordsworth's later work was largely undistinguished. The third major revision of *The Prelude* had been completed in 1838; the poem didn't see the light of day until after his death, when Mary gave it a name and handed it over for publication. But in 1843, on the death of Robert Southey and at the age of 73, Wordsworth's position as Grand Old Man of the literary establishment was confirmed by his appointment as **Poet Laureate**.

After his **death in 1850**, William's body was interred in St Oswald's churchyard in Grasmere, to be later joined by Dorothy (1855) and by his wife Mary (1859).

Travel store

Travel

Andorra The Pyrenees, Pyrenees & Andorra Map, Spain
Antigua The Caribbean
Argentina Argentina, Argentina Map, Buenos Aires, South America on a Budget
Aruba The Caribbean
Australia Australia, Australia Map, East Coast Australia, Melbourne, Sydney, Tasmania
Austria Austria, Europe on a Budget, Vienna
Bahamas The Bahamas, The Caribbean
Barbados Barbados DIR, The Caribbean
Belgium Belgium & Luxembourg, Bruges DIR, Brussels, Brussels Map, Europe on a Budget
Belize Belize, Central America on a Budget, Guatemala & Belize Map
Benin West Africa
Bolivia Bolivia, South America on a Budget
Brazil Brazil, Rio, South America on a Budget
British Virgin Islands The Caribbean
Brunei Malaysia, Singapore & Brunei [1 title], Southeast Asia on a Budget
Bulgaria Bulgaria, Europe on a Budget
Burkina Faso West Africa
Cambodia Cambodia, Southeast Asia on a Budget, Vietnam, Laos & Cambodia Map [1 Map]
Cameroon West Africa
Canada Canada, Pacific Northwest, Toronto, Toronto Map, Vancouver
Cape Verde West Africa
Cayman Islands The Caribbean
Chile Chile, Chile Map, South America on a Budget
China Beijing, China, Hong Kong & Macau, Hong Kong & Macau DIR, Shanghai
Colombia South America on a Budget
Costa Rica Central America on a Budget, Costa Rica, Costa Rica & Panama Map
Croatia Croatia, Croatia Map, Europe on a Budget
Cuba Cuba, Cuba Map, The Caribbean, Havana
Cyprus Cyprus, Cyprus Map
Czech Republic The Czech Republic, Czech & Slovak Republics, Europe on a Budget, Prague, Prague DIR, Prague Map
Denmark Copenhagen, Denmark, Europe on a Budget, Scandinavia
Dominica The Caribbean
Dominican Republic Dominican Republic, The Caribbean
Ecuador Ecuador, South America on a Budget
Egypt Egypt, Egypt Map
El Salvador Central America on a Budget
England Britain, Camping in Britain, Devon & Cornwall, Dorset, Hampshire and The Isle of Wight [1 title], England, Europe on a Budget, The Lake District, London, London DIR, London Map, London Mini Guide, Walks In London & Southeast England
Estonia The Baltic States, Europe on a Budget
Fiji Fiji
Finland Europe on a Budget, Finland, Scandinavia
France Brittany & Normandy, Corsica, Corsica Map, The Dordogne & the Lot, Europe on a Budget, France, France Map, Languedoc & Roussillon, The Loire, Paris, Paris DIR, Paris Map, Paris Mini Guide, Provence & the Côte d'Azur, The Pyrenees, Pyrenees & Andorra Map
French Guiana South America on a Budget
Gambia The Gambia, West Africa
Germany Berlin, Berlin Map, Europe on a Budget, Germany, Germany Map
Ghana West Africa
Gibraltar Spain
Greece Athens Map, Crete, Crete Map, Europe on a Budget, Greece, Greece Map, Greek Islands, Ionian Islands
Guadeloupe The Caribbean
Guatemala Central America on a Budget, Guatemala, Guatemala & Belize Map
Guinea West Africa
Guinea-Bissau West Africa
Guyana South America on a Budget
Holland see The Netherlands
Honduras Central America on a Budget
Hungary Budapest, Europe on a Budget, Hungary
Iceland Iceland, Iceland Map
India Goa, India, India Map, Kerala, Rajasthan, Delhi & Agra [1 title], South India, South India Map
Indonesia Bali & Lombok, Southeast Asia on a Budget
Ireland Dublin DIR, Dublin Map, Europe on a Budget, Ireland, Ireland Map
Israel Jerusalem
Italy Europe on a Budget, Florence DIR, Florence & Siena Map, Florence & the best of Tuscany, Italy, The Italian Lakes, Naples & the Amalfi Coast, Rome, Rome DIR, Rome Map, Sardinia, Sicily, Sicily Map, Tuscany & Umbria, Tuscany Map, Venice, Venice DIR, Venice Map
Jamaica Jamaica, The Caribbean
Japan Japan, Tokyo
Jordan Jordan
Kenya Kenya, Kenya Map
Korea Korea
Laos Laos, Southeast Asia on a Budget, Vietnam, Laos & Cambodia Map [1 Map]
Latvia The Baltic States, Europe on a Budget
Lithuania The Baltic States, Europe on a Budget
Luxembourg Belgium & Luxembourg, Europe on a Budget
Malaysia Malaysia Map, Malaysia, Singapore & Brunei [1 title], Southeast Asia on a Budget
Mali West Africa
Malta Malta & Gozo DIR
Martinique The Caribbean
Mauritania West Africa
Mexico Baja California, Baja California, Cancún & Cozumel DIR, Mexico, Mexico Map, Yucatán, Yucatán Peninsula Map
Monaco France, Provence & the Côte d'Azur
Montenegro Montenegro
Morocco Europe on a Budget, Marrakesh DIR, Marrakesh Map, Morocco, Morocco Map,
Nepal Nepal
Netherlands Amsterdam, Amsterdam DIR, Amsterdam Map, Europe on a Budget, The Netherlands
Netherlands Antilles The Caribbean
New Zealand New Zealand, New Zealand Map

DIR: Rough Guide **DIRECTIONS** for short breaks

Available from all good bookstores

Nicaragua Central America on a Budget
Niger West Africa
Nigeria West Africa
Norway Europe on a Budget, Norway, Scandinavia
Panama Central America on a Budget, Costa Rica & Panama Map, Panama
Paraguay South America on a Budget
Peru Peru, Peru Map, South America on a Budget
Philippines The Philippines, Southeast Asia on a Budget,
Poland Europe on a Budget, Poland
Portugal Algarve DIR, The Algarve Map, Europe on a Budget, Lisbon DIR, Lisbon Map, Madeira DIR, Portugal, Portugal Map, Spain & Portugal Map
Puerto Rico The Caribbean, Puerto Rico
Romania Europe on a Budget, Romania
Russia Europe on a Budget, Moscow, St Petersburg
St Kitts & Nevis The Caribbean
St Lucia The Caribbean
St Vincent & the Grenadines The Caribbean
Scotland Britain, Camping in Britain, Edinburgh DIR, Europe on a Budget, Scotland, Scottish Highlands & Islands
Senegal West Africa
Serbia Montenegro Europe on a Budget
Sierra Leone West Africa
Singapore Malaysia, Singapore & Brunei [1 title], Singapore, Singapore DIR, Southeast Asia on a Budget
Slovakia Czech & Slovak Republics, Europe on a Budget
Slovenia Europe on a Budget, Slovenia
South Africa Cape Town & the Garden Route, South Africa, South Africa Map
Spain Andalucía, Andalucía Map, Barcelona, Barcelona DIR, Barcelona Map, Europe on a Budget, Ibiza & Formentera DIR, Gran Canaria DIR, Madrid DIR, Lanzarote & Fuerteventura DIR Madrid Map, Mallorca & Menorca, Mallorca DIR, Mallorca Map, The Pyrenees, Pyrenees & Andorra Map, Spain, Spain & Portugal Map, Tenerife & La Gomera DIR
Sri Lanka Sri Lanka, Sri Lanka Map
Suriname South America on a Budget
Sweden Europe on a Budget, Scandinavia, Sweden
Switzerland Europe on a Budget, Switzerland
Taiwan Taiwan
Tanzania Tanzania, Zanzibar
Thailand Bangkok, Southeast Asia on a Budget, Thailand, Thailand Map, Thailand Beaches & Islands
Togo West Africa
Trinidad & Tobago The Caribbean, Trinidad & Tobago
Tunisia Tunisia, Tunisia Map
Turkey Europe on a Budget, Istanbul, Turkey, Turkey Map
Turks and Caicos Islands The Bahamas, The Caribbean
United Arab Emirates Dubai DIR, Dubai & UAE Map [1 title]
United Kingdom Britain, Devon & Cornwall, Edinburgh DIR England, Europe on a Budget, The Lake District, London, London DIR, London Map, London Mini Guide, Scotland, Scottish Highlands & Islands, Wales, Walks In London & Southeast England
United States Alaska, Boston, California, California Map, Chicago, Colorado, Florida, Florida Map, The Grand Canyon, Hawaii, Los Angeles, Los Angeles Map, Los Angeles and Southern California, Maui DIR, Miami & South Florida, New England, New England Map, New Orleans & Cajun Country, New Orleans DIR, New York City, NYC DIR, NYC Map, New York City Mini Guide, Oregon & Washington, Orlando & Walt Disney World® DIR, San Francisco, San Francisco DIR, San Francisco Map, Seattle, Southwest USA, USA, Washington DC, Yellowstone & the Grand Tetons National Park, Yosemite National Park
Uruguay South America on a Budget
US Virgin Islands The Bahamas, The Caribbean
Venezuela South America on a Budget
Vietnam Southeast Asia on a Budget, Vietnam, Vietnam, Laos & Cambodia Map [1 Map],
Wales Britain, Camping in Britain, Europe on a Budget, Wales
First-Time Series FT Africa, FT Around the World, FT Asia, FT Europe, FT Latin America
Inspirational guides Earthbound, Clean Breaks, Make the Most of Your Time on Earth, Ultimate Adventures, World Party
Travel Specials Camping in Britain, Travel with Babies & Young Children, Walks in London & SE England

ROUGH GUIDES Don't Just Travel

Computers Cloud Computing, FWD this link, The Internet, iPhone, iPods & iTunes, Macs & OS X, Website Directory
Film & TV American Independent Film, British Cult Comedy, Comedy Movies, Cult Movies, Film, Film Musicals, Film Noir, Gangster Movies, Horror Movies, Sci-Fi Movies, Westerns
Lifestyle Babies & Toddlers, Brain Training, Food, Girl Stuff, Green Living, Happiness, Men's Health, Pregnancy & Birth, Running, Saving & Selling Online, Sex, Weddings
Music The Beatles, The Best Music You've Never Heard, Blues, Bob Dylan, Book of Playlists, Classical Music, Heavy Metal, Jimi Hendrix, Led Zeppelin, Nirvana, Opera, Pink Floyd, The Rolling Stones, Soul and R&B, Velvet Underground, World Music
Popular Culture Anime, Classic Novels, Conspiracy Theories, Crime Fiction, The Da Vinci Code, Graphic Novels, Hidden Treasures, His Dark Materials, Hitchhiker's Guide to the Galaxy, The Lost Symbol, Manga, Next Big Thing, Shakespeare, True Crime, Tutankhamun, Unexplained Phenomena, Videogames
Science The Brain, Climate Change, The Earth, Energy Crisis, Evolution, Future, Genes & Cloning, The Universe, Weather

NOTES

Small print and
Index

A Rough Guide to Rough Guides

Published in 1982, the first Rough Guide – to Greece – was a student scheme that became a publishing phenomenon. Mark Ellingham, a recent graduate in English from Bristol University, had been travelling in Greece the previous summer and couldn't find the right guidebook. With a small group of friends he wrote his own guide, combining a highly contemporary, journalistic style with a thoroughly practical approach to travellers' needs.

The immediate success of the book spawned a series that rapidly covered dozens of destinations. And, in addition to impecunious backpackers, Rough Guides soon acquired a much broader and older readership that relished the guides' wit and inquisitiveness as much as their enthusiastic, critical approach and value-for-money ethos.

These days, Rough Guides include recommendations from shoestring to luxury and cover more than 200 destinations around the globe, including almost every country in the Americas and Europe, more than half of Africa and most of Asia and Australasia. Our ever-growing team of authors and photographers is spread all over the world, particularly in Europe, the US and Australia.

In the early 1990s, Rough Guides branched out of travel, with the publication of Rough Guides to World Music, Classical Music and the Internet. All three have become benchmark titles in their fields, spearheading the publication of a wide range of books under the Rough Guide name.

Including the travel series, Rough Guides now number more than 350 titles, covering: phrasebooks, waterproof maps, music guides from Opera to Heavy Metal, reference works as diverse as Conspiracy Theories and Shakespeare, and popular culture books from iPods to Poker. Rough Guides also produce a series of more than 120 World Music CDs in partnership with World Music Network.

Visit www.roughguides.com to see our latest publications.

Rough Guide travel images are available for commercial licensing at www.roughguidespictures.com

Rough Guide credits

Text editor: Amanda Tomlin
Layout: Sachin Tanwar
Cartography: Maxine Repath and Katie Lloyd-Jones
Picture editor: Nicole Newman
Production: Rebecca Short
Proofreader: Karen Parker
Cover design: Dan May and Chloë Roberts
Photographer: Helena Smith
Editorial: Ruth Blackmore, Andy Turner, Keith Drew, Edward Aves, Alice Park, Lucy White, Jo Kirby, James Smart, Natasha Foges, Róisín Cameron, James Rice, Lara Kavanagh, Emma Traynor, Emma Gibbs, Kathryn Lane, Monica Woods, Mani Ramaswamy, Harry Wilson, Lucy Cowie, Alison Roberts, Joe Staines, Peter Buckley, Matthew Milton, Tracy Hopkins, Ruth Tidball; **Delhi** Madhavi Singh, Karen D'Souza, Lubna Shaheen
Design & Pictures: **London** Scott Stickland, Dan May, Diana Jarvis, Mark Thomas, Sarah Cummins, Emily Taylor; **Delhi** Umesh Aggarwal, Ajay Verma, Jessica Subramanian, Ankur Guha, Pradeep Thapliyal, Anita Singh, Nikhil Agarwal, Sachin Gupta.
Production: Liz Cherry
Cartography: **London** Ed Wright; **Delhi** Rajesh Chhibber, Ashutosh Bharti, Rajesh Mishra, Animesh Pathak, Jasbir Sandhu, Karobi Gogoi, Alakananda Roy, Swati Handoo, Deshpal Dabas
Online: **London** Faye Hellon, Jeanette Angell, Fergus Day, Justine Bright, Clare Bryson, Aine Fearon, Adrian Low, Ezgi Celebi; **Delhi** Amit Verma, Rahul Kumar, Narender Kumar, Ravi Yadav, Debojit Borah, Rakesh Kumar, Ganesh Sharma, Shisir Basumatari
Marketing & Publicity: **London** Liz Statham, Louise Maher, Jess Carter, Vanessa Godden, Vivienne Watton, Anna Paynton, Rachel Sprackett, Laura Vipond; **New York** Katy Ball, Judi Powers; **Delhi** Ragini Govind
Reference Director: Andrew Lockett
Operations Assistant: Becky Doyle
Operations Manager: Helen Atkinson
Publishing Director (Travel): Clare Currie
Commercial Manager: Gino Magnotta
Managing Director: John Duhigg

Publishing information

This fifth edition published May 2010 by
Rough Guides Ltd,
80 Strand, London WC2R 0RL
14 Local Shopping Centre, Panchsheel Park, New Delhi 110017, India
Distributed by the Penguin Group
Penguin Books Ltd,
80 Strand, London WC2R 0RL
Penguin Group (USA)
375 Hudson Street, NY 10014, USA
Penguin Group (Australia)
250 Camberwell Road, Camberwell, Victoria 3124, Australia
Penguin Group (Canada)
195 Harry Walker Parkway N, Newmarket, ON, L3Y 7B3 Canada
Penguin Group (NZ)
67 Apollo Drive, Mairangi Bay, Auckland 1310, New Zealand
Cover concept by Peter Dyer.

Typeset in Bembo and Helvetica to an original design by Henry Iles.
Printed in Singapore

312pp includes index
A catalogue record for this book is available from the British Library
ISBN: 978-1-84836-435-6

1 3 5 7 9 8 6 4 2

Help us update

We've gone to a lot of effort to ensure that the fifth edition of **The Rough Guide to The Lake District** is accurate and up-to-date. However, things change – places get "discovered", opening hours are notoriously fickle, restaurants and rooms raise prices or lower standards. If you feel we've got it wrong or left something out, we'd like to know, and if you can remember the address, the price, the hours, the phone number, so much the better.

Please send your comments with the subject line "**Rough Guide The Lake District Update**" to Ⓔmail@roughguides.com. We'll credit all contributions and send a copy of the next edition (or any other Rough Guide if you prefer) for the very best emails.

Have your questions answered and tell others about your trip at Ⓦwww.roughguides.com

Acknowledgements

Jules Brown would like to thank the following organizations for invaluable information, advice and assistance: Cumbria Tourism, Lake District National Park Authority, English Heritage and National Trust. Special thanks are also due in particular to Nicola Hewiston, David Switzer, Tony Hume, Dave Bailey, Jonathan Robb, Andy and Chrissy Hill, Ellis Butcher, Barry Surtees and everyone else who responded willingly to my endless questions and requests. I'd also like to thank Mandy for her careful editing, and Captain I Little and the Two Marks for various walks up steep mountains in zero visibility and driving rain – our watchword, as ever, what could possibly go wrong?

Photo credits

All photos © Rough Guides except the following:

Introduction

Blencathra (or Saddleback) from Tewet Tarn © Joe Cornish/photolibrary
Shore of Derwent Water near Keswick © Lee Beel/photolibrary
Sign outside the *Wordsworth Hotel*, Cockermouth © Tony West/photolibrary
Tourists browsing Tiberthwaite Avenue, Coniston © Dave Porter/photolibrary
Belle Isle and the town of Bowness © David Lyons/alamy
Agaric toadstools under a silver birch tree © Ashley Cooper/corbis

Things Not To Miss

01 Tarn Hows in autumn © Alan Novelli/photolibrary
02 Honister Slate Mine zip wire, courtesy of Honister Slate Mine
05 Castlerigg Stone Circle in Keswick © Ashley Cooper/corbis
06 Great Langdale and the Langdale Pikes © Jon Allison/photolibrary
07 Cyclists in Grizedale Forest © StockShot/alamy
08 *Full Circle Yurts*, courtesy of Full Circle Yurts
09 Maiden Moor in the Borrowdale Valley © Dave Porter/photolibrary
11 Aira Force © Jason Gallier/alamy
12 Rydal Mount © James Emmerson/photolibrary
13 Osprey © david tipling/alamy
14 Muncaster Castle © Lucy Barden/photolibrary
15 Hardknott Roman fort © Ashley Cooper/alamy

Out and about in the Lakes colour section

A ruined barn above a snowy Mardale Head, Harter Fell and Nan Bield Pass © Andy Stothert/photolibrary
Boats docked on a pier, Keswick © John Short/corbis
Sailing dinghy on Windermere © Tony West/photolibrary
Cumberland and Westmorland Wrestling, Grasmere © Tracy Gunn/alamy
Cyclists with view across Ullswater, near Martindale © Rod Edwards/photolibrary
High Ropes course, Grizedale Forest © StockShot/alamy
Walking boots next to dry-stone wall, Grange-over-Sands © Rod Edwards/photolibrary
Bassenthwaite Lake and Swinside Fell from Cat Bells © Alan Novelli/photolibrary
Beer garden at *Kirkstile Inn*, Loweswater © Tony West/photolibrary
Wasdale Valley © britain on view/photolibrary

Writers and artists colour section

Samuel Taylor Coleridge by Phillips, courtesy of The Wordsworth Trust
Ruskin's Lake District home at Brantwood © Keith Wood/photolibrary
View of Skiddaw & Derwentwater, c.1780 by Joseph Farington © Yale Center for British Art/Bridgeman
Dove Cottage, home of William Wordsworth © 1StopImages/alamy

Black and whites

p.114 Crinkle Crags in winter, Great Langdale © Ruth Tomlinson/photolibrary

Index

Map entries are in colour.

D

E

F

G

M

N

O

P

Q

R

S

T

Map symbols

maps are listed in the full index using coloured text

County boundary
Chapter divisions boundary
National Park boundary
Motorway
Major road
Minor road
Unpaved road
Path
Railway
Ferry route
Waterway
Wall
Bridge/pass
General point of interest
Church (regional maps)
Abbey
Castle
Stately home
Gardens
Cave
Viewpoint

Mountain peak
Hills/mountains
Rocks
Ruin
Waterfall
Campsite
Accommodation
Statue
Hospital
Bus stop
Parking
Petrol station
Tourist office
Post office
Internet access
Swimming pool
Building
Church
Cemetery
Park
Marsh